Court, Credit, and Capital

Seventeenth-century Amsterdam was a city of innovations. Explosive economic growth, the expansion of overseas trade, and a high level of religious tolerance sparked great institutional, socioeconomic and legal changes, a period generally known as "the Dutch Golden Age." In this book, Maurits den Hollander discusses how insolvency legislation contributed to the rise of a modern commercial order in seventeenth-century Amsterdam. He analyzes the procedure and principles behind Amsterdam's specialized insolvency court (the Desolate Boedelskamer, 1643) from a theoretical perspective as well as through the eyes of citizens whose businesses failed. The Amsterdam authorities created a regulatory environment which solved insolvency more leniently, and thus economically more efficiently, than in previous times or places. Moving beyond the traditional view of insolvency as a moral failure and the debtor as a criminal, the Amsterdam court recognized that business failure was often beyond the insolvent's personal control, and helped restore trust and credit among creditors and debtors.

Maurits den Hollander is Assistant Professor of Legal History at Tilburg University. He specializes in legal and institutional developments across the late medieval and early modern eras. This is his first book.

See the Studies in Legal History series website at
http://studiesinlegalhistory.org/

STUDIES IN LEGAL HISTORY

Other books in the series:

Kevin Arlyck, *The Nation at Sea: The Federal Courts and American Sovereignty, 1789–1825*

Alastair McClure, *Trials of Sovereignty: Mercy, Violence, and the Making of Criminal Law in British India, 1857–1922*

James Q. Whitman, *From Masters of Slaves to Lords of Lands: The Transformation of Ownership in the Western World*

Marie-Amélie George, *Family Matters: Queer Households and the Half-Century Struggle for Legal Recognition*

Simon Devereaux, *Execution, State and Society in England, 1660–1900*

Giuliana Perrone, *Nothing More than Freedom: The Failure of Abolition in American Law*

(*Continued after the Index*)

Court, Credit, and Capital

Amsterdam's Insolvency Legislation in the Dutch Golden Age

MAURITS DEN HOLLANDER
Tilburg University

CAMBRIDGE
UNIVERSITY PRESS

CAMBRIDGE
UNIVERSITY PRESS

Shaftesbury Road, Cambridge CB2 8EA, United Kingdom

One Liberty Plaza, 20th Floor, New York, NY 10006, USA

477 Williamstown Road, Port Melbourne, VIC 3207, Australia

314–321, 3rd Floor, Plot 3, Splendor Forum, Jasola District Centre, New Delhi – 110025, India

103 Penang Road, #05–06/07, Visioncrest Commercial, Singapore 238467

Cambridge University Press is part of Cambridge University Press & Assessment, a department of the University of Cambridge.

We share the University's mission to contribute to society through the pursuit of education, learning and research at the highest international levels of excellence.

www.cambridge.org
Information on this title: www.cambridge.org/9781009631051

DOI: 10.1017/9781009631037

When citing this work, please include a reference to the DOI 10.1017/9781009631037

First published 2025

A catalogue record for this publication is available from the British Library

Library of Congress Cataloging-in-Publication Data
NAMES: Hollander, Maurits den, 1994– author.
TITLE: Court, credit, and capital : Amsterdam's insolvency legislation in the Dutch golden age / Maurits den Hollander, Tilburg University.
DESCRIPTION: Cambridge, United Kingdom ; New York, NY : Cambridge University Press, 2025.
IDENTIFIERS: LCCN 2025004902 | ISBN 9781009631051 (hardback) | ISBN 9781009631037 (ebook)
SUBJECTS: LCSH: Bankruptcy – Netherlands – Amsterdam – History – 17th century. | Bankruptcy – Netherlands – Amsterdam – History – 17th century.
CLASSIFICATION: LCC KKM1943 .H65 2025 | DDC 346.49207/809032–dc23/eng/20250520
LC record available at https://lccn.loc.gov/2025004902

ISBN 978-1-009-63105-1 Hardback

To my parents

Contents

Figures

Tables

Acknowledgments

This book grew out of my doctoral thesis at Tilburg University (2018–2021), and accumulated many debts during various rounds of writing and rewriting.

My dissertation was funded by the European Research Council, as part of the Starting Grant project "Coherence in Law through Legal Scholarship" led by my promotor, Professor Dave De ruysscher. I am deeply grateful to him and my co-promotor, Professor Randall Lesaffer, for expertly guiding me towards becoming an independent researcher. I am grateful to my friends and colleagues at Tilburg University and beyond, thanks to whom this potentially lonely academic journey remained ever pleasant and interesting.

I thank Professors Oscar Gelderblom, Thomas Safley, Maria Fusaro, and Maarten Prak for stimulating conversations and advice. The examination committee, consisting of Professors James Whitman, Albrecht Cordes, Manon van der Heijden, and Arnoud-Jan Bijsterveld, provided excellent feedback and stimulating questions that constitute the foundation of this book as a reworked academic monograph.

Much of the research for this book was conducted using manuscripts held by the Amsterdam Municipal Archives. Without the digitization services and support of its staff during the COVID pandemic and lockdowns, it would have been impossible to write this book. I thank the staff of the Tilburg University Library for kindly processing endless IBL requests and acquisition suggestions. Doctor Corine Schouten was most helpful in arranging interviews. I thank Royal

Palace Amsterdam's curator Alice Taatgen for kindly providing the requested illustrations and permissions. I warmly thank Professor Bob Wessels for his interest in this project and for introducing me to new possibilities for the public dissemination of my research.

I thank Cambridge University Press and the editors of the series "Studies in Legal History" for helping me towards the publication of this manuscript. I am grateful to the anonymous reviewers, who gave helpful suggestions for improvement. I am most thankful to my editor, Professor Thomas McSweeney, who over the past years helped me in more ways than could be expected to make this book into its best imaginable version.

My final thanks are to my family. I would like to thank my husband, Rik, for his patience when listening to my recurring stories about yet another fascinating insolvency. I would like to express my deep gratitude to my parents, who have stimulated and supported me in more ways than they probably realize. It is to them that I dedicate this book.

A Note on Currency and Naming Conventions

This book is about the early modern Dutch Republic, a society and period that might be familiar to some but not all of its intended readership. This section will briefly explain some of the basic currency and naming conventions that have been adopted throughout the book.

The Low Countries (roughly the current nation states of the Netherlands, Belgium, and Luxembourg) in the seventeenth century consisted of two main parts: the independent (Dutch) Republic of the Seven United Netherlands in the north; and the Southern Netherlands, ruled by the Spanish branch of the Habsburgs. Within the Dutch Republic, Amsterdam lies in the province of Holland. This book does not adopt the popular use of "Holland" as designation for the Netherlands or Dutch Republic as a whole.

The Low Countries were not "systematically" monetized in the early modern period. Following Burgundian and Habsburg mint ordinances in the first half of the sixteenth century, the guilder or *gulden* became the standard money of account, subdivided into twenty *stuivers* of sixteen *penningen* each. The circulating currency throughout the early modern period consisted of a wide variety of foreign coins, such as *patacons* or *ducatons* from the Southern Netherlands. In this book, sums in guilders are abbreviated as fl. X – X – X (i.e. 1 guilder – 20 stuivers – 16 penningen). When guilders or guilders and stuivers suffice to note an amount of money, I have left out the redundant details. Around 1650, an average unskilled laborer in Holland earned

19 stuivers a day, a skilled laborer (journeyman) 25 stuivers. In this same period, 10 stuivers a day sufficed to properly feed a five-person household.[1]

In sixteenth- and seventeenth-century Dutch sources, surnames are often abbreviated as "-sz." or "-sdr.," which in full would be written out as "-szoon" or "-sdochter." I have generally stuck to the abbreviations as found in the original documents, so "Pietersz." rather than "Pieterszoon," except for titles of secondary literature, where an abbreviation would obscure the reference.

Some of the characters that appear in this book were in possession of an academic degree. In this context, "mr." does not refer to "mister" but to "meester" or *magister*, the title granted to a graduate of a contemporary law faculty. The title "dr." refers to *doctor*, and was granted to an *artes* graduate.[2] As per standard Dutch spelling conventions, academic titles are written in lower case, so not "Dr." or "Dr" but "dr. Ten Grootenhuys," unless they appear at the start of a sentence.

[1] Jan de Vries and Ad van der Woude, *The First Modern Economy: Success, Failure, and Perseverance of the Dutch Economy, 1500–1815* (Cambridge University Press, 1997), 81–83 (currency) and 620–25 (cost of living).

[2] See Chapter 4 below for further details on academic education in this period.

Introduction

> Amsterdam is now undisputedly Europe's most famous city of commerce. Even though it does not possess ancient roots, in its novelty it is happier than many older and once renowned cities. Truly, today it seems like none can be compared to Amsterdam, be it in terms of greatness ... or the amount of people, wealth, and flourishing maritime commerce from all corners of the world.[1]

Seventeenth-century Amsterdam was a city of innovations. Explosive economic growth and the expansion of overseas trade went hand in hand with a high level of religious tolerance. These developments sparked great institutional, socioeconomic, and legal changes. Therefore, it is unsurprising that many histories of the city on the Amstel are success stories. Similar to the contemporary immigrants Jacques Le Moine De L'Espine and Isaac le Long cited above, many historians have tried to explain its remarkable cultural and economic efflorescence in this period.[2]

1 Jacques le Moine de l'Espine and Isaac le Long, *De koophandel van Amsterdam* (Amsterdam: Andries van Damme en Johannes Ratelband, 1714), 3–4.

2 Jonathan I. Israel, *Dutch Primacy in World Trade, 1585–1740* (Oxford: Clarendon Press, 1989); Jan de Vries and Ad van der Woude, *The First Modern Economy: Success, Failure, and Perseverance of the Dutch Economy, 1500–1815* (Cambridge University Press, 1997); Clé Lesger, *Handel in Amsterdam ten tijde van de Opstand. Kooplieden, commerciële expansie en verandering in de ruimtelijke economie van de Nederlanden ca. 1550–ca. 1630* (Hilversum: Verloren, 2001); Oscar Gelderblom, *Zuid-Nederlandse kooplieden en de opkomst van de Amsterdamse stapelmarkt (1578–1630)* (Hilversum: Verloren, 2000); Oscar Gelderblom, *Cities*

However, this does not mean that the seventeenth century was a golden age for all of Amsterdam's citizens. In these same years, many of them actually expressed their concerns about the "expensive and woeful times." Rather than enjoying the fruits of flourishing commerce, these citizens were confronted with *slegte neering* or "bad trade." One of them, the merchant Jan Arnout Wichelhuysen, explained how "the upcoming war, bad debtors, and slow repayments of [his own outstanding] debts" had been important factors contributing towards his insolvency in 1695.[3] As Joseph Schumpeter argued with regard to his concept of "creative destruction," continuous economic growth and innovations are almost necessarily paired with the failure and disappearance of less successful, inefficient business ventures. Therefore, business failure and insolvencies are generally seen as an inescapable feature of the advent of modern capitalism.[4] This book is not a collection of the success stories of merchants and entrepreneurs such as Reinier Pauw, Louis de Geer, or the brothers Louis and Elias Trip.[5] Resisting the attraction of these powerful magnates, it will instead focus on people such as Van Wichelhuysen, whose businesses failed.

This book analyzes the impact of the introduction of the Desolate Boedelskamer or "Chamber of Insolvent and Abandoned Estates" in 1643 on Amsterdam's economy and society between 1578 and 1700. Through a broad archival analysis of the social and economic context in which insolvency legislation was created and applied in seventeenth-century Amsterdam, it will highlight the ways in which innovative governance and legal practices interacted with moral thought in order to produce a liberal, open-access insolvency regime.

As James Whitman argues, it is held as common consensus that "it was in seventeenth-century Holland ... that the most striking and

of Commerce: The Institutional Foundations of International Trade in the Low Countries, 1250–1650 (Princeton University Press, 2013); Maarten Prak and Jan Luiten van Zanden, *Pioneers of Capitalism: The Netherlands 1000–1800* (Princeton University Press, 2023).

3 Gemeente Amsterdam Stadsarchief [GAS], 5072: Archief van de Commissarissen van de Desolate Boedelkamer [DB], inv. nr. 697, nr. 26.

4 Joseph A. Schumpeter, *Capitalism, Socialism, and Democracy* (New York: Harper & Brothers, 1942), 81–86.

5 See e.g. Kees Zandvliet, *De 500 rijksten van de Republiek. Rijkdom, geloof, macht & cultuur* (Zutphen: Walburg Pers, 2018); Menno Witteveen, *Reinier Pauw (1564–1636) en Amsterdam. De macht van een man en een stad* (Amsterdam: Boom, 2022).

seminal developments in the rise of a modern commercial order took place."[6] Amsterdam, being the locus of legal and institutional innovations in the early modern Dutch Republic, has naturally received most attention from economic, social, and cultural historians. This motivated the choice to make Amsterdam the focus of this legal-historical analysis, in order to confront existing theories in its historiography – which will be treated in subsequent sections of this introductory chapter – with new evidence from the city's legal archives.

This book moves beyond important research trends that prevail in both legal and economic historical scholarship. Instead of a singular focus on either legal doctrine or the functioning of markets and economic growth, it approaches the legal, institutional, socioeconomic, and cultural history of early modern Amsterdam as an interconnected whole. It will therefore also argue in favor of an "embedded" perspective on the economy, not separated from but fundamentally related to all these cultural, moral, and social dimensions of life that come together in the archives left behind by the inhabitants of seventeenth-century Amsterdam.[7] The central topic around which this analysis has been constructed is insolvency legislation. Insolvency, as a crucial junction of the fundamental contextuality of commercial law, can illuminate a number of different things about Amsterdam's Golden Age.

First, as Jean Limpens remarks, "insolvency legislation is one of the melting-pots in which all legal affairs amalgamate." Those studying insolvency have to take into account all other legal fields that might have an impact on the person or business in financial distress.[8] At the same time, solid and transparent insolvency legislation is a "vivid and important part of the legal framework of market economies," as it provides creditors with confidence in the rules that safeguard

[6] James Q. Whitman, "The Moral Menace of Roman Law and the Making of Commerce: Some Dutch Evidence," *The Yale Law Journal* 105, no. 7 (1995): 1841–89, 1844.

[7] On the notion of "embeddedness" and the debate on its role in economics, see e.g. Mark Granovetter, "Economic Action and Social Structure: The Problem of Embeddedness," *American Journal of Sociology* 91, no. 3 (1985): 481–510.

[8] Louis F. Ganshof, *Le Droit de la faillite dans les états de la Communauté économique européenne* (Brussels: Centre Interuniversitaire de Droit Comparé, 1969), Preface: "[Le droit de la faillite] est l'un des creusets ou tous les materiaux juridiques s'amalgament."

their investments.[9] Therefore, historical analysis of the phenomenon of insolvency constitutes an important meeting ground for legal and economic historians.

Second, and connected to this observation, insolvency and economic misfortune are not restricted to specific classes or social groups. A singular focus on businesses and the production side of the economy is both one-sided and insufficient to understand processes of change in (economic) history. In the household, important decisions were taken on the size and contents of consumption, labor supply, savings, and investments in human capital through education.[10] An analysis of the broader impact of an institution such as the Desolate Boedelskamer makes it possible to bridge the gap in historiography between the study of (international) merchants and the upper classes on the one hand, and the household economics of the middle classes on the other.

Third and finally, this draws attention to an important debate in economic history and sociology between adherents of the schools of the "new institutional economics,"[11] and a "moral economy."[12] Any analysis which seeks to separate morality and economy, or financial aspects from social relations, can never hope to fully understand people from the past and the societies in which they lived. In this

[9] Bob Wessels, Bruce Markall, and Jason Kilborn, *International Cooperation in Bankruptcy and Insolvency Matters* (Oxford University Press, 2009), 1–2.

[10] Jan Luiten van Zanden and Arthur van Riel, *The Strictures of Inheritance: The Dutch Economy in the Nineteenth Century*, trans. Ian Cressie (Princeton University Press, 2004), 319–27.

[11] Douglass C. North and Robert Paul Thomas, *The Rise of the Western World: A New Economic History* (Cambridge University Press, 1973); Douglass C. North, *Institutions, Institutional Change, and Economic Performance* (Cambridge University Press, 1990); Avner Greif, *Institutions and the Path to the Modern Economy: Lessons from Medieval Trade* (Cambridge University Press, 2006); Sheilagh C. Ogilvie and A. W. Carus, "Institutions and Economic Growth in Historical Perspective," in *Handbook of Economic Growth*, ed. Philippe Aghion and Steven N. Durlauf, 2 vols. (Amsterdam: Elsevier, 2014), IIA:403–513.

[12] Karl Polanyi, *Great Transformation: The Political and Economic Origins of Our Time*, 2nd ed. (Boston: Beacon Press, 2001); Edward P. Thompson, "The Moral Economy of the English Crowd in the Eighteenth Century," *Past & Present* 50 (1971): 76–136; Craig Muldrew, "Interpreting the Market: The Ethics of Credit and Community Relations in Early Modern England," *Social History* 18, no. 2 (1993): 163–83; Craig Muldrew, *The Economy of Obligation: The Culture of Credit and Social Relations in Early Modern England* (Basingstoke: Macmillan Press, 1998); Laurence Fontaine, *The Moral Economy. Poverty, Credit, and Trust in Early Modern Europe* (New York: Cambridge University Press, 2014).

book, insolvency legislation and practices in seventeenth-century Amsterdam will serve as the lens through which the functioning of early modern institutions will be explored and analyzed as part of their broader civic framework.

Insolvency and Bankruptcy

Generally, one can distinguish two major forms of financial demise: "insolvency" (Dutch: *faillissement* or *insolventie*) and "bankruptcy" (Dutch: *bankroet*). "Insolvency" is usually employed as a neutral term, to describe an economic condition. This word is derived from the Latin verb *solvo*, which combined with the negative prefix "-in" can be translated as "to be unable to pay." "Bankruptcy," on the other hand, generally indicates a legal status. According to a widespread story, this term originated in late medieval Italy. When a merchant or money changer was unable to fulfil their obligations, the wooden bench where they conducted their business was broken in half to publicly signify their incapacity to honor their obligations: *banca rotta* or "broken bench." However, Sandor Schick convincingly argues that bench-breaking is a myth, and no evidence can be found to substantiate it. Whatever its origin, "bankruptcy" came to be associated with fraud or dishonesty early on. The malversation of private property made it a deeply offensive phenomenon. This sentiment is also expressed by other recurring terms for bankrupts, such as *decoctor* (lit. "reduced by cooking") – one who consumed their own substance.[13] While in general parlance, insolvency and bankruptcy are often used as interchangeable substitutes, the more precise distinction in meaning between these two terms can be observed in a wide variety of past and present legal systems.[14]

[13] Thomas Max Safley, "Introduction: A History of Bankruptcy and Bankruptcy in History," in *The History of Bankruptcy: Economic, Social and Cultural Implications in Early Modern Europe*, ed. Thomas Max Safley (London: Routledge, 2013), 2–3; Sandor E. Schick, "Globalization, Bankruptcy and the Myth of the Broken Bench," *American Bankruptcy Law Journal* 80, no. 2 (2006): 219–60; Annamaria Monti, "Fallimento-impresa," in *Parole in Divenire. Un vademecum par l'uomo occidentale*, ed. Alberto Sciumè and Aldo A. Cassi (Turin: Giappichelli, 2016), 43–57.

[14] Paolo Di Martino, Mark Latham, and Michelangelo Vasta, "Bankruptcy Laws Around Europe (1850–2015): Institutional Change and Institutional Features," *Enterprise & Society* 21 (2020): 1–55, esp. n. 2.

In his well-known *Hollandsch Rechtsgeleerd Woordenboek* or "legal dictionary," the notorious but best-selling eighteenth-century legal scholar Franciscus Kersteman defines *insolventie* as the situation in which "a person, incapable of repaying his debts due to misfortune, losses, and other disasters, hands over his estate to the local *Desolate Boedelskamer* or relevant local court, to his creditors' benefit."[15] On the other hand, he describes a *bankroetier* as "a person, who after concluding fraudulent debts, and without properly fulfilling his creditors' legal claims, absconds and becomes a fugitive."[16] Grotius had already employed the same widespread designation of bankrupts as "die schuilen ofte weg-loopen met onbetaelde schulden" or "those who hide or abscond while leaving debts unpaid."[17] A similar image emerges from the French *code du commerce* of 1673, in which it is stressed: "La faillite ou banqueroute. Ces mots ne sont point synonymes" – "insolvency" and "bankruptcy" are not synonyms. While a *faillite* was simply someone who could not pay their debts "due to losses resulting from a considerable accident, for which he could in no way be held responsible," a *banqueroute* willingly caused their own financial demise, for instance by "involving [themself] in indiscreet engagements or risky business." The criminal nature of the bankrupt was most fully revealed if they ran off with their creditors' possessions, or tried to rob them through other fraudulent actions such as those covered by the *actio pauliana*.[18] In this book, therefore, the term "bankruptcy" will be reserved for fraudulent insolvencies.

Insolvency Legislation in the Early Modern Dutch Republic

In late medieval Europe, failing to fulfil one's financial obligations was indiscriminately and severely punished. In many cities and states, it

[15] Franciscus Lievens Kersteman, *Hollandsch rechtsgeleerd woorden-boek* (Amsterdam: Wed. van Esveldt en Holtrop, 1777), 205–6.

[16] Ibid. 36.

[17] Hugo de Groot, *Inleidinge tot de Hollandsche rechts-geleerdheid*, ed. F. Dovring, H. F. W. D. Fischer, and E. M. Meijers, 2nd ed. (Universitaire Pers Leiden, 1965), 62, II.5.3; see also J. A. Ankum, *De geschiedenis der "actio Pauliana"* (Zwolle: Tjeenk Willink, 1962), 368.

[18] Daniel Jousse, *Nouveau Commentaire sur l'ordonnance du commerce des mois de mars 1673* (Paris: Jean Debure, 1777), esp. 149–50; Ankum, *De geschiedenis der "actio Pauliana."*

was common to use public shaming sanctions for those unable to pay their debts. The fact that such harsh measures were not just restricted to fraudulent or fugitive bankrupts, but also used for honest but unfortunate insolvents, illustrates the essentially criminal nature that attached to the legal treatment of insolvencies well into early modern times. Contemporary legal scholars in many parts of Europe generally presumed that every insolvent would automatically have committed fraud, as characterized by Baldus's well-known maxim *fallitus, ergo fraudator*.[19] Of course, this did not encourage unfortunate victims of economic circumstances willingly to place themselves in the hands of their creditors: many problematic debtors (initially) chose to run off with their remaining possessions rather than face a court.[20] This negative view is also reflected in much of the insolvency legislation from this period. In his 1540 *Eeuwig Edict* or "Perpetual Edict," for instance, Emperor Charles V even decreed that all fugitive bankrupts had to be punished with a death sentence, regardless of whether they eventually paid their debts or not.[21] However, it seems that in the Low Countries such harsh ordinances were rarely carried out in practice. Quite to the contrary, especially in parts of Holland, the late sixteenth and seventeenth centuries witnessed the development of increasingly liberal local insolvency regimes.

According to James Whitman, this was linked to the "moral lessons" of Roman law, which became ever more influential in the Dutch Republic in this period. The new legal tradition would have provided a way to normalize commercial activities and actions that used to be strongly condemned in the past.[22] However, Wouter Druwé has argued that in the writings of contemporary legal scholars, "no unequivocal weakening effect of Roman Law on shaming practices can

[19] Baldus, Cons. 392; referred to by Willem L. P. A. Molengraaff, *Leidraad bij de beoefening van het Nederlandsche handelsrecht* (Haarlem: Erven F. Bohn, 1925), 882. See also Monti, "Fallimento-impresa," 44–46; Chapter 2 below.

[20] As Forster argues, the fact that late medieval jurisprudence did not allow compositions with a living debtor, unless they formed the incentive for a fugitive insolvent to return and facilitate the execution of their estate, might have been the reason why so many medieval insolvents were forced to become *fugitivi*: Wolfgang Forster, *Konkurs als Verfahren. Francisco Salgado de Somoza in der Geschichte des Insolvenzrechts* (Cologne: Böhlau, 2009), 212–15.

[21] J. Lameere and H. Simont (eds.), *Recueil des ordonnances des Pays-Bas. Deuxième série 1506–1700*, 8 vols. (Brussels: J. Goemaere, 1907), IV:233–34.

[22] Whitman, "The Moral Menace."

be observed."[23] Furthermore, as Griet Vermeesch states with regard to the accessibility of courts, early modern litigants should not be viewed as powerless targets for top-down policies, but actively helped to shape the law and its functioning.[24] Limiting oneself to the study of legal doctrine, therefore, would not suffice to properly analyze a topic that is as rich and multifaceted as insolvency in seventeenth-century Amsterdam. It is crucial to cross-check legislation with historical evidence of its application in practice.

This leads to the important question of how we can explain change in legal history, if not through doctrinal analysis. Randall Lesaffer has stated that legal historians should employ a method which he calls *law in history*: the historical study of law within its broader social, economic, cultural, and political context. This makes sense, as the historian is not primarily concerned with the origins or further evolution of law as such, but studies it as a phenomenon within the particular society and time in history where it occurred.[25] Law, therefore, is always a social construct, and its ethics dependent on a history of communication. This makes it the subject of a history of ideas, which should make use of the proper historical method of interpretation, *Verstehen*.[26] This method should be understood as "a dialogical progression between stored knowledge and new information." In this process, the "complementary imagination" of historians plays an important heuristic role.[27]

As I will argue in this book, the introduction of the Amsterdam Desolate Boedelskamer in 1643 proved to be a crucial step in the consolidation of transparent, widely accessible, and more humane

[23] Wouter Druwé, "Dignity and Cessio Bonorum in Early-Modern Dutch Learned Legal Literature," Max Planck Institute for European Legal History Research Paper Series 2016-08 (2016), 23.

[24] Griet Vermeesch, "Reflections on the Relative Accessibility of Law Courts in Early Modern Europe," *Crime, Histoire & Sociétés / Crime, History & Societies* 19, no. 2 (2015): 53–76, 65.

[25] Randall Lesaffer, "Law and History: Law between Past and Present," in *Law and Method. Interdisciplinary Research into Law*, ed. Bart van Klink and Sanne Taekema (Tübingen: Mohr Siebeck, 2011), 136.

[26] Wolfgang Ernst, "Zur Epistemologie rechtsgeschichtlicher Forschung," *Rechtsgeschichte* 23 (2015): 256–59, 256.

[27] Michael Stolleis, "Methode der Rechtsgeschichte," in *Handwörterbuch zur deutschen Rechtsgeschichte (HRG) Konfliktbewältigung – Nowgorod*, ed. Albrecht Cordes, currently 4 vols. (Berlin: Schmidt, 2016), III:1480.

insolvency procedures. In order to explain these changes, we have to study the law as part of its broader historical context. Therefore, this book will mainly focus on the institutional, procedural, social, and economic dimensions of insolvency legislation. Such reconstructions can only be made through detailed archival analysis.[28] The next sections will introduce and explain both the broader analytical framework and the methodological choices that were made when writing this book.

Amsterdam's Success Story: Institutions and Economic Growth

Historians have suggested many different explanations for Amsterdam's rise to primacy among the Low Countries' trading cities. As the seventeenth-century English ambassador William Temple observed, in the period of its greatest commercial success Amsterdam actually had a very incommodious port, which big ships could only enter during high tide. This led him to conclude that "'tis not an Haven that draws Trade, but Trade that fills an Haven, and brings it in vogue."[29] This "Trade," the general economic climate, was the sum of all the individual merchants, artisans, and entrepreneurs who were based in Amsterdam in this period. Temple, therefore, already points at the tension between structure and agency, endogenous or exogenous factors, as the most important cause for economic growth.

In the historiographical debates on the rise of Amsterdam as a city of commerce, two main positions can be identified. A first strand of argumentation focuses on long-term endogenous economic developments in order to explain the Dutch Republic's economic take-off. Jan de Vries and Ad van der Woude have pointed out that the elastic supply of shipping space, low transaction costs, and the efficiently functioning markets that originated with Amsterdam's traditional

[28] I have published more elaborately about the use of historical research methodologies for legal scholars elsewhere: Maurits den Hollander, "On the Relations between Law and History," *Forum Historiae Iuris* (2019) (online journal).

[29] William Temple, *Ambassadeur in de Lage Landen – Observations upon the United Provinces*, ed. Daniel Jeen Roorda and Y. H. Foppema (Haarlem: Fibula – Van Dishoek, 1978), 135.

Baltic trade formed ideal preconditions for its great expansion in international commerce in the last quarter of the sixteenth century. The fact that merchants reinvested their profits would have stimulated the rise of a more efficient range of institutions, such as the Bank of Exchange; technological innovations, such as the *Fluit* ship; and specialization. All of this combined to reduce transaction costs, which they see as the prime reason why Amsterdam became the world's central, dominant commercial center or "staple market."[30] According to Clé Lesger, Amsterdam functioned as the prime *information* market of the Low Countries rather than as a physical "staple market"; as the Dutch gateway in a developing modern transit trade system. In this information economy, southern migrants would have played a crucial role through the introduction of innovative financial techniques and pre-existing networks in regions where Amsterdam merchants lacked connections up to that time.[31]

This ties in with the second classic argument on the economic rise of Amsterdam, as voiced by Jonathan Israel: Amsterdam owed its rise to immigrants from the Southern Netherlands, especially those who fled Antwerp after the Spanish captured this great city of commerce in 1585.[32] The rich and skilled southern artisans and merchants would have "brought not only their knowledge, capital, and talents, but also the strong motivation to make things work" to Amsterdam, which was said to have turned into "the most Brabantine city of the North" or "the new Antwerp."[33] However, even though a large number of southerners migrated to Amsterdam in the years after 1585, Oscar Gelderblom argues that their influence on the expansion of Amsterdam's commerce should not be overestimated: "the bulk of the immigrants were young men of modest means, ... still at the beginning of their career in international trade." Amsterdam's attractiveness was grounded in pre-existing endogenous factors, but for the immigrants these were formed by its existing integration with Antwerp rather than the Baltic trade. As merchants from north and south successfully collaborated in numerous ventures both before and

30 De Vries and Van der Woude, *First Modern Economy*, 669–71.

31 Lesger, *Handel in Amsterdam*.

32 Israel, *Dutch Primacy in World Trade, 1585–1740*.

33 Gustaaf Asaert, *1585. De val van Antwerpen en de uittocht van Vlamingen en Brabanders* (Tielt: Lannoo, 2004), 136–37.

after the Dutch Revolt, Gelderblom sees them as "part of one single, native merchant community which developed in the Low Countries in the course of the sixteenth century."[34]

How can these factors help us to understand Amsterdam's success story? It is broadly acknowledged that an early market economy, such as late medieval Holland, had the potential to spark "Smithian" economic growth: market exchange leads to specialization – relative productivity gains – which capitalists systematically exploit for profit.[35] Neoclassical economics presumes a world of perfect information, in which all is determined by the utilitarian interests of individual actors and institutions.[36]

The main critique of the important school of new institutional economics (NIE) on this traditional image is that it fails to consider transaction costs. Such costs include that of organizing and obtaining economic information or reducing the risks inherent in commerce, such as piracy or the failure of debtors to repay their loans. Douglass North and other adherents of the NIE made "institutions" into the central subject of their analysis, in order to consider how institutional constraints actually limit actors in their pursuing of self-interest in a reality of imperfect information. If growth is to proliferate, economic organization needs to be efficient. The protection of property rights is seen as essential to attain this goal, as these make it worthwhile for individuals to engage in economically productive activities.[37] North initially emphasized the importance of strong states, which would have possessed the military means to guarantee the legal enforcement of the open-access institutions that helped merchants to overcome the problems caused by early modern Europe's political and legal

[34] Gelderblom, *Zuid-Nederlandse kooplieden*, 250–53; Oscar Gelderblom, "Continuïteit en verandering in de handelsgeschiedenis van Amsterdam," *BMGN – Low Countries Historical Review* 118, no. 1 (2003): 49–57.

[35] Prak and Van Zanden, *Pioneers of Capitalism*, 7; Bas van Bavel, *Manors and Markets: Economy and Society in the Low Countries, 500–1600* (Oxford University Press, 2010).

[36] Muldrew, "Interpreting the Market."

[37] Douglass C. North, *Structure and Change in Economic History* (New York: Norton, 1981); North, *Institutions, Institutional Change*. A useful overview of the development and thinking of the NIE can be found in Rudolf Richter, "The New Institutional Economics: Its Start, Its Meaning, Its Prospects," *European Business Organization Law Review* 6, no. 2 (2005): 161–200.

fragmentation.[38] However, this is difficult to square with the early expansion of European international commerce, in the absence of centralized states.[39]

An entirely different strand of criticism on neoclassical economics is that it fails to take social relations into account. Based upon the substantivist anthropology of Karl Polanyi,[40] historians such as Edward Thompson, Craig Muldrew, and Laurence Fontaine have argued that economic life should not be studied as an autonomous sphere, but as fundamentally submerged or "embedded" in social relations. They argue that the culture of the early modern market was explicitly social, as relations between buyers and sellers were governed by a normative and regulatory morality in which credit was based upon trust and reputation rather than amoral self-interest.[41] Forms of cooperation between merchants such as guilds would have generated the bargaining power necessary to stimulate governments to protect merchants and provide impartial justice in situations where such private ordering mechanisms would not suffice.[42] However, Emily Kadens has shown how ex-post legal enforcement was essential to help constrain low-level cheating among the customers of grocers in early modern London.[43] Furthermore, Amsterdam never had an overarching local merchant guild, and repeatedly refused demands for special privileges from foreign merchant colonies.[44]

Oscar Gelderblom has proposed a solution to this problem by focusing on intercity competition as a driving force of institutional change. According to Gelderblom, "the very problem of Europe's

38 North and Thomas, *The Rise of the Western World*. Later, however, he nuanced this position: North, *Institutions, Institutional Change*.

39 Gelderblom, *Cities of Commerce*, 2.

40 Polanyi, *Great Transformation*.

41 Thompson, "The Moral Economy of the English Crowd in the Eighteenth Century"; Muldrew, "Interpreting the Market"; Muldrew, *Economy of Obligation*; Fontaine, *The Moral Economy*. This can be linked to proponents of private ordering solutions such as, especially, Greif, *Institutions*; Avner Greif, Paul Milgrom, and Barry Weingast, "Coordination, Commitment, and Enforcement: The Case of the Merchant Guild," *Journal of Political Economy* 102, no. 4 (1994): 745–76.

42 Greif, Milgrom, and Weingast, "Coordination, Commitment, and Enforcement."

43 Emily Kadens, "Cheating Pays," *Columbia Law Review* 119 (2019): 528–89; Emily Kadens, "The Dark Side of Reputation," *Cardozo Law Review* 40 (2019): 1995–2027.

44 Sheilagh C. Ogilvie, *Institutions and European Trade: Merchant Guilds, 1000–1800* (Cambridge University Press, 2011), 32–34.

legal and political fragmentation also produced its solution, in the form of urban governments that tried to attract trade through the continuous adaptation of their legal, commercial, and financial institutions."[45] In the early modern period, local governments were able to provide and enforce the efficient open-access public-order institutions heralded by North as the foundation of economic growth just as well and actually even better than centralizing states.[46] As Prak and Van Zanden have emphasized, these also formed the locus of the Dutch "coordinated market economy," which long managed to restrain capitalist rent-seeking impulses through a powerful urban civil society.[47]

It is in their explanations for the proliferation of credit – enabling economic growth – that these debates on social and economic history are of great relevance for this book. While the adherents of NIE generally restrict their analysis to international commerce and "big finance," moral economy scholars tend to focus on poor and middle-class households. The study of insolvency allows us to integrate these strands of research into a unified perspective on the daily operation of the early capitalist economy, allowing us to further our understanding of Amsterdam's early modern efflorescence.

From Personal to Systemic Trust

The ability to obtain credit is strongly linked to reputation, as exemplified by its linguistic origins in the Latin word *credo*, which is closely connected to notions of "faith," "trust," and "authority."[48] At the end of the day, trust is essential for any type of transaction. This was just as true in the early modern period as it is today, for humble shopkeepers and their customers as well as for international merchants. As Peter Mathias states, "if access to credit was the first rule for success in business then creditworthiness was the means to this essential end." A businessman's respectability was created by others, who had to accord them the status of being worthy of trust. This form of credibility could not simply be asserted: it had to be built up

[45] Gelderblom, *Cities of Commerce*, 3. [46] Ibid. 123–25.

[47] Prak and Van Zanden, *Pioneers of Capitalism*, 207–9. See also Harold Joseph Berman, *Law and Revolution*, II: *The Impact of the Protestant Reformations on the Western Legal Tradition* (Cambridge: Harvard University Press, 2006), 348.

[48] Fontaine, *The Moral Economy*, 8–12.

slowly by actions as well as words.[49] In reality, both reputation and more formal "classic" institutions are essential for the functioning of the economy. Good insolvency legislation, as I argue in this book, has the potential to support economic growth through both of these factors. On the one hand, it can provide an external, public form of security to stimulate individual transactions but, on the other hand, it also has the potential to restore part of a debtor's reputation that had previously been damaged by an insolvency through open, independent, and transparent legal procedures.

However, it is easier to describe than to explain these beneficial effects of well-functioning insolvency legislation for the economy at large. This is a problem that one often encounters in studies of institutions as agents of change in history, a problem that might partially be solved by moving beyond and above the institutional framework itself to analyze it from a greater level of abstraction. Sociological analysis, in particular systems theory, allows us to reflect on such relationships between individuals and society as a whole, as well as the functioning of the mechanisms behind institutions such as law or the economy, and how these fit together. The insights gained from such strictly intellectual endeavors must then be tested against empirical evidence obtained from archival research. This allows us to study institutions from an analytical position that has a far greater explanatory potential than one which would remain strictly constrained to the institutional framework itself. I will borrow some relevant concepts from Niklas Luhmann's functional sociology and incorporate these into my analytical framework. This does not mean that I embrace his entire worldview or will seek to test it in a comprehensive manner. That topic would merit another book in itself. Nevertheless, a brief treatment of some of his ideas helps us to reflect on the aforementioned economic and institutional theories that I do intend to engage with.

How, for instance, can we account for the role of trust in human relations? According to Luhmann's functional sociology, our world

[49] Peter Mathias, "Strategies for Reducing Risk by Entrepreneurs in the Early Modern Period," in *Entrepreneurs and Entrepreneurship in Early Modern Times: Merchants and Industrialists within the Orbit of the Dutch Staple Market*, ed. Clé Lesger and Leo Noordegraaf (The Hague: Stichting Hollandse Historische Reeks, 1995), 13–15.

is overly complex.[50] It presents an individual actor with more possibilities than they could ever actualize, which is further complicated by the fundamental unpredictability of other human beings and the changeability of social relations over time. Trust bridges these gaps in time and knowledge, enabling the actor to reduce social complexity by limiting the amount of possible future events. This not only provides psychological relief, liberating the individual from what would otherwise turn into a paralyzing insecurity, but also points to its elementary significance for the functioning of complex social systems such as the economy.[51] It is only on the basis of trust that organized social groups and systems can expand the time horizon of their actions,[52] for instance through the appointment of a managing director (which requires a broad principal–agent trust due to unpredictable future events faced by this employee) or the function of money (relying on the widespread trust that it will also be accepted as legal tender in future).[53]

Luhmann's major contribution to trust research is the notion that *social systems* can also be the proper object of trust. In system trust, an individual actor "basically assumes that a system is functioning and places his trust in that function and not in … people."[54] In Luhmann's theory, social systems are a direct result of the increasing complexity of modern societies, which necessitates the differentiation of social relations into subsystems such as law, politics, or the economy to reduce its inherent chaos and contingency.[55] Law's function, in Luhmann's terms, is "to stabilize normative expectations over time and so avoid reliance on experience."[56] The progression from premodern to modern society would have been accompanied by a reversed prominence of interpersonal versus system trust. If "a social order becomes more

[50] For a very useful summary of Luhmann's ideas on trust and power, from which I have also benefited myself, see Frens Kroeger, "Unlocking the Treasure Trove: How Can Luhmann's Theory of Trust Enrich Trust Research?," *Journal of Trust Research* 9, no. 1 (2019): 110–24.

[51] Niklas Luhmann, *Trust and Power*, ed. Christian Morgner and Michael King (Cambridge: Polity Press, 2017), 5–9.

[52] Ibid. 128. [53] Ibid. 56 and 89.

[54] Ibid. 55; Kroeger, "Unlocking the Treasure Trove," 116.

[55] Reza Banakar and Max Travers, "Systems Theory," in *Law and Social Theory*, ed. Reza Banakar and Max Travers, 2nd ed. (Oxford: Hart Publishing, 2013), 55–56.

[56] Michael King, "The Radical Sociology of Niklas Luhmann," in *Law and Social Theory*, ed. Reza Banakar and Max Travers, 2nd ed. (Oxford: Hart Publishing, 2013), 66–67.

complex and variable, ... the very complexity of the social order creates a greater need for co-ordination and hence a need to determine the future – i.e., a need for trust."[57] Luhmann emphasizes the strong link between trust and self-confidence, which means that a significant breach of trust (such as the failure to repay one's debts) may endanger both the trustor's (creditor's) social image as well as their self-image: it calls into question their ability to make sense of the social world not just through instrumental (economic) but also by means of social (loss of face) embarrassment.[58] This points at the essentially reflexive nature of trust (and credit): trustors will always look to others for confirmation that their own position is sensible. Trust not only underlies social order, but individual trust is also embedded into and conditioned by the social. This group dynamic plays a significant role in the institutionalization of trust to a systemic level.[59] As source of increased stability and hence predictability, this systemic variant of trust, embedded in governmental institutions, is essential in allowing social systems to grow and increase in complexity over time. Today as much as in the early modern age, trust and power, or reputation and legal authorities, exist alongside each other and concurrently serve as functional complements to stabilize social systems.[60]

While Luhmann provides important indications as to the nature and relevance of system trust, he only gave some brief and unspecific comments on its genesis. The conditions under which trust and power impede or amplify one another deserve further study.[61] The same is true for many of the assumptions made by the NIE about the effects of law and legal institutions on economic growth.[62] The example of Amsterdam's early modern insolvency legislation and practices is well suited to take some tentative empirical steps in this direction. The introduction of the Desolate Boedelskamer in 1643 has the potential to serve as a natural experiment, allowing us to determine the effect of

[57] Luhmann, *Trust and Power*, 23–24 and ch. 7. [58] Ibid. 29, chs. 8 and 11.

[59] Ibid. 77. [60] Kroeger, "Unlocking the Treasure Trove," 120–21.

[61] Ibid. 116 and 121; Frens Kroeger, "The Development, Escalation and Collapse of System Trust: From the Financial Crisis to Society at Large," *European Management Journal* 33, no. 6 (2015): 431–37.

[62] Jan Dumolyn and Bart Lambert, "Cities of Commerce, Cities of Constraints: International Trade, Government Institutions and the Law of Commerce in Later Medieval Bruges and the Burgundian State," *TSEG / Low Countries Journal of Social and Economic History* 11, no. 4 (2014): 89–102.

institutional innovations on the relations between creditors and debtors. This book therefore analyzes the interplay between legal institutions and social norms, systemic and personal trust, as mechanisms which provided essential securities for transactions and hence formed a foundation for economic growth.

Research Focus and Sources

This book will analyze the extent to which the introduction of the Desolate Boedelskamer in 1643 had an impact on Amsterdam's economy and society between the 1578 *Alteratie*, which replaced the city's Catholic government with a Protestant one, and 1700. How were insolvency and indebtedness looked upon in general, and in what ways did this influence the procedures and functioning of a legal institution such as the Desolate Boedelskamer? Who were the insolvents that were submitted to the commissioners' care? What were their social backgrounds, and how did this influence the strategies which they had at their disposal to influence the resolution of their financial and legal problems? And, finally, how should the treatment of insolvencies be viewed from the broader perspective of theories about the economic success of Amsterdam in this period? Studying insolvency helps to shed new light on the intriguing debates about Amsterdam's rise, since it allows us to understand how this society coped with failure.

Even though it can hardly be argued that the city of Amsterdam is exemplary or typical for the general situation in the seventeenth-century Dutch Republic, the fact that it pioneered many legal and economic institutional innovations that were subsequently adopted by other cities justifies the choice to make it the focus of this in-depth analysis of early modern insolvency legislation and practices. The mental world that was occupied by Amsterdam's inhabitants and administrators can easily be extrapolated to the entire province of Holland, as well as other (urbanized) parts of the early modern Dutch Republic.[63] Through a broad archival analysis of the social

[63] For the broader dissemination of innovations such as the majority composition, see Chapter 7 below, and especially Maurits den Hollander, "Failliet in de Republiek. Lokale ordonnanties over de omgang met desolate boedels, circa 1643–1713," *Pro Memorie* 24, no. 2 (2022): 190–217.

and economic context in which insolvency legislation was created and applied in seventeenth-century Amsterdam, I will highlight the ways in which innovative governance and legal practices interacted with moral thought in order to produce a liberal, open-access insolvency regime. This book combines an analysis of relevant insolvency ordinances, urban legislation, and legal scholarship with a practical reconstruction of the events and procedures surrounding individual insolvencies.

The primary source material that was used for this book was predominantly found in the Municipal Archives of Amsterdam (GAS) and the National Archives in The Hague (NL-HaNA). These archives not only allow us to reconstruct the daily work and procedures of the Amsterdam Desolate Boedelskamer, but also provide a glimpse of the insolvents' personal stories. The Amsterdam archives constitute the core of my research, and provide the foundation for an in-depth analysis of the ways in which insolvency was dealt with in historical practice, as a mirror of official municipal and academic legal traditions.[64]

The archives of the Desolate Boedelskamer have not been preserved in their entirety. A combination of natural disasters and equally disastrous archival policies in the early modern period resulted in the destruction of part of this valuable collection. On Sunday July 7, 1652, less than a decade after the court had been founded, the old medieval city hall of Amsterdam caught fire in the middle of the night. According to Jan Wagenaar, "on this occasion, many old registers and [archival] pieces were burned."[65] At the same time, thanks to heroic acts of a number of brave citizens many other documents were rescued from the inferno:

Eenige ijveraars voor Stads dienst streefden, midden door de vlammen, naar de Secreterije, en keerden, met armen vol boeken en papieren, te rug. Een was 'er, die naar de Weeskamer liep, toen zij in vollen brand stond, en de boeken en registers, welken hij magtig worden kon, ten vensteren uit, op

[64] The urban ordinances of 1643 and 1659 have been published in Gerard Rooseboom (ed.), *Recueil van verscheyde keuren, en costumen; midtsgaders maniere van procederen binnen de stadt Amsterdam*, 2nd ed. (Amsterdam: Jan Hendricks, 1656), 304–9; Hermanus Noordkerk (ed.), *Handvesten; ofte privilegien ende octroyen: mitsgaders willekeuren, costuimen, ordonnantien en handelingen der stad Amstelredam*, 4 vols. (Amsterdam: Hendrik van Waesberge, Salomon en Petrus Schouten, 1748), II:687–90.

[65] Jan Wagenaar, *Amsterdam in zijne opkomst*, 4 vols. (Amsterdam: Isaak Tirion, 1765), II:583–84.

straat smeet, daar zij waargenomen en gebergd werden: waarna hij zig, bij een touw, langs den tooren, nederliet, alzo de trap, die hij opgekomen was, reeds was afgebrand.

[A number of brave zealots managed to reach the Secretariat through the flames, returning with their arms full of books and paperwork. One of them even entered the Orphan Chamber, which was entirely ablaze, throwing all books and registers on which he could lay his hands out of a window on the street, from where they could be salvaged. Thereafter, he had to escape using a rope lowered from the tower, as the stairway by which he had entered had already burned down.]

Even though it shows some burn-marks, it is probably thanks to these brave citizens that the oldest register of the appointment of curators, which even predates the court itself, has survived to the present date.[66]

Rather more reprehensible is the fact that the burgomasters and the court's commissioners themselves sold off and destroyed parts of this archival collection at various points in its history. Following complaints about the "paper flood" which filled the "book room" and other storage areas, in 1720 it was decided to sell off much of the archives that had been built up from the establishment of the Desolate Boedelskamer up to and including 1684 as wastepaper. For fl. 2,200, Leiden citizen Reinout Gartner bought the whole collection *voetstoots en bij de hoop* or "as a heap, not measured and just as it is in whatever condition." In 1756, archives from 1684–1714 that were stored in the court's warehouse and on the attic of the (new) city hall were sorted and largely disposed of. This time, the wastepaper trader Maarten Neeltjes from Krommenie obtained ninety-seven bales of archival material for the pitiful amount of fl. 517. In 1773 the *opruiming* of documents from 1714–1735 followed, the archives being destroyed in a paper mill in the presence of one of the court's servants.[67] Lastly, between 1805 and 1808 the Amsterdam city hall was rededicated as a royal palace under the Kingdom of Holland. These events, as well as the connected overly swift evacuation of certain warehouses that were used as storerooms by the municipal administration at the time, reportedly resulted in a *verscheurcommissie* or

[66] GAS, 5072: DB, inv. nr. 469.

[67] GAS, 5072: DB, inv. nr. 59, ff. 37–38, 102v–103r, 106, and 160. See also Eric Ketelaar, *Archiving People: A Social History of Dutch Archives* (The Hague: Stichting Archiefpublicaties, 2020), 159–60.

"tearing-up committee" that led to a final destruction of many early modern documents.[68] Whereas the selection criteria that were used in these clean-up operations are unclear, it is likely that many documents and registers containing information about individual insolvency cases similar to those that have survived from the late seventeenth and eighteenth centuries must originally also have existed for the first decades of the court's existence.

Fortunately, however, enough of the fascinating material created and archived by the Desolate Boedelskamer was preserved to allow a reconstruction of its functioning and development over time, as well as the impact of these developments on the legal treatment of financial demise in seventeenth-century Amsterdam. I will briefly describe the main series of records that I used in order to clarify their function, contents, and form.

The *Notulen* or minutes are one of the oldest series of registers, created from the moment the annually elected commissioners started their work in November 1643. During their meetings, structured with headings consisting of the relevant insolvent's name, notes about the commissioners' decisions would be included on a case-by-case basis. The minutes allow us to find information about curators' acts for which they needed the commissioners' permission, orders to execute an insolvent estate, decisions on requests for *cessie van goede* (a voluntary surrender of the insolvent estate) or *seureté de corps* (a protective short-term moratorium), or information about the conclusion of *akkoorden* (compositions). This series of codices, therefore, provides valuable insights into individual cases as well as the commissioners' daily work from the foundation of the Desolate Boedelskamer onwards.[69]

The series of *Resolutiën* or Books of Resolutions starts ten years later, in 1654. For the entire seventeenth century, one codex sufficed to copy and store decisions by the commissioners as well as, sometimes, burgomasters and aldermen, related to procedures, work instructions, staff, salaries, and other organizational matters pertaining to

[68] W. F. H. Oldewelt, "Twee eeuwen Amsterdamse faillissementen en het verloop van de conjunctuur (1636 tot 1838)," *Tijdschrift voor Geschiedenis* 75, no. 4 (1962): 421–35, 425–26.

[69] GAS, 5072: DB, inv. nrs. 1–30.

the Desolate Boedelskamer. Together with the official ordinances, this register is crucial to arrive at a deeper understanding of Amsterdam's increasingly sophisticated way of managing insolvencies over time.[70]

The registers of *Staten der Cessionanten* have unfortunately only survived from 1689 onwards. These collections of insolvents' applications for *cessie van goede* (from the Latin *cessio bonorum*), that were numbered and bundled into a codex on an annual basis, provide deep insight into the identity and background of individual insolvents. *Cessie* granted insolvents protection from debt imprisonment on the condition that they would hand over their entire estate (except for some basic life necessities) to be executed for the benefit of the creditors. Regular inventories of an estate (*boedel-inventarissen*) only include movable goods, while these *staten van goed* provide a much more complete image. Besides listing all outstanding debts, claims, and possessions, the documents usually also include stories about the events leading up to the insolvency and subsequent *cessie*-application.[71]

The *akkoorden* between insolvents and their creditors have, unfortunately, not been bundled and preserved in their entirety. Hundreds of these compositions from the seventeenth century can be found in the archive's category titled *Restant* or "leftovers." While this collection is incomplete, a comparison with the cases and accords mentioned in specific years of the minutes suggests that about a third to half of the accords in every year are still accessible, either as originals or contemporary copies.[72]

These main source series were supplemented by material from the inventories of insolvent estates and other supporting registers, as well as useful references found in a number of notarial protocols and other archives produced by the Amsterdam local authorities in this period.

The core of my archival analysis consists of the creation of two datasets containing, respectively, series of accords between insolvents and their creditors, and applicants for *cessie van goede*. The accords were selected randomly from the exemplars preserved in the Amsterdam archives. I have selected fifteen accords for each of the first two decades of the court's functioning, and ten for each subsequent

[70] GAS, 5072: DB, inv. nr. 58. [71] GAS, 5072: DB, inv. nrs. 689–702.
[72] GAS, 5072: DB, inv. nrs. 1227–2879.

decade. This allows us to study the effect of the 1659 ordinance on the structure and contents of these individually arbitrated agreements. Because of the large consistencies within the sampled cases, as well as their random selection, it is likely that this collection allows us to form a representative view on the practices surrounding the accord in this period. This is supported by a comparison of quantitative information such as debt values in my sample of accords with an overview compiled by the Amsterdam Municipal Archives in 1892, containing summarized data on all 598 surviving accords from the period before 1700.[73] More information on the specific contents of these two datasets as well as the way in which I structured the data can be found in the Appendix.

Unfortunately, unlike the accords, the Amsterdam registers of applications for *cessie* have only been preserved from 1689 onwards. However, the fact that the reconstructed procedure seems to be coherent with the court's oldest ordinances, supplemented by evidence found in the archives of the High Court of Holland (*Hoge Raad*) in The Hague, allows us to regard this collection as representative for at least the second half of the seventeenth century. Machiel Bosman has examined the Amsterdam applications for *cessie* that were sent to the High Court between 1654 and 1659, concluding that "in Rembrandt's time more than half of the Amsterdam insolvents requested a letter of *cessie*," but that studies of this phenomenon are generally lacking.[74] This book will seek to partially fill this lacuna by studying a great number of these cases from the 1690s. The first surviving codex of Amsterdam applications for *cessie van goede* covers the complete year 1690, as well as parts of 1689 and 1691; the second and third registers I selected are restricted to the years 1695 and 1700.[75]

It proved possible to extract 259 unique cases from the Amsterdam sources, which constitute a sufficient sample to draw conclusions about the sorts of people that made use of the benefice of *cessie* and

[73] GAS, 5072: DB, inv. nr. 145.
[74] Machiel Bosman, *Rembrandts plan. De ware geschiedenis van zijn faillissement* (Amsterdam: Atheneum – Polak & Van Gennep, 2019), 106 and 197–198 (n. 6).
[75] GAS, 5072: DB, inv. nrs. 689, 697, and 702. The register with inv. nr. 692, consisting of the originals of the applications of the year 1690 found as "neat copies" in register "A" (inv. nr. 689), was used to complement this data.

the reasons why they were forced to do so.[76] Almost every applicant for the year 1700 could also be found back in the *registeren van curatele*, the register of curators. This indicates that the sample for the given years is more-or-less complete, as every insolvency treated by the Desolate Boedelskamer officially started with the appointment of a curator.[77] From an analysis of the value of debts of each insolvent estate, it appears that in every examined year the population showed a consistent build-up, supporting the representativeness of the sample (see Figure I.1).

Even though privileged debtors such as noblemen or widows would have possessed the right to have their insolvency treated directly by the Court of Holland (*Hof van Holland*) rather than (at first instance) by local aldermen, in practice this court does not seem to have played an important function in the resolution of insolvencies in early modern Amsterdam.[78] Even though the Court of Holland was the institution responsible for treating *cessie* applications in Holland between 1573, when its provincial government ceased to recognize the jurisdiction of the Great Council of Malines, and 1582, when the High Court of Holland was founded and took over this procedural function, this does not seem to have left many traces in the *Hof*'s archives, either.[79] A quick survey of the indices on the website of the National Archives in The Hague did not provide any meaningful results for seventeenth-century Amsterdam, even though the surviving process files or *proceszakken* do contain a small number of *cessie* cases in which an appeal was filed against the judgment of a local court.[80] A sample of Amsterdam *cessie* cases from the year 1700 has been traced in the archives of the High Court (*Hoge Raad van Holland*), in order to arrive at a complete

[76] The term "benefice" might potentially cause confusion here, due to its predominant use for ecclesiastical offices in the literature. In this book, it is used as a translation of *beneficie*, which was the term used by contemporaries to describe legal remedies such as *cessie van goede* that were granted by the sovereign.

[77] GAS, 5072: DB, inv. nrs. 480 and 481.

[78] Maria-Charlotte le Bailly, *Procesgids Hof van Holland, Zeeland en West-Friesland: de hoofdlijnen van het procederen in civiele zaken voor het Hof van Holland, Zeeland en West-Friesland zowel in eerste instantie als in hoger beroep* (Hilversum: Verloren, 2008), 48–52.

[79] Eric Ketelaar, "De procesgang bij het Hof van Holland, Zeeland en West-Friesland," in *Verslag en bijdragen Rijks Archiefschool 1969–1970* (Utrecht: Rijksarchiefschool, 1971), 56–58.

[80] NL-HaNA, www.nationaalarchief.nl/onderzoeken/archief/3.03.01.01.

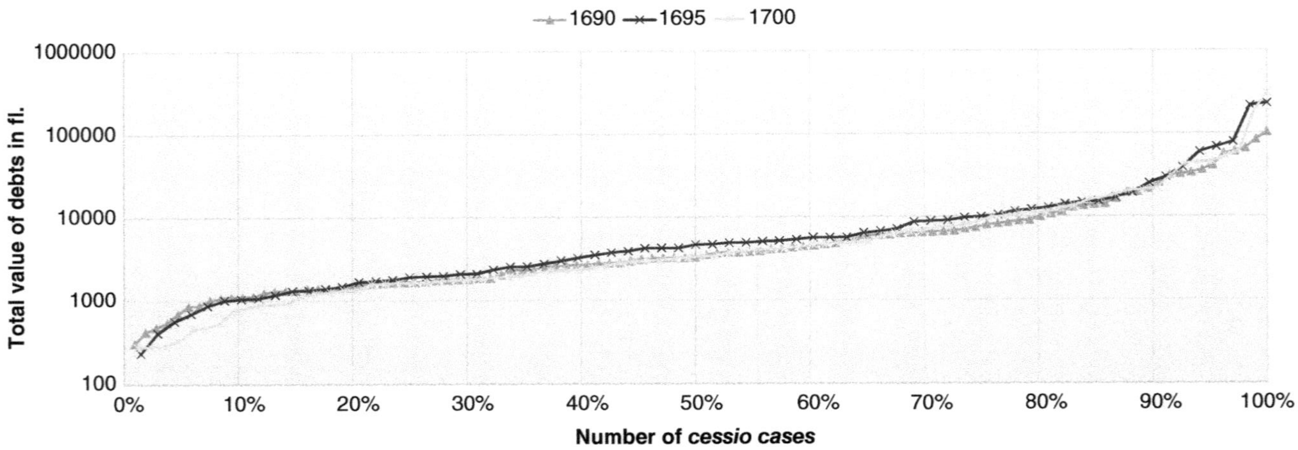

FIGURE I.1 Value of debts per insolvent estate of applicants for *cessie van goede* in 1690, 1695, and 1700 on a logarithmic scale

understanding of the way in which they were processed.[81] It is important to note that these applications to the High Court contain far less information about individual insolvencies than the complete files that have been preserved in the Amsterdam archives from the 1690s onwards. As will be elaborated upon in Chapter 6, they lack the personal stories and detailed information about debts and possessions that make these applications such a valuable historical source.

It is important to note that these applicants for *cessie* constituted the vast majority of Amsterdam insolvents. While Oldewelt has created statistics on the annual number of insolvencies in Amsterdam in the early modern period, these data appear to be partially corrupted.[82] His main source for this period is the registers for *curatele*. However, for the year 1700, I found the actual number to be about a third lower than Oldewelt's count. This new result quite closely corresponds to the number of *cessie* applicants for that year, supplemented by some cases in which an accord could be reached with the creditors. We can draw two important conclusions from this observation. First, one should hesitate to take Oldewelt's data at face value, even though his article might still be useful in its interpretation of long-term economic trends. Second, it is important to realize that the majority of Amsterdam insolvents in the later seventeenth century resolved their financial problems through the *cessie* procedure rather than through an accord, even though the latter received more attention in the older literature. These source collections allow us to arrive at important and meaningful conclusions about the functioning of insolvency legislation as part of its broader social and economic context in seventeenth-century Amsterdam.

[81] NL-HaNA, Hoge Raad Holland en Zeeland, 3.03.02, inv. nr. 104.
[82] Oldewelt, "Twee eeuwen."

PART I

CONTEXT

1

Citizens and Institutions

The first inhabitants of what would become the city of Amsterdam arrived at the river Amstel in the eleventh century. The area, then under the jurisdiction of the bishop of Utrecht, was drained as part of the large land clearings that took place everywhere between the North Sea dunes and the city of Utrecht in this period. In order to control the flow of water to the Zuiderzee, a dam with sluices was built in the Amstel around 1270. The tiny village that had sprung up around these waterworks slowly grew into a proper city.[1] On October 27, 1275, Count Floris V provided its inhabitants with a toll privilege that allowed them to trade and travel freely through the entire County of Holland. This was part of the count's ongoing rivalry with the bishop of Utrecht, as both princes strove to control the Amstelland on their borders. Notwithstanding the toll-privilege, it was Bishop Gwijde van Avesnes who granted Amsterdam its first proper city charter soon after 1300. These and later codifications of the city's privileges and legal framework were prompted by its citizens' own initiatives.[2]

As Amsterdam expanded, its inhabitants continued to develop an extensive trading network. Its fleet connected the Baltic trade with

[1] Ben Speet, "Een kleine nederzetting in het veen," in *Geschiedenis van Amsterdam*, I: *Een stad uit het niets (tot 1575)* (Amsterdam: SUN, 2004), 21–61.

[2] Eef Dijkhof, "Op weg naar autonomie," in *Geschiedenis van Amsterdam*, I: *Een stad uit het niets (tot 1575)* (Amsterdam: SUN, 2004), 62–73; Joost C. M. Cox, *Repertorium van de stadsrechten in Nederland*, 2nd ed. (Oisterwijk: Stichting tot Uitgaaf der Bronnen van het Oud-Vaderlandse Recht, 2012).

(southern) France and the Iberian Peninsula.[3] The greatest expansion of commerce dates to the last quarter of the sixteenth century, after what is often called the *Alteratie*. In the religious conflict between Protestants and Catholics that resulted in the Dutch Revolt against Philip II of Spain, Amsterdam for a long time continued to support the royalist party. On May 26, 1578, however, the Catholic municipal government was overthrown and replaced by its Protestant rivals. Through a shouting crowd of ordinary citizens, kept at bay by the civic militia or *schutterij* and its officers, the old government headed by burgomasters Hendrik Dircksz and Joost Buyck was led to a boat on the Damrak and dropped off on a dike beyond the city's borders. In an era of violent religious upheaval, this was a surprisingly bloodless revolution. This can, perhaps, be explained by the fact that Amsterdam's switch was not born so much out of religious devotion as political necessity. The formerly exiled Calvinists such as Baerdesen and Pauw, who now replaced the Catholic faction, gained broad support for the switch in Amsterdam's political allegiance by emphasizing Amsterdam's isolation. The *Alteratie* was primarily prompted by the fact that Amsterdam started to be isolated in the midst of rebel country: a position that seriously threatened its commerce-driven economy.[4]

After the city had joined the Dutch Revolt, the Amsterdam burgomasters and *vroedschap* or city council were increasingly occupied by matters of (inter)national politics. In turn, because of economic growth and a quickly expanding population, the aldermen's bench faced ever increasing amounts of civil litigation. While in 1578 the city had housed no more than 30,000 people, by the end of the seventeenth century this had increased explosively to more than 200,000 inhabitants.[5] This had two important consequences. In the first place,

[3] Herman Kaptein, "Poort van Holland. De economische ontwikkeling 1200–1578," in *Geschiedenis van Amsterdam*, I: *Een stad uit het niets (tot 1575)* (Amsterdam: SUN, 2004), 109–73.

[4] Henk van Nierop, "Van wonderjaar tot Alteratie 1566–1578," in *Geschiedenis van Amsterdam*, I: *Een stad uit het niets (tot 1575)* (Amsterdam: SUN, 2004), 450–81; R. B. Evenhuis, *Ook dat was Amsterdam. De kerk der hervorming in de Gouden Eeuw*, 2 vols. (Amsterdam: Ten Have, 1965), I:93–97.

[5] Hubert Nusteling, *Welvaart en werkgelegenheid in Amsterdam 1540–1860. Een relaas over demografie, economie en sociale politiek van een wereldstad* (Amsterdam: De Bataafsche Leeuw, 1985).

it became impossible for the burgomasters to remain involved with all the details of local administration. From the beginning of the seventeenth century onwards, legal and administrative tasks that had formerly been conducted by the burgomasters and aldermen were gradually delegated to various subordinate committees and public officials. Second, in order to ensure the stability and continuity of governance in Amsterdam – and thus essentially in the entire Dutch Republic – the group of families from which the burgomasters were elected became rather small. It soon developed into the tight-knit urban oligarchy of patricians known as "regents," who came to dominate Dutch government in the early modern period.[6]

The regents were not just involved with foreign policy. For a long time, for instance, the aldermen personally intervened in the estates of insolvent citizens. Due to demographic pressure and the resulting increase in the amount of litigation, it became ever more difficult to properly supervise the curators who had been appointed to each insolvent estate. As part of the general development towards specialization of governmental offices, on January 30, 1627 the Amsterdam *vroedschap* resolved to establish a *Camere van Desolate Boedels ende Commissarissen daertoe ghestelt.* This Desolate Boedelskamer was the last of five subordinate courts that were created in this period. Henceforth its commissioners would be responsible for the appointment and supervision of curators, the repartition of payments among the creditors, and, if necessary, the liquidation of the insolvent estate – tasks which had previously been conducted by the aldermen. Three urban officials were appointed to design and write down instructions for this new institution *soo haest doenlijck en sijn sal* or "as soon as possible."[7] For unknown reasons, these men do not seem to have attached great weight to this mandate. The new legal institution only began its work on November 6, 1643, more than fifteen years after the original resolution had been passed.[8]

[6] Gerhard Wilhelm Kernkamp, *Regeering en historie van Amsterdam in de 17e eeuw* (Amsterdam: Emmering, 1900), 19–20; Jan Wagenaar, *Amsterdam in zijne opkomst*, 4 vols. (Amsterdam: Yntema en Tieboel, 1767), III:366–67.

[7] Kernkamp, *Regeering en historie*, 48–52; Goswin Moll, *De Desolate Boedelskamer te Amsterdam: bijdrage tot de kennis van het Oud-Hollandsch failliten-recht* (Amsterdam: De Roever-Kröber-Bakels, 1879), 206, Appendix B.

[8] Moll, *Desolate Boedelskamer*, 17–18.

This general increase in the size and organizational complexity of local government occurred not only in Amsterdam, but was typical for many contemporary Dutch cities. The population of Dordrecht, for instance, increased from 12,000 to 18,000 inhabitants between 1575 and 1600. Many series of administrative documents such as protocols, marriage, and burial registers, were either started or vastly expanded in this period, accompanied by a significant increase in the numbers of public officials. Similar demographic developments also catalyzed the growth of public administration in Leiden. Even when in later periods economic growth and population levels stabilized or even decreased, the number of bureaucrats remained the same. As Elise van Nederveen Meerkerk remarks, "once a certain level of bureaucracy had been attained it was neither easy nor desirable to diminish the number of offices." This can be explained by the fact that cutbacks on employee budgets would usually endanger the income and profits of magistrates themselves, as well as those of their families and friends.[9] Again, this illustrates the tension between the tendency towards a professionalization of public governance, on the one hand, and a concentration of power in a limited number of kinship networks, on the other.

Early modern Amsterdam has often been characterized as a "city of commerce," "commercial hub," or "merchant republic." Mary Lindemann states that Amsterdam's citizens rarely divided their political identity as citizens from their identity as economic actors and merchants. They were both simultaneously: "Not everyone in Amsterdam was a merchant … nonetheless, commerce defined them all, or at least, the city they inhabited."[10] While (maritime) commerce was indisputably of great importance for the city on the Amstel, as indicated by the underlying commercial interests that played an important role in the *Alteratie*, such labels have also tended to blind

[9] Elise van Nederveen Meerkerk, "Professionalization of Public Service: Civil Servants in Dordrecht, 1575–1795," *Journal of Urban History* 36, no. 3 (2010): 345–67, 352 and 361; Manon van der Heijden, *Civic Duty: Public Services in the Early Modern Low Countries* (Newcastle upon Tyne: Cambridge Scholars Publishing, 2012), 48–52.

[10] Mary Lindemann, *The Merchant Republics: Amsterdam, Antwerp, and Hamburg, 1648–1790* (New York: Cambridge University Press, 2014), 5 (quote) and 83; see also Oscar Gelderblom, *Cities of Commerce: The Institutional Foundations of International Trade in the Low Countries, 1250–1650* (Princeton University Press, 2013).

historians to the large part of its citizenry whose horizons were more limited. The main motivation to acquire the citizenship of Amsterdam in the early modern period seems to have been the desire to enter one of the important craft guilds rather than to obtain commercial privileges. Even though their direct role in Amsterdam politics was limited, middle-class organizations such as craft guilds, as the foundation of the civic community, played a crucial role in the city's government and were definitely not neglected by the regents.[11] Therefore, an evaluation of the functioning of an institution such as Amsterdam's Desolate Boedelskamer will always need to consider the broader economic, social, and cultural contexts that might have had an impact on the law and those who applied it. As I will argue in this chapter, the law and economy of the seventeenth century did not "happen" in a vacuum, but were intimately embedded in and shaped by the social and cultural notions of the broader corpus of citizens.

This chapter will analyze the shift towards a closer involvement of the Amsterdam authorities with citizens from all layers of society that occurred through various institutional innovations after the *Alteratie* of 1578. First, I will discuss the function of credit as a unifying economic phenomenon, which allows us to shed light on the connections between people from various classes as well as to explore their economic strategies. Focusing on the phenomenon of insolvency, essentially a breakdown of credit, allows us to open up broader perspectives on the early modern economy. Second, I will explore arrangements for social aid, as these formed an important mechanism for coping with economic failure. Guilds and their *burgerlijke* or civic middle-class values shaped social and economic policies of this period in important ways, clearly displaying the integration among different social groups that also came to be reflected in contemporary legal theory and practice. Third, related to this discussion of the general fabric of society in seventeenth-century Amsterdam, I will go on to treat the important function of religious communities in

[11] Erika Kuijpers and Maarten Prak, "Burger, ingezetene, vreemdeling: burgerschap in Amsterdam in de 17e en 18e eeuw," in *Burger*, ed. Joost Kloek and Karin Tilmans (Amsterdam University Press, 2002), 113–32. See also Marco in 't Veld and Maurits den Hollander, "Citizenship in Early Modern Amsterdam: An Artisanal Identity?," in *Citizenship, Identity, and Commerce in Legal History*, ed. Dave De ruysscher, Albrecht Cordes, and Heikki Pihlajamäki (Leiden: Brill, 2021).

financial conflict resolution between creditors and debtors. The moral dimensions of insolvency that become manifest through the acts of various Amsterdam consistories reflect important changes in the attitudes towards – and dealing with – insolvency that are quite typical for the seventeenth-century Dutch Republic.

An Economy of Credit

As a young lawyer in his native Zeeland, the great Dutch moralist, and grand-pensionary Jacob Cats (1577–1660) fell desperately in love with a fair maiden while listening to a sermon in Middelburg's Walloon Reformed Church.[12] Even though he was consumed by his lust for this young woman, the fires of his passion were quickly quenched when he discovered that her father was a bankrupt. While Simon Schama explains Cats's radical turn by stating that "property could prevail over passion," Lotte van de Pol argues that social rather than economic arguments prompted him to look for another partner. Honor was intimately connected with reliability in financial matters. A bankrupt such as the father of Cats's sweetheart had violently disrupted this system of trust and reputation by not only stealing his creditors' money, but also, most importantly, by stealing their confidence. This made the girl instantly unsuitable as a marriage partner for a man of Cats's social standing and reputation.[13] This section will explore these tensions between honor, reputation, trust, and credit as vital factors in economic relations between early modern creditors and debtors.

Early modern entrepreneurs could not do without credit if they wished to make a serious profit. The uncertainties resulting from several types of delays meant that they needed substantial amounts

[12] The grand-pensionary was officially the most senior legal advisor of the States of Holland but, due to the economic and political importance of that province and his influence on their meetings, soon came to occupy a role close to that of prime-minister of the Dutch Republic: J. L. Price, *Holland and the Dutch Republic in the Seventeenth Century: The Politics of Particularism* (Oxford University Press, 1994), 129–33.

[13] Simon Schama, *The Embarrassment of Riches: An Interpretation of Dutch Culture in the Golden Age* (New York: Alfred A. Knopf, 1987), 443–44; Lotte C. van de Pol, "Prostitutie en de Amsterdamse burgerij: Eerbegrippen in een vroegmoderne stedelijke samenleving," in *Cultuur en maatschappij in Nederland 1500–1800*, ed. Peter Boekhorst, Peter Burke, and Willem Frijhoff (Amsterdam / Heerlen: Boom / Open Universiteit, 1992), 185–86.

of capital to finance their stock, to invest in shipping shares, and to provide for delayed payments by their own debtors. If an interesting commercial opportunity arose, merchants often needed to act fast, a capacity which was seriously handicapped or even made impossible if they solely had to rely on their own capital and reinvested profits.[14] In all such relations between creditors and debtors, trust was of vital importance. At the same time, of course, trusting also necessarily entails risk. As John Smail states, "the only way a merchant could minimize the risks associated with credit was by dealing with individuals who could be trusted to pay their debts, a proposition whose inherently circular logic is indicative of the problems they faced."[15] The Dutch author Pieter de la Court (1618–1658) argued that fraud was a grave danger for commerce: "as this entirely depends on trust or good faith (*bona fides*), deceit (*dolus malus*) can cause its utter ruin."[16] When creditors lost faith in a debtor's honesty and capacity to recover from financial misfortune, in an age of imperfect information on the performance of businesses few options remained but to turn to the legal authorities in order to try to limit losses as far as possible. Precisely such an unfortunate sequence of events forced the elderly widow Anna van Loo to seek the protection of the Desolate Boedelskamer on Thursday July 8, 1700.[17]

Four decades earlier, her life had seemed much brighter. On May 3, 1657 Anna, then 32 years old, had married Laurens Jansz. Nooten from Delfshaven, aged 29, in Amsterdam's Dutch Reformed congregation.[18] Nooten was described as a *haringcoper* or herring

[14] Gelderblom, *Cities of Commerce*, 67.

[15] John Smail, "Credit, Risk, and Honor in Eighteenth-Century Commerce," *Journal of British Studies* 44, no. 3 (2005): 439–56, 446.

[16] Pieter de la Court, *Interest van Holland, ofte gronden van Hollands-welvaren* (Amsterdam: Joan. Cyprianus vander Gracht, 1662), 76.

[17] Gemeente Amsterdam Stadsarchief [GAS], 5072: Archief van de Commissarissen van de Desolate Boedelkamer [DB], inv. nr. 702, nr. 54.

[18] GAS, Burgerlijke Stand: doop-, trouw- en begraafboeken [DTB], inv. nr. 477, p. 217. Through her sister Magdalena's marriage with Titus van Rijn in 1668, Anna van Loo eventually became related to Rembrandt van Rijn, who was to become not only one of the most famous Dutch painters of the seventeenth century but also one of its most notorious insolvents. Within one year both Titus, Magdalena, and Anna's mother Anna Huybrechts succumbed to the plague epidemic that ravaged Amsterdam at that time: I. H. van Eeghen, "Het graf van Titus van Rijn," *Maandblad Amstelodamum* 76 (1989): 123–26.

buyer. How should we interpret this occupation? In the commercial landscape of early modern Amsterdam, the *copers* functioned as wholesalers while those businessmen described as *vercopers* worked as retailers. During the seventeenth century, the latter increasingly came to be described as *winkeliers* or shopkeepers, while in earlier times they had been known as *merseman* or *kramer*. The mass of the Amsterdam citizenry consisted of such ordinary self-employed craftsmen and small retailers, who formed the link between the big merchants and entrepreneurs and the masses of humble wage-laborers. Some big *winkeliers* also partially functioned as minor wholesalers for retailers in their direct vicinity, while the proper Amsterdam wholesalers often delivered goods to shopkeepers in a much wider region. The Nooten business clearly belonged to this larger type, as is revealed by the company's debtors. In the *staet* (inventory) of Anna van Loo, we find debtors from Haarlem, Utrecht, Montfoort, Weesp, Elburg, Putten, Muyden, and even Groningen, besides some wealthy Amsterdam citizens such as "the lord Cromhout," together owing fl. 578 – 5. This illustrates how early modern insolvency cases are a useful source to reveal credit networks even across social borders.[19]

On May 12, 1685, Anna and Laurens's sole surviving daughter – yet another Anna – married the merchant Nicolaes van der Meer from Maassluys, who joined the Nootens' fish-trading business.[20] Soon thereafter, disaster struck. In April 1686, Laurens Nooten passed away, leaving it up to the young Nicolaes to continue the family business in company with his mother-in-law. It became his responsibility to manage their external commercial relations and to take care of the books and papers, as having passed the age of 60 by that time Anna "did not possess any knowledge about these things, solely concerning herself with the selling of plaice (*schol*) and salted fish." When her son-in-law died in April 1700, however, it appeared that he had seriously forsaken his duties. In the years directly preceding his death, Nicolaes had completely stopped registering his transactions, while the older books among his administrative documents were both messy and incomplete.

[19] Clé Lesger, *Het winkellandschap van Amsterdam. Stedelijke structuur en winkelbedrijf in de vroegmoderne en moderne tijd, 1550–2000* (Hilversum: Verloren, 2013), 63–72.

[20] GAS, DTB, inv. nr. 514, p. 5.

His unfortunate mother-in-law discovered that her capital had completely evaporated in the course of just a few years. As some of her creditors, who had naturally lost their trust in her capacity to revive the business or provide them with clear information, "threatened her with the apprehension of her person," the widow had no other options but to request "the miserable benefice of *cessie van goede*" at the age 75.[21]

As the entire fifth chapter of this book is dedicated to the *cessie* procedure in all its intricacies, here it suffices to note that this legal benefice protected an insolvent against debt imprisonment if they would cede all their worldly possessions to their common creditors. This type of insolvency procedure is especially interesting for historians because of the *staet en inventaris* that the insolvent had to deliver to the court: a document listing all outstanding debts, claims, and possessions, often accompanied by detailed personal stories. Regular inventories of an estate (*boedel-inventarissen*) only included movable goods, while *staten van goed* provide a much more complete image of its possessions and debts. This also makes such documents a valuable source for social and economic history.

From the (regular) inventory that was drawn up of Anna's movable goods on orders of the Desolate Boedelskamer two days after she had filed her application for *cessie*, we learn that she lived in a house on the Martelaarsgracht. This is currently close to Amsterdam's central railway station, but in the seventeenth century it must have been an ideal location for a fish-trading business due to its immediate outlet to the IJ river. After her furniture and other possessions had been valued at fl. 1,303 – 5 by "sworn appraiser" Catharina Verlaen, on July 22, 1700 the commissioners of the Desolate Boedelskamer granted Anna van Loo her *cessie*. In order to start the liquidation of her estate, they ordered Willem van der Does to "examine and appraise" the fish found in the warehouse and yard situated under the widow's living quarters. On July 26, he valued these *coopmanschappen* or "merchandise" at fl. 482 – 18. Eventually, on September 1, Anna had gathered the fl. 1,800 needed to buy off the claim to her personal possessions.[22]

[21] GAS, 5072: DB, inv. nr. 702, nr. 54. All references to the *staet* of Anna van Loo are based upon this file.

[22] GAS, 5072: DB, inv. nr. 30, ff. 59r–60r; inv. nr. 624, ff. 83v–89v. On Amsterdam's sworn appraisers, see Marleen Puyenbroek, "Gezworen schatsters. Vakvrouwen in zeventiende-eeuws Amsterdam," *Amstelodamum* 108, no. 2 (2021): 103–17.

Anna's *staet* reveals that besides the company with her son-in-law, she also continued to trade on her own account. This personal business resulted in outstanding debts of about fl. 3,500, all for diverse types of fish bought in the year leading up to her insolvency. The greatest part, fl. 2,360, was held by only two trading partners: Annetje van der Burgh from Vlaardingen and Laurens Welbooren from Maassluys. The majority of the debt, however, had been incurred in the company's name. While Anna seems to have paid off her personal creditors promptly enough, her son-in-law's messy administrative management is clearly reflected by the fl. 30,701 of outstanding debts, some of which went as far back as 1684. Of this total amount, fl. 13,600 is explicitly marked as a long-term *obligatie*, and a further fl. 10,000 are *schepenkennisse*, long-term loan contracts that had officially been registered with the aldermen and thereby gained preference over more informal debts. The latter were entirely held by two relatives: Jan Pietersz. Nooten and Jan van der Meer from Maassluys. Early modern entrepreneurs often relied on family and relatives for the provision of such long-term business capital. They were the people one knew best, and who shared common interests, which was always the best guarantee for trust. As the old adage has it, "blood is thicker than water": the weaker the institutional context due to risks and uncertainties, the higher the premium on personal trust and kinship.[23]

At first sight, we might be tempted to equate such a level of indebtedness with poverty. In this period, however, one's ability to amass debt was strongly linked to the possession of property, reputation, and other securities that could be offered to potential creditors in lieu of trust. Hence, the real poor usually did not have much debt at all. Bart Willems's study of the eighteenth-century Antwerp middle classes reveals that house-owners had substantially higher debts from larger numbers of creditors; they were on average five times

[23] Peter Mathias, "Strategies for Reducing Risk by Entrepreneurs in the Early Modern Period," in *Entrepreneurs and Entrepreneurship in Early Modern Times: Merchants and Industrialists within the Orbit of the Dutch Staple Market*, ed. Clé Lesger and Leo Noordegraaf (The Hague: Stichting Hollandse Historische Reeks, 1995), 6–8; Luuc Kooijmans, "Risk and Reputation: On the Mentality of Merchants in the Early Modern Period," in *Entrepreneurs and Entrepreneurship in Early Modern Times: Merchants and Industrialists within the Orbit of the Dutch Staple Market*, ed. Clé Lesger and Leo Noordegraaf (The Hague: Stichting Hollandse Historische Reeks, 1995), 28.

as high as those who did not own immovable property were able to obtain.[24] Conversely, poor Amsterdam widows in this period had much smaller debts at the time of their death than similar lower middle-class households headed by a married couple or a widower. According to Laurence Fontaine, this low level of indebtedness is a strong indication of their economic marginalization rather than of economically rational behavior.[25] Outside investments, such as the aforementioned "obligations," were necessary to sustain a business of any size. Therefore, it is not so much the amount of debt but rather the clear failure to maintain decent and transparent administrative documentation which proved to be problematic for Anna van Loo's business.

While humble households in the Dutch Republic generally obtained their cash through weekly wage payments, many small craftsmen or other service providers actually received the majority of their income on a seasonal basis. These were often connected to the renewal dates of rental and service contracts on May 1 and November 1. This explains why these days also developed into common clearing dates for the settlement of debts. For employers, this payment method made it easier to handle the cash required to pay their workers, as it allowed them to bundle the wages into a few larger silver coins rather than heavy piles of low-value copper currency. The severe cash-flow problems that this system caused for many households were partially solved through the credit that was provided on a substantial scale by bakers and other middle-class retail traders. Almost all transactions were noted down in the shopkeeper's register or notched on a tally: one's *kerfstok*.[26] These phenomena are perfectly illustrated by the *staet* of bread baker Hendrick Schreuder, who became insolvent soon after Anna van Loo.

[24] Bart Willems, *Leven op de pof: Krediet bij de Antwerpse middenstand in de achttiende eeuw* (Amsterdam University Press, 2009), 166–69.

[25] Laurence Fontaine, *The Moral Economy: Poverty, Credit, and Trust in Early Modern Europe* (New York: Cambridge University Press, 2014), 154–55.

[26] Jan de Vries, *The Price of Bread: Regulating the Market in the Dutch Republic*, Cambridge Studies in Economic History (New York: Cambridge University Press, 2019), 111–13; Willems, *Leven op de pof*, 194–98. A tally (Dutch *kerfstok*) was a wooden stick on which a number of notches was carved to indicate a specific amount of debt. It would subsequently be split length-wise, ensuring that only the true creditor and debtor had a perfect matching copy as proof of the obligation.

On November 18, 1700, the day on which his *staet* was handed over to the commissioners, Schreuder had worked as a baker for almost twenty-five years. As his wife and five children were often ill, which resulted in high medical costs, he had been forced to buy grain on credit from a number of merchants. In the years leading up to his insolvency, "the high grain prices as well as bad debts and bankrupt customers" had eroded his profit margins, resulting in a situation in which he could not sustain his family from the "meagre profits." While Schreuder owed fl. 1,182 – 10 to five different grain merchants, the most immediate reason for his insolvency seems to have been the smaller debt of fl. 191 – 13 owed to his landlord Jan Pietersz. van Coeverden for the past year's house rent. This debt had to be repaid on November 1 in order to prolong the contract. The grain merchants did not have a direct motivation to enforce a liquidation of Schreuder's estate, as they had a better chance of recovering their money through the bakery's continued operation. However, when the unfortunate baker could not pay his rent, Van Coeverden had a preferential claim on all movable goods found in the estate except for the tools required for the bakery's operation. After their execution he could simply rent his property to a new, more creditworthy tenant. This shows how the combination of a relatively small debt and a creditor who had little motivation to extend trust in the form of a debt renegotiation scheme could lead to Schreuder's insolvency and his subsequent application for *cessie*.[27]

The unlucky baker's story highlights how the high-risk–low-volume loans that were extended on a large scale by shopkeepers and other members of the lower middle classes also put them at risk of economic shocks. Bart Willems and Craig Muldrew found numerous references to "bad debts" in probate inventories.[28] If too many of their customers failed to repay their debts, shopkeepers such as Schreuder would face similar problems vis-à-vis their own suppliers, which would in turn put wholesalers such as Anna van Loo at serious risk. In her *staet*, the widow also described outstanding debts owed to her as "zoo goed als quaad": some from which repayments could still be expected, others

[27] GAS, 5072: DB, inv. nr. 702, nr. 78.

[28] Willems, *Leven op de pof*, 72–77 and 202; Craig Muldrew, *The Economy of Obligation: The Culture of Credit and Social Relations in Early Modern England* (Basingstoke: Macmillan Press, 1998), 82 and 96.

that would probably prove to be unrecoverable. Sometimes, local governments sought to curtail these risks by introducing a legal limit on the amount of consumer credit that could be provided per individual consumer. In Oudewater, a baker or innkeeper was allowed to "write on the wall" debts worth no more than a total of fl. 16.[29] In Assendelft, the limit was even as low as 30 stuivers. If an innkeeper were to break this rule, they would be unable to execute their claims in court. Such legal limits to credit were often avoided through the practice of pawn-broking, which was also often used as a last resort by poor debtors who had run out of personal credit with shopkeepers, family, or friends.[30]

During the early modern period, all over Europe official pawnshops were established by local governments or religious organizations. These institutions usually had two main goals: on the one hand, they extended credit to the poor at more advantageous rates than unofficial usurers; on the other hand, profits resulting from its business were often allocated to social aid foundations and sometimes also directly benefited the urban treasury. The pawnshops were an important solution for many poor and lower middle-class households, allowing them to monetize their clothes or other possessions if need arose. Some women pawned their Sunday dress every Monday morning to recollect it on Saturday evening, in the meanwhile using the small capital obtained for their commercial activities. This phenomenon occurred with such frequency that some English pawnshops had to refuse winter blankets and coats as deposits during the summer months. Pawnshops were an essential service for many small craftsmen, who used the money borrowed there to buy the materials required for their business. Most of them could not have done without this system due to their lack of sufficient personal credit.[31]

[29] Around 1650, an average unskilled laborer in Holland earned 19 stuivers a day, a skilled laborer (journeyman) 25 stuivers. In this same period, 10 stuivers a day sufficed to properly feed a five-person household. See A Note on Currency above.

[30] Arie Th. van Deursen, *Mensen van klein vermogen. Het kopergeld van de Gouden Eeuw* (Amsterdam: Bert Bakker, 1991), 124; Fontaine, *The Moral Economy*, 96–97. I have, however, not found any references to similar rules that applied to early modern Amsterdam.

[31] Fontaine, *The Moral Economy*, 157–82. See also, for the Low Countries, H. A. J. Maassen, *Tussen commercieel en sociaal krediet. De ontwikkeling van de Bank van Lening in Nederland van Lombard tot Gemeentelijke Kredietbank 1260–1940* (Hilversum: Verloren, 1994).

In Amsterdam, an official pawnshop or *bank van leening* was established in 1614. Even though the practice had officially been forbidden in 1477, individual Lombard merchants had always continued to provide credit at high interest rates. Until 1581 the local authorities had turned a blind eye to these practices, as in the absence of banks they were indispensable for the general functioning of the economy. In that year, the first steps towards regulation of the pawnshops were taken by granting an official license to Johan Laignier. In exchange for an annual fee of fl. 600 and legal limitations on weekly interest rates, he received an official monopoly from the city. In 1591, Laignier was replaced by Sion Luz, who had previously also held a pawnshop in Dordrecht. When Luz's license ended on April 25, 1614, the authorities decided against its prolongation and instead opted for a public institution: the *bank van leening*. This institution offered an interest rate of 16.25 percent for "small pawns" worth less than fl. 100, while under the old system the maximum rate had been 21.67 percent. As in many other cities, the institution's social side was further strengthened by the allocation of its profits to the relief of poverty through the Dutch Reformed Deaconry.[32] For the Amsterdam poor, but also for small shopkeepers and other parts of the lower middle classes, both formal and unofficial pawnshops retained an important role in the proliferation of credit well into the twentieth century.[33]

Interestingly, pawnshops were not only used by the lower classes. Just as bakers and innkeepers acted as a link between the working class and the commercial economy, pawnshops fulfilled the need for short-term credit for both poor widows and merchants operating on an international scale. The fact that in the years after the opening of the Amsterdam *bank van leening* millions of guilders were extended as credit proves the broad and general demand for such an institution. Even though by the later eighteenth century, the Amsterdam *bank van leening* did not extend large sums of commercial credit anymore, in the seventeenth century such operations still formed an important

[32] L. Jansen, *Geschiedenis van de Stads Bank van Lening te Amsterdam 1614–1964* (Amsterdam: Stads-kredietbank voor Roerende Zaken, 1964), 12–21 and 60.

[33] Auke van der Woud, *Koninkrijk vol sloppen. Achterbuurten en vuil in de negentiende eeuw* (Amsterdam: Bert Bakker, 2010), 144–50.

source of revenue.[34] Those who, anxious to preserve their reputation, did not wish to pawn their goods in person, could make use of one of the fifty official brokers or *inbrengsters* for pawns worth more than 25 stuivers. Similar to the situation encountered in sources from Leiden, Rotterdam, and Gouda, in Amsterdam this was a predominantly female occupation. The sole exception from seventeenth-century Amsterdam was Samuel Adamsz., who was allowed to take over his deceased wife's position on January 28, 1668.[35]

Important merchants or *koopmannen* were essentially confronted with the same challenges as wholesalers such as the widow Anna van Loo, but on a larger scale. As credit provided by direct family and kinship networks was usually insufficient to finance their entire commercial operations, merchants also had to rely on external capital. The Amsterdam merchant Hans Thijs, who traded in leather and jewelry between 1589 and 1611, is a perfect example of this development. Initially Thijs almost completely relied on loans supplied by his brothers and sisters. After 1598, however, his business swiftly expanded from less than fl. 20,000 to over fl. 100,000. While he continued to make use of family deposits, these quickly became insufficient for the scale of his commercial activities. Benefiting from the newly arisen possibility of using United East Indies Company (VOC) shares as collateral for informal promissory notes or IOUs, Thijs borrowed on average between fl. 50,000 and fl. 70,000 annually from no fewer than seventy different merchants or their widows. The security offered by these shares, which were a liquid asset because of their regular transfer among shareholders, is illustrated by the fact that interest rates on family and market loans quickly converged in the early seventeenth century.[36] By entering book debts, merchants in effect created money. Nevertheless, many such loans were not backed by VOC shares or real estate, and even for

[34] Maassen, *Tussen commercieel en sociaal krediet*, 137–39; Jansen, *Bank van Lening*, 22 and 50.

[35] Jansen, *Bank van Lening*, 22 and 39–41; Manon van der Heijden and Ariadne Schmidt, "Public Services and Women's Work in Early Modern Dutch Towns," *Journal of Urban History* 36, no. 3 (2010): 368–85, 380.

[36] Gelderblom, *Cities of Commerce*, 67–69; Oscar Gelderblom and Joost Jonker, "Completing a Financial Revolution: The Finance of the Dutch East India Trade and the Rise of the Amsterdam Capital Market, 1595–1612," *The Journal of Economic History* 64, no. 3 (2004): 641–72.

those that were, merchants also had to rely on other mechanisms for maintaining trust and hence liquidity. A creditor always had to rely upon their reputation. Credit relationships between merchants were often maintained by a regular exchange of current account statements and a prompt settlement of outstanding balances. Prompt settlement thus functioned as a check on the proliferation of credit within tight-knit commercial networks, the amount of which could expand or contract according to economic needs in the form of book money.[37]

Movable goods were also used as security for credit between individuals, bypassing the *bank van leening*'s official structures. One especially colorful example of this practice can be found in the diary of Isaac Pool, which provides an authentic view on the life of an Amsterdam merchant in the second half of the seventeenth century. Together with his brother Jacob, Pool owned a house called De Boeier on the Singel near the Rouaanse Kade. The cellar of this property was rented out to various tenants, but not always without trouble. On April 21, 1674, Isaac Pool placed an *arrest* on the estate of his tenant Annetien Hooghenbergh. As we saw in the case of Hendrick Schreuder, this was a common legal strategy for landlords whose tenants failed to pay their rent. However, soon after he had notified Hooghenbergh of the arrest, Pool was warned that she had removed her most valuable property from the cellar, a *kostelijk* or "beautiful" bed. A certain woman named Kristiena, who lived with her, later informed Pool that the bed "as well as a red blanket and a pillow" had been taken to a corset-maker in the Molsteeg. Furthermore, Hooghenbergh had sold two boxes of ribbons to an anonymous buyer in the Kalverstraat. When Isaac Pool arrived at De Boeier, he met two people in the doorway who were carrying away even more goods, at which he exclaimed: "Look ... so they remove the goods, blatantly disregarding a legal arrest!" He threatened to have Hooghenbergh incarcerated until she would pay her rent or told him where she had hidden her possessions. This apparently sufficed to discipline the fraudulent debtor: on that same afternoon the bed,

[37] Mathias, "Strategies," 13–15; Oscar Gelderblom and Joost Jonker, "Enter the Ghost – Cashless Payments in the Early Modern Low Countries, 1500–1800," *SSRN* (2015), http://dx.doi.org/10.2139/ssrn.2604089, esp. 10–11.

pillow, and a box of other goods were delivered to Pool "mynent tot onder pandt" or "as security for his claim."[38]

In this period, creditors always faced an information problem. Solely based upon their impression of their debtor and rumors about his or her success or failure in business, they would have to decide whether to continue granting trust or to seek an execution of their debts. This also explains the great concern for reputation that was displayed by many people in this period. A family's local standing had to be won and maintained through all of its members' actions, even across multiple generations. This was as important for the poor who sought credit with shopkeepers such as their local baker as for internationally operating merchants attempting to finance their commerce. Early modern merchants' vulnerability in this regard probably also explains why "the opinion of the world" and good manners were prominent elements of seventeenth-century education. These were, after all, essential when cultivating the relations that were needed to secure one's social position. It also explains why friends could often be relied upon to help someone who had fallen into financial trouble: they saved their friend's reputation and credit in order to maintain their own.[39]

Of course, early modern businessmen would not drag one another to court at the first sign of repayment issues. They recognized that their trading partners could suddenly be faced by illiquidity, and if the business to which credit had been extended seemed essentially sound, were willing to accept delays instead of jeopardizing business relations with the immediate threat of litigation. Debts were usually prolonged and renegotiated as part of arbitration processes in which floating debt was converted into longer-term debt, smoothened by a reasonable annual interest and securities.[40] Most merchants even reserved

[38] Isaac Pool, *De handelsgeest van Isaac Pool. Dagboek van een Amsterdammer in de Gouden Eeuw*, ed. Laurence Duquesnoy and Jeroen Salman (Hilversum: Verloren, 2018), 23 and 107–8.

[39] Kooijmans, "Risk and Reputation," 30–32; Thomas Max Safley, "Business Failure and Civil Scandal in Early Modern Europe," *BHR* 83 (2009): 35–60, 46.

[40] In Amsterdam, from at least the beginning of the seventeenth century onwards a local law or *willekeur* stipulated that defaulting debtors henceforth had to pay 8 percent interest per year, calculated from the stipulated date of payment in the original contract until the date of the actual payment: Jacob Pieterszoon Wachter, *Handtvesten ofte privilegien, handelingen, costumen ende willekeuren der stadt Amstelredam* (Amsterdam, 1639), 115–16. See also Gelderblom, *Cities of Commerce*, 105 (n. 16).

part of their profits to write off irretrievable debts resulting from single transactions with unfamiliar parties. Sometimes, however, taking one's loss was impossible. Too much money might be involved, or the transaction might be part of a chain of other obligations.[41]

Such cases reveal the importance of well-functioning and freely accessible insolvency procedures for the proliferation of credit and economic growth in this period. Oscar Gelderblom has stressed the importance of the fact that the Amsterdam authorities were always present in the background to support the network-based trade of international merchants by legal means. Business correspondence and other documentation were both generally accepted and frequently used as legal proof in commercial disputes.[42] The credible threat that one could ultimately resort to a court in case of fraud by an agent or other debtor substantially raised the opportunity costs of cheating for the latter. While merchants generally preferred mediation by notaries or externally appointed arbiters to more expensive and time-consuming formal legal procedures, the threat of taking a dispute to court was often enough to reach an agreement even before a judge had arrived at a ruling. In this way, legal institutions were essential to back up the seventeenth-century economy of credit, which was normally characterized by interpersonal trust and private-order arbitration.[43]

Insolvency and especially fraudulent bankruptcy resulted in a severe breach of trust, which endangered the moral grounds on which exchange and the economy normally rested in this period. As I will continue to argue in this book, an institution such as the Desolate Boedelskamer could alleviate part of creditors' insecurity through the replacement of personal trust with system trust. By its resolution of part of the information deficit (i.e. a reduction of complexity) through a transparent, fact-based, and objective insolvency procedure, many businesses which would otherwise have been unable to survive were now granted a second chance through a restructuring of their debts. These increasing possibilities for business turnaround management were an important innovation in seventeenth-century Amsterdam, facilitated by the open-access legal solutions of a public-order

[41] Gelderblom, *Cities of Commerce*, 105. [42] Ibid. 77–78 and 92–94.
[43] Mathias, "Strategies," 9; Gelderblom, *Cities of Commerce*, 104–5.

institution that was nevertheless firmly grounded in interpersonal arbitration strategies.

As I have shown in this section, focusing on the moment of insolvency – essentially the breakdown of credit (i.e. trust) and "normal" economic relations – allows us to illustrate the social embeddedness of the economy in seventeenth-century Amsterdam for merchants and businessmen from all layers of society. People relied on family and friends for long-term capital, while securities such as *panden* or VOC-shares served to bridge the trust deficit with less familiar parties. Ultimately, the system trust that was provided by the Desolate Boedelskamer helped to sustain or revive interpersonal trust and credit even in periods of financial stress, opening up perspectives beyond the moment of insolvency for many honest and industrious citizens. This was a clear and intentional result of the innovative governance that can be observed in Amsterdam from the *Alteratie* onwards; a development that is even better understood if we place it in the wider context of social policy in this period. The next section will explore this supporting evidence for the conscious social integration of all layers of Amsterdam's society at the zenith of its Golden Age.

Guilds and Social Policy

One of the most important social boundaries in seventeenth-century Amsterdam was that between citizens and noncitizens. Citizenship could either be inherited from one's parents or obtained at a later age, through sale or for free after marrying a citizen's daughter. Two important rights that came with *poorterschap* (urban citizenship) were the possibility of joining a craft guild, and – after seven years – the right to be elected to one of the main governmental offices such as those of burgomaster or alderman. In order to be considered fit for such positions, one would need to be a good *patriot* or "lover of the fatherland." Furthermore, one had to support the Reformed religion.[44] This makes sense when we take the events of 1578 into account. As discussed at the beginning of this chapter, during the

[44] Kuijpers and Prak, "Burger, ingezetene, vreemdeling," 115–16; Wagenaar, *Amsterdam* (1767 edition), III:273.

Alteratie the civic militia banished the Catholic government after rumors that it conspired to deliver Amsterdam back into the hands of the new Spanish governor, Don Juan of Austria. In a unique procedure, representatives from their ranks elected a new city council, aldermen, and burgomasters, invariably supporters of the Prince of Orange and the revolt. At this crucial moment, therefore, there was a strong influence of the Amsterdam middle classes on the composition of its government.[45]

Nevertheless, Maarten Prak argues that the history of urban communities has (too) often been studied from an elite perspective, which has strengthened the tendency to characterize their government as being dominated by an oligarchy of regents. As a consequence, the influence of civic institutions such as guilds in normal (non-crisis) years has been systematically underestimated.[46] While the *regeeringhe* or local government of a commercial hub such as Amsterdam actively strove to create a good business climate through institutional innovation, they were joined by bottom-up initiatives through middle-class organizations such as guilds. Amsterdam's political and economic structures were firmly embedded in a broader social context, which is especially visible in various types of social welfare policies that were pursued in this period.

Although citizenship was an essential feature of social, economic, and cultural life in early modern Amsterdam, about half of its population was actually made up of mere *ingezetenen* or "inhabitants."[47] These people were not necessarily poor, as some groups of foreigners such as international merchants might not feel the need to obtain citizenship even if they could easily pay for it, but most of the *ingezetenen* clearly belonged to the lower reaches of the urban community. The majority of citizens, in turn, belonged to what we could describe as the broad middle classes. In seventeenth-century Holland, these artisans and modest shopkeepers made up between 20 and 30 percent of the urban population. Education and craftsmanship separated such citizens from the lower classes, the *grauw* of unskilled laborers who were

[45] Jan Wagenaar, *Amsterdam in zijne opkomst*, 4 vols. (Amsterdam: Isaak Tirion, 1760), I:367–70.

[46] Maarten Prak, *Citizens without Nations: Urban Citizenship in Europe and the World, c.1000–1789* (Cambridge University Press, 2018), 5.

[47] Ibid. 40.

often without fixed employment. A further 8 to 14 percent consisted of government servants (e.g. clerks, schoolmasters) and wealthier specialized shopkeepers. Only the top 6 to 8 percent of Amsterdam's population could be described as the true *bourgeoisie* of international merchants, rentiers, and regents.[48]

In the early modern period, people who had fallen into poverty could not rely on guaranteed support from the national government such as a basic income. However, there were many initiatives for poverty relief on the local level, often connected to religious communities. In late seventeenth-century Amsterdam, both citizens and "outsiders" who needed aid could fall back on a combination of public and private initiatives for poverty relief.[49] The two colleges of *huiszittenmeesters* had been taking care of citizens in need since the Middle Ages onwards, and after the *Alteratie* they continued their work as public institutions. In 1613 the authorities supplemented them by the new college of *Aalmoezeniers*, who took care of poor immigrants and at the same time sought to reduce illegal beggary. Only those unfit to work, deemed *rechte armen* or "true poor," could apply for aid. Beggars, vagabonds, and other *leeglopers* were

[48] Maarten Prak, *The Dutch Republic in the Seventeenth Century*, trans. Diane Webb, 2nd ed. (Cambridge University Press, 2023), 124; Sandra Bos, *"Uyt liefde tot malcander." Onderlinge hulpverlening binnen de Noord-Nederlandse gilden in internationaal perspectief (1570–1820)* (Amsterdam: IISG, 1998), 22; Jan de Vries and Ad van der Woude, *The First Modern Economy: Success, Failure, and Perseverance of the Dutch Economy, 1500–1815* (Cambridge University Press, 1997), 563–64.

[49] A substantial number of studies have been published on poverty relief in the early modern Dutch Republic in general, and Amsterdam more specifically. These paragraphs are based on a selection of this literature: Maarten Prak, "Armenzorg 1500–1800," in *Studies over zekerheidsarrangementen. Risico's, risicobestrijding en verzekeringen in Nederland vanaf de middeleeuwen*, ed. Jacques van Gerwen and Marco H. D. van Leeuwen (Amsterdam: NEHA/Verbond van Verzekeraars, 1998), 49–90; Hendrik C. de Wolf, *Geschiedenis van het R.C. Oude-Armenkantoor te Amsterdam* (Hilversum: Uitgeverij Paul Brand, 1966); Marco H. D. van Leeuwen, "Amsterdam en de armenzorg tijdens de Republiek," *NEHA-Jaarboek* 59 (1996): 132–61; Erika Kuijpers and Maarten Prak, "Gevestigden en buitenstaanders," in *Geschiedenis van Amsterdam*, IIa: *Centrum van de wereld, 1578–1650*, ed. Willem Frijhoff and Maarten Prak (Amsterdam: SUN, 2004), 188–239; Maarten Hell, "De Oude Geuzen en de Opstand. Politiek en lokaal bestuur in tijd van oorlog en expansie 1578–1650," in *Geschiedenis van Amsterdam*, IIa: *Centrum van de wereld, 1578–1650*, ed. Willem Frijhoff and Maarten Prak (Amsterdam: SUN, 2004), 240–97.

incarcerated and subjected to forced labor in the *Rasphuis* for men and the *Spinhuis* for women.[50]

These structures also display the tension between the need for immigrant labor and the public-order issues caused by unwanted beggars. The public institutions were supplemented by a wide variety of private initiatives, organized by religious denomination. The aid provided by the government was limited in size and form, only comprising food, fuel, and clothing, for instance, while religious aid such as that of the Catholic *Armenkantoor* supplemented this with a small amount of money to assist with additional expenses. In a similar fashion, the Dutch Reformed *Diakonie* – which, as discussed above, was partially financed from the profits of the *bank van leening* – not only provided monetary aid, but even had doctors in its service, as well as a private apothecary and bakers who prepared the bread that was handed out to the poor. In 1678 the Lutherans created their own orphanage. In this way, the basic level of vertical public aid was combined with various forms of horizontal social aid: solidarity within the religious groups to provide for the livelihood of the poor.

As discussed above, Amsterdam strove to attract merchants in competition with regional rivals through a combination of diplomacy and favorable open-access institutions.[51] With regard to poverty relief, however, an unlimited open-access policy could cause important free-rider issues. When the numbers of the poor increased in the last quarter of the seventeenth century, cities tried to alleviate the pressure of workless immigrants on their poverty-relief institutions through a system of *borgbrieven*. Before immigrants were accepted into the city, they had to provide a letter from their old place of residence which guaranteed the latter's accountability for costs resulting from poverty aid for at least one year. Surprisingly, Amsterdam did not require such letters from immigrants. Marco van Leeuwen even argues that Amsterdam's functioning as a "safety valve" was the prime reason

[50] This practice closely corresponds to the ideas expressed by sixteenth-century humanists such as Juan Luis Vives, *Over de hulp aan de armen*, trans. Raf Debaene (Zoetermeer: Klement, 2015); and, most notably, Dirk Volkertsz. Coornhert, *Boeventucht of middelen tot mindering der schadelijke lediggangers*, ed. A. J. Gelderbloem et al. (Muiderberg: Coutinho, 1985).

[51] Gelderblom, *Cities of Commerce*.

why the early modern Republic's localized system of social aid did not succumb to such free-rider issues.[52]

Amsterdam's liberal immigration policy is often explained by three factors. First, migration was an absolute necessity to provide sufficient sailors for the fleet. According to the masters of the Nieuwezijds Huiszittenhuis, "het coorn is met caff vermengt en om 't selve te suijveren laeten wij aen den Heere des oogst": they would not throw away the chaff with the grain, in order to attract sufficient labor. The fact that sailors knew that their widows and families would be taken care of in their absence, would be an important encouragement to move to Amsterdam.[53] Second, poverty relief was mainly targeted at the proletariat as a way of incorporating these groups of people who were not participating in "higher" social networks such as guilds or the civic militias into civil society. Social welfare systems were not just a form of one-way wealth redistribution between elites and the poor. They can be understood as an implicit form of social contract or "institutionalized exchange mechanism" in which social groups traded favors. The propertied classes worried about public order, and poverty relief was an important way to ensure the compliance of less well-to-do elements in society.[54] Third, the aid provided by the *huiszittenmeesters*, for which one only became eligible after a few years of citizenship, was much more generous than that of the *aalmoezeniers*, which was the only form of aid for noncitizens that was organized by the urban government. In a similar fashion, the Citizens' Orphanage had more varied and calorie-rich diets than the Almoners' Orphanage. This class-justice helped to reconcile established citizens with the large influx of generally poor immigrants.[55]

Interestingly, this general philosophy of incorporating the poor through public means was also directly supported by the magistrates themselves. After the almoners' college had been introduced, on June

[52] Prak, "Armenzorg," 82–84; Van Leeuwen, "Amsterdam en de armenzorg."

[53] Van Leeuwen, "Amsterdam en de armenzorg," 152–54; Prak, *The Dutch Republic in the Seventeenth Century*, 125–28.

[54] Marco H. D. van Leeuwen, "Guilds and Middle-Class Welfare, 1550–1800: Provisions for Burial, Sickness, Old Age, and Widowhood," *Economic History Review* 65, no. 1 (2012): 61–90, 85; Marco H. D. van Leeuwen, *The Logic of Charity: Amsterdam, 1800–1850* (London: Macmillan Press, 2000).

[55] Kuijpers and Prak, "Gevestigden," 227–28 and 238; Van Leeuwen, "Amsterdam en de armenzorg," 155.

24, 1624 the *vroedschap* decided that all senior and "middling" subordinate officials had to donate a prescribed minimum amount to this institution upon entering their position. In the seventeenth-century *ambtenboeck* or "register of offices," these amounts are neatly noted for every staff member of the Desolate Boedelskamer that fell into the aforementioned categories. Both the secretary and the bookkeeper had to donate fl. 100, every curator was expected to provide half that amount, while for the clerks a minimum contribution of fl. 25 sufficed.[56]

Generally, this system of public and private forms of social aid functioned well enough to guarantee the subsistence of the Dutch Republic's population. While other early modern nations were plagued by recurring periods of famine, in Amsterdam this phenomenon was virtually unknown until the Napoleonic era. In the entire existence of the Dutch Republic, skilled laborers in Holland faced only eleven months of crisis.[57] All spikes of excess mortality in the seventeenth-century Northern Netherlands were caused by plague rather than famine.[58] It is revealing how the Dutch Reformed Synod of Middelburg in 1581 mentions war, epidemics, *dure tijd* or "expensive times," and persecution of faith as proper reasons to organize a day of fasting or public prayer, but did not include hunger in this list. When Petrus Datheen rhymed the Lord's Prayer in Dutch (1566), he made a similar choice: "Deliver us, Lord, from discord and envy / From plague and expensive times."[59] Of course, the large volume of freight shipping available, as well as the strong commercial links with the grain-exporting regions of the Baltic that formed the "mother of all trades" in Amsterdam and the early modern Dutch Republic, must have been an important factor in its successful handling of failed harvests and other food shortages.[60]

[56] GAS, 5031, Burgemeesters – ambten en officiën [BAO], inv. nr. 54, pp. 31–32; Moll, *Desolate Boedelskamer*, 175.

[57] De Vries, *The Price of Bread*, 254–61.

[58] Daniel R. Curtis and Jessica Dijkman, "The Escape from Famine in the Northern Netherlands: A Reconsideration Using the 1690s Harvest Failures and a Broader Northwest European Perspective," *The Seventeenth Century* 34, no. 2 (2019): 229–58.

[59] Van Deursen, *Mensen van klein vermogen*, 73–74: "Behoedt ons Heer, voor twist en nijd, / Voor pest en ook voor duren tijd."

[60] Milja van Tielhof, *The "Mother of All Trades": The Baltic Grain Trade in Amsterdam from the Late 16th to the Early 19th Century* (Leiden: Brill, 2002); Remmelt Daalder et al., eds., *Goud uit graan. Nederland en het Oostzeegebied 1600–1850* (Zwolle: Waanders Uitgevers, 1998).

"Give us this day our daily bread" (Matthew 6:11). For many Europeans, well into modern times, bread was indeed the core of their diet, from which they had to obtain the majority of their calories. It is generally agreed that the capacity to guarantee the material sustenance of their population was of vital importance for the legitimacy of early modern political authorities.[61] Following Thompson, many historians have argued in favor of the concept of a "moral economy," a shared mentality among the commoners which, from the late seventeenth century onwards, would have led them to intervene in food prices through coordinated riots when the authorities failed to protect their interests. From the late seventeenth century onwards, a new liberal ideology would lead authorities in England and France, for instance, to lift controls on bread prices and the grain trade, resulting in endemic rioting. However, according to Jan de Vries, there is little evidence for this move away from the regulatory mind-set until at least the 1750s. In England, for instance, the old Assize of Bread was even more generally enforced after its 1709 reformulation.[62]

Across Europe, governments typically measured grain prices at set temporal intervals to proportionally fix the maximum price of bread. This system favored bakers over consumers, as in times of high grain prices their profits went up due to its failure to distinguish between fixed and variable costs. In the 1590s, Dutch cities introduced a new system called *broodzetting*, which addressed this issue by carefully measuring and establishing the actual production costs paid by bakers. Because prices were adjusted weekly based upon the most recent grain price indexes, the new Dutch system allowed for bread prices that in the years 1594–1600 were on average 11.2 percent lower than they would have been under the old system. This partially benefited consumers, but also helped to finance the state through a newly introduced provincial milling-excise. This was an "optimal" tax, as it was levied disproportionally on more luxurious wheat bread variants, thereby cross-subsidizing the coarser rye bread on which

[61] On the public-order consequences of food shortages resulting from the combination of failing harvests and bad policies that occurred on a global scale over the seventeenth century, see Geoffrey Parker, *Global Crisis: War, Climate Change and Catastrophe in the Seventeenth Century* (New Haven: Yale University Press, 2013).

[62] Edward P. Thompson, "The Moral Economy of the English Crowd in the Eighteenth Century," *Past & Present* 50 (1971): 76–136; De Vries, *The Price of Bread*, 274–75.

the lower classes relied for their diet. This innovative policy accomplished the twin goals of reducing the effects of rising grain prices on the purchase-power of the lower classes while at the same time providing the Dutch government with more than 10 percent of its public revenues. Even if the fear of bread riots might have stimulated the introduction of this intricate system of price regulation, its combination with public and private poverty-relief arrangements was so effective that in practice such popular uprisings were unknown in the early modern Dutch Republic. Perhaps this was an even more perfectly "moral" economy than could have been attained by purely bottom-up initiatives.[63]

As was discussed in the first section of this chapter, in the early modern credit economy – essentially a shame culture – personal honor or reputation was of the utmost importance in all social and economic relations. Especially ordinary middle-class citizens, such as the simple baker Hendrick Schreuder, had to work hard to keep up such *burgerlijke* or civic codes of honor. In their daily struggle to secure their status, they often felt the need to establish a clear social distance between themselves and the "honorless": strangers and more generally the lower classes of society.[64] For such respectable middle-class citizens, the functioning of guilds can be compared to the functioning of poverty-relief institutions for the lower strata of Amsterdam society.

Before the *Alteratie*, guilds had dedicated the vast majority of their members' contributions to religious purposes. The maintenance of an altar or chapel as well as the artwork needed to fill them were costly affairs, joined by religious processions and copious feasts on their patron saint's day that formed an important social dimension of guild membership. However, the new Calvinist government quickly put an end to these practices. On June 21, 1578 it was decreed that henceforth, guilds were forbidden to spend any money on "useless superstitions, drunkenness, and indecent gormandizing."[65] Instead, all contributions were put to more practical use – namely, the support of impoverished, sick, or otherwise incapacitated members. It should

[63] De Vries, *The Price of Bread.*

[64] Van de Pol, "Prostitutie en de Amsterdamse burgerij," 179–86.

[65] I. H. van Eeghen, *De gilden. Theorie en praktijk.* (Bussum: C. A. J. van Dishoeck, 1965), 12.

be noted that this was not exclusively the result of Calvinist values, as over time this (partial) shift of guild funds towards social purposes also occurred in many cities in the Catholic Southern Netherlands. By the late eighteenth century, such policies had resulted in a situation in which even most of the small guilds in Amsterdam had a *bos* or moneybox from which social arrangements were financed.[66]

The guild welfare schemes funded out of these *bossen* offered forms of insurance for burial costs, sickness, sometimes widows' support, and exceptionally even old-age pensions. The illness benefits were normally two to three times higher than regular forms of poverty relief, which allowed artisans and their families to "keep up appearances" at least for a while. Therefore, the guild *bossen* were a true middle-class phenomenon, a tool of mutual support that allowed skilled workers of sufficient financial means to maintain their social status in times of hardship and misfortune. While even master-artisans usually did not earn enough to create private reserves, their income was sufficiently stable to contribute 1 or 2 stuivers a week to the guild *bos*. The government supported these social welfare arrangements by privileges, sometimes even directly subsidizing them through the allotment of specified tax incomes. The Amsterdam peat-porters guild, for instance, received permission to levy a tax on all incoming peat ships, while its shipwrights' guild had received the right to tax all owners of ship wharves and sloops.[67] According to Van Leeuwen, this discreet assistance that helped the middle classes "to secure their social rank even in difficult times" can be seen as "a form of compensation for the political influence denied to [them] under the early modern corporatist political regime."[68] Notwithstanding the merits of this analysis, Amsterdam's social welfare policies in this era might not just be a compensation for the guild's political influence, but could also be interpreted as its direct result.

[66] Bos, *Uyt liefde tot malcander*; Bert De Munck, *Guilds, Labour and the Urban Body Politic: Fabricating Community in the Southern Netherlands, 1300–1800* (New York: Routledge, 2018). See also Maarten Prak, "Guilds and Mutual Aid in the Northern Netherlands," in *Professional Guilds and the History of Insurance: A Comparative Analysis*, ed. Phillip Hellwege (Berlin: Duncker & Humblot, 2020), 47–62.

[67] Prak, *The Dutch Republic in the Seventeenth Century*, 122–23; Van Leeuwen, "Guilds and Middle-Class Welfare," 77–78 and 85.

[68] Van Leeuwen, "Guilds and Middle-Class Welfare," 85–86.

Even though the regent class displayed clear aristocratizing tendencies in this period, this does not mean that the Amsterdam burgomasters and aldermen were blind to the interests and opinions of the broader mass of citizens. Petitions formed an important communication channel between guilds, churches, and the local authorities. For Amsterdam alone, hundreds of early modern petitions from the craft guilds have survived, and many more must have been drawn up, as petitions that were turned down were immediately destroyed. The authorities generally seem to have looked favorably upon these requests. Maarten Prak's survey of local legislation has revealed that more than 40 percent of the petitions led to the introduction of an urban bylaw, most of which copied the text drafted by the guilds verbatim into the Amsterdam books of ordinances. This shows how the voice of the broad middle groups of seventeenth-century Amsterdam was indirectly translated into policy through the important layer of civic institutions such as guilds and militias.[69]

While we might be tempted to view the different classes in early modern Amsterdam in isolation or as segregated social groups, in practice they were closely linked through common interests in public order and social stability. This is not just revealed by social welfare programs such as the direct aid of the *huiszittenmeesters* or publicly subsidized guild welfare programs, but also through liberal, fair, and accessible insolvency procedures that helped honest insolvents from the middle classes and the elite alike to protect and restore their reputation. Before turning to a discussion of how these legal procedures developed over the seventeenth century, we have to examine one final platform for financial conflict resolution that was active in these formative years of the Dutch Golden Age. Similar to the way in which they provided a vital supplement to the general poverty relief through their deaconries, Amsterdam's religious communities also played an important role in the arbitration between insolvents and their creditors well into the seventeenth century.

[69] Prak, *Citizens without Nations*, 72–75; Maarten Prak, "Individual, Corporation and Society: The Rhetoric of Dutch Guilds (18th. C.)," in *Individual, Corporate, and Judicial Status in European Cities (Late Middle Ages and Early Modern Period)*, ed. Maarten Prak and Marc Boone (Louvain/Apeldoorn: Garant, 1996), 255–79; Henk van Nierop, "Popular Participation in Politics in the Dutch Republic," in *Resistance, Representation, and Community*, ed. Peter Blickle (Cambridge University Press, 1997), 284–87.

Law and Religion: Excommunication or Rehabilitation?

It is generally agreed that rapid demographic growth and urbanization were important driving forces behind the expansion of early modern civil services.[70] Over the sixteenth and seventeenth centuries, many urban governments in the northern Low Countries secularized legal instruments such as marriage law that had previously been part of church jurisdiction. However, in both Protestant and Catholic areas the church struggled to accept the expanding interference of secular authorities in what had previously been matters of faith. Even though they were formally no longer allowed to involve themselves in legal matters, Protestant consistories would often refuse to endorse a strict distribution of tasks between church and worldly authorities. The Calvinist *kerkenraden*, in particular, played an important mediating role in early modern Dutch cities, their activities forming "an essential contribution to urban peace and social cohesion." In the field of marriage-related disputes, they even appear to have been more active than official ecclesiastical courts in Catholic areas, striving to reconcile sinners with both the church and the broader community. At the same time, this also points to an important difference between consistory and aldermen, the church, and the court: while the former saw *tucht* (religious "discipline") as a means to reconcile parties with one another, the latter mainly sought to restore public order by punishing criminal offences.[71]

Four decades ago, Alfred Soman argued that legal historians had too often limited themselves to the study of official legal institutions and organized forms of crime, while neglecting individual deviant behavior. Soman pleaded for the study of "infra-judicial institutions" such as church consistories or notaries, which also played an important role in the resolution of conflicts in early modern society.[72] Over the years, various scholars have striven to fill this gap.[73] Aries van

[70] Van der Heijden, *Civic Duty*, 7.

[71] Ibid. 58–60 and 99–100; Manon van der Heijden, *Huwelijk in Holland. Stedelijke rechtspraak en kerkelijke tucht, 1550–1700* (Amsterdam: Bert Bakker, 1998).

[72] Alfred Soman, "Deviance and Criminal Justice in Western Europe, 1300–1800: An Essay in Structure," *Criminal Justice History* 1 (1980): 3–28.

[73] For a good discussion of more recent literature and developments in this field, see Wim Decock (ed.), *Handbuch zur Geschichte der Konfliktlösung in Europa*, III: *Konfliktlösung im Fruhen Neuzeit* (Berlin: Springer, 2021); Vermeesch, "Reflections on the Relative Accessibility of Law Courts in Early Modern Europe."

Meeteren, for instance, has analyzed the phenomenon of "forum shopping" or *Justiznutzung* for the city of Leiden. Over the seventeenth century, various forms of religious and worldly authorities complemented one another to fulfil the growing demand for arbitration and more formal legal variants of conflict resolution among citizens.[74] In order to reach a proper understanding of the general functioning of public services in the early modern period, we have to be aware of the permeable boundaries between private, public, and ecclesiastical initiatives.[75] It is important to stress, however, that the relation between these early modern public and ecclesiastical authorities on the matter of bankruptcy and insolvency was not so much a conscious delegation of governmental tasks, as it was a complementary system, in which both parties in their own ways contributed to a stable public and moral order. In Chapter 5, the important role of public notaries in the creation of the Amsterdam procedure of the *accord* will be treated in further detail. This section, in turn, will discuss how the Reformed consistories and their counterparts in other religious communities played an equally important role in the resolution of insolvency-related conflicts in early seventeenth-century Amsterdam.

In late medieval France, church courts fulfilled an important role in credit relations between the faithful. The annual confession and communion that good Christians were required to take before Easter resulted in a yearly peak of litigation before Lent. Excommunication served as a means to forcefully pressure Christians to restore the broken charity and concord within their community by paying their debts.[76] Tyler Lange found little evidence of excommunication for debt in the northern Low Countries, arguing that "lay courts may well have developed appropriate remedies in the absence of an adequate supply of ecclesiastical justice particularly marked in the vast diocese of Utrecht."[77] Well into the seventeenth century, however, many groups of Dutch Protestants and even Jews used social exclusion sanctions as punishment for bankrupts in ways that were

[74] Aries van Meeteren, *Op hoop van akkoord. Instrumenteel forumgebruik bij geschilbeslechting in Leiden in de zeventiende eeuw* (Hilversum: Verloren, 2006).
[75] Van der Heijden, *Civic Duty*, 178.
[76] Tyler Lange, *Excommunication for Debt in Late Medieval France: The Business of Salvation* (Cambridge University Press, 2016).
[77] Ibid. 211–12.

strongly reminiscent of excommunication for debt. Whereas in some churches, insolvents and their families were completely banned from the community, most often the punishment was less severe, usually taking the form of an exclusion from sacraments such as communion (among Protestants often called the Lord's Supper).

It is important to note that due to its public character, the Dutch Reformed Church never exercised its full-blown disciplinary activity over all who regularly attended its services – including so-called mere *liefhebbers van de gereformeerde religie* or "enthusiasts of the Reformed faith." Only those who had made a public confession of their faith, the *lidmaten* who thereby joined the sacramental community of those allowed to attend communion, willingly subjected themselves to the *tucht*.[78] Calvin had introduced the practice of a home-visit by the elders of the congregation, in which they would prepare the faithful for attendance at the Supper by removing any potential spiritual impediments. The concept of *ergernis* or "offence, annoyance" was of central importance in this regard. Any member of the congregation who had caused offence to a fellow believer would have to redress this sin before being able to rejoin the *corpus Christi* during communion. If only a few were aware of the transgression, it had a secret nature and could be addressed through a private confession during the elders' visit. A public sin such as insolvency, however, would have to be examined and treated by the complete consistory.[79]

The way in which the early modern consistories disciplined their congregations had much in common with the general way of proceeding in contemporary courts of law. Janine Garrisson-Estèbe even states that the French Calvinist consistories would organize sittings like those of a legal court.[80] While Abels is not entirely in favor of this characterization, which would "harm the essentially spiritual dimension of church discipline," he acknowledges that the proceedings bore a close resemblance to those of a worldly *vierschaar*. Already in 1579, for instance, the Delft consistory employed a certain Wouter Pietersz.

[78] Arie Th. van Deursen, *Bavianen en Slijkgeuzen. Kerk en kerkvolk ten tijde van Maurits en Oldenbarnevelt* (Assen: Van Gorcum & Comp, 1974), 128–29.

[79] Paul Abels, *De nieuwe samenleving*, II: *Nieuw en ongezien. Kerk en samenleving in de classis Delft en Delfland 1572–1621* (Delft: Eburon, 1994), 35.

[80] Janine Garrison-Estèbe, *Protestants du Midi, 1559–1598* (Toulouse: Privat, 1980), 100.

as official door-guard. His tasks included summoning suspects before the consistory, and are reminiscent of those of legal *deurwaarders* in governmental service.[81]

Even though in Amsterdam the government-appointed curator (after 1643 supervised by the commissioners of the Desolate Boedelskamer) was the official authority that sought to resolve conflicts between insolvent debtors and their creditors, similar to the situation in Delft, Amsterdam's religious authorities also meddled in these procedures with their own investigations and arbitration efforts. The strong moral condemnations of insolvency and especially a fraudulent bankruptcy were related to the idea that this was a form of theft, a clear breach of the eighth commandment: "Thou shalt not steal" (Exodus 20:12 / Deuteronomy 5:16). Even worse, such actions could cause financial problems for innocent third parties such as small artisans and shopkeepers. The severity of the problem meant that even though honest insolvents were treated somewhat less harshly, they too were subjected to shameful rituals as an example for the rest of the community.[82]

As soon as the elders of the Amsterdam Dutch Reformed Church heard about an insolvency, it was investigated and then publicly proclaimed during a service. Such events occurred with a certain regularity, as Mary Sprunger established a minimum of 459 instances based upon seventeenth-century consistory notes. Likewise, Evenhuis states that "a complete account of all references to insolvencies in the consistory's protocols would easily fill a small book." In order to streamline the *tucht* procedure, the Reformed elders even went as far as to create preprinted insolvency forms on which only a debtor's name had to be entered before they could be used in a service. After such a proclamation, the insolvent was excluded from the celebrations of the Last Supper until their debts had been repaid or a satisfactory agreement

[81] Abels, *De nieuwe samenleving*, II:36. On the history of the *deurwaarder*, see Remco van Rhee, "Geschiedenis van het deurwaardersambt. Van 'nederige dienaar' tot zelfbewuste professional," *Justitiële Verkenningen* 3 (1999): 19–30.

[82] Mary Sprunger, "Faillissementen. Een aspect van geestelijke tucht bij de Waterlands-doopsgezinde gemeente te Amsterdam in de zeventiende eeuw," *Doopsgezinde Bijdragen* 17 (1991): 101–30, 102–3; Herman Roodenburg, *Onder censuur: de kerkelijke tucht in de gereformeerde gemeente van Amsterdam, 1578–1700* (Hilversum: Verloren, 1990), 377–78.

had been reached with their creditors. Often, insolvent members of the congregation were so ashamed of their desperate financial condition that they did not dare to leave their house to attend church anyway. During this exclusion period, the insolvent was also banned from all church offices, such as that of deacon.[83]

Until the consistory's investigations had concluded and resulted in a satisfactory (arbitral) solution, not only the insolvent himself but his wife, too, were banned from communion. There were three main reasons why the consistory took this measure. First, both spouses usually conducted their business together. Sometimes women even (partially) worked and traded on their own account, as exemplified by Anna van Loo. Second, in the case of a fraudulent bankruptcy in which an insolvent had hidden certain goods just before his financial situation became public knowledge, his wife would often know of these actions or even have supported them. Third, the consistories were especially critical if their investigations revealed that an insolvency had been caused by "indecent gormandizing" or other forms of exorbitant spending. In some cases, an insolvent's wife was identified as the source of such prodigality. According to her neighbors, the consistory noted, Janneke Werkijns caused her husband's insolvency due to her being a *costelycke vrouw in bruyloftsmalen voor haer kinderen en anders* or "being an expensive wife, [wasting money] on her children's wedding meals and other things." Often, however, a wife who proved to be innocent was quickly readmitted after the creditors had officially freed her from the blame of her husband's acts.[84]

The insolvent themself would usually only be readmitted after the elders' investigation had revealed that all creditors had been sufficiently satisfied. While the Reformed elders preferred an accord, as this usually resulted in a higher chance for the creditors to be fully repaid, in the seventeenth century *cessie van goede* also became an acceptable solution that could lead to a religious rehabilitation of the debtor. Even if not all debts had been repaid as of yet, the

[83] Sprunger, "Faillissementen," 102–5; R. B. Evenhuis, *Ook dat was Amsterdam. De kerk der hervorming in de Gouden Eeuw*, 2 vols. (Amsterdam: Ten Have, 1967), II:150–51.

[84] Evenhuis, *Ook dat was Amsterdam*, II:151–52.

creditors could allow (*lijden* or literally "suffer") the consistory to prematurely lift an insolvent's exclusion from the sacraments. In a 1606 correspondence between the churches of Amsterdam and the Palatinate concerning the rehabilitation of insolvents, it is stated that even though it was preferable to wait for their readmission to the communion until all terms specified in an accord had been paid, in practice this might take too long. With the creditors' consent, such an unfortunate debtor who was "engulfed in sadness, or totally alienated from the church and its preaching" might be treated with clemency. This usually happened on the condition that the debtor would promise to strive to repay all remaining arrears if they regained any of their former wealth in future.[85] Interestingly, these practices bear a close resemblance to the usual conditions of an accord as concluded before the Desolate Boedelskamer. Both in the case of a readmission to communion and when an estate was freed from the supervision of the commissioners through an act of rehabilitation (this procedure will be treated in greater detail in Chapter 3), this publicly restored part of the insolvent's honor and creditworthiness.

In Amsterdam's English Reformed congregation, founded in 1607 for English-speaking Protestants in the city, elders and deacons were sometimes even directly involved with the financial management of an insolvent estate. In certain cases, such actions of the consistory seemed the only way to solve a conflict between a debtor and their creditors, either because both parties requested that the church provide arbiters or because the creditors believed that its involvement would be their best guarantee to retrieve as much as possible of their claims. While the English Reformed consistory also accepted written evidence of the creditors' satisfaction before they readmitted an insolvent to communion, at times this was deemed insufficient. On February 23, 1639, for instance, an insolvent was only readmitted to

[85] Roodenburg, *Onder censuur*, 180 and 397; Sprunger, "Faillissementen," 104; Evenhuis, *Ook dat was Amsterdam*, II:152. This was also discussed on the Synod of Enkhuizen, which convened from October 9, 1618 onwards: J. Reitsma and S. D. van Veen, *Acta der provinciale en particuliere synoden, gehouden in de Noordelijke Nederlanden gedurende de jaren 1572–1620*, 8 vols. (Groningen: J. B. Wolters, 1893), II:23–24. Citation from the letter printed as a whole in Van Deursen, *Bavianen en Slijkgeuzen*, 382–83.

communion after an elder and deacon had been appointed to supervise his estate and "to receive every six months the accounts of his gains and expenses, the surplus to be reported to the Consistory, for the use of his creditors." This practice was in line with the guidelines provided by the Dutch Reformed synod of North-Holland in 1618, and typical of the way in which Amsterdam's Calvinist consistories dealt with nonfraudulent insolvencies in their midst in the first decades of the seventeenth century.[86]

The active meddling of religious authorities such as Amsterdam's Reformed consistories in insolvency procedures were certainly not undebated or to every citizen's liking. Related to his general criticism of the consistories' recruitment policy, the well-known regent Cornelis Pietersz. Hooft (1547–1626) actually expressed feelings of clemency for insolvent targets of "church justice":

> A church existing under a Christian government should not be allowed to call people before its consistory (which is bound by neither oath, nor instruction) for trifles and matters that are not criminalized according to the laws of the land, nor to shame and scandalize them to the great injury of their good name and credit.[87]

Being called before the elders for an interrogation, or ultimately a temporary exclusion from communion until one had reached a decent solution with one's creditors, clearly inflicted serious harm on one's social position. Hooft believed that such moral reproaches should only be administered by the public (political) authorities. If need arose, they could always summon someone (an insolvent) to the city hall for matters which, if more serious (in cases of fraud), would have resulted in a criminal verdict.[88] While the Dutch Reformed consistories clearly disagreed with such sentiments, an interesting development can be observed in their treatment of economic conflicts in the first decades of the seventeenth century. Even though Van Deursen remarks that citizens who could not pay their debts "were always

86 Alice Clare Carter, *The English Reformed Church in Amsterdam in the Seventeenth Century* (Amsterdam: Scheltema & Holkema / Stadsdrukkerij Amsterdam, 1964), 169–75.

87 Cornelis Pietersz. Hooft, *Memoriën en adviezen*, 2 vols. (Utrecht: Kemink & Zoon, 1871), I:81.

88 H. A. Enno van Gelder, *De levensbeschouwing van Cornelis Pieterszoon Hooft, burgemeester van Amsterdam (1547–1626)* (Amsterdam: A. H. Kruyt, 1918), 106.

regarded as culprits, never as victims," if this sentiment ever prevailed among the majority of Dutch Calvinists it quickly evolved into a more nuanced stance.[89]

While during a small peak of insolvencies in 1597 the Delft consistory acted "ruthlessly," especially in the case of fugitive debtors, a few years later this had clearly changed.[90] The reason for this development seems to have been a discussion at the synod of South-Holland that convened from September 9, 1597 in the small city of Schoonhoven. There, it was decided that in every case of insolvency the consistory was obliged to carefully investigate whether the financial problems had been caused by personal misconduct and fraud, or "originated in simple misfortune, received from our Lord."[91] In 1605, the synod of the Reformed churches in North-Holland discussed similar problems that occurred among their congregations. The representatives found "that many in the cities of Holland become bankrupts, causing great damage for many people, much to the annoyance of the churches." In reaction to this phenomenon, the consistories were also prompted to investigate and punish potential instances of bankruptcy in their communities.[92] Generally, however, from these years onwards a clear distinction started to be made between fugitive bankrupts, who were publicly condemned, and unfortunate insolvents, who were actively encouraged to seek a decent legal solution for their financial problems in order to be readmitted to the Lord's Supper. As had already been remarked at the Schoonhoven synod: "while the former clearly have to be censored for their extravagance and guile, in like manner there is no reason why any form of punishment should be imposed upon the latter."[93]

While in the early seventeenth century, consistories were thus actively involved in the supervision of insolvent estates and directly arbitrated between creditors and their debtors to settle the terms for their repayment, as the century progressed they increasingly agreed that these responsibilities should be borne by the secular authorities.

[89] Van Deursen, *Bavianen en Slijkgeuzen*, 223.
[90] Abels, *De nieuwe samenleving*, II:85–86.
[91] J. Reitsma and S. D. van Veen, *Acta der provinciale en particuliere synoden, gehouden in de Noordelijke Nederlanden gedurende de jaren 1572–1620*, 8 vols. (Groningen: J. B. Wolters, 1894), III:93–94.
[92] Roodenburg, *Onder censuur*, 377; Sprunger, "Faillissementen," 102.
[93] Reitsma and van Veen, *Acta der provinciale en particuliere synoden*, III:94.

If an insolvent could provide an "order from the lords" such as a *cessie* or an accord, the consistory accepted these on the simple promise that the rehabilitated insolvent would honor the obligations laid out therein. This pragmatic and more distant role for the consistories was actually more in line with Calvin's own thoughts about the proper relation between civil and ecclesiastical authorities.[94] At the same time, we should keep in mind that when trying to enforce its dogmas on social and economic matters, the Calvinist church in the Dutch Republic was seriously handicapped by the fact that its actual discipline was restricted to the relatively small "inner circle" of active members rather than to the entire society. According to Simon Schama, "the [small] number of eminent and wealthy (not to mention obscure and poor) figures subjected to the ban suggests that it did not strike terror in the hearts of all believers."[95]

Most probably, this "revolution by evolution" in the treatment of insolvencies by the Reformed consistories was caused by two factors. On the one hand (as I will argue in Chapter 2), Dutch society went through a number of cultural developments in the first half of the seventeenth century. This changing mental world clearly influenced both religious and secular authorities. On the other hand, the rapidly professionalizing treatment of insolvent estates by the Amsterdam legal authorities that culminated in the establishment of the Desolate Boedelskamer (as described in Chapters 3–6) must also have reduced the need for the consistories to initiate their own investigations. As their main goal was the reduction of *ergernis* among the faithful, the Reformed consistories were ready to accept formal legal solutions such as the *akkoord* if these restored peace among their members. Still, this reduction of the consistories' active role should not blind us to their important social and moral authority, which remained more-or-less unchallenged in the entire period treated by this book.

Even stricter than the *tucht* or discipline exercised by the Reformed consistories was that of the *Doopsgezinden* or Mennonites. In their opinion, not living up to one's financial commitments was not just a sin against the creditor, but would also damage the reputation of the whole community towards the outside world. As a result, among the strictest of their congregations, the so-called "Old Flemish"

94 Carter, *English Reformed Church*, 177.
95 Schama, *Embarrassment of Riches*, 335–36.

churches, insolvents and bankrupts alike were completely banished from the community as soon as their financial shortcomings were revealed. After such a sanction had been proclaimed, no member was allowed to even speak to the banished, which resulted in a cruel form of social isolation. Even though banishment was theoretically the most severe stage of escalation of *tucht* among the Reformed congregations, it was very rarely used in practice after the initial stages of the Reformation.[96] The Mennonites, on the other hand, continued to adhere to this harshest form of social discipline for a much longer period. In the early seventeenth century, a conflict about insolvencies even resulted in a minor schism in Haarlem. One of the local elders, Jacob Pietersz. van der Meulen, refused to banish an honest insolvent, who had committed no fraudulent acts, but after his refusal he and those of his opinion – who came to be known as the *Vermeulensvolk* – were themselves banished from the congregation.[97]

In 1642, the Amsterdam Mennonite preacher Cornelis Anslo of the *Waterlandse* congregation went as far as to pay the staggering amount of fl. 60,000 for debts that had been incurred by his insolvent son, even though he was not legally bound to do so. According to one of Anslo's offspring who recorded the event, he would have defended his actions as follows:

> As a preacher, who steps forward to point others to their duties, admonishing them to follow the lesson from Matthew 7:12 to treat others like one would prefer to be treated; ... I would not want this debt (even though I do not have to pay it) to make my preaching fruitless, or to cause my words to lose any of their strength.[98]

Of course, even among the Mennonites most would probably not have gone this far to preserve their reputation. In the course of the seventeenth century their communities also increasingly opened up towards the outside world, leading to the acceptance of the legal intrusion of secular

96 Abels, *De nieuwe samenleving*, II:38–40.

97 Sprunger, "Faillissementen," 101–2; S. Zijlstra, *Om de ware gemeente en de oude gronden. Geschiedenis van de dopersen in de Nederlanden 1531–1675* (Hilversum: Verloren, 2000), 452 and 469–70.

98 Zijlstra, *Om de ware gemeente*, 452; S. A. C. Dudok van Heel, "Doopsgezinden en schilderkunst in de 17e eeuw – Leerlingen, opdrachtgevers en verzamelaars van Rembrandt," *Doopsgezinde Bijdragen* 6 (1980): 105–23, 114.

judges, such as the commissioners of the Desolate Boedelskamer, that would presumably have been contested around 1600.[99]

Interestingly, comparable developments can also be observed among Amsterdam's Jewish communities. For the Portuguese Jews, or Sephardim, who arrived in Amsterdam from the late sixteenth century onwards, the right to use the *herem* or excommunication formed one of the foundations of Jewish autonomy. While no official permission from the Amsterdam authorities to apply this punishment has come down to us, the Sephardic community must have received explicit permission to employ a social sanctioning mechanism of this severity. In 1605, the Jews of Haarlem were granted a charter that explicitly allowed them "to excommunicate and ban from their midst ... those among them who might be found to live a scandalous and offensive life." On January 27, 1683, however, the Amsterdam authorities sought to tighten their control over the Sephardic *herem*: henceforth the *parnassim* – the leaders of the Amsterdam congregation – could only excommunicate members with prior agreement and authorization of the aldermen. Even though this decision was reversed after just a few months, it illustrates the thin line between internal autonomy and top-down municipal control regarding such infrajudicial practices in this period.[100]

The general aim of the Sephardic *parnassim*'s use of these powers was the preservation of peace, order, and union in their community.[101] The functioning of these elders displays great similarities to the Calvinist "disciplinary revolution from below" that, as we saw before, also affected the social treatment of insolvents in Protestant congregations. The mediating efforts of the Jewish *parnassim*, who generally sought to prevent litigation in secular courts by members of their congregations if this could be avoided, thereby soon became "embedded in the city's legal culture and system of arbitration." However, the Sephardic Jews never used the *herem* to

99 Zijlstra, *Om de ware gemeente*, 453.

100 Yosef Kaplan, *An Alternative Path to Modernity: The Sephardi Diaspora in Western Europe* (Leiden: Brill, 2000), 108–10.

101 Evelyne Oliel-Grausz, "Patrocinio and Authority: Assessing the Metropolitan Role of the Portuguese Nation of Amsterdam in the Eighteenth Century," in *The Dutch Intersection: The Jews and the Netherlands in Modern History*, ed. Yosef Kaplan (Leiden: Brill, 2008), 153–55.

ostracize bankrupt merchants from their community, or to exercise moral control over business practices in general.[102] This runs contrary to the practices found in both Calvinist and Mennonite congregations, but intriguingly also diverges from the other substantial organized Jewish community in Amsterdam. Perhaps, this can be explained by the fact that (overseas) trade was the central occupation of many Sephardim, which might have made them less strict about insolvency due to their awareness of the financial risks inherent in this sector of the economy.

In the German Jewish congregation of the Ashkenazim, however, excommunication for debt was practiced. The Ashkenazim used the ban to punish and completely exclude those who had committed financial crimes such as bankruptcy, comparable to the common practice among the strictest Mennonites. Even insolvents who had received *cessie* or had concluded an accord with their creditors were forbidden to hold offices in the religious community. However, as the seventeenth century progressed, the Amsterdam authorities clearly sought to limit this private form of ecclesiastical justice, as testified by their actions against similar ban-practices among the Sephardim.[103] After riots and internal unrest among the Jews in 1710, the aldermen replaced some of their religious leaders, at the same time demanding that henceforth they could not excommunicate any of their flock "without properly notifying the acting burgomasters and aldermen."[104] When in 1736, the *parnassim* of the German Synagogue wished to banish Samson Salomons on the order of his creditors due to a "thievish bankruptcy," they could only do so after having received the aldermen's prior authorization.[105] This clearly illustrates how public authorities increasingly sought to regulate what had previously been these religious communities' internal matters.

[102] Evelyne Oliel-Grausz, "Dispute Resolution and Kahal Kadosh Talmud Torah: Community Forum and Legal Acculturation in Eighteenth-Century Amsterdam," in *Religious Changes and Cultural Transformations in the Early Modern Western Sephardic Communities*, ed. Yosef Kaplan (Leiden: Brill, 2019), 249–51.

[103] Sprunger, "Faillissementen," 104 (n. 12); Joke Spaans, "Stad van vele geloven 1578–1795," in *Geschiedenis van Amsterdam*, IIa: *Centrum van de wereld, 1578–1650*, ed. Willem Frijhoff and Maarten Prak (Amsterdam: SUN, 2004), 445.

[104] GAS, 5061: Archieven van de Schout en Schepenen, van de Schepenen en van de Subalterne Rechtbanken [ASS], inv. nr. 644, ff. 40v–41v.

[105] GAS, 5061: ASS, inv. nr. 644, ff. 108v–109v.

Even when Amsterdam's local government expanded considerably in the period after the *Alteratie*, the consistories of various protestant churches as well as the Jewish *parnassim* continued for a long time to involve themselves with essentially legal problems such as insolvency. All religious communities in Amsterdam attached substantial worldly punishments to what they perceived as serious moral issues, which were regarded as a severe threat to the functioning and integrity of their congregations. The examples discussed in this section point towards this important general trend in which the punishments flowing forth from social disciplinary activities within religious communities were increasingly subjected to the accordance of secular judges. As the seventeenth century progressed, even the most radical Mennonite sects started to show clemency for honest but unfortunate insolvents to a greater or lesser extent. Even though former *cessie* applicants were generally barred from offices like the deaconry, this seems to have been motivated by practical rather than moral concerns: it simply did not make sense to delegate complex financial responsibilities to such former insolvents. The concentration of financial conflict resolution in public-order institutions such as the Desolate Boedelskamer signified a departure from a complete reliance on personal trust, provided by communities and mediated by individuals such as notaries or religious elders, to its increasing complementation by more professional, systemic forms of trust. In seventeenth-century Amsterdam, individual insolvents, their creditors, and the consistories, came to rely upon such forms of innovative governance to restore the public and moral order of the larger civic community.

Conclusion

The last decades of the sixteenth century were a period of great change and upheaval for those living in Amsterdam and the new Dutch Republic. This was not just true for matters of faith, but for all aspects of public and private life. The *Alteratie* of 1578 sparked a period of rapid economic and demographic growth, as well as a greater involvement of local government in matters of national and international politics. This created a tension between the need to uphold public order, while also continuing to facilitate the economic climate which had made Amsterdam such an attractive destination for migrants of many different backgrounds in the first place. At the same time, however, this newly expanded diversity did not signify a complete breakdown of the civic community into segregated social groups, as it went accompanied by a serious growth in the size and complexity of civil services. The local authorities increasingly interfered in matters of private life, thereby compensating, by means of innovative governance, for the breaking apart of the single Christian community of believers that was the result of the Reformation. The changing roles of public and ecclesiastical institutions can therefore at least partially be explained by the pragmatic religious pluriformity and societal dynamism that characterize early modern Amsterdam.

The central example through which this development will be studied in this book is that of financial conflict resolution between creditors and debtors, as its treatment increasingly passed from the hands of aldermen, notaries, and consistories into those of the specialized commissioners of the Desolate Boedelskamer. Even though religious communities continued to play an important role in arbitrating between insolvents and creditors from their own ranks, over time public legal institutions such as the Desolate Boedelskamer came to occupy the central role in the resolution of such financial disputes. Likewise, religious initiatives for poverty relief were supplemented by generally available social welfare policies that were intricately targeted at both citizens and outsiders from all layers of society. Far from neglecting the middle classes and their important civic organizations such as guilds and the militias, the regent oligarchy provided a listening ear to their concerns as expressed in petitions, which were often directly translated into new and innovative policies.

At the same time, merchants and entrepreneurs from all layers of society worked hard to uphold their reputation, which was essential to sustain the interpersonal trust that formed the foundation of credit in a period that was characterized by information deficits. Systemic trust as provided by open-access governmental institutions such as the Desolate Boedelskamer, which provided a fair and transparent insight into an (alleged) insolvent's books and papers and sought to balance the interests of all creditors, went a great way to restore faith in both unfortunate insolvents and the general economic climate. As this chapter has sought to argue, the economy of seventeenth-century Amsterdam was intimately interwoven with the broader social, cultural, and religious aspects of the urban community at large. This became especially tangible at the moment of insolvency: the breakdown of credit, trust, and the general moral order which underpinned all social and economic relations in this period. In Chapter 2, I will go on to explore the legal implications of these important changes in the broader societal context, which allows us to reflect on the mentality of Amsterdam's Golden Age.

2

Morality and Insolvency Legislation

When admonishing Amsterdam's merchants during one of his services, the Calvinist preacher Godfried Udemans (*c.*1581–1649) pointed out that it was better to lose one's material wealth, which might be regained, than one's reputation, which could easily be lost forever:

> Laet een Coopman die maxime vast houden: eere voor gout, want een arm man die in syne vromicheydt wandelt is beter dan een rijck man die verkeert is met syne lippen ... Want een eerlijck man is ende blijft een eerlijck burgher, al is hy arm, maer die syne eere overleeft heeft, die is levende doot.[1]

> [Let a merchant take for his maxim: honor above gold, for it is better to be a poor man than a liar ... For an honorable man is and will always remain a burgher even if he be poor, but if he outlives his honor, that is a living death.]

While Udemans did not hate commerce as such, he was seriously concerned about certain specific commercial practices. Most relevant for present purposes, he considered bankruptcy to be "an abominable species of theft."[2] This line of thought should be interpreted as a direct consequence of the general functioning of the early modern economy and society discussed in the previous chapter.

[1] Godfried Udemans, *'t Geestlyck roer van 't coopmans schip* (Dordrecht: Françoys Boels, 1638), f. 14. Translation: Simon Schama, *The Embarrassment of Riches: An Interpretation of Dutch Culture in the Golden Age* (New York: Alfred A. Knopf, 1987), 331.

[2] James Q. Whitman, "The Moral Menace of Roman Law and the Making of Commerce: Some Dutch Evidence," *The Yale Law Journal* 105, no. 7 (1995): 1841–89, 1857, and 1872.

Insolvency was an inherently problematic phenomenon for two main reasons. First, it was a social and economic problem, as the failure to fulfil one's financial obligations not only endangered the financial health of a range of other businesses and entrepreneurs, but also harmed a city's commercial position. Contemporaries showed a clear concern about the reputation of their city as a place to do business when discussing the proliferation of bankruptcies in their midst.[3] Second, insolvency was also a moral problem. Strongly criminalized, insolvency led to a loss of personal reputation which could ultimately result in one's removal from the civic and religious community. The fact that insolvency (and even more so a fraudulent bankruptcy) put both the public and moral order of society at risk explains why over time, urban public authorities increasingly sought to regulate and restrain what was essentially a private economic phenomenon.[4] In Amsterdam, as I will argue, this was intimately connected with a radical moral reinterpretation of insolvency. As Fockema Andreae points out:

> It is unthinkable to imagine a proliferation of credit if the creditor does not have the certainty that he might be able to force his debtor to honor his obligations if need would arise; and this security he will only truly possess if the state is willing and able to support him.[5]

Even though a creditor's rights were most efficiently secured by public authorities, for a long time insolvency largely remained a matter between private parties that was not addressed in a coherent or

[3] Mary Lindemann, *The Merchant Republics: Amsterdam, Antwerp, and Hamburg, 1648–1790* (New York: Cambridge University Press, 2014), 277.

[4] Annamaria Monti, "Osservazioni sparse intorno alle vicende storiche del fallimento," in *Commentario alla legge fallimentare*, ed. Cesare Cavallini, 4 vols. (Milan: Egea, 2010), IV:12–13 and 23.

[5] Sybrand J. Fockema Andreae, *Het Oud-Nederlandsch burgerlijk recht* (Haarlem: Bohn, 1906), 2. His argument runs contrary to the views of his German contemporary Josef Kohler, who emphasized the difference between public and private approaches towards insolvency legislation, arguing that the public tradition originating in Spain was less efficient than the "Germanic" private tradition, in which the assembled creditors rather than a judge dominated legal insolvency proceedings. According to Dalhuisen, the whole public–private distinction is nebulous and not always warranted by the historical facts. In every country, regardless of its legal orientation, legal authorities exercised a strong supervision over insolvency procedures: Jan Hendrik Dalhuisen, *Compositions in Bankruptcy: A Comparative Study of the Laws of the E.E.C. Countries, England and the U.S.A.* (Leiden: A. W. Sijthoff, 1968), 12 (n. 41) and 17 (n. 72).

significant manner by either central or local governments in Western Europe. The two central issues inherent in insolvency, its socioeconomic and morally problematic nature, formed a dual challenge that legislators and policy makers were confronted with when attempting to deal with this topic.

In this chapter, I will describe in broad strokes the development towards more substantial legislative activity and governmental involvement with financial conflict resolution, with special attention to the Low Countries. First, I will discuss the traditional treatment of insolvency from both Roman and Germanic perspectives. While execution procedures at one time had a strong individual focus, over time creditors' rights were increasingly balanced by collectivizing legal solutions. The second part of this chapter will discuss these developments from the debtor's perspective. For a long time, legal solutions for insolvency strongly criminalized the insolvent (then called bankrupt, *fallitus*), seeking to stimulate honest and prudent conduct among citizens by deterrence. The failure to fulfil one's obligations was indiscriminately punished by shaming rituals in many parts of Europe. While these defamatory practices proliferated well into the early modern period, they seem to have disappeared from the legal treatment of insolvencies in seventeenth-century Amsterdam. This signifies a crucial change in public mentalities, which allowed for the introduction of a more lenient and efficient insolvency regime. The third and final section of this chapter will explore a possible explanation for that intriguing development through an analysis of the mental world of Amsterdam and the Dutch Republic during its formative era. Travelling back to the roots of the legal treatment of insolvencies in European history offers interesting perspectives on the unique character of seventeenth-century Amsterdam's legal culture, economy, and society that will be explored in the remainder of this book.

The Traditional Execution of Debts

In antiquity as well as in most of the medieval period, legislative initiatives in the field of insolvency often remained limited to seizure and execution proceedings that were indiscriminately applied to all who failed to fulfil their financial obligations. Insolvents were generally distrusted and characterized as fraudulent felons, their cases dealt with by harsh private criminal law. The Roman term *decoctor*, used for both insolvents and squanderers, is a telling example of how such matters were viewed for the greater part of our common era. It has been argued that according to the ancient Roman *Law of the Twelve Tables* (*c*.450 BC), through a *manus iniectio* procedure a creditor was entitled to sell their bankrupt debtor as a slave, or even to put them to death. This quite literal, bloody take on the idea of an "execution" of debts returned at various moments in history.[6] In the alternative *nexum* procedure, the debtor had pledged their body as collateral and subsequently defaulted on their loan. However, here forced labor in the form of debt bondage rather than slavery was the result. Supposedly, citizenship would not have been lost.[7] Ancient execution traditions, whether Roman or Germanic, generally show little regard for other creditors: it was literally "he who comes first, grabs first."[8] From the time of the Roman Republic and again from the late medieval period onwards, however, especially in urban commercial hubs merchants and legislators arrived at the insight that cooperation of the insolvent might be beneficial for all parties involved. This led to the creation of ever more intricate legal insolvency procedures.[9]

Under republican and classical Roman law, procedures had been created that focused on an insolvent's goods and possessions rather than on their physical person. Even though these procedures fell into disuse after late antiquity, they merit attention due to their continued influence after interest in Roman law was rekindled in universities

6 Michael Spann, *Der Haftungszugriff auf den Schuldner zwischen Personal- und Vermögensvollstreckung. Eine exemplarische Untersuchung der geschichtlichen Rechtsquellen ausgehend vom Römischen Recht bis ins 21. Jh. unter besonderer Berücksichtigung bayerischer Quellen* (Berlin: Lit, 2004), 3–21; Jacques Brissaud, *Le Créancier "premier saisissant" dans l'ancien droit français* (Paris: Presses Universitaires de France, 1972). Dondorp argues, however, that we should interpret Aulus Gellius's comment on the ancient Roman law in a different fashion: not the insolvents' *body*, but the proceeds from their sale as a slave would be the target of the legal execution: Harry Dondorp, "Partes Secanto. Aulus Gellius and the Glossators," *Revue Internationale Des Droits de l'antiquité* 57 (2010): 131–44.

7 Peter M. Bauer, *Der Insolvenzplan. Untersuchungen zur Rechtsnatur anhand der geschichtlichen Entwicklung* (Berlin: Lit, 2009), 33–35; Spann, *Der Haftungszugriff*, 21–23.

8 Bob Wessels, Bruce Markall, and Jason Kilborn, *International Cooperation in Bankruptcy and Insolvency Matters* (Oxford University Press, 2009), 3–4.

9 Dave De ruysscher, *Gedisciplineerde vrijheid. Een geschiedenis van het handels- en economisch recht* (Antwerp: Maklu, 2014), 76–77.

from the later eleventh century onwards. In the first century BC, the *praetor* received the power to order the execution of an insolvent estate through the procedure of *missio in bona*. During a specified period, a curator guarded the estate on behalf of the creditors while the insolvent and their relatives could try to gather enough funds to avoid an execution. If they failed, the insolvent's possessions were sold as a whole to the highest bidder through a *venditio bonorum*. This procedure resulted in the important innovation that proceeds were shared among all the creditors instead of the older first-come-first-served principles. Augustus's *Lex Julia* introduced another important innovation, *cessio bonorum*, which enabled honest insolvents who had not acted in "bad faith" to willingly surrender their estate to their common creditors in order to regain their physical freedom. Neither remedy officially provided for a discharge of debts, even for a bona fide debtor.[10]

The protection from legal action or "automatic stay" and the exemption from personal execution that were provided as part of the *cessio* equally benefited the insolvent and their creditors. Unlike in the more traditional procedures, it protected the creditors from one another by providing for an orderly execution, just as in the *venditio*.[11] As an alternative to *cessio*, the Justinian Codex provides the procedure of *dilatio* for bona fide debtors. If a majority of the creditors agreed, the emperor could grant a payment extension for five years. Alternatively, if the debtor provided sufficient securities for the repayment of their debts, the emperor could also grant the *dilatio* as a favor – that is, without explicit creditors' consent. Interestingly, in this case the absence of *culpa* ("negligence," "fault") does not seem to have been required.[12]

Finally, the concept of majority compositions was also introduced during the imperial period. If someone died and no heir was available

[10] Ibid. 84–90; Bauer, *Der Insolvenzplan*, 36–40; Dalhuisen, *Compositions in Bankruptcy*, 6–8.

[11] Walter Pakter, "The Mystery of 'Cessio Bonorum,'" *Index : Quaderni Camerti Di Studi Romanistici = International Survey of Roman Law* 22 (1994): 323–42.

[12] Wolfgang Forster, *Konkurs als Verfahren. Francisco Salgado de Somoza in der Geschichte des Insolvenzrechts* (Cologne: Böhlau, 2009), 211; Arnoud J. Noordam, "Schuldsanering en goede trouw" (PhD, Amsterdam, VU, 2007), 136–37; Dalhuisen, *Compositions in Bankruptcy*, 9–12. On the *dilatio*, see Codex Justinianus, C.1.19.2 and 4; C.7.71.8.

or willing to accept their indebted inheritance, the estate would be sold through a *venditio bonorum*, bringing *ignominia* – great shame, dishonor – on the deceased. In the procedure known as *remissio*, a majority of the creditors could allow a (partial) discharge of the total debt if this would convince the heir of an insolvent estate to accept their bad inheritance. The idea of a legal discharge through a majority composition thus originated from the Roman law of succession.[13]

Generally, therefore, under Roman law the treatment of defaulting debtors slowly shifted from an execution on the person to an execution of their estate; while at the same time the idea that an insolvent could be blameless for their condition was introduced in procedures such as *cessio bonorum* and the *dilatio*. While a discharge through majority composition only became available for the unique case of the heir of a deceased debtor, the *remissio* nevertheless signifies an important innovation that was expanded upon in later times. All these elements would continue to be part of the basic repertoire of insolvency legislation throughout Western history.

After the collapse of the strongly commercialized Roman Empire in Western Europe, a renewed focus on the person of the debtor could be observed in its Germanic successor states. In their legal traditions, any failure to repay a debt was seen as a criminal offence that was to be punished by a fine. Such cases were regarded as private disputes between contractual parties: collective procedures such as the Roman *venditio* or *cessio* do not seem to have existed. Land became the most important form of collateral; for any other unsecured debts one was generally held physically liable. Due to the virtual absence of markets and the scarcity of labor, however, land was only of use when it could be worked and efficiently protected against foreign invasions.[14] In the High Middle Ages, creditors were often allowed to resort to private coercive debt imprisonment until their claims had been satisfied. As is revealed in sources such as the *Sachsenspiegel*, in a world accustomed to serfdom, indemnificatory bondage was often seen as

[13] Forster, *Konkurs als Verfahren*, 212; Dalhuisen, *Compositions in Bankruptcy*, 9–12. On the *remissio*, see Codex Justinianus, D. 2.14.8 and 10; D. 2.14.7.17–19; D.17.1.58.1; D. 42.9.23.

[14] Douglass C. North and Robert Paul Thomas, *The Rise of the Western World: A New Economic History* (Cambridge University Press, 1973), 19–24; De ruysscher, *Gedisciplineerde vrijheid*, 90–91.

a useful tool to force an insolvent debtor to repay their arrears.[15] The private incarceration of insolvent debtors also occurred in the high medieval Low Countries, as shown by the 1288 *Handvesten van Waterland*, a collection of ordinances issued by Count Floris V for the region north of Amsterdam. If a debtor persisted in their default for more than two weeks, a *bode* or messenger of the court would lock them up and hand them over to their creditors. While it was expressly forbidden to physically harm the insolvent, a creditor could "keep him on water and bread" as long as they wished, which was probably until the insolvent or their relatives had found a way to settle the unpaid debt.[16]

Over time, however, insolvency legislation and practices had to adjust to increasingly monetized economies. The standard way of dealing with unpaid debts, forced labor, which assumed that landowners were the creditors and peasants their debtors, no longer sufficed in the commercializing economies of late medieval cities. In many parts of Europe, creditor-initiated imprisonment for debt increasingly became standard practice in case of insolvency. Often, such measures were effectuated in one of the official royal or urban jails rather than in the creditor's private residence.[17] In fourteenth-century Florence, for instance, 64 percent of all inmates in the public prison had been incarcerated because of unpaid debts.[18]

In late medieval Amsterdam, if a debtor's assets were found to be insufficient to repay one of their creditors when the latter had initiated a preservatory legal procedure such as *eigenpand*, the debtor could be personally arrested in order to transform the procedure into an executory variant. After the debtor had declared that they lacked possessions that would suffice as pledge for their creditors, they were brought before the municipal court to formally repeat this declaration in the presence of burgomasters and aldermen. Afterwards, the bailiff would bring the debtor outside on the Dam square, where they

15 Jean Dunbabin, *Captivity and Imprisonment in Medieval Europe 1000–1300* (Basingstoke: Palgrave Macmillan, 2002), 76–77; Bauer, *Der Insolvenzplan*, 70–74.
16 Simon van Leeuwen, *Het Rooms-Hollands-regt [etc.]* (Leiden/Rotterdam: Hackens, 1664), 445.
17 Dunbabin, *Captivity and Imprisonment*, 78 and 95–96.
18 Guy Geltner, *The Medieval Prison: A Social History* (Princeton University Press, 2008), 51.

were guided to a *ring, gestraet met het wapen der stad* or a "circle, paved with the arms of the city." After the insolvent debtor had walked around this symbolic pavement three times, their citizenship was officially forfeited. This was necessary to make it legally possible for them to be jailed by the bailiff until their relatives or friends would find a way to fulfil the creditors' demands.[19] Over the course of the sixteenth century, this practice must have disappeared. By the seventeenth century the aforementioned procedure of *eigening van schulden* was no longer practiced, as even for the most informal of debts one could directly initiate an execution proceeding against an insolvent debtor, whether he or she was a citizen or foreigner.[20]

In Brabant and its commercial center Antwerp, creditors also locked up their debtors in order to force them to accept judgment, rather than absconding with their remaining goods. According to Dave De ruysscher, this was inescapable, as in this period only a judgment could form a valid basis upon which to organize an auction of a debtor's assets, movable or immovable. Such legal procedures were often slow, which made them impractical. The imprisonment of a debtor was simply the most efficient method to execute a debt, as it put pressure on the defaulter to arrange new securities or other types of credit. This potentially led to a solution before a trial had finished or even before the case was treated in court. While officially citizens as well as varying groups of foreign merchants were protected against incarceration, in practice there are many examples in which such privileges were neglected and had to be enforced in court. Rather than facing this prospect, debtors confronted with financial problems were stimulated to run off. This had adverse effects on commerce. Even the slightest rumor of default stimulated a debtor's swift and premature detention, which in turn caused a ripple effect of seizures and executions by all of their creditors. This effect was strengthened by the fact

[19] Jeronimo Mattheus Barels, *Onderzoek over de pandingen binnen de stad Amsterdam in gebruik* (Amsterdam: Hendrik Gartman, 1780), 146–48; M. C. van Hall, "Verhandeling over het zinnebeeldige in de Oud-Nederlandse regten," in *Regtsgeleerde verhandelingen en losse geschriften* (Amsterdam: Johannes van der Hey en Zoon / Ten Brink & De Vries, 1838), 233–40.

[20] Gerard Rooseboom (ed.), *Recueil van verscheyde keuren, en costumen; midtsgaders maniere van procederen binnen de stadt Amsterdam*, 2nd ed. (Amsterdam: Jan Hendricks, 1656), 152–54.

that late medieval legislation often continued to focus on individual debt recovery, usually on a crude first-come-first-served basis.[21]

The fact that fleeing bankrupts were not unknown in late medieval Amsterdam is vividly illustrated by a passage in the first of its *keurboeken*, collections of local urban bylaws, which is the oldest Amsterdam example of a legal rule relating to insolvency:

Item nyemant en moet lude uyt der stede vueren die ruymen mit horen inghebuedel, noch dier lude guede die gheruymt sijn dair yemant gebrec an hadde buten den gherechte bij 10 Pond Holl. dat sal staen tots gerechts pruevinge.[22]

[Nobody is allowed to assist people who seek to leave the city with all of their goods, or who had absconded at an earlier stage, while owing money to their creditors, on the pain of a legal fine of 10 lb. Hollands.]

This *keur*, which must have been in effect from before 1422, strongly forbids citizens to extend any form of aid to a fugitive bankrupt. Anyone who aided such criminals to the detriment of their creditors would be punished with a fine of 10 Holland pounds, equal to the later guldens of 20 stuivers each.[23]

From the twelfth century onwards, European commerce had started to flourish again, most prominently in Italian city-states such as Venice, Florence, and Genoa. As time went by and in response to these changing economic circumstances, some cities developed increasingly intricate insolvency proceedings that ensured an equal distribution of all executed movable goods between the creditors. Venice probably had one of Europe's most liberal insolvency regimes in this period. In 1395, its government abolished criminal prosecution for absconded bankrupts who returned and handed over their account books and a

[21] Dave De ruysscher, "Business Rescue, Turnaround Management and the Legal Regime of Default and Insolvency in Western History (Late Middle Ages to Present Day)," in *Turnaround Management and Bankruptcy*, ed. Jan Adriaanse and Jean-Pierre van der Rest (New York: Routledge, 2017), 25–26; Dave De ruysscher, "Jurisprudence & The Formulation of Law in Antwerp: An Academic and Practice-Oriented Tradition in Commercial Law (Sixteenth to Nineteenth Centuries)," in *Nothing Will Come of Nothing. Science and Education in Antwerp since 1500*, ed. Helma de Smedt (University of Antwerp, 2019), 230; Brissaud, *Le Créancier.*

[22] Goswin Moll, *De Desolate Boedelskamer te Amsterdam: bijdrage tot de kennis van het Oud-Hollandsch failliten-recht* (Amsterdam: De Roever-Kröber-Bakels, 1879), 4–5.

[23] Ibid. 1.

survey of their property. The government's administrators sought to stimulate the crafting of an amicable agreement or *concordato* between a cooperative debtor, who was deemed of good intent, and their creditors. Through mediation, deals were struck that had to be supported by the majority of the creditors. Even in Venice, however, voluntary debt negotiation proceedings that were started outside of a formal bankruptcy were very rare. This procedure was always initiated by a dishonorable denunciation of flight, which must have been detrimental for the insolvent's reputation. Even though the government sought to provide elements of systemic trust through its mediating function, this was undermined by the fact that individual creditors lost their claim if they did not submit it within a rather short period of time.[24]

Over the course of the fifteenth century in Antwerp, as well, it became common to accept that movables could serve as general collateral for debts, even if that had not been stipulated in a contract. This important development towards the depersonalization of security for debt probably prompted the move towards new ways of handling insolvency. A solution to the problem of individual debt enforcement in the form of collective insolvency proceedings named *samenloop* was introduced between 1516 and 1518. Henceforth, the proceeds from the liquidated assets of a dead or fugitive debtor were divided proportionally among their creditors, after these had been sold in a public auction in the city's *Vrijdagmarkt* square. However, these rules were only applied to nonfraudulent insolvencies in the new collection of local bylaws or *costuymen* of 1582, which meant that these new municipal insolvency procedures officially continued to have a limited, criminal nature until the end of the sixteenth century.[25] In contemporary legal practice, however, extrajudicial compositions between nonfraudulent insolvents and their common creditors after

[24] Magnus Ressel, "Norms and Practice of Handling Complex and International Insolvencies in Early Modern Venice," in *Dealing with Economic Failure: Between Norm and Practice (15th to 21st Century)*, ed. Albrecht Cordes and Margrit Schulte Beerbühl (Frankfurt am Main: Peter Lang, 2016), 115–38; De ruysscher, "Business Rescue," 30–31; Umberto Santarelli, *Per la storia del fallimento nelle legislazioni italiane dell'età intermedia* (Padua: Cedam, 1964), 290–302.

[25] Dave De ruysscher, *"Naer het Romeinsch recht alsmede den stiel mercantiel." Handel en recht in de Antwerpse rechtbank (16de-17de eeuw)* (Kortrijk-Heule: UGA, 2009), 317; De ruysscher, "Jurisprudence & The Formulation of Law in Antwerp," 230 and 233.

the Venetian model became increasingly popular. It was only in the 1608 *costuymen*, however, that the authorities officially embraced such agreements, known as *akkoord*, provided that a majority of three-quarters of the creditors representing two-thirds of the value of debts (or the other way around) had signed the composition. This had an important advantage for the insolvent: they regained possession of their goods if they adhered to the conditions of the *akkoord*, and could request an official rehabilitation at the Council of Brabant.[26]

The slow acceptance of majority compositions by local authorities in Antwerp and other cities in the Low Countries can be explained by imperial ordinances that sought to curtail this phenomenon. On May 10, 1544, Emperor Charles V decreed:

> Datmen gheen brieven verleenen en sal om te bedwinghen den crediteur te consenteren in appointement ghemaect bi sinen schuldenaer mitte meeste portie van sine crediteuren, so verre dat biden voorschreven appointemente quytschelt eenighe partien vande schult ofte datmen gheve dach van betalinghe sonder caucie.[27]

> [It is forbidden to issue a letter that would force an unwilling creditor to consent to a composition that had been concluded between an insolvent and the majority of his creditors, if this would entail the remission of part of the debt or an extension of the payment term without sufficient securities being provided.]

The emperor's reasoning makes sense in light of the basic rules of medieval contract law, "that the contractor could contract only for [themself]."[28] The glossators had partially solved this problem by arguing that in the classic case of a deceased debtor, granting the composition would also be to the advantage of the dissenting minority of creditors. Rather than facing the complete absence of a debtor when the heir would refuse to accept an insolvent inheritance, the composition would result in a situation in which at least part of the collective debts could be repaid.[29]

[26] De ruysscher, "*Naer het Romeinsch recht alsmede den stiel mercantiel,*" 329–31.

[27] J. Lameere and H. Simont (eds.), *Recueil des ordonnances des Pays-Bas* [*ROPB*]. *Deuxième série 1506–1700*, 8 vols. (Brussels: J. Goemaere, 1910), V:52–56 (Brussels, May 10, 1544) art. 34.

[28] Formulated in the medieval maxim derived from C.5.59.5.2: *Quod omnes tangit ab omnibus debere approbari*. See Dalhuisen, *Compositions in Bankruptcy*, 10.

[29] Forster, *Konkurs als Verfahren*, 212–13.

Well into the seventeenth century, there was a consensus among legal scholars that this reasoning could not be applied to a living debtor.[30] This ran contrary, however, to contemporary legal practice. In late-medieval Italian city-states, majority compositions started to be applied in court to cases with fugitive insolvents – equally absent as the deceased debtor from Roman law.[31] Majority compositions became increasingly popular in many Dutch cities over the seventeenth century. This was also reflected and regulated in Amsterdam's *costuymen*. When discussing such compositions, it is important to differentiate between agreements that only provided for a restructured repayment scheme of the debt as a whole (*dilatio*), or that provided debt relief by acquitting part of the debt (*remissio*). Apart from the classic case of the heir of the absconding debtor, the remission of debts remained impossible, unless all creditors agreed. Officially, as I will argue in Chapter 5, majority compositions or *akkoorden* in Holland kept being limited to payment extensions modelled on the *dilatio*.

In this same period, the development of collective insolvency procedures and the revived prominence of movable goods resulted in an increasing role of public officials in insolvency and bankruptcy procedures. In Antwerp, for instance, seized goods – which could only be officially locked by the *amman* (bailiff) and their helpers, the *knuivers* – always had to be sold in public. If a judgment had been obtained, this took place through the procedure of *executie*, which necessitated an inventory of all the debtor's possessions before the auction could take place; if the seizure was based upon other documentary evidence, an inventory was unnecessary but the execution or *uitwinning* could only take place through the equally cumbersome *evictie* procedure. Both an *executie* and an *evictie* had to be initiated before the civil court or *vierschaar* within six weeks. At the same time, creditors also started to receive a more official role in insolvency procedures through the appointment of a curator as their representative.[32] It was important for the creditors to react quickly when a

30 Cf. the Castilian *Siete Partidas*: Forster, *Konkurs als Verfahren*, 213, referring to SP 1555 V.15.6.

31 See e.g. Raphaelis Fulgosii placentini, *Pandectarum Commentariorum* (Lyon: Servarius, 1554), on D. 4.14.7.19; Dalhuisen, *Compositions in Bankruptcy*, 20, referring to Matthaeus de Afflictis, *Decisiones Neapolitani*, 288.

32 De ruysscher, "*Naer het Romeinsch recht alsmede den stiel mercantiel,*" 310–13.

samenloop had been initiated upon a debtor's insolvency and his or her goods had been seized: if they brought their claims too late they would be lost, just as was the case in Venice.[33] When the 1582 *costuymen* started to differentiate between fraudulent or fugitive bankrupts and innocent insolvents, it became important to determine the precise moment at which the debtor had entered into this state. In principle, a merchant was regarded as bankrupt when they were publicly known as such, which was connected to their disappearing from the *Beurs* or Bourse. It was argued that someone who failed to appear there must have had something to hide. Subsequently, the 1608 *costuymen* provided for a procedure in which the *amman* officially fixed the date of the insolvency based upon facts from an insolvent's correspondence and administrative paperwork.[34]

Well into the seventeenth century, much of Amsterdam's commercial legislation – including the rules on insolvencies – was based upon these older examples from Antwerp.[35] Therefore, it is unsurprising that many of the procedures described in this section show important similarities to those that will subsequently be analyzed in Chapter 3 for the Amsterdam Desolate Boedelskamer, which was founded in 1643. This includes the important idea that all creditors were to be treated as equals as part of a generalized and collective insolvency procedure rather than on an individual first-come-first-served basis. Evidence for collective execution procedures in Holland starts to appear from the late fifteenth century onwards.[36] It can, for instance, be found in an Amsterdam bylaw that was originally issued on February 5, 1530, stating:

> Dat elle die Crediteurs van alzulcke personen, van wien schulden bij obligatiën ofte anders behoorlijcken blijct, gelijckelijcken inne comen zullen ende betaelt werden 't pont ponts gelijck, ten ware enighe van dezelven Crediteurs van hoere schulden schepenen kennisse mochten bijbrengen, gedateert voor de voorsz. suspicie.[37]

[33] Ibid. 322. [34] Ibid. 324–25.

[35] Dave De ruysscher, "Antwerp Commercial Legislation in Amsterdam in the 17th Century: Legal Transplant or Jumping Board?," *Tijdschrift voor Rechtsgeschiedenis* 77 (2009): 459–79.

[36] Dave De ruysscher and Ilya Kotlyar, "Local Traditions v. Academic Law: Collateral Rights on Movables in Holland (*c.*1300–*c.*1700)," *Tijdschrift voor Rechtsgeschiedenis* 86, no. 3–4 (2018): 365–403, 383–84.

[37] Moll, *Desolate Boedelskamer*, 5.

[That all creditors of such persons, whose debts have been proved by obligations or other decent evidence, will be paid out equally as they enter, pound by pound, unless any of these creditors might hold a *schepenkennisse* (i.e. a privileged, registered proof of their debt) dated before the legally established moment of the debtor's insolvency.]

The fact that this was already regarded as an old and fixed custom by the seventeenth century is further illustrated by an attestation registered before the public notary Jan Fransz. Bruijningh on September 19, 1617. The lawyers Jan de Wit, Cornelis van Davelaer, and Anthonis Hagenoy; the procurators Willem de Vinck and Arent van Gent; notaries Frederick van Banchem, Jacob Meerhout, and Sijbrant Corneliss; and the merchants Hillebrant den Otter, Hans van Loon, and Jan Loots declared that "if someone becomes insolvent here [in Amsterdam] or elsewhere and various creditors initiate an *arrest*, the first to do so has no stronger claim than the last." While it is not entirely clear why Jacques Niquet asked them to confirm this practice, the attestation shows that by the seventeenth century, collective insolvency procedures were widely accepted in Amsterdam.[38]

The Desolate Boedelskamer was in important ways indebted to prior legal developments in sixteenth-century Antwerp, but at the same time introduced important innovations regarding the involvement of public officials in the resolution of insolvencies. Even though the Antwerp archives contain a collection that is similarly named *Insolvente Boedelskamer*, this was an early twentieth-century archival invention that had never been a true institution during the *Ancien Régime*, but merely brought together a collection of (originally separate) early modern merchants' books and papers.[39] In Amsterdam, as we will see, the fact-based approach that ensured an equal treatment of both the insolvent and their creditors was honed to a much greater degree of perfection. These developments also had an important impact on the decriminalization of insolvency, which is especially visible in the treatment of applicants

[38] Gemeente Amsterdam Stadsarchief [GAS], 30452: Toegangen Notarieel Archief S. Hart, inv. nr. 511, "Failliet," referring to GAS, Notarieel Archief [NA], inv. nr. 119, f. 250 (September 19, 1617).

[39] Elien Doesselaere, "Archiefvormer, bewaarplaats of constructie? Een onderzoek naar de context van de Antwerpse Insolvente Boedelskamer" (MA thesis archivistiek, Brussels, Vrije Universiteit Brussel, 2011).

for the reintroduced benefice of *cessio bonorum*. I will now turn to a discussion of this legal solution for insolvency, to which strongly defamatory rituals had come to be attached as it was reintroduced in the late medieval period.

Defamatory Rituals and Legal Innovation

"I declare bankruptcy!" In late medieval Italy, one could hear these words in many public squares, uttered by people who were hitting the special bankrupts' rock with their naked backsides. These peculiar ceremonies can be linked to the revival of the old Roman concept of *cessio bonorum*. In the medieval and early modern period, insolvency procedures often contained defamatory elements that were meant to placate the creditors' desire for a punishment in some form, as already noted with regards to the Amsterdam *eigenpand*. Even though it contained perversely shameful elements, the Italian *cessio* was an innovation in the sense that provided some agency to the debtor, while satisfying the creditor's wish for revenge and encouraging other debtors to repay their loans in order to save their reputations.[40] In this section, I will discuss how as proper, collective insolvency procedures spread throughout late medieval and early modern Europe, governments also introduced defamatory rituals in order to prevent fraudulent insolvents from abusing the new legislation. At the same time, however, in some areas and most prominently in the Dutch Republic, an alternative position was developed in which greater clemency for the insolvent debtor became a prominent feature of both legal doctrine and practice.

While the insolvency procedures that were developed in late medieval Italian cities in response to commercial developments were partially inspired by the rediscovered Roman law that was taught at universities such as that of Bologna, they also remained rooted in medieval ideas.[41] Perhaps one of the most important new features that was fused into the old Roman procedures was the idea of the

[40] Hans Planitz, "Der Schuldbann in Italien," *Zeitschrift der Savigny-Stiftung für Rechtsgeschichte. Germanistische Abteilung* 52, no. 1 (1932): 134–259, 229–34; Whitman, "Moral Menace," 1872–73.

[41] De ruysscher, *Gedisciplineerde vrijheid*, 91; Santarelli, *Per la storia del fallimento*, 23–25.

insolvent as a fraudulent thief, as typified by Baldus de Ubaldis's (1327–1400) statement *fallitus, ergo fraudator*.[42] As discussed in the previous section, the strong focus on a swift execution of debts and limited possibilities for compositions in medieval insolvency proceedings stimulated insolvent merchants to run off to another city rather than face the legal authorities. In many Northern Italian cities, in legal practice it was presumed that all debtors who were insolvent would also be contemplating flight and should therefore also be classified as flight risks. This criminalization of insolvency enabled the urban courts to use inquisitorial powers against the insolvent debtor and their estate, which made it possible to declare void all transactions that had taken place after the official insolvency date that could then be established based upon the debtor's books.[43] Only in the sixteenth century did jurists such as Benvenuto Straccha (1509–1578) begin to differentiate between innocent and fraudulent insolvents, stressing that only a debtor who fled or *fugitivus* should be classified as a true bankrupt and punished as such.[44]

The classic procedure of *cessio bonorum* that was reinstituted in the late medieval period gained acceptance as a more humane alternative to the debtor's ban, which was then widely practiced in Northern Italy.[45] It is illustrative of the original criminal nature of bankruptcy that the Italian term *fallimento* can be traced back to *fallere*, "to defraud," which just like the aforementioned term *banca rotta* is reflected in Western European languages to the present day (Dutch *fallissement*; French *faillite*). These linguistic connections point at the important influence that Italian legal and commercial innovations in

[42] Baldus, Cons. 392; referred to by Willem L. P. A. Molengraaff, *Leidraad bij de beoefening van het Nederlandsche handelsrecht* (Haarlem: Erven F. Bohn, 1925), 882.

[43] Jussi Sallila, "Insolvency, Commercial Utility and the Principles of Justice: The Making of Bankruptcy Law in Sweden and Finland, *ca.*1680–1868" (PhD, University of Helsinki, 2015), 52–53; De ruysscher, *Gedisciplineerde vrijheid*, 93; Santarelli, *Per la storia del fallimento*, 47–69.

[44] Benvenuto Straccha, *De Mercatura* (Amsterdam: Jan Jacobsz. Schipper, 1669), 433–71. This "bestseller" was first published in Venice in 1553.

[45] Walter Pakter, "The Origins of Bankruptcy in Medieval Canon and Roman Law," in *Proceedings of the Seventh International Congress of Medieval Canon Law*, ed. Peter Linehan (Vatican City: Bibliotheca Apostolica, 1988), 488–89. On the role of the ban, see also Marta Lupi, "Ius Mercatorum and Statutes of Florence during the 14th and 15th Centuries: The Case of Bankruptcy," *GLOSSAE. European Journal of Legal History* 16 (2019): 205–27.

general had on wider parts of Europe in this period.[46] The *cessio* as it came to be applied in late medieval Antwerp, for instance, also clearly resembled prior French and Italian developments. This can probably be explained by the presence of large communities of Italian merchants in the commercial hubs of Flanders and Brabant.[47]

Unlike in the Italian city-states, urban legislation in the Low Countries was also influenced by the centralizing initiatives of the Burgundian rulers and their Habsburg successors. The local legal traditions consisted of varying combinations of urban privileges and (oral) customary laws that were in part officially homologized as collections of *costuymen* from the sixteenth century onwards. At that time, these local collections had already been influenced for centuries by elements of the learned *ius commune* that was taught at universities, which makes them interesting combinations of local and Roman- or "learned" law.[48] In the field of insolvency, it is important to note that whereas the Italian and French procedures were often part of a specific commercial law that only applied to merchants, insolvency procedures as they developed in the German territories were more general in nature.[49]

For the Low Countries, the first half of the sixteenth century was especially important in this regard due to a number of central ordinances or *placaten* that were issued by Emperor Charles V in this period. In 1536, a new ordinance fundamentally changed the existing insolvency practice in many Brabantine cities by reestablishing the Roman law-inspired procedure of *cessie van goede* as a general right for honest insolvents. Henceforth, insolvents could theoretically always petition for a royal *lettre de cession*, to be validated by a local court in a procedure known as *interinement*. Creditors could not

[46] Annamaria Monti, "Fallimento-impresa," in *Parole in Divenire. Un vademecum par l'uomo occidentale*, ed. Alberto Sciumè and Aldo A. Cassi (Turin: Giappichelli, 2016), 44–46; Wessels, Markall, and Kilborn, *International Cooperation*, 5–6.

[47] Philippe Godding, *Le Droit privé dans les Pays-Bas méridionaux du 12e au 18e siècle* (Brussels: Académie Royale de Belgique, 1987), 218–19. On communities of foreign merchants in the Low Countries, see Bruno Blondé, Oscar Gelderblom, and Peter Stabel, "Foreign Merchant Communities in Bruges, Antwerp and Amsterdam, *c.*1350–1650," in *Cultural Exchange in Early Modern Europe*, II: *Cities and Cultural Exchange in Europe, 1400–1700*, ed. Donatella Calabi and Stephen T. Christensen (Cambridge University Press, 2013), 154–74.

[48] Beatrix Jacobs, "Ius Patrium en Ius Commune. Twee zijden van een medaille," *Pro Memorie* 19, no. 1 (2017): 22–46.

[49] Sallila, "Insolvency," 48.

deny this right, unless they provided evidence of fraud.[50] The fact that they were issued by the central authorities, however, did not mean that such ordinances were immediately adopted into all local legal traditions. In Antwerp, for instance, the 1536 ordinance was only slowly and partially merged into its existing insolvency legislation and procedures.[51] Therefore, the reinvention of the old benefice of *cessio bonorum* as *cessie van goede* in the Low Countries is a good example of the tensions and interplay between varying top-down and bottom-up sources of legislation.

The older medieval Brabantine *abandonnement* procedure nevertheless influenced the application of the newly introduced and more debtor-friendly *cessie van goede* through the inclusion of defamatory elements, just as had happened before in Northern Italy. The old Antwerp *abandonnement* procedure had included a ceremony in which the debtor had to swear that they had not hidden anything from their creditors. After the oath, they had to raise the tail of their coat – *zijn slippe presenteren*, which humiliatingly exemplified that they had concealed nothing. In 1541 and again in 1544, Charles V issued a new ordinance that contained some further instructions regarding *cessie* that were even more similar to these older Brabantine traditions. In the new ordinance, it was decreed that an applicant for *cessie* had to appear in court bare-headed and *ongegort* or without a belt if they wished to officially register the benefice.[52] These successive ordinances thereby display a tension between the wish to secure more

[50] J. Lameere (ed.), *ROPB. Deuxième série 1506–1700*, 8 vols. (Brussels: J. Goemaere, 1902), III:549–550 (Brussels, August 30, 1536). See also Dave De ruysscher, "Reconciling Old and New. Imprisonment for Debts and Cessio Bonorum, in Antwerp and Mechelen (*c.*1500–*c.*1530)," in *European Traditions: Integration or Dis-Integration?*, ed. J. Oosterhuis and Emanuel van Dongen (Oisterwijk: Wolf Productions, 2012), 35–48. The *interinement* had originally been introduced to placate resistance from important Flemish and Brabantine cities, who feared abuses if the benefice was obtained without their involvement: Véronique Demars-Sion, "La Réglementation de la cession de biens dans les Pays-Bas méridionaux: copie ou modèle des solutions francaises?," in *Commerce et droit*, ed. Jean-Marie Cauchies and Serge Dauchy (Brussels: Facultes Universitaires Saint-Louis Bruxelles, 1996), 137–39; Godding, *Le Droit privé*, 219.

[51] De ruysscher, "*Naer het Romeinsch recht alsmede den stiel mercantiel,*" 354–57.

[52] J. Lameere and H. Simont (eds.), *ROPB. Deuxième série 1506–1700*, 8 vols. (Brussels: J. Goemaere, 1907), IV:325–329 (Bruges, October 20, 1541), 528; for the later Dutch version of this same ordinance, see ibid. 52–56 (Brussels, May 10, 1544), preprint 35.

proceeds for the creditors through the cooperation of the debtor, on the one hand, and the tradition of punishing insolvency, which was perceived as a malicious affair, on the other. Imprisonment for debt had not only been used for practical legal reasons, but had also been intended to damage an insolvent's reputation. When it was replaced by procedures such as *cessie*, this led to the idea that even honest debtors could only receive this "benefice" *vituperose*, or "amidst shame." Such shaming rituals therefore remained an important part of *cessio bonorum*-inspired procedures as they spread over the Low Countries and other parts of Western Europe.[53]

The city of Leiden, for instance, used a defamatory *cessie* procedure that was quite similar to that of Antwerp. In 1664, when members of the short-lived Amsterdam College van Commercie presented potential solutions for the problem of bankrupts who hid their fraudulent actions by administrative tricks in order to be treated as honest insolvents, they also referred to Leiden's defamatory ceremonies for *cessie* applicants. According to what the committee "had heard," the unfortunate applicants were humiliated by being forced to present themselves in their underwear on a *verheventheit*, an elevated platform, in front of the city hall for the duration of one hour on three consecutive days. This apparently resulted in a situation in which no one dared to apply for *cessie* at all, insolvents trying to avoid it at all costs by seeking to arrive at an accord with their creditors.[54]

There is some confusion about the moment at which such defamatory practices fell into disuse. Its oldest description is found in Duke Philip the Fair's confirmation of the Leiden insolvency statute of July 30, 1501.[55] A letter of Stadtholder Maurits of Orange from 1622 suggests that the defamatory procedure was still in use at that time.[56] While Brugmans remarks that he could not find references in the local

[53] Whitman, "Moral Menace," 1873; Demars-Sion, "La Réglementation de la cession de biens," 147–49; De ruysscher, "Reconciling Old and New," 37 and 45–47.

[54] Hajo Brugmans, "De notulen en munimenten van het College van Commercie te Amsterdam, 1663–1665," *BMGN – Low Countries Historical Review* 18 (1897): 181–330, 249–52.

[55] Frans van Mieris (ed.), *Bundel van handvesten [etc.] der stad Leyden* (Leiden: Abraham Kallewier, 1759), 193–94.

[56] Wouter Druwé, "Dignity and Cessio Bonorum in Early-Modern Dutch Learned Legal Literature," Max Planck Institute for European Legal History Research Paper Series 2016-08 (2016), 11–12, referring to Van Mieris, *Handvesten der stad Leyden*, 194–95.

Leiden ordinances confirming the facts mentioned by the Amsterdam College van Commercie, Van Mieris has actually published an ordinance which suggests that the defamatory elements of the Leiden *cessie* were only officially abolished on September 30, 1671.[57] However, in 1666 the Leiden-born legal scholar Simon van Leeuwen remarked that while such practices had been observed in the past, in his own days (1626–1682) they had long since fallen into disuse.[58] Although Grotius went into the mechanics of *cessie* when writing his *Inleidinge* around 1620, he does not mention that any shameful sanctions could be attached to it.[59] This strongly suggests that soon after the first quarter of the seventeenth century, in Leiden as well as the rest of Holland, the *cessio vituperose* must have disappeared. Seen in this light, it is puzzling that the 1664 Amsterdam committee chose to refer to a seemingly outdated practice, especially since they also expressed their doubts about whether its introduction would be beneficial for a "city of commerce such as Amsterdam." It is therefore unsurprising that, similar to many other activities of the College, the report did not result in any practical effects.

In many other parts of Europe, the sixteenth and seventeenth centuries are actually typified by an increasing criminalization of insolvency rather than by softening attitudes towards this phenomenon. It was perceived to be a rapidly spreading and dangerously immoral practice that had to be punished. This attitude is also reflected in a number of additional ordinances of Charles V targeted at the Low Countries, by which he strove to prevent the occurrence of fraudulent and fugitive bankruptcies with harsh penalties. Five years before authorizing *cessie van goede* for innocent insolvents, in 1531 Charles issued an ordinance that provided a "remedy against all bankrupts and fugitives." Such felons were to be treated as "public thieves" that had to be "punished and hurt in public, without mercy." If a merchant had absconded, public announcements would compel them to return to

57 Brugmans, "De notulen en munimenten van het College van Commercie," 249 (n. 1); Van Mieris, *Handvesten der stad Leyden*, 197–98.

58 Whitman, "Moral Menace," 1878.

59 Hugo de Groot, *Inleidinge tot de Hollandsche rechts-geleerdheid*, ed. F. Dovring, H. F. W. D. Fischer, and E. M. Meijers, 2nd ed. (Universitaire Pers Leiden, 1965), 327–29. See also Maurits den Hollander, "Grotius and Insolvency," *Grotiana* 44 (2023): 276–92.

face their creditors within forty days, under threat of eternal banishment.[60] In 1540, however, the emperor concluded that his previous ordinance had not had its intended effect. Henceforth, judges were to condemn such fugitive bankrupts to "death by hanging, without possibility for grace or pardon." If they failed to pronounce such verdicts, they would themselves be liable to repay the entire outstanding debt to the creditors. Accomplices who had assisted a bankrupt in any way would also be heavily punished.[61] The third ordinance, which entered into effect in 1544, is somewhat milder. Even though it forbids majority compositions that would force an unwilling creditor to remit part of his or her claim, it does appear to create legal space for more merciful creditors to conclude some form of private composition with an insolvent debtor of good faith. While these ordinances do seem to have been in effect in sixteenth and early seventeenth-century Amsterdam, their application was selective. There is no evidence, for instance, of death sentences for bankrupts in practice.[62]

Although fifteenth-century French legislation started to differentiate between the criminal *banqueroute* and the innocent *faillite*, there, too, insolvents were indiscriminately stripped of their civil rights and subjected to public humiliation. A limited rehabilitation was possible for merchants in some cases through a debt-restructuring *concordat* with a qualified majority of the creditors but, as was typical for this period, a discharge of debts remained impossible.[63] Imprisonment was not just restricted as a form of punishment for fraudulent bankrupts, but also viewed and employed as a way to incentivize insolvents and their relatives to pay their debts and to prevent them from hiding any remaining money.[64] In a series of ordinances issued between 1490

[60] Lameere (ed.), *ROPB*, III:265–273 (Brussels, October 7, 1531), 267–68; for a Dutch translation, see Johan van de Water (ed.), *Groot placaatboek* (Utrecht: Jacob van Poolsum, 1729), 415–16.

[61] Lameere and Simont (eds.), *ROPB*, IV:232–38 (Brussels, October 4, 1540); Van de Water, *Groot placaatboek*, 421–25.

[62] Noordam, "Schuldsanering en goede trouw," 140–42; Moll, *Desolate Boedelskamer*, 2. For the ordinance, see Lameere and Simont (eds.), *ROPB*, V:52–56 (Brussels, May 10, 1544).

[63] Sallila, "Insolvency," 58–59; Claude Dupouy, *Le Droit des faillites en France avant le Code de Commerce* (Paris: R. Pichon & R. Durand-Auzias, 1960), 153–54.

[64] Amalia D. Kessler, "Enforcing Virtue: Social Norms and Self-Interest in an Eighteenth-Century Merchant Court," *Law and History Review* 22, no. 1 (2004): 71–118, 114–15.

and 1673, it was gradually made impossible to declare bankruptcy by attorney. The debtor had to come before a judge in person, their clothes hanging open so that their naked body was displayed to the public "to mark and augment his infamy." Apart from that, an insolvent who had received *cessio* (which does seem to have been available to wider parts of the population, unlike the *concordat*) had to wear the shameful green cap or *bonnet vert* for a stipulated period.[65] In Rouen, this practice was motivated by the wish to protect other merchants, unaware of the insolvent's true condition, against the danger of doing business with those who would likely be unable to live up to their promises.[66]

Probably influenced by these French ceremonies, the francophone parts of the Swiss Confederacy adopted similarly humiliating *cessio* procedures. A Genevan statute of 1505 decreed that the insolvent debtor had to declare their debts, possessions, and incapacity to pay their creditors while standing in the midst of the community. They were then led around the city sitting on a donkey, accompanied by a blaring trumpet-player to ensure public attention. Arriving at St. Pierre's cathedral, the insolvent would ungird their belt, take off their boots and raise their cloak up to their shoulders. With their bare backside, they would have to hit a designated pillar three times, shouting in loud voice: "Cedo bonis, cedo bonis, cedo bonis, et omnia bona mea in solutum creditoribus meis relinquo!"[67]

Throughout the Holy Roman Empire, penalties for fraudulent bankrupts also became much stricter in this period, as exemplified by Charles V's laws from the 1530s. Similar to the ordinances for his Dutch possessions, these rulings officially introduced the death penalty for bankrupts throughout the Empire. While imperial authority over local rulers in the Empire was often limited, imperial legislation did offer a general framework upon which local authorities based their bankruptcy statutes. The ordinances stressed that it was the duty of local rulers to punish insolvency with shaming sanctions,

[65] Whitman, "Moral Menace," 1874–75; Sallila, "Insolvency," 59.

[66] Daniel Souterius, *Praxis Banccaeruptorum* (Leiden: Godefridus Basson, 1615), 50–51.

[67] Adrian Staehelin, "Zwangsvollstreckung in älteren Schweizer Stadtrechten," *Zeitschrift der Savigny-Stiftung für Rechtsgeschichte: Germanistische Abteilung* 93, no. 1 (1976): 184–256, 252.

regardless of any leniency on the part of the creditors. In many cities, a "bell of shame" or *Schandglocke* was rung to the humiliation of those who had become bankrupt due to extravagance or other forms of disorderly conduct.[68] In Frankfurt, where a *cessio* procedure for honest insolvents had been introduced in 1578, only three years later the aldermen's fear that debtors would voluntarily misuse it to their own advantage led to the introduction of much stricter rules. Insolvents would now have to provide evidence of their honest misfortune, and were forced to wear a shameful yellow cap for three years after the procedure. Jewish insolvents would even be chased out of the city together with their families, just like those bankrupts who were found to have committed fraud.[69] The city of Augsburg also introduced detailed *Faillitenordnungen* between 1564 and 1580, which prescribed increasingly severe, shameful sanctions.[70]

At the same time, however, these laws provided for the proper management of insolvent estates by curators selected by the creditors from their ranks. It also became possible for a majority of the creditors to make binding decisions about compositions that would restructure their insolvent debtor's estate.[71] Such agreements had long remained controversial, as exemplified by Charles V's 1544 ordinance, but in the course of the seventeenth century opposition to them also seems to have weakened in the Empire. The scholar David Mevius, for instance, who had been a staunch opponent of such forms of relief for innocent debtors, in 1661 changed his position as he came to realize that compositions might be advantageous for creditors, too.[72] This

[68] Sallila, "Insolvency," 66–71.

[69] Justinius Verus, *Discurs von verdorbeten Kaufleuten, Bancorottirern und Falliten* (Frankfurt-Leipzig: Esaias Fellgibeln, 1669), 58–62. This will probably be related to general, and at that time widespread, notions of Jewish perfidy. See Francesca Trivellato, *The Promise and Peril of Credit: What a Forgotten Legend about Jews and Finance Tells Us about the Making of European Commercial Society* (Princeton University Press, 2019).

[70] Mark Häberlein, *Brüder, Freunde und Betrüger. Soziale Beziehungen, Normen und Konflikte in der Ausgburger Kaufmannschaft um die Mitte des 16. Jahrhunderts* (Berlin: Akademie Verlag, 1998), 333–37.

[71] Remko Mooi, "Without Regard to Foreignness: The Emergence of Equal Treatment in Early Modern German Insolvency, 1648–1806" (PhD, Tilburg University, 2023), 87–88 and 112–14; Sallila, "Insolvency," 69; Thomas Max Safley, "Business Failure and Civil Scandal in Early Modern Europe," *BHR* 83 (2009): 35–60, 46.

[72] Forster, *Konkurs als Verfahren*, 215–17; Dalhuisen, *Compositions in Bankruptcy*, 19–21.

is similar to the growing acceptance of majority compositions in the Dutch Republic in this period, as will be discussed in Chapter 5.

English judges, in contrast, rejected *cessio*. Insolvents could be shamed by the use of the pillory, and the bankruptcy statutes of 1604 and 1624 provided that those who concealed property could lose an ear.[73] In a limited number of cases from 1543 onwards, the court of Chancery forced unwilling minorities of creditors to accept a composition through a bill of conformity procedure that is reminiscent of Dutch majority compositions. However, in 1621 this was forbidden by means of a royal proclamation.[74] Even if, in theory, out-of-court compositions between creditors and their insolvent debtor formed an alternative to the slow and restrictive official bankruptcy procedure, the crucial weakness of such agreements was that they could only be enacted with the cooperation of all creditors involved.[75]

Similar to its strictness in dealing with insolvency, England also witnessed the introduction of increasingly harsh criminal laws in the late sixteenth and early seventeenth century, ever more felonies becoming punishable by a death sentence. This development is often linked to the English Revolution of 1640–1689, which established the supremacy of Parliament, landed gentry, and wealthy merchants over the Crown and nobility. Unsurprisingly, many of the new statutory capital crimes resulted in an improved protection of property rights that was beneficial to these victorious social classes.[76] Douglas Hay points out, however, that this went hand in hand with a substantial decline in the percentage of indictments for capital offenses resulting in actual hangings. Juries would generally reduce indictments to charges of lesser offenses, or transmute capital punishment into "transportation" to the colonies for a number of years. Hay argues that ruling-class judges, prosecutors, and jurors would have used terror

[73] Schick, "The Myth of the Broken Bench," 252–56; Whitman, "Moral Menace," 1874.

[74] Fleur Stolker, "The Forgotten History of Bankruptcy, 1543–1624," *The Journal of Legal History* 44, no. 3 (2023): 295–324.

[75] Aidan Collins, "Bankruptcy in the Court of Chancery, 1674–1750" (PhD, University of York, 2020), 24–25.

[76] Harold Joseph Berman, *Law and Revolution*, II: *The Impact of the Protestant Reformations on the Western Legal Tradition* (Cambridge: Harvard University Press, 2006), 314–15; Leon Radzinowicz, *A History of English Criminal Law and Its Administration from 1750*, 5 vols. (London: Stevens, 1948).

and mercy to deter potential criminals and uphold the class system. This theory has been vigorously challenged by John Langbein, who does, however, not offer his own explanation for Hay's paradox.[77]

Berman solves the paradox by pointing at England's prevailing Calvinist moral theology in this period. This system of beliefs encouraged maximum severity of formal legal rules, coupled with "a high degree of humaneness and conscientiousness" in their application to concrete cases. As God by His grace could provide salvation from even the most grievous sins, so the jury, representing the community that bore a collectively responsibility to uphold public morality, could withhold the death penalty from penitent offenders who were not malicious, but simple victims of an infirm will.[78] This important debate clearly shows that legal developments can only be understood as part of their context. Statutes and ordinances cannot be taken at face value, but have to be carefully combined with empirical results obtained through archival research, revealing the true application of the law in historical practice. How are these important developments reflected in contemporary English insolvency procedures?

English legislation knew many restrictions on execution against property, expressed by the idea that "a man's home is his castle." As discussed in the previous section, this meant that creditors were usually forced to resort to execution against the person in the form of debt imprisonment.[79] Even when, in 1706, a new bill introduced the revolutionary idea of a potential discharge of debts for honest insolvents, this was counterbalanced by the bill's central purpose, to classify financial fraud as a felony, to be punished with death by hanging. However, similar to developments in English criminal law as a whole, bankrupts were rarely hanged in practice. A 1707 amendment decreased the possibility of obtaining a discharge through the introduction of the requirement that three-fifths of the creditors in number and value had to consent to the insolvent receiving a certificate

[77] John H. Langbein, "Albion's Fatal Flaws," *Past & Present* 98 (1983): 96–120. Langbein responded to Hay's contribution in the volume Douglas Hay et al., *Albion's Fatal Tree: Crime and Society in Eighteenth-Century England*, 2nd ed. (London: Verso, 2011). For a famous response to Langbein's critique, see Peter Linebaugh, "(Marxist) Social History and (Conservative) Legal History: A Reply to Professor Langbein," *New York University Law Review* 60, no. 2 (1985): 212–44.

[78] Berman, *Law and Revolution*, II:317–24.

[79] Sallila, "Insolvency," 77.

of discharge, which often failed. In practice, therefore, early modern English prisons were full of insolvent debtors. Whereas in France this phenomenon was equally widespread around 1700, there debt imprisonment decreased over the course of the eighteenth century. In the aftermath of the economic crisis of 1771, for example, 125 people were imprisoned for debt in Paris. In London, however, in this same period 1,250 insolvents were incarcerated.[80] Only in the Victorian era would criminal offenses clearly begin to surpass insolvency as ground for incarceration.[81]

Even though it was not nearly as widespread as in England or France in this period, civil debt imprisonment did occur in seventeenth-century Amsterdam from time to time. When creditors provided guarantees for the incurred costs, they could lock up their debtor in an inn such as the *Witte Wambuis* against fixed tariffs. The *Schild van Frankrijk* on the Kalverstraat and the *Munt* were also sporadically employed for this purpose. Within twenty-four hours after the creditors had obtained a court order to this end, their unfortunate debtor was forced to go to the stipulated inn. If this civil *gijzeling*, or hostage-taking, did not result in the repayment of the debts (for instance, by friends or relatives) within two weeks, the debtor would be moved to the public prison or *boeien*, where he or she would be kept until the debts were paid.[82] Usually, however, this fate was avoided by obtaining *cessie van goede*. This represents an important difference from the situation of insolvent debtors in other parts of Europe; rather than running away from legal procedures, Amsterdam applicants for *cessie* such as Geertruy de Ridder, widow of the baker Paulus Volckerse, actually sought the protection of the law against their uncompromising creditors.[83] In Chapter 6, I will discuss the

[80] Emily Kadens, "The Last Bankrupt Hanged: Balancing Incentives in the Development of Bankruptcy Law," *Duke Law Journal* 59, no. 7 (2010): 1229–1319; Laurence Fontaine, *The Moral Economy: Poverty, Credit, and Trust in Early Modern Europe* (New York: Cambridge University Press, 2014), 199 and 210.

[81] Daniel Lord Smail, *Legal Plunder: Households and Debt Collection in Late Medieval Europe* (Cambridge: Harvard University Press, 2016), 156–57. See also Margot Finn, *The Character of Credit: Personal Debt in English Culture, 1740–1914* (Cambridge University Press, 2003).

[82] Maarten Hell, *De Amsterdamse herberg 1450–1800. Geestrijk centrum van het openbare leven* (Nijmegen: Vantilt, 2017), 270–71.

[83] GAS, 5072: Archief van de Commissarissen van de Desolate Boedelkamer [DB], inv. nr. 697, nr. 46.

Amsterdam *cessie* procedure and individual stories of applicants for this benefice in further detail.

Stories such as that of the widow De Ridder suggest that the city of Amsterdam formed an early and intriguing exception in a general European landscape of strict and criminalizing insolvency legislation. For both creditors and debtors, even the Venetian procedure could not match the level of service that was reached by Amsterdam and its Desolate Boedelskamer over the course of the seventeenth century. Instead of introducing more stringent criminal procedures, its regents moved towards penalizing acts such as the concealment of assets rather than the financial problems themselves.

The idea that repayment could be suspended in case of a debtor's incapacity was not new. It had already been recommended by the fourteenth-century scholastic Duns Scotus, who argued that an "impotent" debtor should be treated with clemency, if only they would repay as soon as they "came to fatter fortune." In his wake, the canon lawyers and moral theologians belonging to the sixteenth- and seventeenth-century School of Salamanca also supported the principle of debt renegotiation schemes. At the same time, however, they continued to uphold the maxim *pacta sunt servanda*: contractual promises could not be unbound. Postponed payment was the most appropriate way to deal with insolvent debtors, while debt remissions were viewed with suspicion. According to the moralists, this could only be the result of an entirely free decision by the creditor(s). Interestingly, some of them pleaded explicitly in favor of the public management of insolvent estates, in order to avoid fraud and to secure all of the creditors' rights.[84]

According to the contemporary Dutch moralist Udemans cited at the beginning of this chapter, applying for *cessie van goede* was the only possible honorable act that was left to insolvents: "want soo doende sal hy syne ziele ende eere bewaren" – "by doing so, he will save his soul and his honor."[85] After their case had been treated by the competent local court, insolvents could even regain their honor. This was separated by a long shot from the widespread defamatory

[84] Wim Decock, "Law, Religion, and Debt Relief: Balancing above the 'Abyss of Despair' in Early Modern Canon Law and Theology," *American Journal of Legal History* 57, no. 2 (2017): 125–41.

[85] Udemans, *Geestlyck roer*, f. 13.

ceremonies connected to insolvency procedures in other parts of Europe discussed above, even if these were also ultimately based upon the Roman *cessio bonorum*.[86] As imprisonment for debt quickly lost its relevance in the Dutch Republic, insolvents were positively incentivized to be honest and transparent through a realistic prospect of their social and economic rehabilitation. The ideas expressed by the School of Salamanca closely resemble the principles that came to be applied by the Desolate Boedelskamer in seventeenth-century Amsterdam. Therefore, it is interesting to analyze whether or not we can also trace such lines of thinking in the writings of other contemporary Dutch moralists and legal scholars. I will now turn to a discussion of the ways of thinking about insolvency that might give us an indication of the public mentality related to this theme in the early modern Dutch Republic.

The Mental World of a Golden Age

In his inaugural lecture to the new Amsterdam *Athenaeum Illustre* in 1632, Professor Caspar Barlaeus (1584–1648) stated that "a large and prosperous community should not solely devote its attention to flourishing companies, full harbors, and opulent buildings; but should also heed the importance of spiritual values." These values would support the businessmen in their daily work, Barlaeus argued, as they might find inner peace and inspiration in the lectures that would allow them to conduct their business even more prudently and successfully.[87] Such inspiration could not only be found in the lectures of professors or Calvinist preachers such as Udemans, but also in Amsterdam's material culture. As part of his well-known description of Amsterdam, Caspar Commelin described the art that could be found in its glorious new city hall:

> Above the door or entrance to the Desolate Boedelskamer one can see the embellished history of Daedalus, and his son Icarus ... This has been constructed so that we might learn that temperance is always wholesome, while excesses lead to great harm ... A decoration that is wonderfully well suited to the affairs that are being treated in this room.

[86] Whitman, "Moral Menace," 1882–83.

[87] Caspar Barlaeus, *Mercator Sapiens*, trans. S. van der Woude (Amsterdam: Universiteitsbibliotheek, 1967), 17–18.

FIGURE 2.1 Artus Quellinus, *De val van Icarus* (1657)
(Royal Palace Amsterdam, photo: Tom Haartsen)

This *Fall of Icarus* had been sculpted by the great sculptor Artus Quellinus, surrounded by "chests, cases, sealed letters, paper, and account books, which are being gnawed at by rats." (See Figure 2.1.) Perhaps inspired by Barlaeus's moral program, Commelin remarked that this art matched the purpose of the court very well, for if one failed to be temperate, "one would, together with Icarus, fall into a sea of troubles, and decay amidst shame and slander."[88] Of course, this application of Ovid's classical tale to the new center of law and governance in Amsterdam sought to convey a powerful message to any visitors: *onmaat vergaat* or "pride goeth before the fall." This is closely connected to the idea of the insolvent as *decoctor*, who due to their spendthrift ways, had caused their own financial demise. Both the moral and the socioeconomic problems of insolvency are closely connected to the person of the debtor in Quellinus's sumptuous sculpture, which might suggest that the legal institution situated behind

[88] Caspar Commelin, *Beschryvinge van Amsterdam* (Amsterdam: Wolfgang, Waasbergh, Boom, Van Someren, and Goethals, 1693), 288–89.

this door would harshly condemn such acts in a way reminiscent of other contemporary legal traditions.

Nothing, however, was less true. Inside the Desolate Boedelskamer, an additional piece of art also built upon Greek mythology to provide a radically positive turn to this story. On the central mantelpiece, a 1657 painting by Thomas de Keyser depicted Odysseus kneeling in front of Nausicaä, daughter of King Alcinous of the island of Phaeacia. (See Figure 2.2.) When he washed up on its shores poor, naked, and unkempt, after ten years of travels and a shipwreck, Odysseus was clothed and cared for by Nausicaä. This symbolized the relationship between the commissioners of the Desolate Boedelskamer and those committed to their care: rather than just condemning the insolvents, the commissioners guided them towards a new start. Simon Schama typifies their work as a balancing act "between prodigality and avarice, between risk and security that had to be upheld," which aimed at reconciliation between debtor and creditors rather than punishment. The commissioners, like the deacons of the orphanage or the city sheriff, were both judges and stewards, bearing responsibility for civic peace as much as to equity.[89] One has to keep in mind that the proliferation of fraudulent bankruptcies would not just endanger the moral order of society, as expressed by the Church synods discussed in the previous chapter, but would also endanger Amsterdam's reputation as an international commercial hub. If a debtor's liquidity issues, essentially the direct consequence of a lack of trust between them and their creditors, could be solved and a dishonorable execution sale averted, this would not only benefit the insolvent themself but also result in beneficial effects for their creditors and society in general. Both in their roles as elders of religious congregations and as judges of urban courts such as the Desolate Boedelskamer, the Amsterdam regent-elite tried to maintain public order by providing systemic trust through legal and institutional innovation in the form of policies that were explicitly aimed at reconciliation.

It is interesting to examine how contemporaries felt about these developments. Laurence Fontaine argues in favor of the use of theater, dramatic works in particular, to understand people's experience

[89] Schama, *Embarrassment of Riches*, 343–44.

FIGURE 2.2 Thomas de Keyser, *Odysseus en Nausicäa* (1657) (Royal Palace Amsterdam, photo: Tom Haartsen)

of the economy in a certain period. Such sources "translate the shared ways in which author and public think and discuss the world."[90] In his play *De Spaensche Brabander*, the great poet and playwright Gerbrand Adriaensz. Bredero (1585–1618) criticizes *moetwillige bankroetiers*, who lightly accepted debt only to flee to free cities such as Vianen or Culemborg when they could not fulfil their financial obligations (this practice will be treated in further detail in Chapter 5). In his *Klucht van de Koe* from 1612, he again fulminates against such bankrupts

> who scandalously steal the common man's money, and even for a flimsy sum rush to seek asylum in Culemborg.[91]

[90] Fontaine, *The Moral Economy*, 5.

[91] Gerbrand Adriaenszoon Bredero, *Klucht van de koe* (Amsterdam: Cornelis Lodewijckszoon van der Plasse, 1619), lines 41–42: "die 't so byster en grof de mienteman ontstelen en om een haverstro eens haes-op na Kuylenburgh spelen."

To this day, the expression "going to Vianen" or *naar Vianen gaan* means "to go bankrupt." Bredero thought that such people should not be treated as kindly as they were, even arguing that they should be hanged in front of their own doors. This hostile sentiment was relatively common among many layers of society in seventeenth-century Amsterdam.[92]

As a matter of fact, the grain merchant and regent Cornelis Pietersz. Hooft (1547–1626), one of Amsterdam's wealthiest and most successful businessmen in the decades after the *Alteratie*, shared Bredero's hostile sentiment towards bankrupts. If this represents the way in which people generally felt about insolvency in this period, how can we then explain the clear development towards a more merciful, debtor-friendly insolvency legislation in the seventeenth-century Dutch Republic? In order to understand such sentiments, we have to stress the importance of the conceptual separation that came to exist between fraudulent bankrupts and unfortunate insolvents, who were victims of ecological or economic circumstances beyond their control. Hooft's distaste for "nefarious bankrupts" was actually closely connected with his xenophobia towards immigrants from the Southern Netherlands.[93] He complained that for many years, the government had stood by as the church appointed immigrants as deacons and elders of the Dutch Reformed congregation. This was "a clear cause of our current troubles":

> Among these same [immigrants] here in our city, from the beginning of our reformation onwards, we have encountered large amounts of bankruptcies and other forms of misconduct, which among such a relatively small number of them as have served in these offices up to this moment, is all too strange and ridiculous.[94]

As discussed in the previous chapter, according to Hooft the increased influence and control of the government over such appointments would suffice to resolve these issues. Even though he generally

[92] J. G. van Dillen, "Amsterdam in Bredero's tijd," *De Gids* 99 (1935): 308–36, 314–15 and 335; Marijke Gijswijt-Hofstra, *Wijkplaatsen voor vervolgden. Asielverlening in Culemborg, Vianen, Buren, Leerdam en Ijsselstein van de 16e tot eind 18e eeuw* (Amsterdam: De Bataafsche Leeuw, 1984).

[93] Cornelis Pietersz. Hooft, *Memoriën en adviezen*, 2 vols. (Utrecht: Kemink & Zoon, 1871), I(2).

[94] Ibid. I:66.

thought that the government should abstain from regulating the economy, if a few malevolent gripers could put the broader civic community at risk the authorities should act to protect the common good. At the same time, however, Hooft expressed clemency for unfortunate insolvents, especially those who had become victims of the consistories' strict "church justice."[95]

Similar sentiments can be encountered in the work of Pieter de la Court, another influential contemporary political thinker. At first sight he seems to display great distaste for those who did not honor their financial obligations, arguing that fraudulent bankrupts should be persecuted and killed like "tossing and thievish bumble bees."[96] When expressing such hostile feelings towards bankrupts, Bredero, Hooft, and De la Court were probably thinking of men like Isaac Le Maire, an ex-director of the United East Indies Company (VOC) who had been removed from his office due to a corruption charge. Le Maire's subsequent (failed) attempt to seek personal profit by undermining the company's financial position through the world's first stock syndicate resulted in his flight from Amsterdam to the village of Egmond aan den Hoef. Having caused a chain of insolvencies among his accomplices and their creditors, he was generally regarded with contempt.[97] Le Maire is an excellent example of De la Court's "thievish bumblebees." However, the Dutch lawyer juxtaposed this group with unfortunate "good honeybees," who were to be treated with compassion rather than shameful punishment. According to De la Court, those "honest merchants" who had lost their fortune through natural disaster, defaulting debtors, piracy, or war had to be treated with clemency. They should even be allowed to keep a tenth of their goods in order to attempt to restore their business to its previous state, unharmed by their creditors or further lawsuits.[98]

[95] H. A. Enno van Gelder, *De levensbeschouwing van Cornelis Pieterszoon Hooft, burgemeester van Amsterdam (1547–1626)* (Amsterdam: A. H. Kruyt, 1918), 43–44.

[96] Pieter de la Court, *Interest van Holland, ofte gronden van Hollands-welvaren* (Amsterdam: Joan. Cyprianus vander Gracht, 1662), 86–87.

[97] Lodewijk Petram, *The World's First Stock Exchange* (New York: Columbia University Press, 2014); Dirk J. Barreveld, *Tegen de Heeren van de VOC. Isaac le Maire en de ontdekking van Kaap Hoorn* (The Hague: SDU, 2002).

[98] De la Court, *Interest van Holland*, 86–87.

This represents a revolutionary change in public mentalities with regard to insolvency when compared to the legal practice in many other parts of early modern Europe. The shift from a criminalization of the person of the debtor towards the condemnation of certain specific acts leading up to that state created legal space for the differentiation between the innocent and those guilty of fraud or irresponsible conduct. In his treatise *Praxis Banccae-ruptorum huius seculi*, published in 1615, the Haarlem minister Daniel Souterius (1571–1634) already worked out the distinction between two categories of debtors: those "who by misfortunes have their substance wasted," and they "who by their own default are impoverished." Souterius argues that it would be inhumane if someone whose goods were wasted by evident misfortunes should take the blame for their misfortune and be punished. It would even be "contrary to natural equity," if "out of a hatred to the guilty, one would lay blame on the guiltless." Providing several examples of the potential dangers and risks of maritime commerce taken from the work of ancient authors, Souterius concludes his brief analysis by offering honest insolvents struck by such accidents the consolations of faith and philosophy.[99]

Another popular and well-read minister, Godfried Udemans, also harshly condemned the fraudulent concealing of assets:

> But all these thoughts come from Satan, from the old serpent, from the great red dragon, who is a liar, and a father of lies, and a seducer of the whole world. *Apoc. 12, 9.*[100]

As we saw before, however, he regarded a proper legal solution for insolvency, such as *cessie van goede*, as entirely acceptable. The growing distinction between insolvents and bankrupts explains why *cessie* as it came to be applied in legal practice in the seventeenth-century Dutch Republic was no longer associated with shameful defamatory rituals. Unless the creditors could provide evidence of fraud, insolvents were in principle never refused this benefice in Amsterdam, and

99 Souterius, *Praxis Banccaeruptorum*, 4–9. On Souterius, see also Joost Hengstmengel and Henri Krop, "De gereformeerde religie en economie in de vroege republiek. Daniël Souterius (1571–1634) over de plichten van kooplieden," *Documentatieblad Nadere Reformatie* 42, no. 1 (2018): 2–22.

100 Whitman, "Moral Menace," 1881–82.

definitely did not have to parade through the city while sitting on a donkey. Whereas until the seventeenth century and much later in many other parts of Europe, insolvency remained intimately associated with fraud, in the Dutch Republic that presumption seems to have flipped in this period. The insolvent debtor was regarded as unfortunate, unless proved otherwise. As Bredero ironically stated:

And even if he should go bust, leaving his bills unpaid –
well then, it's off to file a quick *cessio*. Presto!, an honorable man again.[101]

In practice, however, this was slightly more nuanced than Bredero suggests. Early modern Amsterdam has been classified as a "class society," in which social mobility was in part influenced by success in business and the wealth accumulated (or lost!) in such ventures. While wealth alone was not enough to win political power and prestige, it definitely went a long way. In the seventeenth century, it was generally believed that rich men could not easily be bribed. This was important, as the higher public officials often received what amounted to, at most, a symbolic remuneration for their work. Therefore, material wealth qualified one for a political career, as it displayed independence, wisdom, and competence.[102]

Therefore, even though unfortunate insolvents were treated with clemency and often even received a "second chance" to revive their business, this does not mean that an insolvency did not have any effects on one's reputation or social position at all. Some members of the *vroedschap* or city council, for instance, were removed from their offices after having been subjected to the care of the commissioners of the Desolate Boedelskamer. In 1644, Diederick Tholincx had to quit the council after his insolvency and subsequently left Amsterdam to become *ritmeester* or cavalry captain in the service of the States of Holland. Rather than being allowed to retain his respectable function of board member of the *voetboogdoelen*, one of Amsterdam's citizen militia companies, after his insolvency in 1638, Jacob Hooghkamer

[101] Udemans, *Geestlyck roer*, f. 14. Translation: Whitman, "Moral Menace," 1883.

[102] Peter Burke, *Venetië en Amsterdam. Een onderzoek naar elites in de zeventiende eeuw*, 2nd ed. (Amsterdam: Agon, 1991), 37–38; Clé Lesger, "Merchants in Charge. The Self-Perception of Amsterdam Merchants, *ca.*1550–1700," in *The Self-Perception of Early Modern Capitalists*, ed. Margareth C. Jacob and Catherine Secretan (New York: Palgrave Macmillan, 2008), 81–82.

was made *concierge* of this same society as an act of charity.[103] These examples highlight the devastating impact financial problems could have on the social and political functioning of individuals even in early modern Amsterdam.

Much depended on one's actions when faced with financial trouble. Even though he was a devout Calvinist, the merchant Andries van der Meulen (*c.*1549–1611) believed that one should never depend on God alone to solve financial problems. He scorned merchants who hoped that they would soon be rich enough to repay their debts through a windfall, as such naïve businessmen would display "more fantasy than faith." When a colleague discretely asked his advice when he found himself in financial trouble, Van der Meulen argued that he had to inform his creditors about his situation as soon as possible. Otherwise, people might say that he was unreliable, and rightly so. One could not make devout statements and at the same time continue to borrow money while essentially being insolvent, as such immoral and treacherous behavior made one a fraudulent bankrupt who had broken the trust of their creditors.[104]

In seventeenth-century Amsterdam, the tension between *Icarus* and *Nausicaä* was evident in the ways in which businessmen, moralists, and political thinkers alike dealt with insolvency. In the early modern "economy of trust," one was expected to help friends and relatives who faced liquidity problems. At the same time, however, irresponsible behavior and the failure to fulfil one's obligations seriously endangered one's reputation. Such actions harmed the moral capital that was essential to be successful in business, which hinged on one's all-important capacity to mobilize sufficient credit. At the end of the day, however, the introduction of institutions such as the Desolate Boedelskamer helped many unfortunate insolvents to restore trust and to revive their businesses through generalized, widely accessible, and fair legal procedures. The discourse of contemporaries clearly reflects the growing acceptance

[103] Johan E. Elias, *De Vroedschap van Amsterdam 1578–1795* (Amsterdam: N. Israel, 1963), 323 and 365.

[104] Luuc Kooijmans, "Risk and Reputation: On the Mentality of Merchants in the Early Modern Period," in *Entrepreneurs and Entrepreneurship in Early Modern Times: Merchants and Industrialists within the Orbit of the Dutch Staple Market*, ed. Clé Lesger and Leo Noordegraaf (The Hague: Stichting Hollandse Historische Reeks, 1995), 27.

of the systemic trust that was essential to facilitate this revolutionary development. In this way, innovative governance helped a demographically expanding community to preserve both economic growth and its spiritual values in a world of increasing complexity.

Conclusion

In the seventeenth-century Dutch Republic, one was ultimately judged based upon one's actions. Reputation and social standing could be won through honesty, trustworthiness, making good on one's promises, and success in business. Similarly, they could be lost through fraud, treacherous dealings, and the failure to meet one's obligations because of risk-taking and generally irresponsible conduct. In a combined development, insolvency proceedings became collective rather than individual, while execution on the person through imprisonment for debt was largely replaced by execution on property. The gradual replacement of personal by systemic trust that became possible as a result of institutional innovations in cities such as Amsterdam in this period must also have contributed to the important changes in the treatment of insolvents that were discussed in this chapter. Over the course of the seventeenth century, the most successful elements of private arbitration practices were combined and concentrated in the public Desolate Boedelskamer, resulting in an open-access and transparent insolvency procedure. While much in-depth research on similar legal practices remains to be done for other European states such as France or Spain, the current literature suggests that the Dutch Republic diverged in a positive way with regard to its insolvency legislation that, as I will argue, must have benefited debtors and creditors alike.

These different paces of development could be viewed as a consequence of the evolution of the functioning of commerce and the Dutch economy in general, in which innovative governance and institutional change backed up private commercial initiatives. The move towards more debtor-friendly insolvency procedures in the Dutch Republic was accompanied and made possible by important changes in the general way of thinking about the moral dimensions of debt and insolvency. Through the clear separation of criminal acts of bankruptcy on the one hand, and insolvency as an economic condition on the other, Amsterdam's legal institutions managed to restore public order both in its socioeconomic and moral sense. Contemporary art and literature clearly illustrate this important change in public mentalities, which accompanied and underpinned the legal and institutional innovations discussed in this book. In subsequent chapters, an empirical analysis of the procedures that were employed by the Amsterdam Desolate Boedelskamer will reveal how exactly this mental framework was translated into legal practice.

PART II

PROCEDURE AND STAFF

3

Procedure

When he returned to his native Amsterdam after a long foreign commercial expedition in 1678, the young merchant Abraham van Helsdingen was confronted with a delicate situation.[1] Infuriated, he discovered that in his absence, Jacob van Dael – who had been appointed as a curator of the Desolate Boedelskamer three years earlier[2] – had unjustly reported his estate as insolvent to the commissioners. According to the young merchant who, judging from the registration of his marriage with Cornelia de Harde on October 16, 1671, appeared to have been about 33 years old at the time of this conflict, two central issues were at stake.[3] First, not a single creditor had tried – or would have possessed the right – to execute his debts during Van Helsdingen's absence, which clearly spoke against the latter's alleged insolvency. Second, if "not even one of his creditors" had delivered his estate to the court, how could a curator, who could only become legally involved in its management after being appointed by the commissioners, have taken the initiative to do so? As a result of Van Dael's illegal acts, the merchant had not just been harmed in his *goeden naem ende faem* or reputation, but he lamented *dat alle sijn*

[1] Gemeente Amsterdam Stadsarchief [GAS], 5072: Archief van de Commissarissen van de Desolate Boedelkamer [DB], inv. nr. 58, ff. 26v–28r contains the entire story of this case.

[2] GAS, 5072: DB, inv. nr. 58, f. 20.

[3] GAS, 5001: Burgerlijke Stand: doop-, trouw- en begraafboeken [DTB], inv. nr. 497, f. 92r.

crediet [te] sijn geruineert ende benoomen, or "that his entire personal credit had been ruined and stolen." How did the commissioners react to this clear and serious breach of the venerable procedure of *curatele* that had been entrusted to them?

When Amsterdam residents were unable to repay their debts and became insolvent, "of old, the aldermen took over the management of their estates and, to the benefit of the creditors, appointed curators, who had to account to the [aldermen's] bench."[4] As I have discussed in previous chapters, the Dutch Revolt and Amsterdam's *Alteratie* over time resulted in such increased workloads for the aldermen that they delegated these tasks to the commissioners of the newly found Desolate Boedelskamer in 1643.[5] Dave De ruysscher has pointed out that the Amsterdam *curatele* procedure, which became the standard way of handling all insolvencies under the Desolate Boedelskamer, constitutes a clear example of the way in which the Amsterdam insolvency legislation moved away from the Antwerp model on which it had been based. The Amsterdam insolvency procedure was innovative for two main reasons. First, it unified the enforcement of debts, conducted by a judge, with the management of the insolvent estate. This constituted a solution to the problematic information asymmetries that had previously hampered the work of judges and curators. Second, facts gained the upper hand over rumors. While in late sixteenth-century Antwerp, the *failliet* of a debtor who had not run away from their creditors was based upon rumors, such as stories about their failure to attend the Exchange, in seventeenth-century Amsterdam the factual establishment of overindebtedness became the formal starting point of the insolvency procedure. Through the investigation of a debtor's possessions and books and papers which started every *curatele* procedure, it was possible to make decisions based upon facts and figures rather than hearsay and rough estimates.[6]

4 Jan Wagenaar, *Amsterdam in zijne opkomst*, 4 vols. (Amsterdam: Yntema en Tieboel, 1767), III:461.

5 The 1643 founding ordinance was printed in Gerard Rooseboom (ed.), *Recueil van verscheyde keuren, en costumen; midtsgaders maniere van procederen binnen de stadt Amsterdam*, 2nd ed. (Amsterdam: Jan Hendricks, 1656), 304–9.

6 Dave De ruysscher, "Designing the Limits of Creditworthiness: Insolvency in Antwerp Bankruptcy Legislation and Practice (16th–17th Centuries)," *Tijdschrift voor Rechtsgeschiedenis* 76 (2008): 307–27. Cf. for seventeenth-century France, Marta Lupi, "Insolvent Merchants and Royal Jurisdictions in Early Modern Lyon

The way in which Van Helsdingen's case was wrapped up clearly shows the thorough and fact-based manner in which the Desolate Boedelskamer treated individual (alleged) insolvents. The indignant merchant demanded that the erring curator Van Dael be punished, and that he himself receive an official reification to mend the damage inflicted upon his economic and social reputation. The commissioners drew up a declaration of the merchant's good name, and vouched that not a single reference to his estate would be entered into their documentation. As I have not been able to locate Van Helsdingen in the official registers of *curatele*, this promise seems to have been kept. As for Van Dael, due to his abusive, *qualijck, ende te onrechte* or "erroneous, bad and unjust" acts, which had not only endangered Van Helsdingen's reputation but also put the good name of the commissioners at serious risk, he was suspended from their service for six months as a final and serious warning. An official notice of these deliberations signed by secretary Frans Bruijningh was handed over to the merchant, wherewith the case had been closed to the satisfaction of all parties.

In this chapter, which will describe the daily functioning of the Desolate Boedelskamer, I will seek to examine the Amsterdam insolvency procedure through the eyes of the actors involved. How did the court evolve over time, and where is it possible to discern the influence of its staff on such changes? In the preceding chapters, I have argued that social and cultural attitudes towards overindebtedness and the insolvents themselves softened during the seventeenth century. While one might expect that such developments were detrimental to the position of creditors, they actually went hand in hand with important changes to Amsterdam's legal institutions that also sought to protect the creditors' interests. This chapter will discuss to what extent the introduction of the Desolate Boedelskamer had an impact on the management of the insolvent estates that were placed in its care. Through a careful combination of formal work instructions and archival evidence from daily practice, it analyzes the functioning of the Desolate Boedelskamer as part of its broader legal and institutional context.

(1600–1660): The Role of Royal Notaries and the Conservation Des Privilèges Royaux Des Foires" (PhD, Tilburg University, 2023), 81.

Curatele

In this section, I will discuss the general procedure for the management of insolvent estates called *curatele*, which might be translated as "guardianship." Through their transparent management of estates, the commissioners sought to preserve as much as possible of their value for the creditors. As soon as the commissioners were notified of an insolvency, two of them had to go to the debtor's house. There, they would confiscate the paperwork, or the *Boecken, ende Papieren* belonging to the estate, and draw up an inventory of all movable goods that could be found on the premises. Within a few days, these would then be valued by a "sworn appraiser." It seems that the continuing growth of insolvency cases that had led to the establishment of the Desolate Boedelskamer in turn led to a delegation of these tasks to its subordinate officials early on in its history. This had already been allowed for in the 1643 ordinance, in the event that all of the commissioners were unavailable. Soon, it appears to have become common practice for the secretary to fulfil the important inventorying duties, perhaps assisted by one of the two clerks. They also managed the correspondence and public announcements related to newly reported insolvencies. As soon as the commissioners had been notified about a case, the *coopmansbooden*, the *aanteeckenders aen de binnenlandse verschuyten*, and the *bestelders van der brieven* – the early modern mail carriers – had to be notified to spread this news through placards. These notifications served to secure any goods, rights, or claims belonging to the estate both within and outside of the city of Amsterdam. Anyone who was in possession of goods that belonged to the insolvent had to deliver these to the commissioners. Such announcements would be placed in well-frequented locations, for instance close to the city hall. In the late eighteenth century, for instance, citations for proposed compositions would be placarded at the city's bourses.[7]

[7] GAS, 5072: DB, inv. nr. 58, f. 16r; Goswin Moll, *De Desolate Boedelskamer te Amsterdam: bijdrage tot de kennis van het Oud-Hollandsch failliten-recht* (Amsterdam: De Roever-Kröber-Bakels, 1879), 49, 112–13. On the placards and such communications about insolvencies in general, see Maurits den Hollander and Remko Mooi, "Protecting the Foreign Creditor: International Insolvency in Early Modern Amsterdam and Frankfurt Am Main," *TSEG/ Low Countries Journal of Social and Economic History* 16, no. 3–4 (2020): 37–57.

Soon, it became clear that the small number of supporting officials was insufficient to manage the great number of estates that were placed in the court's care. In order to alleviate this burden, on May 5, 1654 the *Oud-Raad* allowed for the employment of an extra clerk.[8] In order to compensate for the extra annual salary of fl. 120 that would now have to be paid out for the additional clerk, however, the other clerks had to give up part of their supplementary emoluments: these were henceforth to be "enjoyed as salary by the three clerks in common, one-third each."[9]

While the bookkeeper started work on the insolvent's books and papers, the commissioners were formally charged with the active management of the insolvent's estate. In the first six weeks after the initiation of the procedure, the insolvent could attempt to reach an accord with their creditors (this process will be treated in Chapter 5). This phase could be prolonged at the commissioners' discretion. If the negotiations succeeded, the estate was placed in the hands of the guarantors of the accord or representatives of the creditors, together with the rehabilitated insolvent. If the insolvent could not gather sufficient support, the commissioners appointed curators, who would liquidate the estate and try to collect its outstanding debts in favor of the creditors. However, the revised 1659 ordinance stipulated that curators would be appointed at an earlier stage, immediately after the inventory had been processed by the Desolate Boedelskamer. This change meant that the commissioners played a more distant role in the management of the estate. Their role shifted to supervision of their subordinates' work, a shift which is reflected by a number of detailed instructions for various types of subordinate staff members that can be found in the court's Book of Resolutions.

A list of regulations from 1663, for instance, provides more insight into the bookkeeper's tasks. As soon as an insolvent's books and papers as well as the inventory of their possessions had been delivered at the court, the bookkeeper was required to produce two copies of the balance. One of these would be placed in the archive, while the

[8] Moll, *Desolate Boedelskamer*, 186. The *Oud-Raad* was a college of all active and former burgomasters, which met four times per year to decide on appointments to substantial offices. See Antonio Porta, *Joan en Gerrit Corver. De politieke macht van Amsterdam (1702–1748)* (Assen: Van Gorcum, 1975), 23.

[9] GAS, 5072: DB, inv. nr. 58, ff. 1v–2v.

other would be handed over to the curators who had been appointed to the estate, together with its books and papers. A so-called *partiment register* had to be added behind every copy of the balance, with separate sections for creditors and debtors.[10] The original account books and documents would be labelled alphabetically, after which the bookkeeper would make clear which entry from the balance corresponded with each original document. After the repartition of goods had taken place, either a register of this arrangement had to be attached to the balance, or a reference had to be made detailing in which register it could be found.[11]

In practice, it was not always as easy to structure the data found in an insolvent's paperwork. In September 1661, bookkeeper Willem Muylman complained that he spent a great deal of extra time each day in order to restructure old books, and transport data to new ledgers. While his predecessor Jorijs Hansen had always received an annual bonus to compensate for the extra work needed to restore order to such messy documentation, described as those that *geembrolieert, ofte verachtert staen*, this had recently been cancelled by the commissioners. Because of the burden of his job, Muylman pleaded for the reinstitution of this compensation.[12]

While the commissioners recognized and appreciated his hard work, they did not wish to overturn their decision to abolish the annual benefice. Muylman would have to conduct his job according to the instructions, without "tiring the commissioners by asking to receive more than his fixed salary" in the future. As a compromise, he would receive a one-time bonus of fl. 250 in compensation for his extra work in the past year. Henceforth, the costs for restoring order to messy documentation would have to be paid from the proceeds of the estate, based upon the commissioners' judgment. Thereby, the court avoided increased overhead costs in its management of a small number of estates, which would eventually have harmed all insolvents and their creditors.[13] It appears that soon after this decision, Muylman started to be assisted by his relatives. On December 2, 1661, the first administrative documents that had to be restructured were handed

[10] Unfortunately, these documents have not been preserved for the seventeenth century.
[11] GAS, 5072: DB, inv. nr. 58, f. 10. [12] GAS, 5072: DB, inv. nr. 58, ff. 6v–7r.
[13] GAS, 5072: DB, inv. nr. 58, ff. 7–8r.

over to "Willem Muylman de Jonge," who had to promise to keep secret anything he might learn from them.[14]

As soon as administrative order had been restored and the balance of an insolvent estate had been drawn up, its active management by the court could begin. The legal date of the insolvency could be established with relative certainty from these documents. This was important in order to reject fraudulent claims by either malicious creditors or scheming friends of the insolvent. In seventeenth-century Amsterdam, all sales of movable goods conducted before the aldermen or a notary needed to be registered with the municipal secretariat within eight days. At least by 1700, any such *transporten* or *schepenkennissen* which concerned the payment or securitization of older debts would only retain their legal validity if they had been registered at least four weeks before the official date of an insolvency. Using such a "look-back period" was important, because transactions directly preceding an insolvency "were often of a dubious nature, to the detriment of other creditors": *alzo die menigmaal simutaal en fraudulent zyn, en tot nadeel van andere Crediteuren gedaan worden.*[15]

The supervision and auditing of curators had always been regarded as one of the commissioners' core responsibilities. When the bookkeeper had drawn up the balance of an insolvent estate, one of the clerks would be instructed to write and deliver an appointment letter or *commissie* to the curators who were to be assigned as its guardians. If a designated curator refused, they would have to appear before the commissioners on the next day. They would then be expected to clarify their reasons for the refusal to take on this case, "and to request [their] release [therefrom] in person." If the curator failed to make an appearance, the commissioners could issue a second call *ter vermaeninge* or "as admonition."[16] Every new curator had to provide sureties for fl. 6,000 as a guarantee for their good conduct.[17]

For each estate that was assigned to a particular curator, they would be listed as indebted in the "register of the curator's accounts." A related credit would be entered every time they delivered payments

[14] GAS, 5072: DB, inv. nr. 58, f. 8v.

[15] Anon., *Amsterdamsche secretary [etc.]*, 2 vols. (Amsterdam: Jacob van Royen, 1700), I:35–38.

[16] GAS, 5072: DB, inv. nr. 58, ff. 17v–18r.

[17] Moll, *Desolate Boedelskamer*, 145.

to the court on behalf of an estate, or made a declaration for their salary or other expenses.[18] Only when one of the commissioners had closed and approbated the final balance of an insolvent estate, were its curators allowed to hand in the final account of their salary and expenses.[19] In 1663 it was decided that the commissioner who was delegated to conduct the audit was authorized to amortize any entries, not exceeding fl. 6, of which they could prove that the costs of collection would exceed their value. These could then be added to the credit side of the curator's account.[20]

Sometimes a curator would be unable to account for their management because they passed away before an estate was discharged from the court's custody. This issue was formally addressed for the first time in the curators' instruction of 1676. The succeeding curator would have to receive a proper account from the deceased curator's widow or heirs. Having received this information and the estate's books and papers, they would formally take over responsibility for the case and the final audit of the account of its management. When nobody wanted to take over a deceased curator's cases, however, they would be delivered back into the hands of the commissioners, who were then responsible for bringing them to their proper conclusion as they saw fit.[21]

The 1643 ordinance of the Desolate Boedelskamer ordained that its commissioners would meet on a daily basis. However, from a 1655 instruction for the clerks, it appears that the commissioners did not meet on Mondays or Saturdays.[22] Further evidence also suggests that their duties were not as heavy as they might have seemed at first sight. They enjoyed five annual holiday periods of twenty-one days each, in April, May, July, September, and December. The holiday in July appears to have lasted even longer than the regular term. This means that the college was off duty for more than a third of the year. The regulations recognized that the commissioners might not always be scrupulous about their attendance, stipulating a fine of 11 stuivers for arriving too late, and fl. 3 for being absent without prior notification of the president.[23]

[18] GAS, 5072: DB, inv. nr. 58, ff. 10v–11r; Rooseboom, *Recueil*, 309.
[19] GAS, 5072: DB, inv. nr. 58, f. 31v; Rooseboom, *Recueil*, 309.
[20] GAS, 5072: DB, inv. nr. 58, f. 12. [21] Moll, *Desolate Boedelskamer*, 213–14.
[22] GAS, 5072: DB, inv. nr. 58, f. 16r. [23] Moll, *Desolate Boedelskamer*, 165–69.

On regular days, insolvents, curators, and other people who had gathered to meet the commissioners would be found waiting in the antechamber to the actual Desolate Boedelskamer. One can easily imagine the unease of the insolvents, who were faced with sculptures of rats gnawing on piles of decaying paper as a symbolic representation of their economic misfortune (see Figure 2.1). One of the clerks, serving as the doorkeeper of the day, would note down their names and the reason why they wished to meet the commissioners. The president would use this to determine the order of the proceedings of that morning. Visitors who appeared too late to be registered on the first *memory* would in principle have to join the back of the queue, formed by a second list. However, when a *gequalificeert* or "important" person would arrive at the court in the midst of its proceedings, the clerk could break the order of the day and ask the commissioners if he or she should be allowed to enter the room straight away. Every time the commissioners rang a bell, the doorkeeper would be allowed to respectfully enter their room *ongedect*, or "bare headed," in order to receive instructions and allow the next visitor into the commissioners' presence.[24]

The clerks would fulfil this door-keeping duty in turn. The others would spend the morning in their office, copying decisions and other acts passed by the commissioners, which could then be collected by those whom they concerned. Their afternoon would be spent copying inventories and other paperwork, until the secretary went home and relieved them of their duty. On the days on which the commissioners did not convene and the secretary was not present either, the clerks had to come to the president's house in the morning to receive instructions about the work that should be done. Any letters or other important messages arriving on such days would likewise have to be delivered to the president's home straight away.[25] This suggests that even if the commissioners were not always present, the court must generally have been manned during working hours.

Every day on which the commissioners convened, each curator would have to call at least six parties to the roll session. It is not entirely clear which kinds of people would have to be called before the commissioners, but given the expected numbers, this probably

[24] GAS, 5072: DB, inv. nr. 58, f. 14r–16v.
[25] GAS, 5072: DB, inv. nr. 58, ff. 14v–16r and 19r.

concerned debtors of estates under their management. If a curator failed to meet the quota, they would be punished. For one missing party, they would be fined 25 stuivers. Two missing parties would result in no further appointments to estates, three in an immediate dismissal from the job.[26] While this sounds severe, the punishments were probably used as a way to stimulate the curators to process estates as quickly as possible. From January 24, 1676 onwards, a new instruction ordered the curators to be present at all times during the commissioners' meetings, in order to answer questions that might arise. When the commissioners had a question for a curator who failed to be present without their explicit permission, he or she would receive a fine of 6 stuivers for the first instance, and 12 stuivers if this occurred again. If a curator failed to meet this expectation more often than that, they would not be assigned any new estates for a while.[27] This rule was obviously made with the creditors' interests in mind, as they directly benefited from a swift end to any *curatele* to limit the management costs incurred by the curator and other supporting officials. Since curators were remunerated per action, such as attending a sitting (see Chapter 4), it was in their personal interest to draw out cases and to increase the number of meetings and amount of travel that could subsequently be declared. Countering such harmful behavior was an important part of the commissioners' work.

The court's minutes provide an idea of the kind of issues which the curators discussed with the commissioners during their meetings. On July 25, 1678, for instance, curator Abraham van Libergen received permission to travel to the court of Alphen, in order to transfer some auctioned pieces of land from the insolvent estate of Isaac van Buren to their new owner.[28] The Desolate Boedelskamer made use of an account in the Bank of Exchange to process transactions on the financial market. On February 15, 1690, curator Jan Bruyn received permission to cash a bill of exchange from the estate of merchant Jan Hill. Broker Guillem Looten was ordered to sell the bill at "the highest possible price," after which he would have to deposit the proceeds in the commissioners' bank account.[29] In some cases, a curator needed to delegate part of their work due

[26] GAS, 5072: DB, inv. nr. 58, f. 11r. [27] Moll, *Desolate Boedelskamer*, 214.
[28] GAS, 5072: DB, inv. nr. 24, ff. 67v–68r. [29] GAS, 5072: DB, inv. nr. 26, f. 148r.

to geographical constraints. On April 5, 1701, for instance, curator Bruyn received permission to employ the services of Abraham Veris to collect all outstanding claims of the partnership of Elias and David Gaon on Curacao.[30] Curators had to be able to put aside moral scruples when fulfilling their job, as illustrated by the case of the insolvent widow Geertruyd Ansloo. On February 26, 1701, the commissioners ordered the sextons of the Old and New Church to appraise the value of two graves that were part of the estate. It appears that Geertruyd had to find a way to redeem the graves of her deceased husband Adriaan van Alderwerelt and his older relative Cornelis Jans van Alderwerelt. On May 12, 1701, Cornelis and Anna van Alderwerelt were able to pay the fl. 380 plus taxes required to save their valuable family graves.[31]

As these examples illustrate, the commissioners' meetings with the curators primarily concerned the liquidation of insolvent estates and the collection of their outstanding claims on behalf of the creditors. In principle, curators strove to sell the (trade) goods and furniture found in an estate as soon as possible. If the curator, in consultation with the creditors, decided that it would be beneficial to postpone selling certain goods due to then prevailing market conditions, this was possible, but always with the commissioners' consent. Immovable goods could only be sold according to the city's standard procedure of the *twaelf nachten* or "twelve nights," through the aldermen. Any money collected by the curators had to be paid into the court immediately.[32] These sums were initially received and managed by the city's general secretariat, as had been the case before the creation of the Desolate Boedelskamer in 1643. If someone had a claim to funds held by the court, its commissioners would issue a written authorization for its payment by one of the secretaries.[33]

On January 26, 1655 the burgomasters decided that henceforth, the most senior clerk of the Desolate Boedelskamer would manage these funds instead. Cornelis Molensteen, who occupied that position

[30] GAS, 5072: DB, inv. nr. 30, f. 110v.

[31] GAS, 5072: DB, inv. nr. 30, ff. 95v and 116v–117r.

[32] Rooseboom, *Recueil*, 306–9. On the traditional execution of immovable property in sixteenth-century Holland at the bailiff's court or *Hoge Vierschaar*, see Oscar van den Arend, *Zeven lokale baljuwschappen in Holland* (Hilversum: Verloren, 1993), esp. 307–310.

[33] Moll, *Desolate Boedelskamer*, 201.

at the time, would have to provide sureties worth fl. 6,000 before he could be entrusted with this new responsibility.[34] It is slightly puzzling why, if the active management of the court's capital had passed into the hands of its commissioners and senior clerk, the burgomasters felt a need to issue a special ordinance which regulated the secretary's management of these same funds on December 7, 1656. On that date, it was decided that the secretaries would not be allowed to write off any debts before the court's bookkeeper had registered the name and amount paid by the person concerned. Henceforth, the bookkeeper would be held accountable for the correct processing of such transactions.[35] This suggests that at least until 1656, both the court's senior clerk and the city's ordinary secretaries could still receive payments intended for the Desolate Boedelskamer. Perhaps this can be explained by the simple fact that all cash held by the municipal government would have been stored in a single safe room in the city hall; as long as payments were registered by the relevant bookkeeper, it was not of great importance who physically delivered them to the vault.

An entry from the Book of Resolutions reveals that it was not always easy to trace and execute an insolvent estate, especially if part of its assets were located outside of Amsterdam. On October 9, 1687, as we read in the minutes of the Desolate Boedelskamer, a certain Claes Cock found himself incarcerated in the Amsterdam prison or *boeien* and had applied for the benefice of *cessie van goede*. Therefore, the commissioners ordered his curators to seize and liquidate all the movable and immovable goods found in his estate, "wherever these might be located."[36] After seeking the advice of his creditors, the commissioners granted Cock his benefice on October 23, 1687.[37] One day earlier, however, the court had received an intriguing letter about this case from the city of Zwolle. Its burgomasters and aldermen had refused to hand over to the Amsterdam curator the proceeds from Cock's goods that had been seized locally. According to the Zwolle magistrates, creditors from Holland would have to file their claims with the local court if they wished to receive their share of Cock's

[34] GAS, 5072: DB, inv. nr. 58, ff. 19v–20.

[35] GAS, 5024: Burgemeesters: dagelijkse notulen, resoluties en missivenboeken [Burg], inv. nr. 99, f. 7r.

[36] GAS, 5072: DB, inv. nr. 26, ff. 40v–41r.

[37] GAS, 5072: DB, inv. nr. 26, f. 42r.

possessions, in order to safeguard the interests of the Zwolle creditors. Being "good friends" of their Amsterdam counterparts, however, they did promise that in case any disputes arose between the different groups of creditors, they would *aen deselve onpartijdigh reght laten wedervaren* or "ensure that justice would have its way in a fair and impartial manner."[38]

Eight years earlier, in 1679, the States of Holland and Utrecht had concluded a bilateral treaty to avoid exactly such competence conflicts. If an insolvency procedure was initiated in either territory, curators would also be invested with the power to collect and administer assets located in the other state. Subsequently, they would be allowed to order their liquidation and to distribute the proceeds according to the laws of the city in which the procedure had been initiated.[39] A potential precedent for this treaty is an agreement between Leiden and Delft from 1668, stipulating that a curator appointed in the city "where the estate had become *desolaat*" – insolvent, abandoned – would automatically possess the authority to execute related goods in the other city.[40] Doubtless such treaties must have eased the lives of both curators and creditors involved in such cross-border insolvencies considerably.[41]

Before the curators could actually start selling parts of an estate, however, creditors who possessed legal claims to part of the insolvent's goods had to be satisfied. Those who held *panden* or pawns that had been obtained before the legally fixed date of the insolvency could have these sold by the concierge of the city. Claimants whose goods were physically present on the premises of the insolvent estate, including unpaid goods sold *à contant* – whose ownership had therefore not been transferred at the time of the insolvency – could take them back.[42] The 1659 ordinance provided details about the way in

[38] GAS, 5072: DB, inv. nr. 58, f. 37.

[39] Kurt Nadelmann, "Bankruptcy Treaties," *University of Pennsylvania Law Review* 58 (1944): 58–97, 62.

[40] Frans van Mieris (ed.), *Bundel van handvesten [etc.] der stad Leyden* (Leiden: Abraham Kallewier, 1759), 192–93.

[41] On bilateral treaties for the legal treatment of early modern cross-border insolvencies, see Remko Mooi, "Without Regard to Foreignness: The Emergence of Equal Treatment in Early Modern German Insolvency, 1648–1806" (PhD, Tilburg University, 2023). Some first results have been included in Den Hollander and Mooi, "Protecting the Foreign Creditor."

[42] Rooseboom, *Recueil*, 183–84.

which such cases were treated by the Desolate Boedelskamer. The creditor had to make their *actie* or legal action known to the curators and deliver the evidence to them "in proper time, but always before the treatment of cases of preference or concurrence, and the sale of the goods." Whenever a creditor chose to place an *arrest* on any of their own goods, they had to notify the curators about this within three days *op pene van desertie* – the claim would be nullified if the creditor failed to respect the proper proceedings. If the defendants, in this scenario the curators, failed to appear before the commissioners after two summonses, they would judge based upon the written evidence and the curators would have to pay the process costs *propter contumaciam*, or due to their default. If the curators did appear, however, the case would have to be *voldongen ende afgepleyt* or "treated and pleaded in full" on the spot. Only the commissioners could decide that there was a need for further litigation in the form of a replication, duplication, etc. Similarly, when curators pressed a claim on behalf of an estate, they would have to notify the commissioners within three days after placing an *arrest* on a person or goods. This was described as *eysch doen ende conclusie nemen*: "positing one's claim and arriving at a conclusion." When the defendant did not react to those legal steps, they would be prosecuted at the next *Vierschaar* – the local aldermen's court – "as in the old days."

While the creditors sought to execute their pawns and tried to establish an order of preference among themselves, the insolvent – supported by the arbitration efforts of curators and commissioners – attempted to conclude an agreement with them. During this intermediate phase, when the debtor was not protected by legal solutions such as an accord or *cessie van goede* as of yet, they had to look for other means to safeguard their physical integrity. I will now briefly turn to the benefice of *seureté de corps*, which was the most important legal strategy utilized for this purpose in the seventeenth-century Dutch Republic.

Seureté de Corps

The poet Bredero described the benefice of *seureté de corps* as the "paper armor" used by insolvents to gain leverage over their creditors when seeking to obtain a favorable resolution of their financial problems. He saw this as a negative phenomenon: in his eyes insolvents tried to run away from their obligations "by donning paper armor": *[door sich] een pampieren harnas aan te trekken*.[43] In reality, the use of this benefice was rather more nuanced. In Chapter 2, we saw how insolvency legislation in preceding centuries often focused solely on the creditors' interests. In order to protect honest but unfortunate insolvents from debt imprisonment in the form of hostage taking, *seureté de corps* became an important tool to facilitate a more humane arbitration process between a debtor and their creditors.[44]

The benefice, which seems to have come into existence in the second half of the sixteenth century, was officially granted by the sovereign.[45] After the Dutch Revolt, the sovereign's legal function in this regard had been taken over by the *Gecommitteerde Raden* – the executive committee of the States of Holland. However, in practice the investigations that needed to be conducted before such letters could be produced were always delegated to local authorities. In Amsterdam, the burgomasters assigned such requests to the commissioners of the Desolate Boedelskamer after 1643. Their motives for doing so were the prevention of *alle abuysen, en sinistre practiquen, die dagelijcx gebruyckt worden by veel personen* or "all abuses and sinister practices daily committed by many persons" who wished to obtain the benefice.[46] On October 19, 1605, the States of Holland had ordained that letters of *seureté de corps* could only be granted with the approval of the majority of the creditors and curators of an insolvent estate. Therefore, the commissioners would only give their approval or *favorabel advijs* after consulting the affected creditors.[47]

In an exemplary sample of seventeenth-century applications for *seureté de corps*, we encounter some of the main reasons for granting this protective benefice. While at first sight, one might expect

[43] Gerhard Wilhelm Kernkamp, *Regeering en historie van Amsterdam in de 17e eeuw* (Amsterdam: Emmering, 1900), 52.

[44] Simon van Leeuwen, *Het Rooms-Hollands-regt [etc.]* (Leiden/Rotterdam: Hackens, 1664), 444–46, IV.41.

[45] Marijke Gijswijt-Hofstra, *Wijkplaatsen voor vervolgden. Asielverlening in Culemborg, Vianen, Buren, Leerdam en Ijsselstein van de 16e tot eind 18e eeuw* (Amsterdam: De Bataafsche Leeuw, 1984), 36.

[46] Rooseboom, *Recueil*, 307.

[47] Anon., *Amsterdamsche secretary*, 321; Joannes van der Linden, *Verhandeling over de judicieele practijcq, of form van procedeeren, voor de Hoven van Justitie in Holland gebruikelijk*, 2 vols. (Leiden: A. en J. Honkoop, 1798), II: 286–87.

that *seureté* only benefited the insolvent themself, in some cases it could also work to their creditors' advantage. Sometimes, one or a few creditors would immediately try to arrest their debtor when they were notified about his or her financial difficulties. While such actions might help them to execute their own claims, they would also make it impossible for an insolvent who still possessed some land or other immovable goods to sell these at a regular market price rather than through an execution sale. If they were protected against such legal actions through *seureté de corps*, the insolvent might eventually be able to realize much higher proceeds from the liquidation of their estate, which would ultimately also be to the advantage of their common creditors.[48] While the benefice was usually granted for a maximum of six months, this was often prolonged if it was judged to be advantageous for all parties involved. From September 15, 1654 onwards, all such requests for a prolongation of the benefice needed to specify the number of times it had already been prolonged after the original application. If this information was found lacking, the request would not be taken into consideration.[49]

The archives of the Desolate Boedelskamer contain an interesting example of a letter of *seureté de corps* that was issued by the States of Holland to Mathijs de Gomse on July 23, 1650. As noted in its closing formula, the document was originally sealed with the *cleijn segel van haere edele groot mogende* or "small seal of the venerable States of Holland" by their secretary, dr. Herbert van Beaumont. Based upon prior advice issued by the Amsterdam authorities on July 20, 1650 after a consultation of his principal creditors, De Gomse received permission to travel throughout the province of Holland and West-Friesland for a period of six months, "in order to conclude the unresolved matters with his creditors there." The letter explicitly forbids "every officer or magistrate in these lands" to "trouble or molest his person" for the duration of the safe-conduct. Interestingly, it is stipulated that "*arresten* of the High Court of Holland, or any other sentences or provisions by judges of the common land," as well

[48] Willem van Alphen, *Papegay, ofte formulier-boek van allerhande requesten, mandamenten, conclusien, schrifturen, als anders, in de dagelijksche practijke dienende voor de respective hoven van justitie in Hollandt*, 2 vols. (The Hague: Johannes Steucker, 1682), I:622–24.

[49] Ibid. I:624; Van der Linden, *Verhandeling over de judicieele practijcq*, II:287.

as any debts relating to public taxes and the old comital domains, were excluded from this general protection.[50] It makes sense that the States did not wish their own rights to be harmed in any way by the benefice. Through these general exceptions, the States always retained the option to incarcerate the insolvent based upon their own rights if they might later wish to do so. Unfortunately, the court's archives do not contain any details on the final resolution of De Gomse's case. Perhaps he successfully concluded an agreement with his creditors before a notary. I will go deeper into the nature of such compositions in Chapter 5.

According to Gijswijt-Hofstra, requests for letters of *seureté de corps* such as the one issued to De Gomse became very popular in the first decades of the seventeenth century, with a peak of about eighteen applications per year between 1610 and 1628. Even though she reports that after this period, the requests for the benefice steadily declined and virtually disappeared around 1730, I have found numerous examples of its use in many Amsterdam insolvencies in the entire second half of the seventeenth century.[51] In about one-third of the cases in the qualitative dataset in which an accord was concluded after 1643, I have found references to a request for *seureté de corps*. In one-sixth of these cases, the insolvent even received one or more prolongations of the benefice. Therefore, it seems safe to conclude that it continued to be widely used by Amsterdam insolvents until at least the early eighteenth century.[52]

Even though *seureté de corps* was meant to facilitate the arbitration of an accord between insolvents and their creditors, it was also used by insolvents who eventually resolved their repayment conflict through a *cessie van goede*. An example of such a case is that of Elias Gaon, also known under his alias Frans de Hoge. The merchant, who traded both on his own account and in company with David Gaon, could no longer fulfil his financial obligations. On January 26, 1700, his creditors agreed to a grant of *seureté* for a period of six months. When this first term expired, on July 13 they agreed to prolong Elias's *vrijgelij* one last time, but *niet langer als ses maanden* – "no longer

[50] GAS, 5072: DB, inv. nr. 7359 (letter); inv. nr. 6, f. 157 (favorable *advijs*).
[51] Gijswijt-Hofstra, *Wijkplaatsen*, 37.
[52] See Chapter 5 below and the Appendix for more details on this data.

than six months."[53] In the meantime, both the estate of his business partner David Gaon and their company had been liquidated.[54] It appears that while Elias had hoped to be able to conclude an amicable accord with his private creditors, his efforts were unsuccessful. In the first months of 1701, his estate was also liquidated through a *cessie*.[55] Presumably, if an insolvent did not expect to be able to conclude an accord anyway, he would not have tried to obtain *seureté* at all but immediately have sought to obtain *cessie*. In practice, its usage was therefore restricted to the insolvents described by Van Leeuwen who "hoped to be able to save their estate": *wanneer den Schuldenaar hoop heeft sijnen Boedel te kunnen redden*.[56]

Sometimes, procedural problems arose. On September 21, 1673, David and Jeronimo Schobinger had received a favorable response to their request to apply for *seureté de corps* after the commissioners had consulted their creditors.[57] When, a few months later, they had not yet succeeded in gathering enough support for an accord, the curators agreed to ask for a prolongation of the protective benefice on March 23, 1674. Interestingly, a marginal annotation describes how on July 21 of that year, it was discovered that the original letter to the States of Holland containing this request had somehow been lost in The Hague. Apparently, this did not have a detrimental effect on the insolvent brothers' legal protection, as the burgomasters simply wrote a new letter in which they repeated their request.[58] One year later, the Schobingers had finally concluded an accord with their creditors, after which an act of rehabilitation was issued on July 12, 1675.[59] This suggests that the States of Holland played an entirely formal role in this regard, and that the real power to grant or prolong the benefice was vested in the local authorities.

When the temporally limited protection of *seureté de corps* ended, an insolvency had to be wrapped up by means of one of the aforementioned legal solutions. Even though insolvency legislation and practices

[53] GAS, 5072: DB, inv. nr. 30, ff. 30–31r and 56v.
[54] GAS, 5072: DB, inv. nr. 30, ff. 34v–35r.
[55] GAS, 5072: DB, inv. nr. 30, f. 87r and inv. nr. 702, nr. 2.
[56] Van Leeuwen, *Rooms-Hollands-regt*, 446, IV.41.4.
[57] GAS, 5072: DB, inv. nr. 21, f. 122v.
[58] GAS, 5072: DB, inv. nr. 21, ff. 148v–149r.
[59] GAS, 5072: DB, inv. nr. 1568 and inv. nr. 22, ff. 52v–54r.

in the Dutch Republic became more debtor-friendly during the seventeenth century, at the end of the day their central goal remained to repay as much as possible of the creditors' claims. I will now move on to the important final phase of the Desolate Boedelskamer's procedure, in which all creditors hoped to receive their due.

Repartition

Whether an insolvency ended with an accord or with the liquidation of the entire estate, the central goal of the Desolate Boedelskamer's procedure was always to collect and distribute the resulting proceeds fairly among all creditors involved. In this section, I will discuss the most important rules which regulated this important closing phase of the Desolate Boedelskamer's procedure.

The 1643 ordinance stipulates that the commissioners would organize an *uytdeelingh* or "distribution" at least twice a year, or more often "as soon as this would be possible."[60] First of all, preferential claims would be paid out. The remaining proceeds of the liquidation would then be shared *pro rata* or *penninghs pondts gelijck* among all unsecured creditors. Anyone who received money from the court had to provide sufficient sureties or *cautie de restituendo* for this sum at the general municipal secretariat, in case creditors with better claims later appeared.[61] This guarantee was strengthened by an oath made before the aldermen, which was formulated in different ways for preferential and regular claims. The guarantors for the first partial repayment of unsecured claims were also sureties for all such repartitions that might be made in the future, when more proceeds had been gathered by the court. For each payment of a preferential debt, however, a new oath would need to be sworn by sufficient guarantors.[62]

Unsurprisingly, soon after the new court started its work disputes arose among creditors about questions of preference of one claim over another. An addition, or *ampliatie*, to the original ordinance

[60] Rooseboom, *Recueil*, 309.

[61] Ibid. 309. A famous example of such a case is that of Rembrandt van Rijn, in which the commissioners withdrew an earlier payment to creditor Isaac van Hertsbeeck in favor of Rembrandt's son Titus: Paul Crenshaw, *Rembrandt's Bankruptcy: The Artist, His Patrons, and the Art Market in Seventeenth-Century Netherlands* (Cambridge University Press, 2006), 80–81.

[62] Anon., *Amsterdamsche secretary*, 70–74.

of March 6, 1644 provided the commissioners with the competence to judge in such cases of *concurrentie ende praeferentie*.[63] Once all goods in an estate had been sold, the creditors would be convoked in order to provide evidence for their claims. While most would have been known from the insolvent's books and papers, any potentially unknown creditors were invited to present their claims by means of placards. Foreign creditors had the option to strengthen their claim through an oath before the aldermen of their place of residence. These would then send a written report of these proceedings to the Amsterdam commissioners. However, when one of the curators or the insolvent themself protested the claim, the foreign creditor would still have to provide written evidence if he or she wished to enforce it. This was also required from creditors with preferential debts. Presumably, the commissioners could then order their bookkeeper to check such written proof against the insolvent's confiscated documentation.[64]

The list of creditors who asserted they held a preferential claim against the estate would have to be accepted by the other creditors. If the latter wished to counter such claims of preference, a written *eysch* or "demand" and supplementary documentation would have to be handed over within fourteen days. The other party would receive a copy of these documents, likewise receiving fourteen days to present documents in their defense called *debat* or *contradictie*. When one of the parties was unsatisfied with the commissioners' judgment, they could file an appeal with the aldermen through the court's secretary within ten days of the original verdict. An appellant had to pay a fl. 3 fee, which they would only retrieve if the aldermen judged their appeal favorably and altered the original verdict. By 1656, this fine for "false appeals" had been doubled to fl. 6. The fact that creditors could proceed against one another in cases of preference on their own initiative had the great advantage that the resulting process costs would not have to be paid out of the insolvent estate, but by the proceeding parties themselves. For an unknown reason, this was altered in the 1777 ordinance. This change was detrimental for the common creditors' interests, who saw their potential proceeds dwindle in favor of the interests of a few of their number.[65]

[63] Rooseboom, *Recueil*, 309–10.

[64] Moll, *Desolate Boedelskamer*, 75–76 and 112–14.

[65] Ibid. 115.

This raises the question of which debts were actually considered preferential in this period. As a general rule, older claims always had preference over younger claims of similar ranking.[66] First of all, the costs incurred by the Desolate Boedelskamer during its management of the estate would be withheld from the proceeds. These consisted of procedural costs, the curator's salary, and emoluments of officials such as the secretary and concierge. In case of a deceased insolvent, the doctor's bill for their fatal illness also gained preference over other claims. The same was true for wages and materials needed for the repair of ships or houses. When an estate contained one or more ships, overdue wages of seamen (which were usually paid out in full at the end of a voyage) and costs made for rope and other supplies needed to sail a ship home from a foreign port would also be repaid before other debts. In the case of a shipwreck, salvage costs to save the ship or at least its cargo were also preferential, as the failure to incur such expenses would likely result in even greater losses for the other creditors.[67]

The 1659 ordinance also contains provisions on the preferential status of house rents. If a tenant became insolvent between May 1 and December 1, only the rent of the current year and unpaid rent from the directly preceding year were considered to be preferential claims. When the insolvency occurred between December 1 and May 1, however, the whole year starting from the next May, as well as the directly preceding year, would be considered a preferential debt. Any further arrears were regarded as regular rather than preferential claims. Thus, a tenant who became insolvent between December and May could be forced to pay one year extra due to breaking their multiple-year contract.[68] This rule makes perfect sense when one takes the customs of the early modern Amsterdam housing market into account. Like many other cities, Amsterdam had used a fixed moving-day since

[66] On this issue, see also Dave De ruysscher and Ilya Kotlyar, "Local Traditions v. Academic Law: Collateral Rights on Movables in Holland (*c.*1300–*c.*1700)," *Tijdschrift voor Rechtsgeschiedenis* 86, no. 3–4 (2018): 365–403.

[67] Moll, *Desolate Boedelskamer*, 12–13; Rooseboom, *Recueil*, 182–89.

[68] Hermanus Noordkerk (ed.), *Handvesten; ofte privilegien ende octroyen: mitsgaders willekeuren, costuimen, ordonnantien en handelingen der stad Amstelredam*, 4 vols. (Amsterdam: Hendrik van Waesberge, Salomon en Petrus Schouten, 1748), II:688–89.

some time before 1413. This was *Meyeavont*, or April 30. On this date, all rent contracts were either renewed or terminated. Departing tenants had to move out before noon, after which the new rent would start on May 1. When a rent was to be terminated, this had to be announced by either owner or tenant in December, to allow the other party to find a replacement before the next *Meyeavont*. This explains why breaking a contract due to insolvency between December and May resulted in a preferential claim of the house owner for the next rent term, as it would be difficult to find a new tenant so close to the annual moving-day.[69]

Related to the problem of house rents was that of interest on capital. Over time, questions arose about the preferential status of interest, and whether this would continue to accrue at all after the insolvency. In 1655, the commissioners decided that creditors of insolvent estates would always act as "competing claimants ... for their capital and its interest, calculated until the precise day of the insolvency, and nothing more." Only those who possessed a hypothec on one of the possessions of their debtor were privileged for one and a half years' interest, but if there were further arrears these would have to compete with all others.[70]

Finally, in 1676 the commissioners requested the opinion of two legal scholars on the preferential nature of tax debts. On January 8 of that year, the lawyers Jacob de Lamine and Altetus Tolling advised as to whether the tax known as the *tweehonderdsten penningh* should be regarded as competing with or privileged over all other claims.[71] The "200th penny" was a 0.5 percent extraordinary tax on capital that had been levied by the States of Holland on a recurring basis since the end of the Twelve Years' Truce in 1621. According to

[69] Clé Lesger, *Huur en conjunctuur. De woningmarkt in Amsterdam, 1550–1850* (Amsterdam: Historisch Seminarium van de Universiteit van Amsterdam, 1986), 26–29.

[70] GAS, 5072: DB, inv. nr. 12, f. 7v and 84v.

[71] De Lamine was active as lawyer in Amsterdam, for instance representing Anna Pauw in her process against Hendrik van Hoven in 1669: Hans Bontemantel, *De regeeringe van Amsterdam, soo in 't civiel als crimineel en militaire (1653–1672)*, ed. Gerhard Wilhelm Kernkamp (The Hague: Martinus Nijhoff, 1897), 484–87. Tolling appears to have been active as lawyer at the Court of Holland until his death in 1691. They appear in various legal opinions from the second half of the seventeenth century in the third volume of the *Nederlands Advysboek*.

the legal scholars, it was important to note that the tax was levied to finance the "common defense and protection of the country and its inhabitants." The *beschreven recht*, or learned law, found in the *Corpus Iuris Civilis* dictated that the fisc always had a *stilswijgende, ende legael hypotheecq*, or a "tacit hypothec," on any of its subjects, and was being placed above other privileged creditors by convention. As they went on to argue, this was affirmed by Grotius's *Inleidinge*, with the limitation that such debts owed to the public purse (*gemeene land*) would only hold preference over other privileged creditors if the latter's claims were dated after the moment at which the resolution on the aforementioned tax had been issued by the States of Holland. De Lamine and Altetus note that, given the fact that it is impossible to know what the exact value of an estate would have been at the moment at which the resolution on the tax was passed, lacking a proper inventory (which would not be made up as long as someone was considered to be *in bonis*), one could argue that it would be very difficult to calculate the respective claims of the fisc and other creditors. However, as anyone who had been taxed too much could file a protest against their assessment, if such a *doleantie* had not been issued by the insolvent, it would be safe to assume that the fisc would be privileged for the full value of its claim against any privileged creditor of a more recent date.[72]

Once the order of preference among the creditors had been thus determined, the commissioners could start to wrap up the procedure. This could in principle be done in three ways: an accord, *cessie van goede*, or a simple execution. As I will argue, the last option was used very rarely in practice.[73] All strategies ultimately resulted in money being paid into the court and being divided among the correct creditors. The major differences between these methods were whether (1) the insolvent themself handed over the instalments into the court after they had been freed from the curator's guardianship, or (2) the curator liquidated the estate on behalf of the creditors; as well as (3) the varying degrees of harm inflicted upon their personal reputation. I

[72] GAS, 5072: DB, inv. nr. 58, ff. 20v–23r.

[73] GAS, 5072: DB, inv. nr. 59, ff. 11–12r. See also Machiel Bosman, *Rembrandts plan. De ware geschiedenis van zijn faillissement* (Amsterdam: Atheneum – Polak & Van Gennep, 2019), 37 (n. 17).

will now briefly discuss the procedural mechanisms for rehabilitation, which developed over the seventeenth century.

Rehabilitation

In much of the literature on insolvency in early modern Amsterdam, there has been confusion about the matter of the rehabilitation of insolvents after their procedure before the court of aldermen or (after 1643) commissioners of the Desolate Boedelskamer had finished. The main reason for this confusion is that neither the ordinance of 1643 nor its 1659 successor included any official provisions on this matter. In this section, I will therefore briefly discuss the issue, and seek to provide clarification based upon my research of the archival material at our disposal.

Goswin Moll states that after an insolvent estate had been executed and the proceeds had been distributed among its creditors, the insolvent (*failliet*) was once again allowed to trade and negotiate as they wished, while their creditors could no longer proceed against them to execute their old debts. If the insolvent managed to obtain sufficient funds to revive their business, therefore, "[they] could act without fear that [their] old creditors would trouble [them] in any way."[74] Here, Moll clearly confuses the procedure for those insolvents who managed to conclude an accord with that for applicants for *cessie*, or for fraudulent bankrupts. He may also be projecting later developments back into the seventeenth century. The last ordinance for the Desolate Boedelskamer, issued in 1777, apparently included the possibility of a separate rehabilitation procedure, which provided for a discharge of all remaining debts for a *bona fide* insolvent if five-eighths of their creditors in number, holding at least one-half of the debts in value, gave their consent to the arrangement. Unlike the compositions known as *akkoord* that were used from the late sixteenth century onwards, this new type of rehabilitation would even have affected preferential claims.[75] This is clearly a phenomenon different from the *rehabilitatie* as we encounter it in the later seventeenth century, which is only mentioned after an accord had reached its majority.

[74] Moll, *Desolate Boedelskamer*, 142.

[75] Ibid. 135–38; Arnoud J. Noordam, "Schuldsanering en goede trouw" (PhD, Amsterdam, VU, 2007), 169–72.

Unlike in cases such as that of Abraham van Helsdingen, discussed at the beginning of this chapter, in which an official letter sought to restore public faith in the financial position of his business after it had unnecessarily been taken into the care of the commissioners, the *acten van rehabiliteyt* that begin to be mentioned in all accord cases from the 1660s onwards primarily seem to have had a procedural function. If a majority of the creditors agreed to sign the composition that had been proposed to them, this was affirmed by an official entry in the minutes of the commissioners, through which the estate was taken out of the hands of the curator. The former insolvent regained full possession of their business and assets, now being free to act as they wished without any involvement of the court and its staff as long as they or their guarantors made sure to pay the amounts that had been agreed upon in the accord at their stipulated dates. It is unclear whether these "rehabilitation entries" were also turned into a real letter that was handed over to the insolvent, as I have not found any traces of such documents in the court's archives. The main importance of such events seems to have been that the former insolvent officially regained control over their estate, which certainly must have had a positive impact upon their personal reputation in the outside world.

While it is clear that a fraudulent bankrupt lost their honor and reputation after a legal execution, as has been discussed in previous chapters, it is less clear what happened to an innocent insolvent who had been forced to make use of the *cessie* procedure. Because of one especially notorious applicant for this benefice, the painter Rembrandt van Rijn, a number of misconceptions have entered into the literature that have sparked much debate. Machiel Bosman has reconstructed how through a mistaken interpretation of Moll's description of the *interinement* procedure by the archivist I. J. Loeff, Gijswijt-Hofstra and Roodenburg came to believe that *cessie van goede* would be a *voldongen feit* or "fait accompli" for the creditors, which in turn caused Dudok van Heel to argue that Rembrandt had made the strategic choice to maliciously force his creditors to accept the *cessie*, which would somehow have been to their disadvantage.[76]

[76] Bosman, *Rembrandts plan*, 37–39 (n. 22), referring to Moll, *Desolate Boedelskamer*, 124–25; I. J. Loeff, *Inventaris Desolate Boedelkamer Amsterdam* (Amsterdam, 1892), 5; Gijswijt-Hofstra, *Wijkplaatsen*, 135; Herman Roodenburg, *Onder*

This created the idea that a *cessie* would be more reprehensible and dishonorable than an accord, even though, as discussed in previous chapters, this is not at all warranted by the way in which the benefice was generally viewed and applied in seventeenth-century Holland. Through the *interinement* before the Amsterdam court, creditors had the opportunity to provide evidence of fraud, as only honest debtors would be allowed to officially register their letters of *cessie* so that they would have legal effect. Therefore, as Kersteman argues, while no such thing as an official rehabilitation was issued for successful applicants for *cessie van goede*, in practice this was implied by and part of the official registration of the benefice.[77] In Chapter 6, I will go further into the legal, social, and economic consequences of *cessie* for its applicants. As I will argue, the *cessie* and *akkoord* procedures were simply targeted at different groups of equally innocent insolvents. For nearly every incapacitated debtor, a proper legal solution for his or her repayment problems resulted in a more-or-less successful reintegration into the civic community.

Conclusion

The introduction of the Desolate Boedelskamer represents a watershed in the management and resolution of insolvencies in the early modern Low Countries in general, and especially for the city of Amsterdam. Insolvency can in part be reduced to an information problem. Without direct access to their debtor's books, creditors were forced to rely on the latter's reputation, outward appearances, and ability to make good on his or her promises. Whereas earlier procedures such as those in sixteenth-century Antwerp had therefore been based upon rumor, with a strong focus on the individual creditor, the Amsterdam *curatele* as it developed in the first half of the seventeenth century unified a fact-based approach towards the insolvent with the

censuur: de kerkelijke tucht in de gereformeerde gemeente van Amsterdam, 1578–1700 (Hilversum: Verloren, 1990), 379; S. A. C. Dudok van Heel, "Rembrandt van Rijn (1601–1669). Een veranderend schildersportret," in *Rembrandt. De meester en zijn werkplaats*, ed. Christopher Brown (Amsterdam/Zwolle: Rijksmuseum/Waanders, 1991), 61.

[77] Franciscus Lievens Kersteman, *Hollandsch rechtsgeleerd woorden-boek* (Amsterdam: Wed. van Esveldt en Holtrop, 1777), 178.

collectivization of the claims and interests of all creditors. The case of Van Helsdingen at the beginning of this chapter clearly illustrates the advantage of an insolvency procedure that was able to separate fact from hearsay. The Amsterdam institutional innovations resulted in benefits for all parties involved in insolvency procedures.

On the one hand, insolvents were treated fairly through a detailed investigation into the true financial condition of their estate before any further steps were taken. The government-appointed curators were independent actors, but a system of various penalties and fines incentivized them to act quickly and to seek the benefit of the estate as a whole rather than representing the interest of a (sub-)group of creditors. The supervision of curators by a public court also helped prevent their acting in collusion with the insolvent or part of the creditors. If they had acted honorably before their insolvency, the physical integrity of the insolvents was ensured through the liberal application of protective beneficces such as *seureté de corps*. The central goal of the court's actions – the maximization of monetary proceeds from the estates in its care – did not just benefit the creditors, but also the insolvents themselves, as this would result in a smaller residual debt after the end of the procedure. All these factors incentivized the insolvent to cooperate, largely removing the need to abscond or hide assets, a typical occurrence in earlier and foreign types of insolvency procedures.

On the other hand, creditors also clearly benefited from these actions. While they generally lost the power to take their debtor hostage or to liberally seize his or her possessions in order to enforce their private claims, the procedure that was imposed collectively by the Amsterdam authorities provided them with the reassurance that their rights would be respected on an equal basis with all other claimants. The simple fact that an insolvent estate was managed by an impartial, open-access, and public institution, must have gone a long way to solve the creditors' basic information problem. Through its transparent, fact-based procedure, the Desolate Boedelskamer actively reached out to creditors in order to investigate their debtor's actions leading up to the insolvency. The centralized collection and distribution of proceeds, together with a clear procedure to establish issues of preference and the hierarchy of claims, ensured that all would receive their due wherever possible.

Thanks to its procedure, the Desolate Boedelskamer could function as an "agency of accountability" for the creditors, generating systemic trust that could replace lost faith in their insolvent debtor. The court could realize this potential thanks to four factors: first, ensuring the insolvent's non-anonymity through the official inventory of the allegedly insolvent estate; second, their vulnerability to the court's power, thanks to its full legal authority to appoint and supervise curators; third, the Desolate Boedelskamer's complete material control over the estate, ensuring that all resources could be sequestered as collateral; fourth, its easy and broad accessibility for both insolvents and creditors, those (far) abroad being treated completely equal to local parties. The systemic trust generated by the Desolate Boedelskamer incentivized creditors to accept restructuring schemes that would otherwise have been deemed too risky and thus unacceptable. This therefore allowed at least a temporary saving of capital and restoration of credit. If the continued business proved successful, that would benefit both creditors and insolvent.[78]

Altogether, for the average creditor and insolvent, the introduction of the Desolate Boedelskamer and its procedure were a clear improvement over the old ways of dealing with insolvencies. Then, an already overworked college of aldermen had to carry out or supervise all these tasks in addition to its other duties. The actions and decisions described in this chapter resulted in a great quantity of documents and administrative entries that had to be processed and ordered in their corresponding registers. Of course, this does not mean that the court always functioned as a well-oiled bureaucratic machine. The great amount of work and the small number of officials processing these cases occasionally resulted in mistakes. Sometimes, these inaccuracies were not accidental, but a clear result of fraud. In the next chapter, the expertise of the Desolate Boedelskamer's staff will be the focus of our attention, with a special focus on the story of one especially error-prone bookkeeper.

[78] Maurits den Hollander, "Restoring Trust and Credit through Innovative Governance in 17th-Century Amsterdam," *Tijdschrift voor Rechtsgeschiedenis* 89, no. 3–4 (2021): 481–99; Piotr Sztompka, *Trust: A Sociological Theory* (Cambridge University Press, 1999), 86–90.

4

Staff

On November 19, 1680, a problem arose in the Desolate Boedelskamer. At that time, the insolvent merchant Isacq Nunes Bernal had managed to conclude an accord with his creditors.[1] In order to validate such an agreement, it had to be signed by the secretary of the Desolate Boedelskamer. However, the 70-year-old Frans Bruijningh appears to have been ill. Fortunately, Clerk Johannes van Willen was able to stretch the formal procedures enough to sign the agreement in Bruijningh's place "because of his indisposition."[2]

While Bruijningh quickly recovered, in subsequent years his physical condition deteriorated until he passed away and was buried in the Old Church on April 5, 1684.[3] Bruijningh had served the Desolate Boedelskamer for more than forty years, which resulted in a small succession crisis. The burgomasters and aldermen fell out among one another about the question of whether or not the latter should play a role in the appointment of a new secretary. The fact that various aldermen confirmed that they had heard Bruijningh himself say that he had been appointed by both burgomasters and *schepenen* after the creation of the Desolate Boedelskamer in 1643 constituted sufficient evidence for the *Oud-Raad*, a college of former officeholders who had

[1] Gemeente Amsterdam Stadsarchief [GAS], 5072: Archief van de Commissarissen van de Desolate Boedelkamer [DB], inv. nr. 1651.

[2] GAS, 5072: DB, inv. nr. 24, f. 75v.

[3] GAS, 5001: Burgerlijke Stand: doop-, trouw- en begraafboeken [DTB], inv. nr. 1047, p. 316.

the right to decide on this matter.[4] In a resolution of May 10, 1684, they ordered that henceforth both burgomasters and aldermen would be involved in a new secretary's appointment. Every year, once the new commissioners had been installed, the secretary would officially have to ask the aldermen to be permitted to continue in office.[5]

Bruijningh's story highlights some important characteristics of the functioning of the Desolate Boedelskamer in the second half of the seventeenth century. First, all members of such governmental institutions attached great value to procedures, especially when this concerned safeguarding their own rights and influence. Second, however, even though most local institutions displayed tendencies towards bureaucratization in this period, individual characters remained very important to their success or failure. The Desolate Boedelskamer was sufficiently flexible to allow important processes, such as the conclusion of accords, to continue in the absence of the main responsible official. As Paul Knevel argues in his study of contemporary civil servants in the service of the Estates-General in The Hague, bureaucratic processes in this period were first and foremost shaped by human actors.[6]

Early modern governance and public administration have often been described as "elitist," "nepotistic," or "oligarchic," characterized by a certain degree of arbitrariness. This perception can at least partially be explained by the fact that individual officials in this period enjoyed a relatively large degree of discretionary space, especially when compared to their modern counterparts. However, the freedom and flexibility to make individual choices does not necessarily mean that there were no standards to which officials had to adhere.[7] Historical notions of what constitutes corruption or good governance can only be understood in the context of contemporary

[4] On the *Oud-Raad*, see Antonio Porta, *Joan en Gerrit Corver. De politieke macht van Amsterdam (1702–1748)* (Assen: Van Gorcum, 1975), 23.

[5] Goswin Moll, *De Desolate Boedelskamer te Amsterdam: bijdrage tot de kennis van het Oud-Hollandsch failliten-recht* (Amsterdam: De Roever-Kröber-Bakels, 1879), 173.

[6] Paul Knevel, *Het Haagse bureau. Zeventiende-eeuwse ambtenaren tussen staatsbelang en eigenbelang* (Amsterdam: Prometheus / Bert Bakker, 2001).

[7] Jeroen van Bockel, *Gevormde kaders. Bureaucratische en professionele regulering van het werk van ambtenaren in de Republiek der Zeven Verenigde Nederlanden* (Delft: Eburon, 2009), 2–3 and 16.

institutions.[8] While full-fledged modern bureaucracies did not exist in seventeenth-century Amsterdam, the Desolate Boedelskamer's officials were kept in check by a combination of formal and informal norms that helped to regulate the ways in which they fulfilled their important roles in the local insolvency procedures.

The Desolate Boedelskamer consisted of a clear hierarchy of offices, headed by the annually elected commissioners. Ultimately, they were accountable to the aldermen and burgomasters. The fact that during their meetings the clerks could only enter the commissioners' room bare-headed, thereby showing proper respect to their superiors, shows the clear sense of hierarchy within the institution.[9] This displays the dual structure of the Desolate Boedelskamer, consisting of political officials or "regents" – the commissioners – who usually managed the institution for just a few years, and subordinate officials, the longer-term staff members such as the secretary, bookkeeper, curators, and clerks.[10] The "political management" was organized in a collegiate form, with only the most senior member styled as president and possessing some additional management tasks. While the curators operated in a more freelance way than the other staff members, the fact that they needed the commissioners' approval for all important decisions related to their management of the insolvent estates confirms their subordinate status in the institutional hierarchy.

In this chapter, I will subsequently discuss the background and characteristics of both main groups of the Desolate Boedelskamer's staff, in order to analyze how they contributed to the professionalization of insolvency procedures in seventeenth-century Amsterdam. Through a closer examination of the ways in which the institution dealt with fraud or mistakes, it will become clear how it helped to create a more professional and trustworthy insolvency procedure. Ultimately, it was the daily labor of commissioners and subordinate

[8] Toon Kerkhoff et al., *A History of Dutch Corruption and Public Morality (1648–1940)* (Newcastle upon Tyne: Cambridge Scholars Publishing, 2020), 7.

[9] GAS, 5072: DB, inv. nr. 58, f. 15r.

[10] On the distinction between "regents" and "subordinate officials," see e.g. Oebele Vries, "Geschapen tot ieders nut. Een verkennend onderzoek naar de Noordnederlandse ambtenaar in de tijd van het Ancien Régime," *Tijdschrift voor Geschiedenis* 90, no. 3–4 (1977): 328–49.

officials that constituted the foundation of the systemic trust generated by the Desolate Boedelskamer, as a crucial means to repair broken relations between insolvents and their creditors.

Commissioners

In the troublesome year 1672, many of the officials and magistrates of Amsterdam were replaced due to a regime change in the Dutch Republic as a whole. The "statist" regents, loosely grouped around the grand pensionary of Holland, Johan de Witt, were removed from power in favor of Prince Willem III of Orange, who was inaugurated as stadtholder. In Amsterdam, existing factions within the city council successfully used these events to remove their adversaries from power. In January 1671, the faction of Andries de Graeff had managed to trigger the downfall of the local magnate Gillis Valckenier, who used the victory of the "Orangist" faction to recover his lost power. After he had incited the people against the government led by De Graeff, Valckenier prompted the *vroedschap* or city council to send the Prince of Orange a request to restructure their council as he pleased. Thus, all of Valckenier's opponents were replaced in September 1672, and he and his faction regained the upper hand in Amsterdam.[11] On November 10, the old commissioners of the Desolate Boedelskamer had to step down due to these events, after which their replacements were inaugurated on the fifteenth of that month. This means that for 1672, a set of commissioners *before* and *after* the regime-change of that year has to be considered. It appears that these events did not influence the functioning of the court's subordinate staff. Unlike their more political managers, the secretary, bookkeeper, and clerks simply continued their work under the new authorities. This episode therefore illustrates an important difference in the recruitment of the court's regents and administrative staff.

Even though no such thing as formal schooling catering to the needs of administrative functions existed in the early modern period, this did not mean that the commissioners lacked the expertise to fulfil their responsibilities. Some were required to have personal

[11] Johan E. Elias, *Geschiedenis van het Amsterdamsche regentenpatriciaat* ('s-Gravenhage: Martinus Nijhoff, 1923), 157–72.

commercial experience, which would provide them with the necessary skills to supervise the management of insolvent estates placed into their care. The fact that two or more of the five annually elected commissioners had to be former aldermen ensured that there would always be sufficient judicial expertise among them.[12] An examination of the lists of commissioners between 1643 and 1700 reveals an interesting development regarding their academic backgrounds (see Figure 4.1).[13]

One immediately notices the variations in the number and types of academic titles used among the commissioners. In some years, such as 1645 or 1658, not a single commissioner bore the title *doctor* or *magister* (Dutch: *meester*). By contrast, in 1670 (four *doctors* and one *magister*) and 1683 (five *magisters*) all commissioners possessed an academic degree. In the second half of the seventeenth century, a trend towards increasing numbers of academically schooled commissioners can be observed. Interestingly, the numbers of *doctors* declined in the first decades, disappearing after 1675, while the number of *magisters* steadily rose over the whole period. In some years, six commissioners were appointed rather than the usual five, but this was always caused by the replacement of an official during the year. Dr. Gerard van Hellemond (1654) and Jean Appelman (1681) moved to the Orphan's Chamber; dr. Gerard Bors van Waveren (1665), mr. Joan Corver (1672), François de Vicq (1673), and mr. Gerbrand Pancras (1693) were elected as aldermen. Mr. Joan Munter (1674) even got promoted to the High Court of Holland. For five commissioners, there was a less positive reason for their replacement: mr. Jonas Witsen (1675), mr. Rombout Hudde (1679), mr. Cornelis Bicker van Swieten (1689), mr. Nicolaas Corver (1692), and mr. Pieter Hulst (1696) died in office. For an unknown reason, Hudde and Hulst were not replaced, but unfortunately neither Commelin nor Wagenaar provides an explanation for this fact.

[12] Gerard Rooseboom (ed.), *Recueil van verscheyde keuren, en costumen; midtsgaders maniere van procederen binnen de stadt Amsterdam*, 2nd ed. (Amsterdam: Jan Hendricks, 1656), 304.

[13] These data were gathered from Caspar Commelin, *Beschryvinge van Amsterdam* (Amsterdam: Wolfgang, Waasbergh, Boom, Van Someren, and Goethals, 1693), 363–88; Jan Wagenaar, *Amsterdam in zijne opkomst*, 4 vols. (Amsterdam: Yntema en Tieboel, 1767), III:461–69.

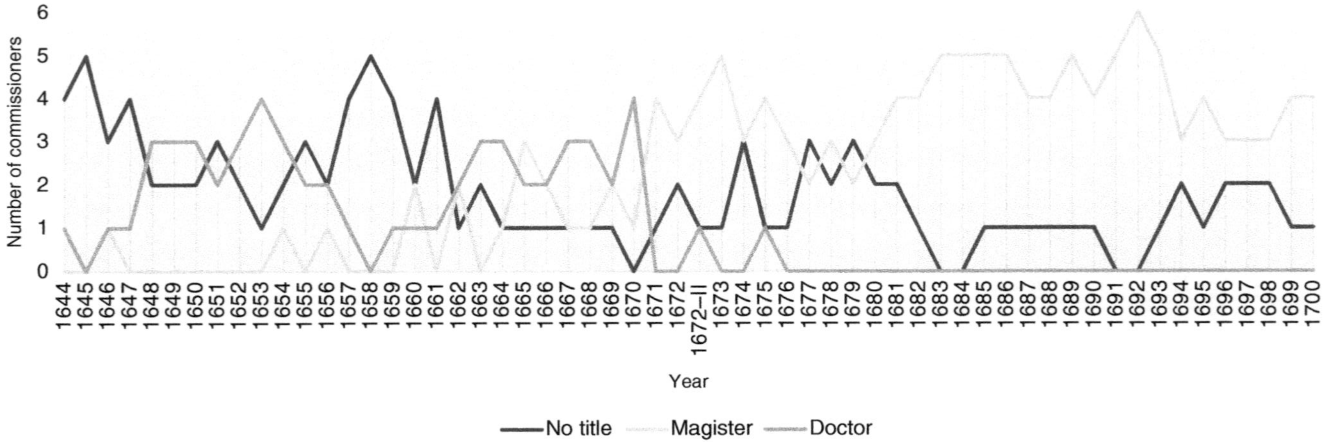

FIGURE 4.1 The educational background of commissioners of the Amsterdam Desolate Boedelskamer

The Desolate Boedelskamer was hardly unique in the rising numbers of university graduates among its commissioners. Between the fifteenth and the eighteenth century, the percentage of Antwerp aldermen who had studied at university rose from 38 to 72 percent. Whereas by 1675 roughly half of the councilors in Amsterdam, Rotterdam, Gouda, and Zierikzee were in possession of a degree, in the eighteenth century this rose to two-thirds.[14] The data above show that these estimates were rather conservative where they concerned Amsterdam's legal officials. In order to understand these developments, we need to take the changing academic environment at the universities of this period into account. In the Middle Ages, academic studies could easily last for a decade. Most students left the university without a doctorate, as the extraordinary costs of the accompanying ceremony prevented them from obtaining this highest degree.[15] This was not problematic, as professions that demanded an academic qualification were rare until well into the seventeenth century. Often, it was sufficient to show a letter of testimony signed by the professor or dean to prove that one had spent a given period at university. The main differences between a doctorate and licentiate were that the former included a longer examination, greater dignity, and granted the graduate the possibility to enter into a professorship. The graduation formed a "set of symbolic exercises" rather than a real "cognitive sanction."[16]

During the early modern period, the duration of academic studies generally decreased to a few years. The examination requirements were also watered down. This might have stimulated the elite to send rising numbers of their offspring to university for a few years. By 1600, the bachelor and by 1650, the licentiate titles had virtually disappeared from Leiden University. The vast majority of degree-taking students finished their studies with the *doctor* exam. In this period "doctor" became a synonym for "graduate," even if the candidate actually just possessed a *licenciate*.[17] This development is linked to the gradual replacement of

[14] Willem Frijhoff, "Graduation and Careers," in *Universities in Early Modern Europe (1500–1800)*, ed. Hilde De Ridder-Symoens (Cambridge University Press, 1996), 412–13.

[15] James A. Brundage, *The Medieval Origins of the Legal Profession: Canonists, Civilians, and Courts* (University of Chicago Press, 2008), 258–62.

[16] Frijhoff, "Graduation and Careers," 363–66.

[17] Helmut Coing, "Die juristische Fakultät und ihr Lehrprogramm," in *Handbuch der Quellen und Literatur der Neueren Europaïschen Privatrechtsgeschichte*, I(2):

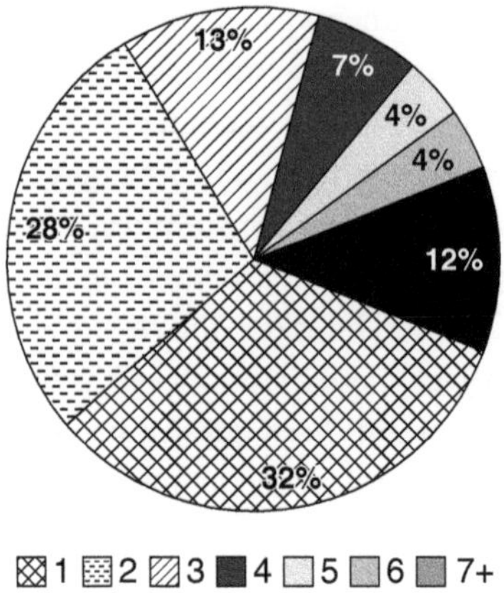

FIGURE 4.2 Number of terms per individual commissioner (1643–1700)

the "dr." title by the "mr." or *magister* variant during the seventeenth century, as shown in Figure 4.1. In the sixteenth century, almost all students who took a degree did so in the arts, and a few in medicine. However, over the course of the seventeenth century the number of law graduates in Holland increased tenfold. This is connected with a general trend, in which legal studies enjoyed greater popularity as the general preparation for a public career. Law graduates used to style themselves as "mr," which explains the observed shift in the Amsterdam data.[18] While not necessarily having followed a truly professional education, increasing numbers of the court's commissioners therefore had obtained the basic academic skills that were starting to be perceived as essential to fulfil higher public offices during this period.

The Desolate Boedelskamer's ordinances stipulate that every year, two out of five commissioners would continue for a second term. Each individual was allowed to fulfil a maximum of three consecutive terms.[19] However, this rule was clearly neglected in a number of cases (see Figure 4.2).

While three-fourths of the commissioners served a maximum of three years and did not therefore transgress the rule laid down in the

Neuere Zeit (1500–1800). Das Zeitalter des Gemeinen Rechts, ed. Helmut Coing (Munich: C. H. Beck'sche Verlagsbehandlung, 1977), 50–53; Frijhoff, "Graduation and Careers," 364–65.

18 Frijhoff, "Graduation and Careers," 365, 379 and 413.

19 Rooseboom, *Recueil*, 304 (art. 2).

ordinance, the average number of terms per commissioner between 1643 and 1700 was a relatively high 2.98, which means that the remainder served the Desolate Boedelskamer for a (much) longer period. Of course, these terms could be spread out over decades in order not to transgress the maximum number of consecutive years, but this rule often seems to have been neglected in practice for the longest-serving commissioners.

Dr. Pelgrom ten Grootenhuys (1618–1660), for instance, worked as commissioner for nine years between 1649 and 1657, similar to mr. Dirck Munter (1648–1701), who served the court continuously between 1680 and 1689. Ten Grootenhuys, who lived in the Bataniëstraat, came from a merchant family. His father Jan was the first curator of the *Athenaeum Illustre*, which would have provided Pelgrom with a solid academic background.[20] Pelgrom's brother, dr. Joan ten Grootenhuys (1621–1679), also served as commissioner for four years, but only after Pelgrom had passed away.[21] Dirck Munter was also born into a wealthy family of merchants, and lived on the Herengracht 54, "situated near the Korsjessteeg." Besides functioning as commissioner, he fulfilled a wide variety of other offices. His career culminated in two terms as burgomaster in 1698 and 1700. Dirck's brother, mr. Joan Munter (1643–1713), also served as commissioner for four years, preceding Dirck in this office. He is described as *de jonge*, probably to distinguish him from their father, who was also named Joan.[22]

This was not necessarily a bad development. The greater personal continuity among its management definitely had the potential to be a positive influence on the Desolate Boedelskamer's daily functioning. Rather than devoting their full-time attention to the court, the commissioners usually combined their office with other occupations and responsibilities. When a merchant was elected to a public office, he or she could not be expected to put their business on hold for its entire duration. The commissioners' regular meetings and the fact that usually one or more of them served the institution for many years on end, ensured sufficient expertise among them to properly supervise the court and its procedures.

[20] Johan E. Elias, *De Vroedschap van Amsterdam 1578–1795* (Amsterdam: N. Israel, 1963), 275 and 512.
[21] Ibid. 541. [22] Ibid. 625–26.

While the position of commissioner was honorable, being one of the city's higher-ranking legal offices, its corresponding monetary rewards were rather symbolic. The commissioners received an annual salary of fl. 400, as well as fl. 50 clothing money (*mantelgeld*), similar to the remuneration of, for instance, the Orphan Masters.[23] If this had been their only source of income, it would have meant that the commissioners earned no more than an ordinary self-employed craftsman or modest shopkeeper, who earned an average income of fl. 350 to 500 per year (see Chapters 5 and 6). Even when considering that the commissioners had other part-time activities, this would miss the point that, as political officials, their salary should be seen as an allowance rather than as a veritable compensation for their invested time and effort. In this same period, for instance, the two *stadsclerken ter secretarije*, or the senior secretaries of the municipal administration, who were expected to fulfil their offices full-time, earned fl. 1,030, which was raised with a further fl. 500 in 1702.[24] For regents, on the other hand, political influence and prestige were the main reasons for their involvement with institutions such as the Desolate Boedelskamer. To a certain extent, the fulfilment of such offices was also considered the "civic duty" of the wealthiest citizens. While serving some terms as commissioner of one or more of the city's subordinate courts, regents could both display their goodwill to serve the community and earn the necessary experience that was required to become eligible for higher political offices.[25]

The collegiate form of governance that was utilized in all courts in seventeenth-century Amsterdam ensured that the commissioners were kept in check by their peers if they were tempted to abuse their power for private purposes. Once they had been elected to office, each commissioner was required to swear a formal oath before the burgomasters. They had to promise "to manage and protect the goods

[23] GAS, 5024: Burgemeesters: dagelijkse notulen, resoluties en missivenboeken [Burg], inv. nr. 1, f. 152r; GAS, 5031: Burgemeesters – ambten en officiën [BAO], inv. nr. 54, p. 31 and 181.

[24] GAS, 5031: BAO, inv. nr. 54, p. 25.

[25] Manon van der Heijden, *Civic Duty: Public Services in the Early Modern Low Countries* (Newcastle upon Tyne: Cambridge Scholars Publishing, 2012), 139 and 148–53.

and affairs of the desperate estates in [their] care diligently, and to the best of [their] knowledge," as a "faithful guardian" or *getrouw opsiender en verzorger*. The oath concluded with the sincere promise to act according to the provisions specified in the court's ordinance.[26] This ordinance was the main set of rules which regulated the commissioners' conduct. Ultimately, if insolvents or their creditors were displeased with the way in which they were treated by the Desolate Boedelskamer, they could always file an appeal with the aldermen's bench. This legal backstop must have motivated the commissioners to live up to their promises. The office rotation system, in which varying groups of regents managed the court for a limited number of years, was a good additional safeguard against a development towards ownership of such positions by a certain family or kinship network.

Subordinate Officials

Soon after the Desolate Boedelskamer had been established, its commissioners started to delegate additional tasks to their subordinate staff. Especially after the new 1659 ordinance entered into effect, which resulted in the appointment of curators at an earlier stage of the procedure, the need to regulate and control their subordinates impelled the commissioners to compile several series of working instructions. While some of them were later published as appendices to the court's ordinances, most were simply noted in the Book of Resolutions, from where they could be copied and distributed among the clerks and other subordinate staff. The larger, formal ordinances or work instructions were made up on the orders of the burgomasters and only afterwards copied into the commissioners' resolutions. Smaller adaptations or additions to these main documents were usually issued on the commissioners' own authority. Table 4.1 provides a brief overview of the various ordinances and instructions that were issued over the seventeenth century.

Unlike the part-time commissioners and curators, the court's secretary, bookkeeper, and clerks generally display clear signs of full-time, specialized occupation of their offices. Since the curators operated in

[26] GAS, 5031: BAO, inv. nr. 50, p. 5 (neat version of the text on f. 14r of this same register).

TABLE 4.1 *Ordinances and work instructions issued by the Amsterdam burgomasters and commissioners for the Desolate Boedelskamer's staff up to 1700*

Date	Targeted staff	Reference
September 5, 1654	Secretary and clerks (on salaries)	Inv. nr. 58, ff. 1r–2v
January 25, 1655	Clerks and some provisions for curators	Inv. nr. 58, ff. 14r–20r
July 6, 1661	Single instruction bookkeeper and curators	Inv. nr. 58, f. 6
November 21, 1661	Single instruction curators	Inv. nr. 58, f. 8
April 24, 1663	Bookkeeper and curators (includes separately issued instructions 1661)	Inv. nr. 58, ff. 10r–12r
January 24, 1676	Curators (amplified: February 9, 1677)	Inv. nr. 58, ff. 23r–26r
September 7, 1685	Explicit orders for Bookkeeper Van Poelwijck, amplifications to older instructions curators and clerks	Inv. nr. 58, ff. 33r–35r
December 1688	New model for the oath and surety of curators	Inv. nr. 58, ff. 39r–40r
June 11, 1693	Single instruction (reissue) curators	Inv. nr. 58, f. 52r

a different manner, resembling present-day freelance professionals, I will discuss them separately before turning to the court's full-time subordinate staff.

Curators

Until 1643, the curators were directly appointed by the aldermen. After that date, the commissioners took over this responsibility.[27] At first there appears to have been no official limit to the number of curators who were actively working for the Desolate Boedelskamer at any moment. By 1682 at the latest, however, the urban *ambtenboek* or "register of offices" mentions a limit of seven curators. The curators' assignment to one of these positions was officially registered in the court's Book of Resolutions. At first sight this might seem superfluous,

[27] On continuity and change in the management of insolvent estates in Amsterdam before and after 1643, see also Maurits den Hollander, "Law as Resource" (*forthcoming*).

as the curators were assigned to insolvent estates and paid on a case-by-case basis. However, this official registration can be explained by the need for every new curator to provide sureties for fl. 6,000 as a safeguard for their good conduct, a rule which was already in place before 1643.[28]

The curators were usually selected from a group of people who possessed a certain level of legal knowledge, but did not work for the court in a subordinate position as yet. The only exception to this unwritten rule occurred in 1661, when clerk Hendrick van Borkelo was appointed a reserve-curator.[29] Sometimes, family relations played a role in the selection of curators. When Jan Bruijn provided sureties in order to start his work as curator on January 29, 1687, one of the guarantors was the widow Maria van der Trille, his mother-in-law or *behoudmoeder*. Interestingly, it is noted that her late husband (and thus Bruijn's father-in-law) Hendrick de Vries had formerly served as curator. It is likely that his family's connections at the court would have helped to secure Bruijn's curatorship once a position became available.[30] Two curators, Alwijn de Jager and Simon van Assingh, were active as notaries at the time of their appointment.[31]

While the curators clearly had a "serving" function and did not belong to the political management formed by the commissioners, they also did not have a fixed, full-time position with the court. Even though all curators were officially registered before any insolvent estates could be assigned to them, they essentially formed a group of freelance professionals whose remuneration was based upon the number of cases they handled and the costs incurred during these operations. This probably also explains why they worked from home, a clear "traditional" element which separates them from some of the court's other officials who actually worked in a more modern office environment. Through a tracking system, the commissioners sought to maintain control over the insolvents' confiscated books and papers. When a balance had been drawn up, curators collected the books relating to the new estate in their care to be used during its management, but only after the clerks had precisely noted the references

[28] GAS, 5031: BAO, inv. nr. 54, p. 32; Moll, *Desolate Boedelskamer*, 144–45.
[29] Moll, *Desolate Boedelskamer*, 146. [30] GAS, 5072: DB, inv. nr. 58, f. 35v.
[31] GAS, 5072: DB, inv. nr. 58, ff. 5v and 32.

attached to these items and the address to which they had been taken by the curator.[32]

Even though the curators worked on their own, the majority of their tasks taking place beyond the court's premises, their acts were closely monitored by the commissioners. Upon their assignment to an estate, a curator became accountable for the entire amount of its book value. This fictional debt to the Desolate Boedelskamer was then gradually redeemed through proceeds resulting from the collection of outstanding debts and the liquidation of assets belonging to the insolvent estate. Once a curator's management ended – either through an accord or because no more future gains could be expected – they were allowed to present their account to a commissioner delegated for that purpose. The latter would check their acts and discharge the curator from their responsibilities if all was found to be well. Only after this formal discharge would the salary and further declarations be paid out. The curators received a variable salary, consisting of 12 stuivers for every *termijn, ende vacatie* or "sitting." Examples of such legal acts were the curator's presence at a hearing or the delivery of a writ to a debtor on behalf of the estate in their care. When it was necessary to travel beyond the borders of Amsterdam, these costs would be covered by a daily compensation of no more than fl. 4 for general expenses or *teercosten*, plus transport fees.[33]

When, over time, curators started to try to obtain payment even before a case had been properly closed, the commissioners reconfirmed in a resolution of January 22, 1683 that "no declarations of curators, lawyers, and procurators will be paid out, before the estates to which such expenses can be related will have been closed and the curators will have received their discharge."[34] Besides the substantial surety of fl. 6,000 that was required for their appointment, the audits must have formed a potent tool to discipline the curators. A payment conflict from 1688 shows that the commissioners treated these events as serious business. This was important, as too high an overhead cost would result in great disadvantages for the creditors.

Curator Simon van Assingh had handed in an invoice of fl. 1,434 for his management of the estate of Estienne Ponthon, which had

[32] GAS, 5072, inv. nr. 58, f. 16v. [33] GAS, 5072: DB, inv. nr. 58, ff. 11v–12r.
[34] Moll, *Desolate Boedelskamer*, 156.

resulted in an accord in which his creditors would be repaid 20 percent of their claims. Even though these amounted to the considerable sum of fl. 105,901, the commissioners judged Van Assingh's account to be *zoo enorm en ter quader trouwe gestelt* or "so enormous and made up in bad faith" that they would not allow it to pass their audit. As they had also discovered that the curator had received certain pistols from Ponthon "in an unusual manner," the latter received permission to reclaim these possessions. At the end of the day, Van Assingh would receive no more than fl. 500 as his salary and, "to show their great dissatisfaction with his actions" or *om haer merckelijck misnoegen in dezen te bethoonen*, it was decided that he would not be allowed to carry out any work for the court in the next three months, starting from April 5, 1689. The commissioners warned that if, in future, the curator would dare to display even signs of such unseemly behavior again, they would punish this rigorously, or *na rigeur van zaecken*.[35] Notwithstanding such rare conflicts, the curators' salary was only standardized in 1805, as a fixed percentage of the value of the repartitioned proceeds in every estate. This suggests that in most insolvencies the curators' accounts were judged to be reasonable by all parties involved.[36]

Secretary, Bookkeeper, and Clerks

In the Desolate Boedelskamer's hierarchy, the secretary was the most important subordinate official. Together with the bookkeeper, they managed the institution's daily administrative processes. They also functioned as the primary supervisor of the clerks, the longest-serving (and thus most senior) of whom had additional financial responsibilities. While many contemporary public officials worked at home, only using government buildings for particular purposes, such as formal meetings, the clerks had to attend the Desolate Boedelskamer on a daily basis, supervised by the secretary.[37] They had to continue their

[35] GAS, 5072: DB, inv. nr. 58, f. 41; inv. nr. 145, p. 35.

[36] Moll, *Desolate Boedelskamer*, 156–57.

[37] Officials in the village of Westzaan, for instance, only utilized their *raadhuis* or town hall for official meetings, but not as a real *bureau* or office: A. van Braam, "Bureaucratiseringsgraad van de plaatselijke bestuursorganisatie van Westzaandam ten tijde van de Republiek," *Tijdschrift voor Geschiedenis* 90 (1977): 457–83, 474.

work in the court until the secretary's tasks were finished and they were given their leave. Even during official holidays, they had to be available in case unexpected events required (administrative) actions to be sanctioned by the president of the court. On January 8, 1655 the burgomasters decided that if the commissioners were displeased with the clerks, who "always had to follow their orders," they could suspend them from their service for six weeks.[38] This clearly shows the clerks' subordinate, serving role in the institution.

As we saw in the introduction to this chapter, the secretary was appointed by both burgomasters and aldermen. While their position was fixed, every year once the aldermen's bench had been renewed the secretary would be required to officially present themself for their appointment to be prolonged. The bookkeeper and clerks were appointed by the burgomasters. While there were no formal recruitment requirements for any of these offices, it is clear that all officials needed to have a certain degree of administrative and financial experience in order to be able to carry out their jobs. The fact that all appointments were handled by colleges rather than individuals, such as the president, will have limited the risk of nepotism.

While, in principle, the secretary and bookkeeper fulfilled a true "profession" in a manner similar to that of the clerks, the first secretary, Frans Bruijningh, is somewhat exceptional in this regard (see also Chapter 5). Stemming from a family of notaries, Bruijningh had his own notarial practice from 1636 onwards.[39] Before the establishment of the Desolate Boedelskamer, notaries played an essential role in the conclusion of accords between insolvents and their creditors. When the authorities chose to regulate this private form of conflict resolution, it made sense that they asked a legal specialist such as Bruijningh to lead this operation as secretary of the new Desolate Boedelskamer. Through his long involvement with this institution during the first decades of its operation, he probably represents its most continuous, professional element, and must have had a major influence on the structure and evolution of its procedure.

[38] GAS, 5072: DB, inv. nr. 58, f. 4v.

[39] A. I. Bosma, *Repertorium van notarissen residerende in Amsterdam Amstelland, ambachtsheerlijkheden en geannexeerde gemeenten 1524–1810* (Amsterdam: Gemeentearchief Amsterdam, 1998), 43.

Still, much like the curators, Frans Bruijningh did not devote all his time exclusively to the court. In its archives, a few interesting documents have been preserved among the collection of accords that have no clear relationship to an insolvency. One of these concerns Jannetje Fierlings, described as *producente* or "producer," widow of Jan Jansz. Cruijsheer. On September 30, 1642, a number of witnesses declare that they have known Jannetje for a long time, and confirm that she married Cruijsheer six years ago. One of them, a former employer whom she had served as maid before her marriage, declares that she had been present at the wedding dinner.[40] While the purpose of this notarial attestation, drawn up by Bruijningh himself, is unclear, it is safe to assume that it is unrelated to the Desolate Boedelskamer, which would only be established one and a half years later. Furthermore, Bruijningh's notarial protocol was not terminated when he entered his office as secretary, but continued until 1675. Interestingly, his private archive also contains a small number of inventories of insolvent estates, from both before and after the establishment of the Desolate Boedelskamer.[41] This shows that his private and public work were not entirely separate, or at least took place in the same office.

However, the fact that even after his long involvement with the court, Bruijningh was not succeeded by one of his relatives, suggests that this intermingling of private and public business did not automatically result in ownership of the office of secretary. While Balthasar Huydekooper only temporarily replaced Bruijningh from the latter's death until early 1685, subsequently secretary Coenraad de Wilhem served the Desolate Boedelskamer until 1724. This means that there was a great personal continuity in the court's principal supporting office.[42]

In the first Book of Resolutions, I encountered an interesting agreement between bookkeeper Willem Muylman and his successor Isaacq van Zon. In a time when pensions were uncommon and people generally had to provide for themselves, Muylman was granted a royal retirement scheme. He immediately received fl. 3,000 in cash or

40 GAS, 5072: DB, inv. nr. 1231. Other examples of such documents are inv. nrs. 1229, 1230, and 1232.

41 GAS, 5075: Notarieel Archief [NA], inv. nrs. 1407–19.

42 GAS, 5031: BAO, inv. nr. 54, p. 31.

gereeden gelde, and it was even agreed that he would retain much of his salary in a different form. This *tractement*, paid by his successor Van Zon, amounted to fl. 500 every six months. Accepting this deal allowed the commissioners to indirectly take care of their infirm former bookkeeper without substantial additional expenses. Most likely, Van Zon agreed to this type of arrangement to ensure that he would obtain the lucrative position of bookkeeper, making it worthwhile to function on half-pay for what would eventually be the first two years of his service in order to fully benefit from the position in future.[43]

An agreement such as that between Muylman and Van Zon did not necessarily result in the recruitment of less capable officials. No matter how they were appointed to their office, any bookkeeper was forced to master the financial and administrative skills that were essential to process the great amount of insolvent estates in the court's care. Manon van der Heijden argues that even though the rationale of early modern public services might not have valued capability according to modern professional standards, "it did recognize the value of experience and commitment."[44] Although some commissioners served more terms than officially allowed by the ordinances, secretary Frans Bruijningh did not fully separate his public from his private paperwork, and bookkeeper Muylman in a way "sold" his office to his successor in exchange for a retirement scheme, these were isolated events that did not result in the domination of the institution by certain families or kinship groups. In all the aforementioned cases, one might actually argue that the court's functioning was positively influenced by these individuals. By contrast in Dordrecht, for instance, the office of urban secretary was completely dominated by the Berck family between 1591 and 1667. Its occupants often had important side-jobs and regularly employed replacements to fulfil their duties.[45] Such practices were rather different from what became the norm in Amsterdam.

Both for insolvents and their creditors, a competent and independent staff of the Desolate Boedelskamer was important for a fair

[43] GAS, 5072: DB, inv. nr. 58, f. 13. This type of arrangement is also known as *belast ambt*, literally "encumbered office." See Vries, "Geschapen tot ieders nut," 346.

[44] Van der Heijden, *Civic Duty*, 176.

[45] Elise van Nederveen Meerkerk, "Professionalization of Public Service: Civil Servants in Dordrecht, 1575–1795," *Journal of Urban History* 36, no. 3 (2010): 345–67, 354–55.

treatment of their cases. In part, the integrity and independence of the staff could be secured through a stable income, which would decrease the attraction of corruption. Emoluments or other payments in kind that are directly assigned to an official often result in an increased chance for the appropriation of such sources of public revenue as private property.[46] All of the subordinate officials working for the Desolate Boedelskamer were paid a fixed salary, sometimes supplemented by monetary emoluments.

At the time of the court's creation, the *Oud-Raad* had granted the bookkeeper a substantial annual salary of fl. 1,200.[47] At least by 1682, they were also paid fl. 50 clothing money per year.[48] Moll wrongly asserts that until 1730, the bookkeeper received 5 percent of the value of estates in which an accord was concluded.[49] He bases this upon an entry in the court's resolutions from that year, which actually orders the bookkeeper to *stop* collecting 5 percent of the value of each accord to the benefit of the secretary and concierge, who (unlike the bookkeeper themself) were entitled to these proceeds up to that moment.[50]

The salary of the secretary was not extremely high, but it was supplemented by generous emoluments for a variety of services. In 1645, the secretary received an annual wage of fl. 200, as well as fl. 40 clothing money. On January 28, 1649 and October 28, 1660, their fixed salary was raised in steps of fl. 100 to the annual wage of fl. 400 that would thereafter remain at this level until 1778.[51] The remuneration paid to the secretary was related to those of the clerks. Each of them received an annual salary of fl. 120, besides a variety of emoluments that seem to have functioned as derivatives of the secretary's tasks and their corresponding rewards.[52] The list of remuneration per task that was made up in 1654 in the first Book of Resolutions suggests that the clerks were paid one-third or one-fourth of the amount that the secretary would have received for similar tasks (see Table 4.2).[53]

[46] Max Weber, *Gezag en bureaucratie*, ed. A. van Braam, trans. J. J. M. de Blok (Rotterdam: Universitaire Pers Rotterdam, 1972), 158 and 167–70.

[47] GAS, 5024: Burg, inv. nr. 1, f. 152r.

[48] GAS, 5031: BAO, inv. nr. 54, p. 31.

[49] Moll, *Desolate Boedelskamer*, 177.

[50] GAS, 5072: DB, inv. nr. 59, f. 42r.

[51] GAS, 5024: Burg, inv. nr. 1, f. 152r; GAS, 5031: BAO, inv. nr. 54, p. 31; Moll, *Desolate Boedelskamer*, 173–75.

[52] GAS, 5031: BAO, inv. nr. 54, p. 31.

[53] GAS, 5072: DB, inv. nr. 58, ff. 1r–2v.

TABLE 4.2 *Remuneration of the secretary and clerks per specific task*

Task	Secretary	Clerk
Drawing up an inventory (proportionally related to hours)	fl. 8 / day	fl. 2 / day
For a *grosse* or authorized copy of an inventory (each page to contain 6 large or 10 small entries)	7 st. / page	2 st. / page
Writing out judgments or acts of authorization	6 st. / page	1 st. / page
For "authentic, or simple" copies of these documents, or all other types of acts and their copies	12 st. / page	2 st. / page
Writing out the two official *grossen* of an accord	fl. 9 – 10 st.	fl. 2

Slightly different rules were established for *citaties*, or summonses. The emoluments for such documents were to be "enjoyed as salary by the three clerks in common, one-third each," while the secretary could also claim their share. For regular summonses, an estate would be charged with 4 stuivers, one of which would be reserved for the secretary. Summonses related to presenting and signing an accord were charged at the rate of 5 stuivers, possibly because they were longer or more complex, with the secretary again being allowed to withhold 1 stuiver for themself before paying out the clerks' share.[54] In 1660, an addition to the original list was made in the margin of the document. Henceforth, everyone who would "present a case on the roll of the city of Amsterdam" related to the Desolate Boedelskamer also had to pay the secretary 1 stuiver for the administrative acts flowing from this legal procedure.[55]

On April 5, 1689, it was discussed how clerks and curators had received money from insolvents who had concluded an accord with their creditors before their case had been brought to its official conclusion. Hoping to smoothen the process of obtaining their act of rehabilitation, the insolvents had happily paid the amounts requested by clerks and curators without receiving a proper accounting thereof. As this ran contrary to the official instructions, which the commissioners had reconfirmed a few years earlier in 1683, they admonished their subordinates to adhere to the correct procedure. Doing

[54] GAS, 5072, inv. nr. 58, ff. 1v–2r. [55] GAS, 5072, inv. nr. 58, f. 1.

otherwise, they feared, would harm the "reputation and general respect of this court."[56]

As discussed above, such notions of reputation and honor were of great importance for the regents who managed legal institutions such as the Desolate Boedelskamer. The court would only be able to fulfil its role for Amsterdam society at large if its reputation allowed for the generation of system trust.[57] Even if the ruling class of Amsterdam in this period can be characterized as oligarchic rather than professional, such "elites in control" might have had an equally positive impact on their subordinates' adherence to fair and regulated procedures.[58] By solving the information problem that might otherwise have made creditors wary of accepting a legal solution such as an accord that eventually benefited all parties involved, repeated successful interventions by the Desolate Boedelskamer could, over time, foster a "trust culture" that allowed more insolvents to try to restore their businesses.[59] Both in their roles as businessmen and administrators, the commissioners would reap the benefits of an equal and transparent treatment of insolvencies and their related legal issues. It is no surprise that they tightened their control over their subordinates in the late 1680s. In this period, the fraudulent acts of bookkeeper Balthasar van Poelwijck gravely endangered the reputation that was so crucial to the Desolate Boedelskamer's functioning. I will now discuss this intriguing exception to the generally positive image of the Desolate Boedelskamer's officials in greater detail.

Fraud

When Abraham Ruttens was appointed as bookkeeper of the Desolate Boedelskamer in 1687, his colleagues met him with a certain degree of mistrust. In order to ensure his faithful management of the court's finances, or *voor zijn getrouwicheyt*, he was required to provide sureties for an amount of fl. 12,000. This was much more than was required from any of the court's other officials, an amount almost ten times his

[56] GAS, 5072: DB, inv. nr. 58, f. 41v.

[57] Niklas Luhmann, *Trust and Power*, ed. Christian Morgner and Michael King (Cambridge: Polity Press, 2017), 55 and 77.

[58] Van Bockel, *Gevormde kaders*, 16.

[59] Den Hollander, "Restoring Trust and Credit."

salary. Jeweler Jan Teyt and broker Jacob de Marre were willing to act as guarantors for Ruttens, which enabled him to accept the lucrative office.[60] As Ruttens was the first bookkeeper who had to provide such extensive safeguards upon entering this office, this change must have been caused by events in the years leading up to his appointment. In this section I will discuss the story of his corrupt predecessor, Balthasar van Poelwijck, who seems to have tried to solve his personal financial problems with public money taken from the court.

In 1689, it was reported to the commissioners that the name of Balthasar van Poelwijck had appeared on the list of requests for the *interinement* of *cessie van goede* (this procedure will be treated extensively in Chapter 6). A resolution from April 27 of that year describes how it had been discovered that as bookkeeper, he had "erroneously taken great amounts of money, rightfully owned by the city as well as various others." The case was brought before the burgomasters. These argued that, as nothing could reasonably be expected to be claimed from the insolvent estate of Van Poelwijck, it would be best for all concerned "to allow the case to pass with a light hand."[61] What had happened in the preceding years? How did the bookkeeper end up in such a desperate financial condition that he was reduced to theft?

While we do not possess genealogical information about his immediate background, it is safe to assume that Van Poelwijck stemmed from the higher reaches of the Amsterdam citizenry. Elias describes him as a "merchant living on the Herengracht." His social status is also testified by his marriage with the rich widow Susanna van der Straeten on February 29, 1680, who had previously been married to the lawyer and regent mr. Jan Clifton.[62] The couple enjoyed some happy years together in their house on the Keizersgracht, situated close to the *uyterste veer* or the "outermost ferry." A daughter and two sons were born, Debora, Leonard, and Abraham.[63]

[60] GAS, 5072: DB, inv. nr. 58, f. 35v. The salaries paid to the bookkeeper and other officials can be found in the *ambtenboek*: GAS, 5031: BAO, inv. nr. 54, p. 31.

[61] GAS, 5072: DB, inv. nr. 58, f. 42r. [62] Elias, *Vroedschap*, 104–5.

[63] Debora and Leonard are mentioned in the baptismal registers of the Amsterdam Westerkerk (GAS, 5001: DTB, inv. nr. 107, pp. 348 and 382), but I could not find any references to Abraham's baptism. However, Abraham must have been born before, and Leonard must have died no later than August 1685, as the burial registers of the Zuiderkerk mention that Susanna left behind three (instead of four) children at the time of her death.

In the meanwhile, Balthasar had started working as bookkeeper of the Desolate Boedelskamer. On March 21, 1682 he swore the oath that was required of senior subordinate officials.[64] Sadly, his life together with Susanna was short. On August 27, 1685 she was buried in the Zuiderkerk in a purchased grave, or *eygegraff*.[65] A few days later, on September 7, the commissioners instructed their bookkeeper to carry out his work with *uyterste vlijt en naerstigheyt*, or "with the utmost diligence." As if they already anticipated the problems that would later arise, they reminded Van Poelwijck to take great care that no more money would be assigned from an estate than had already been deposited in the Desolate Boedelskamer.[66]

It seems that Van Poelwijck's personal financial troubles can be traced back to the early death of his wife. Susanna had one son from her first marriage, Joannes Clifton. His share in Susanna's inheritance would need to be paid out, together with the claims of his remaining half-brother and half-sister, Van Poelwijck's two surviving children with Susanne. The final liquidation of her estate with Balthasar van Poelwijck resulted in a balance of more than fl. 15,000 in favor of the children. That money was not handed over to the minors directly, but managed and invested on their behalf by the commissioners of the Orphan Chamber.[67] Unsurprisingly, given the fact that he had just lost access to his former wife's sizeable capital, Balthasar van Poelwijck was unable to pay this sum directly into the Orphan Chamber. On July 27, 1689 he declared that he remained indebted to the three children of Susanna van der Straeten for an amount of fl. 15,029, which was strengthened by a *weesmeesterkennisse*, a registration that ensured the debt's preferential status.[68]

In the meantime, Balthasar's personal creditors had started to proceed against him for various outstanding debts. In October 1686, David Lopes de Pas had obtained the aldermen's permission to execute a claim of fl. 300 that had been secured by a pledge on a house and

[64] GAS, 5023: Grootmemoriaal Burgemeesters [GB], inv. nr. 7, f. 48v.

[65] GAS, 5001: DTB, inv. nr. 1092, p. 76. [66] GAS, 5072: DB, inv. nr. 58, f. 33.

[67] On the Orphan Chambers in the early modern Dutch Republic, see Josje Schnitzeler, "Financial Care for the Vulnerable: Rise and Decline of Holland Orphan Chambers" (PhD, Utrecht University, 2022).

[68] GAS, 5073: Weeskamer, inv. nr. 807, f. 322 and inv. nr. 808, f. 292.

dye-works on the corner of the Spiegelgracht and the Prinsengracht. While the auction of the property was originally planned on January 18, 1687, this was put on hold by order of the commissioners of the Desolate Boedelskamer.[69] Presumably, they had been notified about the financial problems of their bookkeeper and wished to inspect and restore some order to his estate before allowing any further legal actions to take place. On the date originally scheduled for the auction, an inventory of Van Poelwijck's personal goods and possessions was compiled instead. Among other furniture and decorative items, this included some paintings of himself and his deceased wife Susanna.[70] Due to his personal insolvency Balthasar's position as bookkeeper of the court had become unsustainable, which explains why he was dismissed and replaced by Abraham Ruttens on January 22, 1687.[71]

In order to safeguard his physical freedom and to find a proper legal solution for the repayment conflicts with his creditors, Van Poelwijck filed an application for *cessie* with the High Court of Holland in The Hague. This request, which listed mr. Coenraed Blom, lawyer of the Court of Utrecht; the widow Voet; Lucas Vergeel; and Francois Mollo Moses alias David Lopes de Pas as his main creditors, was received by the Court on March 4, 1687. As usual, the councilors proceeded to forward the application to the relevant local legal authorities, in this case the Amsterdam Desolate Boedelskamer, which would then investigate in order to unearth potential instances of fraud, being the only legal ground on which one could block *cessie* requests. On April 8, the commissioners concluded that the application was valid after a consultation with the creditors, and one day later this was reported to the burgomasters. The High Court had also received an answer or *rescriptio* confirming the commissioners' green light, after which it issued Van Poelwijck's letter of *cessie* with a *committimus* to the local authorities in Amsterdam. Once he had officially registered this document with the burgomasters, it would finally enter into effect.[72]

[69] GAS, 5061: Archieven van de Schout en Schepenen, van de Schepenen en van de Subalterne Rechtbanken [ASS], inv. nr. 2129, f. 102v

[70] GAS, 5072: DB, inv. nr. 613, f. 136.

[71] GAS, 5031: BAO, inv. nr. 54, p. 31; GAS, 5023: GB, inv. nr. 7, ff. 48v and 162r.

[72] National Archives in The Hague [NL-HaNA] 3.03.02, inv. nr. 91, p. 404; GAS, 5072: DB, inv. nr. 26, f. 23.

While, in principle, a *cessie* resulted in the execution of all of an insolvent's possessions in order to redistribute the proceeds among his creditors, in Van Poelwijck's case his personal creditors were overruled by the Orphan Chamber's preferential claim on behalf of the inheritance of his children. On January 17, 1688, the house and dye-works which had originally been executed by David Lopes de Pas were auctioned for an amount of fl. 5,000. The buyer, Cristoffel Luytjes, worked as a silk-painter.[73] On January 23, 1687, curator Adriaen van Roosebeeck had received permission to sell part of a house owned by Van Poelwijck on behalf of the Orphan Masters. This property was described as "situated on the *uyterscht schietschuyteveer*, where the [symbol of a] cuirassier hangs out."[74] The *cessie* did not end the curator's involvement with this insolvency, as testified by an order to the *Roymeesters* – the surveyors of the city – to draft a report on the necessary expenses that had to be incurred to restore the immovable property in Van Poelwijck's estate to its proper condition.[75] While at first the commissioners of the Desolate Boedelskamer had ordered curator Van Roosebeeck to collect the "proceeds from the auction of the house of Balthasar van Poelwijck held by burgomaster Hudde" in order to bring them into the court for the estate's benefit, they quickly revoked and crossed out this order. This makes sense when we consider that the Orphan Chamber had such a large preferential claim upon the estate that no money would be left for the other creditors.[76] On January 24, 1688, the auction of the last remaining property from Van Poelwijck's estate took place. It concerned a yard or *erve* located "on the northern side of the Prinsengracht, between the river Amstel and the Utrechtsestraat," worth fl. 1,570. Interestingly, its buyers were Johan Hudde and Jeronimo d'Haze d'Giorgio, as legal guardians of Abraham and Debora van Poelwijck.[77] Perhaps they believed this property to be valuable enough to physically retain it as part of the children's inheritance.

[73] GAS, 5061: ASS, inv. nr. 2129, f. 161v

[74] GAS, 5072: DB, inv. nr. 26, f. 17. The *schietschuit* was a rapid variant on the regular *beurtvaart* or "packet trade" between Amsterdam and Utrecht, offering scheduled departures at fixed times for both passengers and goods transport. The *uyterscht schietschuyteveer* would have been located on the eastern side of the Singel, near the Gasthuismolensteeg.

[75] GAS, 5072: DB, inv. nr. 26, ff. 42v and 51v.

[76] GAS, 5072: DB, inv. nr. 26, f. 51r. [77] GAS, 5061: ASS, inv. nr. 2129, f. 174r.

While managing the insolvent estate of their former bookkeeper, the commissioners also started an investigation into his management of the estates that had been placed under their authority. After an extensive archival operation, in January 1688 Abraham Ruttens presented a list of (old) estates from which no future profits were to be expected. Even worse, it appeared that in a number of cases more had been paid out than actually should have been. Intriguingly, while Ruttens had found 80 faulty cases from the long years in which Willem Muylman and Isaacq van Zon had been bookkeepers, 220 problematic estates emerged from the five years in which Van Poelwijck had been responsible for the court's financial administration. Ruttens remarked that this last group even contained cases from which "never a single stuiver had reached the court." The commissioners, judging the matter to be "of such weight" that they could not proceed without the backing of their superiors, decided "to bring the matter in the *schoot* or 'bosom' of the lords burgomasters."

On January 24, 1688, therefore, the commissioners went as a body to the burgomasters to consult them about their problem. When they only found burgomasters Van Maarseveen and Hudde present, they decided to deliver Ruttens's list to the presiding burgomaster, Borst van Waveren, that same night, in order to allow him to study its contents. A few days later, on January 30, the commissioners mr. Cornelis Cloeck and mr. Coenraet van Klenck joined the burgomasters in a special meeting to discuss the proper course of action. Together, they arrived at the conclusion that all "hopeless cases" should be closed to avoid any further costs arising from them. The commissioners were authorized to scrap any entries that were judged to be *volcomentlick desperaet* or "entirely desperate," and all those from which they expected the costs of collection to outweigh the potential monetary benefits. As for the entries on which too much had been paid out, it was decided that the commissioners would have to try to recover these sums "with all possible diligence and assiduousness," in order to minimize the losses incurred in this administrative operation.[78] On the order of the burgomasters, Ruttens received a bonus of fl. 600 as a reward for his "extraordinary effort" to unearth these cases.[79]

[78] GAS, 5072: DB, inv. nr. 58, f. 38. [79] GAS, 5072: DB, inv. nr. 58, f. 39r.

It is clear that the problems encountered in Van Poelwijck's books and papers cannot be separated from his personal insolvency or the accusations of fraud on his account discussed by the commissioners and burgomasters early in 1689. During their 1688 meeting on how to deal with the estates for which too much had been paid out, the burgomasters had also ordered the commissioners to investigate who was responsible for the losses that could not be recovered from the creditors or their sureties. These careless officials were to be held liable for the squandered public funds, which had to be repaid if possible. Of course, this also concerned Balthasar van Poelwijck, who was the one responsible for the great majority of these administrative errors.

The discussion of how to deal with Van Poelwijck one year later suggests that, in his case, two problems had become intertwined. On the one hand, he had used part of the proceeds from the tax paid to the Desolate Boedelskamer known as the "city's right" for his individual expenses, possibly when trying to cover up his financial problems. On the other hand, Susanna van der Straeten's death and the problems this caused related to her inheritance must have mentally preoccupied the unfortunate bookkeeper. It is unsurprising that this resulted in sloppy paperwork and many errors that had now been discovered and redressed by his successor Ruttens. Perhaps, the burgomasters felt pity for Van Poelwijck's situation, and had already expected that the sums which could not be retrieved from the creditors would have to be written off. This, together with his insolvency, may explain why they decided that it would be best for all involved "to allow the case to pass with a light hand."[80]

While the scale of his erroneous acts and the fraudulent use of public money for private purposes was extraordinary, of course Balthasar van Poelwijck was not the only bookkeeper who made mistakes from time to time. Inspired by Ruttens's reward after the archival research that unearthed Van Poelwijck's failings, on February 3, 1689 the clerks of the Desolate Boedelskamer presented the commissioners with findings of their own, hoping to receive a similarly generous bonus. The clerks described how between February 17, 1668 and March 8, 1679, under the old bookkeeper Van Zon, they had reordered all archives

[80] GAS, 5072: DB, inv. nr. 58, f. 42r.

of cases processed between 1663 and 1668. They stressed multiple times how much effort it had taken to reorganize these "documents, which were in great disarray, one buried under many others." This operation resulted in a list of 251 creditors who had mistakenly been paid out more than the total proceeds from the estate in which they possessed a claim, amounting to a total loss of fl. 152,000 for the court. The clerks had managed to reclaim fl. 36,000 of this sum, as could be found back in Van Zon's accounts. Having conducted this strenuous labor "without ever having enjoyed sufficient rewards," the clerks petitioned the commissioners to take this situation into consideration. The commissioners were very pleased with their staff's effort in unearthing these cases and recovering the money. Especially in light of recent events, as well as "to animate [the clerks] with an even greater motivation to properly serve this court," the commissioners rewarded them with a bonus of fl. 150. Besides that, the clerks would henceforth receive 2.5 percent of any money they managed to retrieve that had been paid out mistakenly to any "persons, or their guarantors and heirs."[81]

Even though these numbers suggest that the Desolate Boedelskamer regularly lost great amounts of money due to the incompetence or even corruption of its staff, the picture becomes much more nuanced when one takes into account that this erroneously paid-out money consisted of (1) a large number of small payments, (2) in many individual cases, (3) that were spread out over decades of its operation. In this period, the court annually dealt with more than a hundred new insolvencies.[82] The value of some of these estates even amounted to many times the fl. 152,000 that the clerks reported as the total value of the mistakes they had uncovered in the court's administration.[83] These numbers, as well as the fact that the Desolate Boedelskamer itself discovered, reported, and addressed such problems, suggest that it functioned relatively smoothly and transparently, especially according to early modern standards.

[81] GAS, 5072: DB, inv. nr. 58, ff. 40–41r.

[82] W. F. H. Oldewelt, "Twee eeuwen Amsterdamse faillissementen en het verloop van de conjunctuur (1636 tot 1838)," *Tijdschrift voor Geschiedenis* 75, no. 4 (1962): 421–35, 432.

[83] The size of insolvent estates will be discussed in far greater detail in Chapter 5 below. This information is based upon my quantitative dataset.

Conclusion

The Desolate Boedelskamer displays an interesting combination of political and professional urban officials. This duality is an important characteristic of early modern institutions, which constitute a middle ground between traditional and modern forms of governance. As Manon van der Heijden argues, the "communal system" which is often found in the early modern period displays bureaucratic characteristics, "but had its own logic and rationale, based on notions of common interest, voluntarism, and civic activism."[84] The Desolate Boedelskamer represents a clear move towards a more professional treatment of insolvencies in seventeenth-century Amsterdam. Its formal, written procedures were carried out according to increasingly detailed working instructions. These were based upon a clear hierarchy of offices within the institution, while its managing commissioners were ultimately accountable to the burgomasters. Even though mistakes occurred from time to time, and not all of its officials were of irreproachable behavior, when the fraud committed by bookkeeper Balthasar van Poelwijck was discovered, this resulted in a rather comprehensive quality-control system that sought to prevent similar abuses from occurring in future. Even though the Desolate Boedelskamer occupied a real office as the working space of its full-time secretary, bookkeeper, and clerks, the commissioners and curators served the institution on a rather less continuous basis.

While all officials were paid a salary, this was not always fixed and in part (for the secretary and clerks) or wholly (for the curators) determined by the amount of work performed through a system of declarations and emoluments. Such remuneration practices were typical for early modern institutions.[85] Even today, however, many public institutions make use of large numbers of freelance professionals and other types of flex workers, who are hired and dismissed based upon the available amount of work. Seen in this light, the occupation and remuneration structures of the Desolate Boedelskamer were quite professional, both according to contemporary and current standards.

[84] Van der Heijden, *Civic Duty*, 29–30. Cf. Jos C. N. Raadschelders, *Handbook of Administrative History* (Oxford: Routledge, 1998), 117.

[85] Knevel, *Het Haagse bureau*, 162.

At the same time, to fully appreciate this court within the logic of premodern governance necessitates moving beyond such classic dichotomies of traditional versus bureaucratic, communal versus professional government. The Desolate Boedelskamer's staff could restore trust between insolvents and their creditors because they were embedded in and aware of the same social, economic, and religious networks. For the creditors, the increased possibilities of appeal and control created by the introduction of the Desolate Boedelskamer must have formed a clear improvement over the old situation, in which an overworked college of aldermen had to keep the curators in check and public notaries had to be relied upon to respect the interests of all creditors who were involved in an insolvency.[86] From a functional perspective, therefore, the Desolate Boedelskamer's staff managed to introduce clear improvements to the Amsterdam insolvency procedure and practice. They could fulfil their important role for insolvents and creditors thanks to being firmly embedded in the early modern mental world and its communal culture of governance.

[86] This development can also be observed in other contemporary subsidiary courts and institutions, such as the Orphan Chambers: Schnitzeler, "Financial Care for the Vulnerable." See also Den Hollander, "Law as Resource."

PART III

INSOLVENTS

5

The Accord

In his inaugural lecture to the new Amsterdam *Athenaeum Illustre* in 1632, Professor Caspar Barlaeus (1584–1648) warned his audience about avarice:

> They who hunt for excessive profits will also suffer from great losses, and when they entrust their hope for good fortune to sea and wind, their greed will be punished with poverty and infamy ... Wisdom admonishes us to be careful when signing IOUs or other written contracts. Although one might seek security in thousands of legal restrictions to bind the debtor, the cunning Damasippus will mock his creditors ... and laugh with their jaws.[1]

Notwithstanding this prudent advice, Amsterdam citizens engaged in numerous credit relationships, which sometimes resulted in disputes about the repayment of debts. As I have argued, the legal and moral dimensions of such conflicts often interacted, especially in the case of insolvency. Creditors and debtors alike had access to a broad variety of social and legal strategies to arrive at an arbitrated settlement, supported by the Amsterdam Desolate Boedelskamer's functioning as a platform for such matters.

In this chapter, I will focus on one of the most important legal solutions in case of insolvency: the *akkoord* or accord (composition). These agreements between insolvents and their creditors sought to prevent an execution sale of the estate. As Lagerwey argues, the

[1] Caspar Barlaeus, *Mercator Sapiens*, trans. S. van der Woude (Amsterdam: Universiteitsbibliotheek, 1967), 65 and 75.

central goal of such legal arrangements is to further the common good. On the one hand, a composition might result in higher repayment percentages thanks to reduced procedural costs; on the other hand, it means that the insolvent can continue to administer their own affairs and seek to continue their business, "saving [them] from personal financial demise and at the same time preserving a laborious citizen for society."[2] The Amsterdam Desolate Boedelskamer helped to obtain the creditors' trust, which was vital for the conclusion of increasingly favorable accords in this period.

This analysis is based upon a qualitative and a quantitative dataset. The Appendix provides more information on their contents and representativeness. First, it will be made clear how such agreements were concluded privately before notaries, until, in the second quarter of the seventeenth century, the Amsterdam burgomasters sought to subject their effectuation to prior consent of a public authority. I will then proceed to discuss how the delegation of this responsibility to the commissioners of the Desolate Boedelskamer in the 1640s eventually resulted in some important changes to the accord procedure in 1647 and especially 1659. The Desolate Boedelskamer played an important role in making the Amsterdam insolvency procedure more transparent for creditors in general, improving the security of debts through its inclusive and standardized administration of the estates in its care. Next, I will discuss the important role of guarantors in the conclusion of accords. Through their role as security for the agreements, they provided an important advantage to such arbitrated solutions when compared with simple execution sales.

In addition to these important structural developments in Amsterdam's insolvency procedure, the agency of debtors should not be neglected, as it was often in response to their actions that institutional innovation occurred. Insolvents had various strategies at their disposal to put pressure on unwilling creditors in order to force them to accept an accord. They mainly did so through the use of asylum-cities like Culemborg or Vianen. Finally, an analysis of the general characteristics of those insolvents who successfully used the accord procedure will reveal interesting details on their social and

[2] Antonie Cornelis Lagerwey, *Het accoord van den gefailleerde met zijne schuldeisers* (Utrecht: T. de Bruyn, 1862), 72–73.

economic background, especially when compared to those who had to resort to less generous legal arrangements such as a *cessie van goede* (this group of insolvents will be the focus of Chapter 6). Through their extension of public control over former private-order solutions for insolvency such as the accord, the Amsterdam authorities went a long way towards curtailing Barlaeus's cunning Damasippus.

Notarial Accords

On Monday October 25, 1604, merchant and sugar baker Hans van den Bergh arrived at the office of the public notary Lieven Heijlinc in the Amsterdam Warmoesstraat, the core of the city's commercial districts at that time. Heijlinc, originally from Ghent, had been admitted to the notarial office in 1591 and continued to work in Amsterdam until 1612.[3] Van den Bergh faced serious illiquidity. As soon as his creditors heard rumors that he was thought to be *gefailleert ende insolvent* or "bankrupt and unable to repay his debts," they attempted to cash in their bills of exchange and other claims through notarial *insinuaties* – "notarial summonses," usually the first step in legal action. In order to resolve his financial troubles, Van den Bergh now proposed that these creditors conclude an accord secured by two guarantors, Pieter van Eegen and Paulus Sterlincx. He promised to repay *12 schellingen vlaems in het pond groten*, or 60 percent of his debts, in two instalments: one in eight months, and the next in sixteen. The remaining debts would not be annulled, but Van den Bergh's creditors renounced their right to proceed against him in court in order to enforce further repayment. As soon as his business generated some profits again, he would strive to pay all remaining arrears from the period before the conclusion of his accord. After the creditors had signed the agreement on these conditions, it was registered in Heijlinc's protocol for verification, and secured by the guarantors' signatures on December 3, 1604.[4]

Van den Bergh quickly managed to revive his business. In 1605, he was able to buy a sugar bakery and brewery, and only in 1624 do

3 A. I. Bosma, *Repertorium van notarissen residerende in Amsterdam Amstelland, ambachtsheerlijkheden en geannexeerde gemeenten 1524–1810* (Amsterdam: Gemeentearchief Amsterdam, 1998), 70.

4 Gemeente Amsterdam Stadsarchief [GAS], 5075: Notarieel Archief [NA], inv. nr. 58, ff. 122v–126r.

we find signs of new financial problems, when he could not repay a loan extended by the merchant Jan van der Straten. This suggests that he must have had ample opportunity to repay the remaining arrears of his old creditors in the two preceding decades. The creditors only signed an accord such as that concluded by Van den Bergh when they trusted their creditor and his guarantors to be honest and creditworthy enough to actually meet its conditions. Clearly, the sugar merchant's reputation proved decisive in allowing him to renegotiate his obligations and to obtain sufficient credit when trying to revive his business.[5]

The fact that these accords were not just concluded privately between an insolvent and their creditors but were registered with a public notary, such as Lieven Heijlinc, greatly strengthened the chance that the creditors would actually agree to sign the agreement. Public notaries were only admitted after an official examination by the States of Holland, preceded by a training period as clerk with an active notary. The local authorities of the city where he had served as apprentice would have to provide a letter of recommendation before the aspiring notary could be admitted to the central exam. Notaries were bound to regulations imposed by the States of Holland. They were strictly forbidden to pass formal documents in which creditors' rights were harmed, for instance by removing assets from the estate that should be divided among the common creditors.[6] The increasing complexity of society that was caused by demographic and economic growth in seventeenth-century Amsterdam stimulated the demand for legal advice among its citizens. The notaries, who were bound to strict rules laid down by both central and local authorities, increasingly framed and "translated" daily transactions and dealings between merchants and others into legal terms, which resulted in the office of notary becoming a full-time occupation rather than an ancillary

[5] Arjan Poelwijk, "*'In dienste vant suyckerbacken'.*" *De Amsterdamse suikernijverheid en haar ondernemers, 1580–1630* (Hilversum: Verloren, 2003), 161–63.

[6] R. Huijbrecht, "Het notariaat in de gewesten Holland en Zeeland," in *Het notariaat in de Lage Landen (1250–1842)*, ed. A. FL. Gehlen and P. L. Nève (Deventer: Kluwer, 2005), 145–90; Wim Heersink et al., *Register Notarium. De notarissen van het Hof van Holland 1525–1811* (The Hague: Algemeen Rijksarchief, 1999); A. F. L. Gehlen, "De notaris in de Republiek der Verenigde Nederlanden (17de–18de eeuw)," in *Gepasseerd. De rol en positie van notarissen in het verleden*, ed. C. C. T. M. Van Haren, J. Ch. Janssens, and M. J. Swenker (Nijmegen: Gerardt Noodt Instituut, 1987), 60–64.

activity.[7] This legal framework helped to add trust to legal agreements such as accords, providing an alternative to a simple execution of the estate, which would most often yield smaller proceeds for the creditors in the long run than a revived business.

It is difficult to quantify the number of accords that were concluded on an annual basis before the creation of the Desolate Boedelskamer in 1643. Not all notarial protocols from this period have survived, but even those that do remain in the archives contain far too much information to be viably analyzed within the scope of this book. However, based upon references in secondary literature, as well as the partial index on the notarial archives created by the Amsterdam archivist Simon Hart, I have been able to locate nineteen accords concluded between 1592 and 1643.[8]

All of the accords, both before and after the establishment of the Desolate Boedelskamer, share a number of fixed elements. After an opening formula in which the insolvent acknowledges that they are unable to pay their debts, it states that they propose an accord to their creditors in which X percentage of the debt is to be repaid in a number of instalments, usually specified in terms of either months or years after the majority of the creditors have signed the composition. Usually, the larger part of the sum that is to be repaid is secured by guarantors, by real estate, or by movable goods, often supplemented by a small part on the insolvent's own credit. Finally, the insolvent and their guarantors signed the accord, accompanied by the notary or, after the establishment of the Desolate Boedelskamer, its secretary. Lists with creditors' signatures have not been found in notarial protocols, but must have existed, as these were essential for the accord to have its effect. Perhaps they were handed over to the insolvent after the procedure had finished.

Early accords were drawn up by notaries Jacob Gijsbertsz., Lieven Heylinc, Salomon Henrix, and Willem Cluyt.[9] Among these notarial

[7] Wim Heersink, "'Van oude tijden bij alle volkeren geacht.' Amsterdamse notarissen van schrijftafel tot schepenbank, 1600–1800," in *Nieuw licht op oude justitie. Misdaad en straf ten tijde van de Republiek*, ed. Sjoerd Faber (Muiderberg: Coutinho, 1989), 48–63.

[8] GAS, 30452: Archief S. Hart. See the information in the Appendix on the qualitative dataset for more information about these accords.

[9] GAS, 5075: NA, inv. nrs 9, f. 32 (Henrix); 12, ff. 186v–187v (Henrix); 32, ff. 101–2v (Gijsberts); 58, ff. 122v–126r (Heijlinc); 360A, nr. 371 (Cluyt).

agreements, a substantial variety of formulations and writing and composition styles can be observed. Later, however, a standard format and distinct "accord style" arose among a group of notaries who can be linked to one another, and which also became the standard for accords drawn up under the supervision of the Desolate Boedelskamer after 1643.[10] The central figure in this group is notary Jan Fransz. Bruijningh, father of the first secretary of the Desolate Boedelskamer, Frans Bruijningh, who played an important role in the establishment of the court's procedures. Bruijningh Sr. was an important figure in the commercial landscape of early seventeenth-century Amsterdam. As a specialist in trade and navigation, he wrote out more than 6,000 freight contracts between merchants and sailors in his house "De Schrijvende Hand" ("The Writing Hand") at the corner of the Heintje Hoeksteeg in the period 1593–1624.[11] Therefore, when the Amsterdam Chamber of the United East Indies Company (VOC) organized the subscription for its founding capital in August 1602, it made perfect sense to have this supervised by Jan Fransz. Bruijningh.[12] His office must have been the largest notarial practice in the entire city in this period. Bruijningh's father Frans Anthonisz.; brother Albert Fransz.; brother-in-law Jacob Meerhout; as well as his three sons Hendrik, Jacob, and Frans all functioned as public notaries at some point, while many of his former clerks became independent notaries themselves.[13]

In the notarial archive, a very interesting source from Jan Fransz. Bruijningh's hand has survived, described as his *Memoriaal*. The volume contains examples of the various types of acts that must have been drawn up in his office on a regular basis. An index was added for quick referencing. It is likely that Bruijningh himself and especially his sons and other apprentices would have used this material in their daily work. The *Memoriaal* can be characterized

[10] Bosma, *Repertorium van notarissen*, 43–44, 51, 100, and 126.

[11] Clé Lesger, *Handel in Amsterdam ten tijde van de Opstand. Kooplieden, commerciële expansie en verandering in de ruimtelijke economie van de Nederlanden ca. 1550–ca. 1630* (Hilversum: Verloren, 2001), 238; Oscar Gelderblom, *Cities of Commerce: The Institutional Foundations of International Trade in the Low Countries, 1250–1650* (Princeton University Press, 2013), 93.

[12] Lodewijk Petram, *The World's First Stock Exchange* (New York: Columbia University Press, 2014), 7–8.

[13] Bosma, *Repertorium van notarissen*, 23 and 44.

as an instruction manual or formulary. Most importantly, it contains the basic accord design which proliferated among Bruijningh's apprentices until it evolved into the standard format of the Desolate Boedelskamer in the 1640s. The format is dated to May 5, 1622, and displays great similarities to the accord drawn up by Bruijningh in the Quingetti case one year later. While some passages were shortened or fell into disuse in later accords, the basic elements and structure of this design continued to appear word-for-word in accords until at least the end of the seventeenth century.[14] Intriguingly, the archives of the Desolate Boedelskamer contain a document which must have fulfilled a similar function as Jan Fransz.'s *Memoriaal*, but then in the form of what could be described as an accord template written in the hand of his son Frans Bruijningh, the court's secretary. Perhaps this document, which reflects the common style of accords drawn up in this period but includes capital letters "A" or "B" rather than the actual names of the insolvent or their creditors, was intended to instruct the clerks in a similar way as Bruijningh had been tutored by his father. The template treats an exemplary accord in which an insolvent promises to repay 27.5 percent, 7.5 percent of which would be paid in cash, the remainder being secured by a brewery and its tools situated in Weesp, on the Hoogstraat, close to the Muiderpoort.[15]

The relations between Bruijningh Sr. and his apprentices have been worked out in Figure 5.1. One accord in the qualitative dataset was drawn up by Bruijningh himself.[16] His former clerk Jan

[14] GAS, 5075: NA, inv. nr. 202, ff. 127–8. Other contemporary examples of such manuscript notarial formularies have been found in the Southern Netherlands: G. van Dievoet, "Notarisboeken en formulierboeken voor notarissen in de Zuidelijke Nederlanden van 1500 tot 1800," in *Forma Servata. Vijf opstellen over formulieren en formulierboeken in het notariaat van de middeleeuwen tot vandaag*, ed. P. L. Nève and J. J. Verbeek (Deventer: Kluwer, 1998), 51–84. In the *Amsterdamsche secretary*, one can also find examples of 'standard accords' with and without guarantors that were much used around 1700: Anon., *Amsterdamsche secretary [etc.]*, 2 vols. (Amsterdam: Jacob van Royen, 1700), I:323–25.

[15] GAS, 5072: Archief van de Commissarissen van de Desolate Boedelkamer [DB], inv. nr. 7307.

[16] GAS, 5075: NA, inv. nr. 201, ff. 122v–125v (Jasper Quingetti, 1623). For more information on this case, see Oscar Gelderblom, *Zuid-Nederlandse kooplieden en de opkomst van de Amsterdamse stapelmarkt (1578–1630)* (Hilversum: Verloren, 2000), 191 and 216.

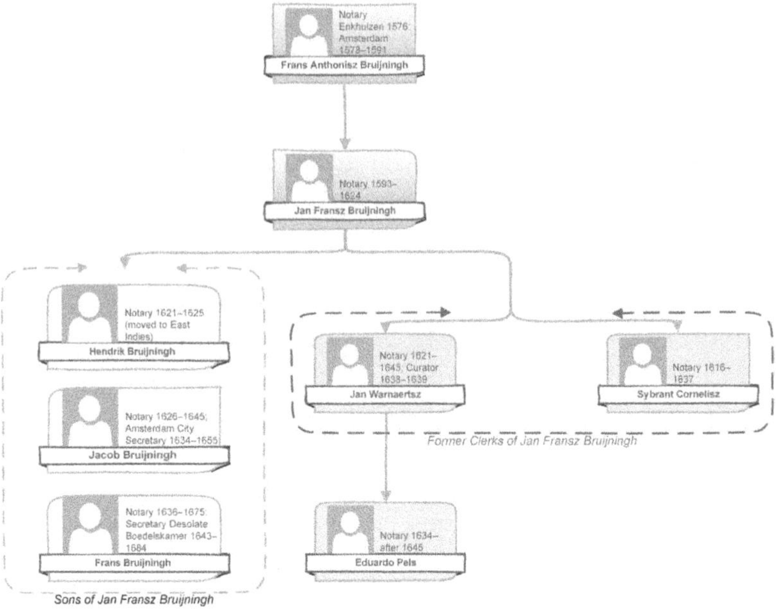

FIGURE 5.1 The Bruijningh family and related notaries in seventeenth-century Amsterdam

Warnaertsz. drew up seven of the twenty accords found before 1643, in a style which he clearly learned from Bruijningh.[17] Sybrant Cornelisz., another former apprentice, drew up two more accords.[18] Jan Warnaertsz.'s former clerk Eduardo Pels in turn drew up an accord in a somewhat different style, probably because this document was primarily intended to officially register the guarantor's backing of the agreement rather than the conditions of the accord itself.[19]

It is striking how most of the early accords, unlike later examples, cover the repayment of the entire debt. Through such agreements, repayment was postponed rather than annulled. This was in line with the aforementioned imperial decrees on insolvency issued by

[17] GAS, 5075: NA, inv. nrs: 700 (Hans Boor, 1625; Jacques Bollaert, 1626; Jeronimo Gailliart, 1626); 835B / 9 (Bartholomeus Reael, 1630); 701, f. 43 (Daniel van der Einde, 1631); and 702 (Nicolaes Ruts, 1638).

[18] GAS, 5075: NA, inv. nr. 633, ff. 70–72v (Jochum Blaeu, 1626) and f. 114v (Cornelis Jansz Goutsbloem, 1626).

[19] GAS, 5075: NA, inv. nr. 1609, f. 1 (Jacob Bosman, 1639).

Charles V in 1540 and 1544. The first ordinance strongly condemned the ratification of agreements with "bankrupts and fugitives, be it for the acquittal of their whole debt or part thereof." Those who had committed fraud were to be given the death sentence: they would end up *ter doot mette koorde* or "executed by strangulation."[20] Article 35 of the 1544 ordinance adds to this prohibition, stating that majority accords are forbidden if they contain the acquittal of part of the debt.[21] While in 1596, the States of Holland stated that they would continue to uphold the imperial decrees, as the seventeenth century progressed it became increasingly common to conclude accords that *de facto* – though explicitly not *de jure* – acquitted part of the debt. From mid-century onwards, in various cities institutions like the Amsterdam Desolate Boedelskamer even made it possible to do this through majority compositions, without the consent of all of the creditors.[22]

Van den Bergh's 1604 accord is the earliest example I have encountered in which the creditors give up their right to enforce the repayment of part of their claims in court, by agreeing to a composition that comprised the repayment of only 60 percent of their claims. Even though the remainder was never officially acquitted, such as in the Roman *remissio*, this must in practice have resulted in a situation in which the remaining arrears of former insolvents who had not been able to regain enough of their former wealth to repay all their old creditors "evaporated" at their death. It is intriguing to note how, over time, ever smaller repayment percentages were concluded with creditors. Whereas in the four accords I have found before 1610, three arrange for repayment of the entire debt – and Van den Bergh's provides for the repayment of 60 percent – as the seventeenth century progresses the average repayment percentages agreed in accords continue to fall to levels as low as 1 percent of the debts.[23] In Figure 5.2,

[20] Lagerwey, *Accoord*, 58–59; J. Lameere and H. Simont (eds.), *Recueil des ordonnances des Pays-Bas* [*ROPB*]. *Deuxième série 1506–1700*, 8 vols. (Brussels: J. Goemaere, 1907), IV:232–38 (Brussels, October 4, 1540).

[21] J. Lameere and H. Simont (eds.), *ROPB. Deuxième série 1506–1700*, 8 vols. (Brussels: J. Goemaere, 1910), V:52–56 (Brussels, May 10, 1544).

[22] Lagerwey, *Accoord*, 58–60; Jan Hendrik Dalhuisen, *Compositions in Bankruptcy: A Comparative Study of the Laws of the E.E.C. Countries, England and the U.S.A.* (Leiden: A. W. Sijthoff, 1968), 15 and 22.

[23] This concerns the accords found in: GAS, 5075: NA, inv. nr. 9, f. 32 (Ambrosius Laurens, 1592); GAS, 5075: NA, inv. nr. 32, ff. 101–2v (Philips Noblet, 1593);

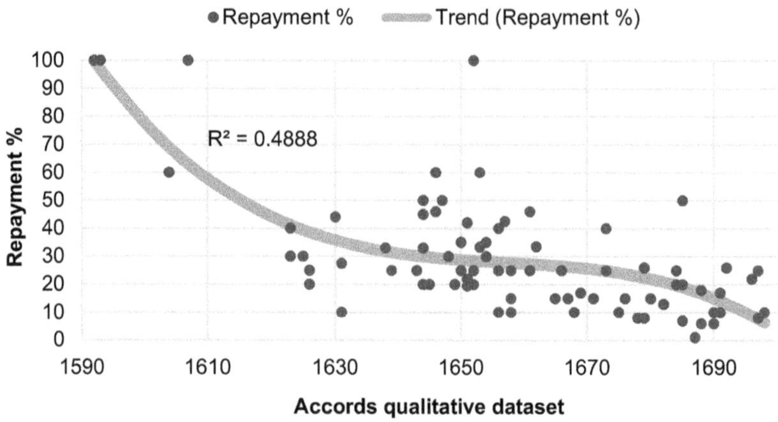

FIGURE 5.2 Repayment percentages per accord in the qualitative dataset (1592–1700)

every dot represents one accord from my qualitative dataset.[24] It is clear that well before the establishment of the Desolate Boedelskamer in 1643, the average repayment percentage – which at that time still had to be agreed upon by all creditors involved in an insolvency – markedly decreased, and continued to do so over the remainder of the seventeenth century.

This general trend, which displays a second substantial decrease in the repayment percentages that were agreed upon in the average accord in the 1660s, can most probably be linked to the updates of the ordinance of the Desolate Boedelskamer in 1647 and 1659, which seriously influenced the accord procedure that had developed under the public notaries in the first half of the seventeenth century. We will now turn to these important innovations.

GAS, 5075: NA, inv. nr. 58, ff. 122v–126r (Hans van den Bergh, 1604) and GAS, 5075: NA, inv. nr. 12, ff. 186v–187v (Sion Luz, 1607). Luz also operated as *tafelhouder* or pawnbroker in Amsterdam until the establishment of the local pawnshop in 1614, see L. Jansen, *Geschiedenis van de Stads Bank van Lening te Amsterdam 1614–1964* (Amsterdam: Stads-kredietbank voor Roerende Zaken, 1964), 14–19.

24 This dataset contains seventeen accords registered by notaries before 1643, as well as randomly selected samples from the collection of accords preserved in the archives of the Desolate Boedelskamer after that date, which were analyzed in their entirety. In order to be able to study the effect of the new 1659 ordinance, I selected thirty accords from the first two decades of the court's functioning, and about ten from each of the last four decades of the seventeenth century. See the Appendix for more information.

Accords under the Desolate Boedelskamer

On November 6, 1643, the commissioners of the Desolate Boedelskamer started their work, in accordance with the instructions of its rather succinct founding ordinance.[25] In the first decades of its operation, these instructions were elaborated upon in two "amplifications" of March 25, 1644 and, more important for our present purpose, April 19, 1647. On April 2, 1659, a completely revised and expanded ordinance went into effect. In this section, I will discuss these changes to the ordinances and how they impacted the procedure and form of the accords.

In 1643, the only regulations stipulated for the accord were that it had to be concluded within six weeks after an insolvent estate had been taken into the court's care, unless the commissioners decided to prolong this term. Once the insolvent had determined how much of their debts were covered by their estate, they would propose the conditions for a potential accord to the commissioners. On January 5, 1644, the commissioners decided that after such a proposal had been worked out on paper by secretary Frans Bruijningh, it would be *omgedragen* or "carried around" to be signed by all creditors by one of the clerks.[26] For the late seventeenth century, we know that insolvents often gathered at least some of their creditors in an inn such as *De Witte Molen op 't Singel over de Warmoesgracht*. There, they would discuss the conditions of the proposed accord before it was presented to the commissioners of the Desolate Boedelskamer and deposited for signing, which presumably increased the likelihood of obtaining sufficient support. It is possible that such gatherings might have taken place from a much earlier period, but their informal nature makes it unlikely to find evidence for them in the official records.[27]

If an accord was concluded with the creditors' approval, the estate's management and documentation were once more handed over to the insolvent, upon payment of an allowance for expenses incurred by

[25] Gerard Rooseboom (ed.), *Recueil van verscheyde keuren, en costumen; midtsgaders maniere van procederen binnen de stadt Amsterdam*, 2nd ed. (Amsterdam: Jan Hendricks, 1656), 304–9.

[26] GAS, 5072: DB, inv. nr. 1, f. 28r.

[27] W. F. H. Oldewelt, "Twee eeuwen Amsterdamse faillissementen en het verloop van de conjunctuur (1636 tot 1838)," *Tijdschrift voor Geschiedenis* 75, no. 4 (1962): 421–35, 422; Anon., *Amsterdamsche secretary*, 322.

the court during the *curatele*. When the commissioners asked the burgomasters how high this allowance should be, on January 30, 1644 it was decided that insolvents who managed to conclude an accord would have to pay 0.5 percent of the net amount paid out to the creditors as the court's due. If no accord could be reached and the estate needed to be executed, 1 percent of the proceeds from the auctions were to be assigned to the Desolate Boedelskamer.[28]

A few years later, in 1647, the burgomasters decreed that henceforth, no accords could be concluded between insolvents and their creditors without involvement of the Desolate Boedelskamer. This most likely ended the practice of concluding accords before notaries. This move towards a closer supervision on the conclusion of such agreements would have helped to ensure that the rights of all creditors were respected. At the same time, however, majority compositions were explicitly allowed for the first time. As I have not found any archival evidence of this phenomenon before 1647, it must have constituted an important innovation in the Amsterdam insolvency procedure. The *ampliatie*, a later addition to the original ordinance, states that when a majority of the creditors representing three-quarters of the debts supported an accord, it would enter into effect. If there were any creditors who opposed the agreement, they would be given the opportunity to appoint one or more "subrogated curators," who would manage the estate together with the guarantors who had undersigned the agreement. From time to time, they would have to account for their administration to the commissioners. Any proceeds were to be handed over to the court, in order to be distributed *pro rata* to signed and unsigned creditors alike.[29]

The new ordinance of 1659 was a much more elaborate revision and expansion of the original instructions from the 1640s. While before this date, a curator was only appointed if no accord could be concluded, henceforth this was one of the first steps in the insolvency procedure (as discussed in Chapter 3). Instead of the commissioners themselves, the curators would now manage the estate during the period in which the insolvent tried to arrive at an agreement with their creditors. The new ordinance also expanded the rules for majority compositions. After 1659, an accord would enter into effect once

[28] GAS, 5072: DB, inv. nr. 1, f. 52. [29] Rooseboom, *Recueil*, 310–11.

either three-quarters of the creditors holding two-thirds of the total debts, or two-thirds of the creditors holding three-quarters of the total debts had signed the proposal.[30] From this moment onwards, increasing numbers of accords began to include a list of all signed and unsigned creditors, specifying the magnitude of their claims and including a calculation to show whether a majority had been reached or not. This provides valuable data on the number of creditors and the size of their claims.[31]

In order to create sufficient support among the creditors to conclude a legally valid accord, it was of crucial importance to notify them of the insolvency and the fact that an agreement had been proposed. This would have been easy if they lived in Amsterdam, but when they resided abroad the chance that they would hear of a debtor's financial problems in time to influence the procedure was much smaller. Informing both domestic and foreign creditors was important for the insolvent themself, who needed their signatures for the accord, but also ensured the inclusiveness and transparency of the insolvency procedure as a whole. The creation of the Desolate Boedelskamer, which employed standardized procedures for the notification of creditors all over Europe, was an important innovation in this regard.

The efforts made in Amsterdam to protect the rights of foreign creditors were remarkable when compared to procedures in other early modern commercial hubs.[32] While originally, the clerks of the Desolate Boedelskamer actively gathered the creditors' signatures, these visits seem to have been replaced by convocations of all creditors in the court after 1659. Article 7 of that year's new ordinance is dedicated to the procedure for accords, "to ensure that such compositions are concluded in an orderly fashion." Amsterdam residents

[30] Hermanus Noordkerk (ed.), *Handvesten; ofte privilegien ende octroyen: mitsgaders willekeuren, costuimen, ordonnantien en handelingen der stad Amstelredam*, 4 vols. (Amsterdam: Hendrik van Waesberge, Salomon en Petrus Schouten, 1748), II:687–88.

[31] The first example I encountered: GAS, 5072: DB, inv. nr. 1400 (Jan Mathes Smits, 1661).

[32] For an elaborate discussion of this development, see Maurits den Hollander and Remko Mooi, "Protecting the Foreign Creditor: International Insolvency in Early Modern Amsterdam and Frankfurt Am Main," *TSEG/ Low Countries Journal of Social and Economic History* 16, no. 3–4 (2020): 37–57.

would be notified through a citation and placards, while "informing letters" or *weetbrieven* would be distributed to (foreign) creditors outside of the city.[33] A thorough analysis of one of the registers of the commissioners' minutes, covering the period between August 1699 and February 1702, uncovered twenty-four cases in which an act of rehabilitation was issued after an accord had been concluded between debtor and creditors. In twenty-two of these cases, the commissioners communicated with creditors through placards and/or letters. Out of the 171 creditors who were informed about one of these insolvencies, 60 (or 35 percent) were foreigners who were contacted through *weetbrieven*. The actual number of foreign creditors involved in these insolvencies must have been even higher, as some of the people contacted through placards (because they lived in Amsterdam) acted as *procureurs* or representatives of foreign parties rather than on their own account.[34] It is clear that these proactive communication policies resulted in a rather more transparent and inclusive insolvency procedure, which might have supported the proliferation of (foreign) credit available to Amsterdam merchants and businessmen. Perhaps the commissioners or the Amsterdam municipal government felt that they needed to strengthen creditors' rights by actively reaching out to them when an accord was proposed after majority compositions had been introduced in 1647. Henceforth, inaction might result in a *de facto* acquittal of part of their claims, necessitating action on the part of unwilling creditors. In order to enable them to do so, extra efforts would need to be made to ensure that all voices would be heard.

However, a survey of older minutes suggests that the situation around 1700 is typical of the way in which the Desolate Boedelskamer had communicated with creditors outside of Amsterdam from its establishment in 1643 onwards. In the minutes regarding one of the first accords discussed by the commissioners, that of Fransoys Lodewijckx and Emanuel Pelt from December 1643, it is explicitly mentioned that "because part of their debt concerns creditors from outside the country," letters had to be sent before the accord could be ratified, as the commissioners argued that it was undesirable to deprive them of the chance to sign or oppose the arrangement as it

[33] Noordkerk, *Handvesten*, II:687. [34] GAS, 5072: DB, inv. nr. 30.

had been drawn up by those present.[35] This highlights that the commissioners' concern for an inclusive treatment of all creditors, both local and foreign, was voiced from the very beginning of the court's functioning.

While Magnus Ressel justifiably draws parallels between the insolvency regimes of Venice and Amsterdam, with regard to creditor-friendliness the Amsterdam commissioners definitely surpassed their Venetian counterparts. In Venice, creditors who did not register in time would lose their claims at the conclusion of an accord.[36] In Amsterdam, the Desolate Boedelskamer itself proactively compiled a list of creditors from the books and papers of the insolvent and secured their claims. Before an insolvent could receive their act of rehabilitation after concluding an accord, they had to deliver to the bookkeeper sufficient means to repay to their unsigned creditors all future instalments that had been agreed upon. Rather than making it their own responsibility to be informed and to react on time, the commissioners actively reached out to foreign creditors and safely stored their share of the proceeds. If at a later time they satisfactorily proved their claims, this money would be handed over to them straight away.[37]

Of course, some creditors never claimed the sums that had been allocated to them during a procedure. According to the commissioners serving in 1800, this often happened when the amount was simply too low to warrant the effort of its collection, or when a creditor was "lost" and could not be reached by notifications about the insolvency procedure and its resulting proceeds. The fact that commissioner Jacob Reynst had already made similar remarks on this phenomenon in January 1666 suggests that the Desolate Boedelskamer's reserves must have grown substantially throughout its existence. This meant that the commissioners managed a great amount of capital, the interest of which was used as an addition to the city-tax or *stadsregt* to pay for the court's expenses. Sometimes, the commissioners – after receiving the permission of the burgomasters – even extended loans to the city.

35 GAS, 5072: DB, inv. nr. 1, ff. 26v–27v.

36 Magnus Ressel, "Norms and Practice of Handling Complex and International Insolvencies in Early Modern Venice," in *Dealing with Economic Failure: Between Norm and Practice (15th to 21st Century)*, ed. Albrecht Cordes and Margrit Schulte Beerbühl (Frankfurt am Main: Peter Lang, 2016), 124–27.

37 GAS, 5072: DB, inv. nr. 58, f. 54r.

Moll remarks that the first of these transactions concerned a loan of fl. 200,000 in 1654, but that he had not encountered any other examples until a similar-sized transaction occurred in 1759. If we can believe the alderman Hans Bontemantel as informed by Reynst, however, at least one further loan of fl. 250,000 was extended to the city's *tresoriers* in January 1666. The fact that in 1800, the court's capital amounted to a staggering fl. 1,229,217, safely suggests that these banking operations never endangered the interests of the creditors.[38]

As discussed in Chapter 2, Charles V's ordinances from the 1540s completely ruled out the possibility of majority compositions that would bind unwilling creditors. However, the development towards a broader acceptance and application of majority compositions in contemporary practice is also reflected in the writings of Dutch legal scholars from this period onwards. In 1662, Simon van Leeuwen stated that a *pactum remissorium* with a majority of creditors binding a minority was lawful if no harm was done to the minority – that is, if the acceptance of the *pactum* improved their situation. This could be the case, for instance, when heirs refused to accept an inheritance unless some debts were acquitted, the traditional example from Roman law in which a legal *remissio* was possible. Another example in which a partial acquittal of debts would be acceptable were cases in which a fugitive debtor offered to return in exchange for a reduction of their debts. This was also accepted by later authors such as Johannes Voet.[39] This signifies an important development, in which the possibility for majority compositions was broadened from the single case, as it was in Roman law, to a much larger group of insolvent estates.

It is important to keep in mind that even when the agreed-upon repayment percentages only covered part of the debt, in principle accords that

[38] Goswin Moll, *De Desolate Boedelskamer te Amsterdam: bijdrage tot de kennis van het Oud-Hollandsch failliten-recht* (Amsterdam: De Roever-Kröber-Bakels, 1879), 198–200; Hans Bontemantel, *De regeeringe van Amsterdam, soo in 't civiel als crimineel en militaire (1653–1672)*, ed. Gerhard Wilhelm Kernkamp (The Hague: Martinus Nijhoff, 1897), 524.

[39] While Dalhuisen states that the ban on majority compositions would still be present in the work of Van Leeuwen or Voet, this is actually more nuanced. Both authors argue against a *remissio*, a reduction of debt, but do not preclude a majority-imposed *dilatio*, a delay of its repayment: Dalhuisen, *Compositions in Bankruptcy*, 22 (n. 101), referring to Simon van Leeuwen, *Het Rooms-Hollands-regt [etc.]* (Leiden/Rotterdam: Hackens, 1664), lib. 4, ch. 41, nr. 7; Gisbertus Voetius, *Commentarius Ad Pandectas*, 2 vols. (Leiden: Johannes Verbessel, 1698) I:lib. 2, tit. 14, nr. 23 ff.

were concluded in seventeenth-century Amsterdam never truly acquitted an insolvent of their responsibility to repay the remainder. Even though creditors could no longer "molest" their debtor or start a lawsuit over debts falling under the ratified accord, it always remained an insolvent's moral obligation to repay the creditors if they ever managed to revive their business and gain new wealth. Almost every accord included a formula that expressed this principle, as exemplified by this passage from the accord of Abraham Boddens, dated on July 3, 1662:

> Voorts hebben de crediteuren van haerder sijde op conditien als voiren, ende van haer voorscreven drie-en-dartich ende half percento voldaen sijnde den voornoemde Abraham Boddens haeren debiteur gequiteert, als sij hem quiteeren mits desen haer vordere reste van haer respective achterwesen mits dese conditie nochtans soo hij hiernae tot prosperiteijt quaeme, ende middelen vercreech hij hem sal hebben te quijten ende daerinne doen naer sijn vermogen, sonder nochtans in rechte noch daer buijten daeromme aengesproocken, oft gemolesteert te mogen werden …[40]

> [Furthermore, provided that the aforementioned thirty-three and one-half percent has been repaid, the creditors from their side promise to acquit the aforementioned Abraham Boddens, their debtor, from all his further arrears, upon the express condition that if he might reverse his fortune at some future moment to the extent that he might once more have the means at his disposal to repay the remainder of their claims, he would have to make good on these old debts, however, [the creditors] could not legally harass or prosecute him for these claims, whether in court or otherwise …]

This knowledge would have made it easier for creditors to accept accords which directly covered only a small part of their outstanding debts. In this sense, one might argue that the accords from seventeenth-century Amsterdam were actually closer in nature to the Roman *dilatio*, which also failed to provide for an official discharge of debts, than to the *remissio*, even if they generally comprised an unspecified and thus potentially eternal extension of the repayment date.

The Amsterdam example of a Desolate Boedelskamer was soon followed up in other cities in the Dutch Republic.[41] When observing these developments, it is unsurprising that at just this moment scholars

[40] GAS, 5072: DB, inv. nr. 1418.

[41] See section "Insolvency in the Dutch Republic" in the final chapter below; Maurits den Hollander, "Failliet in de Republiek. Lokale ordonnanties over de omgang met desolate boedels, circa 1643–1713," *Pro Memorie* 24, no. 2 (2022): 190–217.

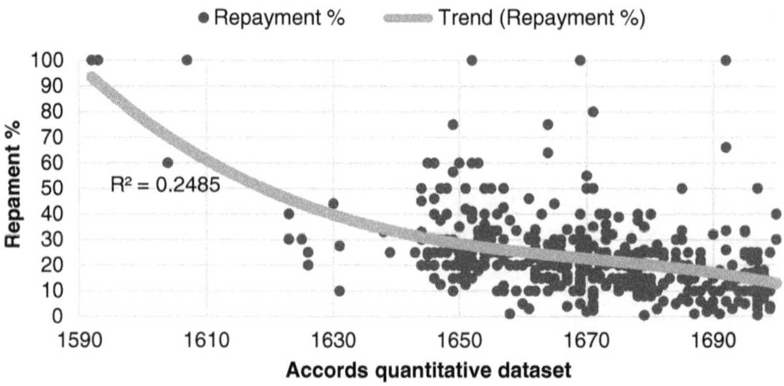

FIGURE 5.3 Repayment percentages per accord in the quantitative dataset (1592–1700)

such as Van Leeuwen also start to include this legal technique in their doctrine. The possibility of a majority composition should be characterized as one of the major innovations of insolvency legislation in the seventeenth-century Dutch Republic, a clear example of how its legal scholarship was open to the adoption of legal techniques and concepts from contemporary practice.

The possibility of concluding accords based upon a majority composition after 1647 was most likely the factor that caused the further decline of average repayment percentages in Amsterdam accords concluded after that date, which we saw in Figure 5.2. These findings are backed up by similar data from the quantitative dataset, each dot again representing one accord (see Figure 5.3).

An accord which guaranteed larger immediate returns would also have a greater chance of being accepted by all creditors, while as the repayment percentage dwindled more and more of them would be prone to oppose the agreement. The possibility of overruling a number of unwilling creditors increased the chance that a less generous accord would still be accepted. However, the downward trend of repayment percentages over time might also be related to other variables, such as increasing amounts of debts per accord over time. Larger debts could potentially be more difficult to repay, which would result in a lower repayment percentage. However, the quantitative dataset does not support this reasoning. In Figure 5.4, the total value of the debts in each insolvency that was resolved through an accord has been plotted

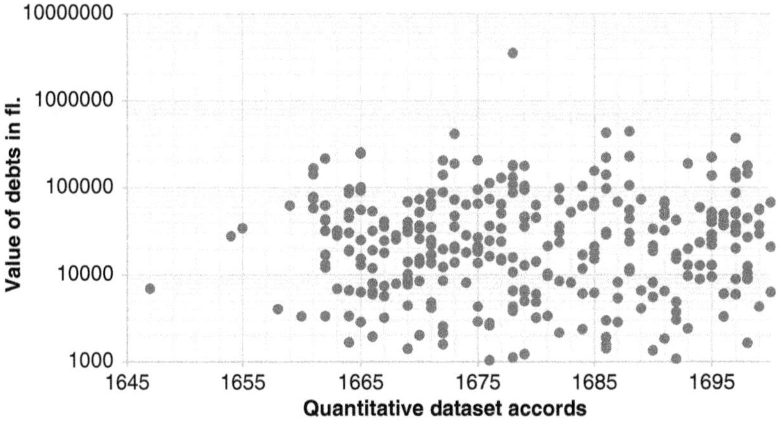

FIGURE 5.4 Value of debts per insolvency in which an accord was concluded in the quantitative dataset on a logarithmic scale (1647–1700)

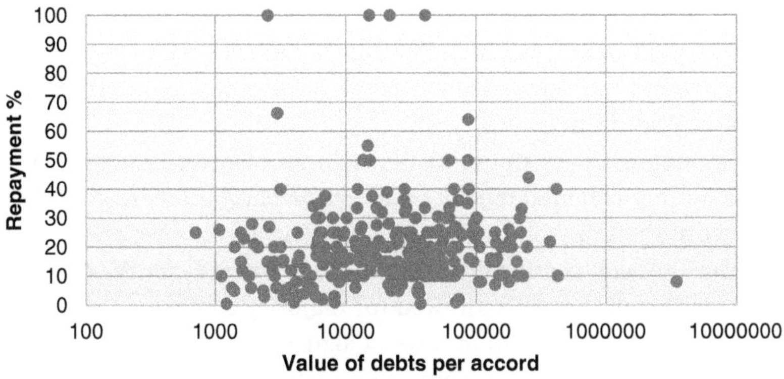

FIGURE 5.5 Repayment percentages related to the value of debts per insolvency in which an accord was concluded in the quantitative dataset (1592–1700)

on a logarithmic scale. As the datapoints are quite evenly scattered over the entire second half of the seventeenth century – the horizontal axis represents the chronology in this graph – this suggests that the average size of insolvent estates did not markedly increase during this period. Therefore, this variable cannot explain the further decrease in average repayment percentages that we observe in this period.

Furthermore, there is no quantitative evidence that the total amount of debt had a large influence on the repayment percentages agreed upon by creditors. In Figure 5.5, the value of debts linked to each individual accord (on the horizontal axis) has been related to the repayment percentage that was agreed upon in each of these compositions (on the vertical axis). Once more, the size of the insolvent estate does not appear to have influenced the repayment percentages.

It is interesting to observe that the vast majority of the accords concluded before the Desolate Boedelskamer agreed upon repayment percentages of 40 percent or less. How can we explain this phenomenon? It is possible that when an insolvent was able to cover as much as 80 percent or 90 percent of their debts, their liquidity was simply too high to warrant involvement of the Desolate Boedelskamer and the costs related to its management of an estate in the first place. Especially when personal relations with the creditors, most of whom would be long-term business contacts, were good, in such cases some (unregistered) delayed payments or interest renegotiations would suffice to secure financial continuity. Only when a debtor ran out of such options, or their creditors urgently needed the money themselves, would the debtor truly become insolvent and end up in the commissioners' care.

The number of creditors involved in an insolvency might have had a more substantial impact on the insolvents' ability to conclude an accord than the total value of debts. For accords between 1647 and the 1660s, it is difficult to establish the precise number of creditors. Although the court allowed for majority compositions in this period, it did not yet require lists of signed and unsigned creditors to be produced. Therefore, some unsigned creditors may be missing from the totals for the twenty-two accords from these years in the qualitative dataset. Still, these data remain too valuable to neglect, as they do provide us with a sense of magnitude. Figure 5.6 displays the relation between the number of creditors per accord (on the horizontal axis) and the repayment percentage that was eventually agreed upon (on the vertical axis), based upon my qualitative dataset. For the sake of transparency, the accords from the period in which we cannot be sure about the total number of creditors have been plotted as dark gray dots, while the other accords are all displayed in pale gray.

One might expect that a higher number of creditors would make it harder to form a majority for an accord that only guaranteed a

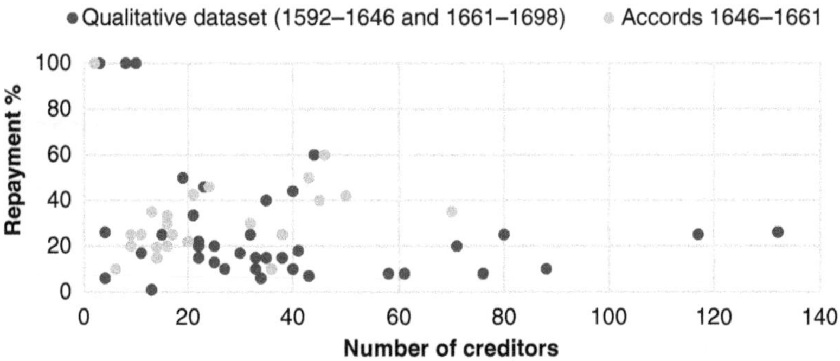

FIGURE 5.6 Repayment percentages related to the number of creditors per insolvency in which an accord was concluded in the qualitative dataset

relatively low repayment percentage. Interestingly, the accords with the highest repayment percentages actually all concerned insolvencies with limited numbers of creditors. Even if this might in part be explained by the fact that these were early cases, concluded in a period when accords generally covered the entire amount of debt, the fact that this concerns only four cases makes it impossible to derive any meaningful conclusions from this observation. In 1684, for instance, Jan Verbiest concluded an accord with his nineteen creditors that covered 50 percent of his debts worth fl. 15,178; this shows that high numbers of creditors did not necessarily preclude high repayment percentages.[42] Even after the 1659 ordinance created ample space for majority compositions, in some cases, relatively small numbers of creditors could still expect considerable repayment percentages if warranted by the condition of the estate. If we can conclude anything from this data, it is that the dynamics of the negotiations between creditors and debtors must have played an important role in the ultimate conditions of a proposed accord and whether or not that could secure majority support. While repayment percentages must have been an important factor for creditors when deciding whether or not to support a proposed accord, such agreements tended to have at least one further characteristic that made them preferable to a simple execution sale: guarantors. I will now turn to this essential form of security, which supported the credibility of the insolvents' proposed solutions for their repayment problems.

[42] GAS, 5072: DB, inv. nr. 1689.

Guarantors

Accords were always agreements full of promises, and creditors could never be completely sure that their conditions would actually be fulfilled in practice. Therefore, such agreements were almost always backed up by one or more guarantors, who pledged their own person and possessions for one or all of the instalments agreed upon in the accord. Through their involvement, the creditors received an additional security that at least the part of their claim that was included in the accord would be repaid.[43] In this section, I will examine this practice in further detail. Who were these guarantors? Why were they willing to risk their own goods to support the insolvent? And which legal rules shaped such constructions in seventeenth-century practice? In order to illustrate these practices I will describe the case of the Portuguese-Jewish merchant Isacq Nunes Bernal in great detail. This interesting figure concluded not just one, but a whole series of accords. What happened to these old debts, and can we find his old creditors and guarantors in the new agreements of the 1670s?

The first time we encounter Isacq Nunes Bernal and his business partner Abraham de Castres in the Desolate Boedelskamer is on December 16, 1668, when they conclude an accord with the creditors of their ailing business partnership. In two instalments of six months each, the creditors would receive one-third of their claims. The creditors Michiel Marcelis and Isacq de Mercado would aid Bernal, De Castres, and their guarantors Raphael Bernal and Simon Francisco Bernal in the management of the estate, in order "to ensure that the instalments shall be fulfilled promptly."[44] Apparently, their actions to liquidate the effects of the business and pursue its outstanding claims were rather less successful than they expected in December 1668. Just before the first six months had passed, instead of paying out the first instalment promised in their accord, Bernal and De Castres recalled their creditors to the Desolate Boedelskamer to renegotiate the agreement.

While, unfortunately, we do not possess an overview of signed and unsigned creditors and the values of their debts for the original 1668 accord, this was included in the new agreement concluded on May 20, 1669. When comparing the creditors to those whose signatures could

[43] Anon., *Amsterdamsche secretary*, 60. [44] GAS, 5072: DB, inv. nr. 1491.

be identified under the 1668 accord, six new signed creditors and four new unsigned creditors can be added to the case. Interestingly, three creditors who signed the original agreement now feature among the unsigned creditors. Perhaps they did not wish to accept the new conditions, which were rather less appealing than those from December 1668. As part of the revised accord, Bernal and De Castres would pay their creditors 24 percent of their claims, 12 percent within one month (i.e. at the time at which the first instalment of the 1668 accord would have been paid out) and the remainder six months after the first instalment. It seems that this new agreement was necessitated by the guarantors' inability to cover the entire gap between the promised payments and the proceeds from the insolvent business. The total debts of fl. 30,909 would have resulted in repayments exceeding fl. 10,000 under the original conditions, which were now reduced to about fl. 7,418. This reasoning is supported by the fact that in the 1669 accord, only the second term of 12 percent is secured by Raphael Bernal and Simon Francisco Bernal, while the first term is now underwritten by Daniel Vaez. Besides that, all three guarantors promise that all preferential creditors would be paid out at the time of the first instalment, one month after the accord "obtained its members."[45]

As we do not find any further traces of this case in the archives, it is probably safe to assume that the obligations agreed upon in the revised accord were met by the insolvents and their guarantors. In both accords, the guarantors renounced their right to make use of a legal benefice called *ordinis divisiones et excussiones*. This would have provided each of them with the protection that they could only be executed for their share, rather than the whole, of the debt that they had undersigned.[46] Of course, the *ordinis divisions et excussiones* undermined the creditors' security, which was the principal reason why almost every accord with multiple guarantors included a formal renunciation of this form of legal protection. Since the guarantors had renounced this protection, the creditors could seek the entire debt from any one of them.

45 GAS, 5072: DB, inv. nr. 1500.

46 Hugo de Groot, *Inleidinge tot de Hollandsche rechts-geleerdheid*, ed. F. Dovring, H. F. W. D. Fischer, and E. M. Meijers, 2nd ed. (Universitaire Pers Leiden, 1965), 211–12; Martinus Caesar, *Ius hodiernum ofte hedens-daaghs recht beschreven ende gecolligeert naer ordre ende tot elucidatie van de vier boecken der institutien des keizers Justiniani* (Amsterdam: Dirck Meyer, 1656), 214–15.

When in 1676, Isacq Nunes Bernal was again unable to meet his personal financial obligations, it is interesting to note that only five creditors match the list of those involved in the 1669 insolvency. Three of them had minor claims, and the remaining two were probably relatives: (H)esther Vaez, who signed for a claim on her personal account and as representative of Elias Nunes Bernal from Bayonne, was the widow of Daniel Vaez, who featured as guarantor in 1669. Interestingly, she is also described by the alias Beatrix Bermuda, similar to Isacq Nunes Bernal's alias George Bermuda. This strongly suggests that she was a sister or other close relative who supported her kin in times of financial hardship. It is clear that after wrapping up his former business with Abraham De Castres, Bernal had managed to revive his commercial activities on a considerable scale, as the accord concluded with his personal creditors on September 28, 1676 concerns debts valued at fl. 36,311.

Bernal promised to pay his creditors 7.5 percent of their claims in cash as soon as the accord had been accepted by a legal majority, and another 7.5 percent six months after the first instalment. The widow Hester Vaez, assisted by mr. Nicolaes Eversdijck – a public notary who also acted as her legal guardian – would serve as guarantor for the complete 15 percent. Eversdijck, "speaking the Spanish and Portuguese languages," translated the conditions of the accord for Vaez. This ensured that she understood the implications of her renunciation of the benefice *senatus consulti velliani*, which stipulated that women could not legally bind themselves, and the Amsterdam bylaw or *keure* that sought to protect women by forbidding them to serve as guarantors.[47] If she had been Bernal's wife rather than a widowed relative, it would also have been necessary to renounce the benefice *authenticae siqua mulier*, which made it impossible for a married woman to legally bind herself in favor of her husband.[48] According to the anonymous author of the *Amsterdamsche secretary*, the renunciation of the two aforementioned benefices should be

[47] De Groot, *Inleidinge*, 210; Jacob de Coeur, *Styl der notarissen; zynde een verzameling van actens, contracten en instrumenten, dagelyks dienende tot de notariale practyk* (The Hague: Cornelis van Zanten, 1740), 351.

[48] De Groot, *Inleidinge*, 210; Bernhard van Zutphen, *Practycke der Nederlansche rechten vande daghelijcksche soo civile als criminele questien* (Leeuwarden: Dominicus Lens, 1664), 57.

sufficient to effectuate a (married) woman's surety for a debt, but it was common practice to explicitly include the reference to the protective Amsterdam bylaw *om alle questien van twistgierige en pleitzieke menschen te voorkomen*, or "to avoid troublesome questions from contentious and litigious people."[49]

After 1676, Bernal seems to have continued his business on a much smaller scale. The last time we encounter him in the Desolate Boedelskamer, at the conclusion of his final accord on July 22, 1680, his estate is indebted for a sum of fl. 14,146. The great majority is owed to Hester Vaez, probably a remnant of her surety for the 1676 agreement. Bernal, who is once again unable to fulfil his outstanding obligations to a large number of small creditors, offers them 7.5 percent of their claims within three months, and another 7.5 percent three months after the first instalment. Hesther Vaez, even though she is by far his largest creditor, again supports the accord as guarantor, this time together with Ester Nunes. The widow Vaez is assisted by Isaacq Vaez Henriques, Ester Nunes by Jacob de Cordoña, while the notary Hendrick Outgers confirms that he has "faithfully translated, interpreted and read out" the accord and especially the passages concerning the guarantors in the Portuguese language.[50] On November 19, 1680, the commissioners provided Isacq Nunes Bernal with his final act of rehabilitation after the accord had been accepted by a legal majority of his creditors.[51]

So far, so good, one would think. However, this story becomes even more intriguing once we consider that the widow Hesther Vaez was forced to conclude an accord with her own creditors under her alias Beatrix Bermuda on May 13, 1680, less than two months before Bernal's final accord! Judging from the inventory of her personal estate, which only consists of a single page listing a number of old pieces of furniture, and which states that she and her late husband "had been living on the Swanenburgh Burghwal," it appears that by the time of her insolvency she might have moved in with one of her children.[52] As only two out of twelve creditors can be linked to one of Bernal's accords, Hester's debts worth fl. 5,994 must have resulted from her personal acts, even if we cannot exclude the possibility that

[49] Anon., *Amsterdamsche secretary*, 66. [50] GAS, 5072: DB, inv. nr. 1651.
[51] GAS, 5072: DB, inv. nr. 24, f. 75v. [52] GAS, 5072: DB, inv. nr. 607, f. 171r.

acting as guarantor for Bernal might have forced her to enter into additional loans. The accord proposed by the widow, in which she promised to repay 20 percent of all debts within five months, was signed by all but one of her creditors. Isaacq Vaes Henriques and Rachel Nunes de Castres acted as guarantors, the latter assisted by Isaacq Mendes de Aquirre (if need arose).[53] Notary Hendrick Outgers once again made sure that Hester and Rachel understood the contents of the document through the provision of a Portuguese translation.[54] On June 18, 1680, the commissioners concluded that after a notification had been issued, the majority of the creditors had signed the agreement. Therefore, they issued Vaez's act of rehabilitation on that same day.[55]

Inserted into the accord file, we find a separate document drafted on May 1, 1679 by the public notary Nicolaes Brouwer in which he provides an overview of transactions between Daniel Vaez and Thomas van Hoffland between 1675 and 1678. This is slightly puzzling, as Hester Vaez is already described as a widow in Bernal's 1676 accord. Presumably, she continued her deceased husband's business, perhaps assisted by her children or relatives. The registered transactions resulted in a balance of fl. 437 in favor of Van Hoffland, which closely corresponds with the fl. 400 for which he is noted as unsigned creditor in Hester's accord one year later. Perhaps, it is unsurprising that Van Hoffland, as the only nonsigning creditor, does not seem to share the Jewish-Portuguese background of Hester's other major creditors.[56] Of course, this raises a number of questions. Why, for instance, was Hester Vaez able to act as guarantor for Bernal's 1680 accord with any degree of credibility? How can we explain the different treatment of Van Hoffland's claim in her personal accord file? And what was the role of the Sephardic Jewish community in the crafting of this specific series of legal agreements?

[53] It is interesting to note that Isaacq Vaes Henriques also became insolvent himself about eight years later, proposing an accord to his creditors for debts worth fl. 29,954 on June 1, 1688. As part of the agreement, which was, however, not secured by any guarantors, the insolvent promised to repay 18 percent of his debts: GAS, 5072: DB, inv. nr. 1726. On this case, which eventually resulted in an act of rehabilitation on November 2, 1688, see also GAS, 5072: DB, inv. nr. 26, ff. 75r, 90 and 91.

[54] GAS, 5072: DB, inv. nr. 1647.

[55] GAS, 5072: DB, inv. nr. 24, ff. 54 and 59.

[56] GAS, 5072: DB, inv. nr. 1647.

Before migrating to Amsterdam, the Vaez family had played a prominent role in sixteenth-century Lisbon, even though they were part of the *Marranos*, Jews who had been forcibly converted to Christianity. One of its members, Ayres Vaez, functioned as personal physician to King John III of Portugal, but later lost royal favor and even had to defend himself against charges by the Inquisition. He was saved by his brother Salvador, who acted as page to the papal nuncio Hiernoymo Ricenati Capodiferro. Abraham Vaez is mentioned as an important scholar and *hakam* of the Jewish community in seventeenth-century Bayonne, while Daniel Vaez acted in a similar scholarly role in Amsterdam. Together with Joseph Athias, he wrote a prayer-book titled *Orden de las Oraciones del Todo el Anno* that was published in 1677.[57] On January 24, 1657, Daniel Vaez "aged around forty" acted as witness in an attestation drafted by public notary Benedict Baddel related to a medical dispute.[58] It is probably no coincidence that Jacob d'Acosta Athias appears as an important creditor to Isacq Nunes Bernal as well as Hester Vaez, and that both Daniel (in 1669) and Hester (in 1676) acted as procurator of "Elias Nunes Bernal of Bayonne" in Isacq's accords.

This explains how social capital in the form of a family's standing within a subcommunity in seventeenth-century Amsterdam might help to obtain majorities for accords that would not have been concluded based upon strictly rational economic criteria. In this sense, Hester Vaez might still have been a valuable guarantor in 1680 due to her name and reputation rather than her solid finances, especially as Bernal's accord was also secured by Ester Nunes. Of course, the trust and credit obtained through such social capital would not count outside of the Jewish community, since it was based on respect for her family's scholarly credentials rather than on her standing as a merchant. The official calculation and registration of the balance between Vaez and Van Hoffland by a public notary and his subsequent refusal to sign her accord, clearly illustrate the difference between creditors

[57] Schulim Ochser, "VAEZ," in *The Jewish Encyclopedia: A Descriptive Record of the History, Religion, Literature, and Customs of the Jewish People from the Earliest Times*, ed. Isidore Singer (New York: Ktav Publishing House, 1906).

[58] A. M. Vaz Dias, "Geneeskundige archivalia. Sprokkels uit het oud notarieel archief te Amsterdam," *Nederlands Tijdschrift voor Geneeskunde* 76, no. 4 (1932): 5584–86.

from within and outside of such social networks. At the same time, it shows how the Jewish religious community could help to smoothen conflicts between debtors and creditors by stimulating the conclusion of an amicable accord in a similar way as the Calvinist consistories strove to arrange arbitrated solutions for honest insolvents in their own communities, as described in Chapter 1.

It is precisely here, where interreligious business contacts resulted in financial problems, that the impartial and professional procedure of the Desolate Boedelskamer could substitute system trust for personal trust in seventeenth-century Amsterdam. Without this institution, someone like Van Hoffland might very well have been unwilling to extend credit to Vaez in the first place, because as an outsider to the Jewish community he could not enforce repayment through private ordering strategies. Because of the existence of a transparent, open-access subsidiary court for insolvency procedures, creditors such as Van Hoffland, and even foreigners, could trust that their interests would be protected to the same extent as those of family members or others who were part of the insolvent's direct social network.[59]

While the number of accords in which Isacq Nunes Bernal and his relatives were involved is exceptional, the ways in which they were supported by varying combinations of guarantors is exemplary for the wider population of insolvents in the qualitative dataset. Of ninety-two accords, in about one-third (thirty-one) no guarantors are mentioned and/or their identity remains unspecified. In another third of the accords (thirty-one), guarantors with a surname different from that of the insolvent are mentioned while no family information is provided. Some accords were secured by the insolvent's wife (five), while in the remainder at least one confirmed family member is mentioned as guarantor, often supported by others (twenty-five). Of course, as we have seen in the accords concerning Isacq Nunes Bernal, family members would often not be directly recognizable through their name. Given the strong reliance of early modern merchants and businessmen on family and kinship networks, it is likely that many guarantors of the second category would also have been relatives of the insolvents whose accords they supported.

[59] See also on this topic Den Hollander and Mooi, "Protecting the Foreign Creditor."

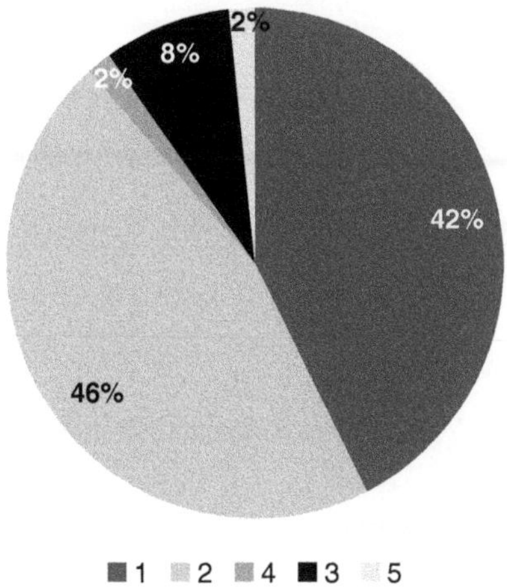

FIGURE 5.7 Number of guarantors per accord in the qualitative dataset

In all four accords, Bernal was aided by various relatives, who provided the financial means needed to secure and eventually fulfil the promises made to his creditors. Without their support, it would probably have been impossible to gather sufficient signatures to create a legal majority. The legal protection flowing forth from the accords allowed Bernal to continue his commercial activities for at least a decade, in which he would otherwise have been incapacitated by lawsuits and other conflicts related to the debts that remained after the execution of his estate. Through the protection and support of the Desolate Boedelskamer and his relatives, Bernal was probably able to generate some profit in the years between his insolvencies, which would ultimately have resulted in larger returns on his creditors' claims than could otherwise have been realized. In all but one of his accords, Bernal was supported by multiple guarantors. This is in line with data found for the population in the qualitative dataset, as displayed in Figure 5.7.

Whereas a slight majority of the accords was supported by more than one guarantor, examples such as the accord concluded in 1669 between Bernal, Casseres, and their creditors were rather exceptional. From the creditors' perspective, a higher number of guarantors would generally have been positive, as this potentially increased their chance of actually receiving the promised repayments. However, there appears to be no correlation between the number of guarantors

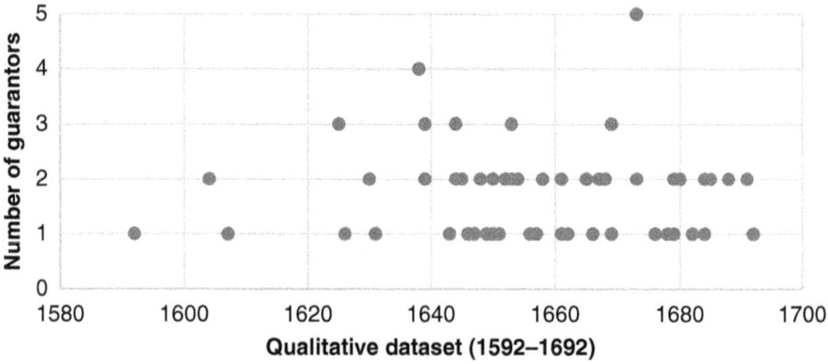

FIGURE 5.8 Chronologic development of the number of guarantors per accord in the qualitative dataset

and the amount of debts in the data from the qualitative dataset. Furthermore, while one might expect that, with the arrival of majority compositions in the second half of the seventeenth century, a demand for higher numbers of guarantors might arise among creditors, as displayed by Figure 5.8 no such conclusion can be derived from the qualitative dataset.

This suggests that the reputation and creditworthiness of the guarantors was more important than their number. In an accord concluded by Pieter Croon and his creditors in 1652, the two guarantors explicitly promise that they will not act as guarantor in any other case for twelve months after the conclusion of the accord.[60] While I have not encountered many examples of such provisions, they clearly constituted an additional strategy to increase the security of the creditors and thus their willingness to sign the accord.

Notwithstanding the increasing opportunities to arrive at an accord through a majority composition with the support of one or more guarantors, many insolvents were faced with a situation in which it was impossible to conclude such amicable agreements. The sixteenth-century princely ordinances already pointed to "fugitive bankrupts" who chose to run off with their remaining possessions rather than face their creditors. While this was strongly condemned, under special conditions it was possible and acceptable to temporarily move to a place of asylum such as Culemborg or Vianen while trying

60 GAS, 5072: DB, inv. nr. 1318.

to come to terms with one's creditors. I will now examine a group of such insolvents, in order to determine to what extent this strategy was successful.

Asylum and the Insolvents' Agency

Jacques Turpijn was probably one of the most notorious Amsterdam insolvents of the seventeenth century. Even though he was a member of the Mennonite Church, which strongly condemned the failure to repay debts in general and harshly punished fraudulent bankrupts, in 1662 the trader in tobacco and jewels absconded with many valuable possessions.[61] This was not something which his creditors, to whom he owed fl. 62,200, would easily accept.[62] Initially, Turpijn fled to Vianen, an old feudal enclave in the province of Holland. Its overlord, the dowager countess Louise Christine of Brederode, regularly extended asylum to various categories of people who had fled their places of residence, after an insolvency or accidental manslaughter, for instance, in exchange for a fee. This practice had arisen in the second half of the sixteenth century, and did not just include the person of the applicant, but also covered their possessions. Other places of asylum in the Dutch Republic included semiautonomous high seigniories such as Culemborg, Buren, Leerdam, and IJsselstein. During their stay abroad, the asylum-seekers would try to conclude an agreement with their creditors, after which they could return home again.[63]

While mocked by authors such as the poet Bredero, the practice of temporarily moving to a place of asylum in order to escape debt imprisonment was quite acceptable for seventeenth-century insolvents. However, when someone who displayed clear signs of fraud, such as Turpijn, received asylum, the Amsterdam authorities would protest. Turpijn's file in the archives of the Desolate Boedelskamer includes a letter from 1662 to the dowager countess of Brederode in

[61] Mary Sprunger, "Faillissementen. Een aspect van geestelijke tucht bij de Waterlands-doopsgezinde gemeente te Amsterdam in de zeventiende eeuw," *Doopsgezinde Bijdragen* 17 (1991): 101–30, 110 (n. 33).

[62] GAS, 5072: DB, inv. nr. 145, p. 44.

[63] Marijke Gijswijt-Hofstra, *Wijkplaatsen voor vervolgden. Asielverlening in Culemborg, Vianen, Buren, Leerdam en Ijsselstein van de 16e tot eind 18e eeuw* (Amsterdam: De Bataafsche Leeuw, 1984).

which Louis Crayers, who had been appointed curator of Turpijn's estate, and various creditors asked her to withdraw her protection from the Amsterdam bankrupt. They describe him as a "seer schandelyck en schelmachtigh bancquerout" or "very outrageous and knavish bankrupt," who had fled the city carrying "diverse kostelycke juwelen ende een grote somme geldts, midsgaders al datter meer voor de hand was" or "diverse valuable jewels and a large sum of money, as well as all other precious goods he had at hand." They requested that they might incarcerate Turpijn in order to take him back to his Amsterdam creditors.[64]

It seems that this request did not have its intended result, as soon afterwards we encounter Turpijn in Culemborg rather than in the Amsterdam prison. On December 11, 1662 Turpijn and his brother-in-law Harman van Uden, who worked in Amsterdam as a wine-buyer, appeared before the public notary Anthonij Govertsz van Gaesbeecq, witnessed by mr. Cornelis van Diemen. Through this act, Turpijn empowers Van Uden to conclude an accord with his creditors. He would retain fl. 6,000, the best bed found in his house, together with its appurtenances, as well as the woolen and linen clothes owned by himself, his deceased wife, and his children. Turpijn would deliver all his jewelry and other remaining possessions to his common creditors if they would acquit him of their claims in exchange.[65]

This proposal was not very advantageous for Turpijn's creditors. Therefore, it is unsurprising that they did not sign it straight away. They seem to have secured the cooperation of the count of Culemborg, just as they were previously assisted by the dowager countess of Vianen, but again the devious Turpijn managed to escape. In 1664, when the accord was finally concluded, he resided in the small city of Buren. On March 21 of that year, co-curator Marcus Broen as well as two commissioners of the Desolate Boedelskamer met Van Uden before the Court of Holland in order to finalize the negotiations for Turpijn's accord. They were aided by a new procuration for Van Uden issued in Buren on February 6, 1664, as well as an inventory of Turpijn's possessions that had been drawn up before the aldermen of that city on February 22. On March 7, 1664, Van Uden

[64] GAS, 5072: DB, inv. nr. 1423, pp. 2–5.
[65] GAS, 5072: DB, inv. nr. 1423, pp. 12–15.

had received a list "to be forwarded to Jacques Turpijn" of the gold, silver, porcelain, and other goods that he would have to give up in order to be able to conclude an accord with his creditors. Apparently, the meeting of March 21 was successful, as a note from April 1664 confirms that Turpijn accepted the conditions that had been agreed upon by his brother-in-law. On April 21, Jacques Turpijn, Van Uden, and his creditors signed the definitive accord.[66]

Even though he had committed fraud and run off to three different asylum cities with his most valuable possessions, eventually Turpijn managed to conclude a generous accord with his creditors. He would be allowed to keep the fl. 6,000 and the possessions already specified in his first instruction for Van Uden in 1662, and based upon the accord he was "completely acquitted and liberated from all actions and pretenses that his common creditors or any one of them individually might sustain or hold against him." In exchange, Turpijn would cede all his other goods and possessions and his own outstanding claims to his creditors. They would also receive his entire books and papers, in order to properly pursue the execution of these debts.[67] On May 30, 1664, the commissioners of the Desolate Boedelskamer confirmed that they had approved the accord concluded between Turpijn and the majority of his creditors. The unsigned creditors would have to adhere to its provisions, and Turpijn was restored to his former freedom.[68] This did not mean that the involvement of the court with this estate was over, however. As the accord had entailed the rather uncommon provision that all goods and effects would be ceded to the creditors, rather than providing for the payment of a certain percentage of the debts, it seems that curator Louys Craeyers remained involved in the management of Turpijn's estate in order to capitalize these assets to the benefit of the common creditors. On November 13, 1665, for instance, the commissioners permitted him to sell "the single grave, situated in the Westerkerk in this city."[69] It is unknown when exactly this case was wrapped up, but it is clear that it was only closed years after the conclusion of the accord.

66 GAS, 5072: DB, inv. nr. 1423, p. 11 (note March 7), p. 23 (note March 21), p. 10 (note April 1664).

67 GAS, 5072: DB, inv. nr. 1423, pp. 6–9 (concept) and pp. 16–17 (neat concept); GAS, 5072: DB, inv. nr. 1434, pp. 6–9 (definitive, signed version).

68 GAS, 5072: DB, inv. nr. 18, f. 38.

69 GAS, 5072: DB, inv. nr. 18, f. 135.

Turpijn, who requested asylum in three different cities, is a spectacular but atypical example of the asylum cases. Besides him, Gijswijt-Hofstra mentions sixty-two other requests for asylum that can be linked to Amsterdam for the seventeenth century. These were all directed at the city of Culemborg, except for the case of Jacob Janssen Weijns, who applied for asylum in Leerdam in 1661.[70] Most of these applicants can be characterized as merchants, while only a handful of artisans attempted to pressure their creditors into an accord by means of a relocation to one of the asylum cities. This can be explained by the fact that asylum was not granted for free. The insolvents had to pay a recognition tax to the authorities who extended their protection, which was progressively increased based upon the value of their debts. Penniless insolvents were not accepted, as they would place a burden on the local social welfare system. This explains why half of the insolvents who obtained asylum in Culemborg had amassed debts worth over fl. 20,000.[71]

While sixty-three insolvents could be linked to Amsterdam, only forty of them can actually be found in the archives of the Desolate Boedelskamer. For eleven cases before 1643, this makes sense, but this leaves a group of eleven insolvents who are not accounted for.[72] It is questionable whether they were really Amsterdam residents, as in that case a curator would always have been appointed as soon as their insolvency became public knowledge. This would certainly have been the case if they fled to Culemborg or Vianen. It is possible that the city that is mentioned might not point to their place of residence, but simply the last place they had visited before arriving at their asylum location. For five of the forty insolvents that could be found back in the Amsterdam archives (12.5 percent), no information could be found about the final resolution of their insolvency.[73] In one case,

[70] Gijswijt-Hofstra, *Wijkplaatsen*, 118–19 and 203–22. Culemborg and Vianan seem to have been the most popular destinations for Amsterdam asylum-seekers, however, this image might be distorted because in Vianen very few records from before 1725 have been preserved (ibid. 101).

[71] Ibid. 66–67 and 89–90.

[72] Three of the eleven Amsterdam cases before 1643 involved bankrupts whose asylum was ended after a request of the Amsterdam authorities. This concerned the cases of Guilian van den Keyboom (1618), Dirck Verstel (1622), and Heijndric van Delhoven (1642). See ibid. 78–79.

[73] This concerns the insolvencies of Mattheus Luls (1654), Jan Janssen Brouwer (1656), Jacob Ruts (1661), Paulus Orth (1663), and Hubert van der Mortel (1697).

that of Hubert van der Mortel, this can be explained by the fact that he passed away while his estate was being managed by the court. On March 6, 1698, an entry in the minutes speaks of the estate of *wijlen* or "the late" Huijbrecht van der Mortel.[74] This might also be true for the other four cases in this category.

It is very interesting to see how the thirty-five cases of which we do know how they were eventually resolved ended. Insolvents would not have gone through the trouble and costs of seeking asylum if they had not expected that this would increase their chances of negotiating an accord with their creditors. An accord was more beneficial for the insolvent than the alternative legal solution of *cessie van goede*, because unlike *cessie* it offered protection against future litigation. Through asylum, the insolvent was able to pressure unwilling creditors, who might reconsider their former resistance and sign the proposed agreement rather than having to wait for years before they could execute their claims by means of a different procedure. For twenty-six Amsterdam insolvents (65 percent) this actually worked out: they managed to end their insolvency with a composition. However, nine of them (22.5 percent) were unable to convince a majority of the creditors, and eventually opted for an application for the benefice of *cessie van goede*. While it saved them from debt imprisonment and formed a socially acceptable legal solution for insolvency, *cessie* could also have been obtained without asylum, and therefore signifies a failure from these insolvents' perspective.

Two of the Amsterdam asylum-seekers who eventually managed to conclude an accord could be characterized as bankrupts rather than unfortunate insolvents. In November 1662, the asylum of Manuel Rodrigues Carion was officially terminated on request of the Amsterdam authorities, who described him as a bankrupt who had acted in bad faith. However, he was only taken into custody in May 1663.[75] It is even more surprising that the commissioners' minutes reveal that shortly afterwards his unsigned creditors received a letter from the Desolate Boedelskamer asking them to sign or refuse Carion's accord, which resulted in his rehabilitation on May 21.[76] Similarly, Melchior Robijn lost his asylum in 1663 due to being accused of false

[74] GAS, 5072: DB, inv. nr. 29, f. 81. [75] Gijswijt-Hofstra, *Wijkplaatsen*, 80.
[76] GAS, 5072: DB, inv. nr. 18, ff. 98 and 102v.

bookkeeping. However, in March 1664 a majority of his creditors complied with his request for *seureté du corps*. On September 15, 1664, his unsigned creditors were asked to sign or refuse a proposed accord, which resulted in Robijn's rehabilitation on May 5, 1665.[77]

It might seem strange that creditors still wished to conclude an accord with bankrupts such as Carion and Robijn, who – unlike Turpijn – were no longer protected by asylum and had committed fraud. Presumably, they expected to be able to arrive at a more favorable agreement when the debtor was at their mercy, but at the same time expected higher yields from an accord than from an execution of the estate. As the contemporary Dutch author Pieter de la Court argued, even though bankrupts should in principle be punished and were undeserving of an accord, for the creditors it was *res nummi*, or "a matter of money": they were always allowed to conclude an accord with their debtor if they judged it to be in their favor to do so.[78]

Trying to force an accord upon one's creditors by seeking legal protection in one of the asylum cities was clearly not an option that was available to every Amsterdam insolvent in this period. In line with Gijswijt-Hofstra's findings for Culemborg, the five insolvents for whom I could find the value of their debts all amassed very substantial amounts of credit in the years leading up to their insolvency.[79] While all of these succeeded in concluding an accord, this was generally true for only two-thirds of the insolvent asylum-seekers from Amsterdam in the seventeenth century. The majority of this group consisted of important merchants. But was this also the case for the larger population of insolvents who managed to resolve their cases through an accord? I will now proceed to analyze the characteristics of this larger population.

Characteristics and Identity of the Accord Population

On September 6, 1646, the twenty-three creditors of Anthonij Roesingh signed an accord in which their debtor promised to pay

[77] GAS, 5072: DB, inv. nr. 18, ff. 19v, 53v, and 99v.

[78] Pieter de la Court, *Interest van Holland, ofte gronden van Hollands-welvaren* (Amsterdam: Joan. Cyprianus vander Gracht, 1662), 86.

[79] GAS, 5072: DB, inv. nr. 145: Baltasar Alvares Nogera alias Aelbert Dircks (1659, fl. 62,036); Jacques Turpijn (1664, fl. 62,200); Isaacq del Soto alias Del Monte (1678, fl. 181,509); Henry Hampson (1680, fl. 63,022); and Abraham van Harsele (1691, fl. 65,921).

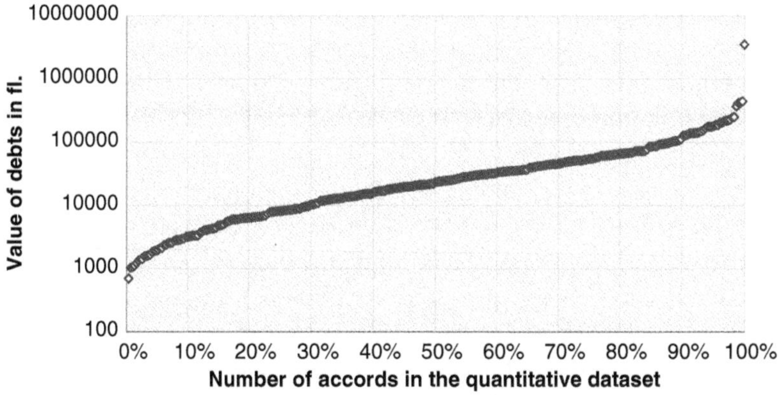

FIGURE 5.9 Value of debts per insolvency in which an accord was concluded in the quantitative dataset on a logarithmic scale (1592–1700)

46 percent of the debts in cash to every creditor who would sign the agreement, in exchange for which they would acquit him and his wife of the remaining debts. This necessitated the support of all creditors, who collectively signed the accord "uyt commiseratie die syluyden metten voornoemde Roesingh ende des selfs huysvrouw ten regarde van haeren hoogen ouderdom sijn hebbende," or "out of the compassion that they felt with Roesingh and his wife because of their old age."[80] According to the inventory made up on July 12, a *toombanck* or counter was situated in the front room of their house in the Bloemstraat, which suggests that the Roesingh family tried to make a living with a small store.[81]

Up to this point, we have encountered a fraudulent jeweler, a sugar entrepreneur, and a small shopkeeper among the people who make up the datasets of insolvents who were able to conclude an accord with their creditors. How representative is each of these cases of the whole population? It is unfortunate that most of the accords do not contain information about the insolvents' occupations. However, based upon the size of their debts – that is, the amount of credit they were able to obtain – we can draw some conclusions about their position in the Amsterdam society. Figure 5.9 displays the size of debts per accord in the quantitative dataset.

[80] GAS, 5072: DB, inv. nr. 1253. [81] GAS, 5072: DB, inv. nr. 573, ff. 1–2r.

It is interesting to observe that the majority of the accords concern debts in the range of fl. 10,000 to fl. 100,000 (58 percent). Roughly one-tenth of the insolvents amassed truly substantial debts of several hundred thousand guilders. What does this say about their position in society?

If we interpret the amount of debts at the time of the insolvency as representative of the size of the insolvent's business, this allows us to compare their cases to the size of other, better-known enterprises from this period. In his study of Dutch trading houses, for instance, Joost Jonker provides information on the development of the size of Amsterdam businesses between 1550 and 1750. Around the middle of the sixteenth century, tax registers show that most businesses were relatively small when compared to Antwerp standards, averaging between fl. 6,000 and fl. 8,000.[82] This quickly increased as the Amsterdam economy boomed in the last decades of the century. A company for Baltic trade like that of Daniel van der Meulen and his brothers-in-law, worth fl. 72,000, should according to Jonker be judged as "belonging to the top layer of society, but not extraordinarily large." During the Dutch Golden Age, famous merchants such as Jan Poppen, Jan Jansz. Kaerel, and Cornelis Pietersz. Hooft were able to amass fortunes worth hundreds of thousands of guilders. However, according to the Amsterdam property tax register of 1631, only twenty-four citizens owned more than fl. 200,000.[83] Their stories were exceptional: most of the businessmen active on the Amsterdam market in the seventeenth century operated on a much more modest scale. Only in the first half of the eighteenth century did modal businesses typically reach the size of fl. 100,000 to fl. 200,000 in the scope of a single generation.[84]

While this data only covers the top segment of society, based upon our knowledge of the prevailing interest rates on Holland state bonds and private loans in this period, it is possible to estimate the income that could flow forth from varying amounts of invested capital in the seventeenth century. A comparison of such proceeds with the annual incomes of various categories of citizens in this period allows us to

[82] Joost Jonker and Keetie Sluyterman, *Thuis op de wereldmarkt. Nederlandse handelshuizen door de eeuwen heen.* (The Hague: SDU, 2000), 17.

[83] Ibid. 53–55. [84] Ibid. 88.

estimate the potential standard of living and social position of a much broader group of insolvents from the accord population.[85] In 1660, the interest rate on Holland bonds was 4 percent, declining to 3 percent in the last decade of the seventeenth century. Rates charged in private markets were roughly 4.75 percent throughout this period.[86] From data on the composition of fortunes at the death of members of the Leiden elite, we know that around 1660 the ratio of investments in bonds versus private loans was 60:40, whereas around 1700 this had shifted in favor of bonds to 93:7.[87] Given the fact that the interest on bonds only decreased to 3 percent in the last decade of the century, 4 percent can be used as a rough estimate of the returns on invested capital in the second half of the seventeenth century. This means that a capital of fl. 10,000 resulted in an annual income of fl. 400, a capital of fl. 100,000 in an income of fl. 4,000, and a capital of fl. 250,000 in an income of fl. 10,000.

When we compare these amounts to the debt values displayed in the quantitative dataset, as displayed by Figure 5.9, we can deduce that all layers of the Amsterdam community of citizens or *burgerij* were represented among the accord population. About one-third of the accords were concluded by people from the lower levels of burghers. These ordinary self-employed craftsmen and shopkeepers with a modest turnover as well as lower salaried public officials earned fl. 350 to fl.500 on an annual basis, and formed about 30 percent of the Amsterdam population in this period. Another quarter of the insolvents who concluded an accord with their creditors can be classified as belonging to what we would call the broad middle classes, varying from successful craftsmen and retailers with an income up to fl. 1,000 to lesser merchants, notaries, and senior public officials. They made

85 I would like to express my thanks to Oscar Gelderblom for this suggestion.

86 Oscar Gelderblom, Mark Hup, and Joost Jonker, "Public Functions, Private Markets: Credit Registration by Aldermen and Notaries in the Low Countries, 1500–1800," in *Financing in Europe: Evolution, Coexistence and Complementarity of Lending Practices from the Middle Ages to Modern Times*, ed. Marcella Lorenzini, Cinzia Lorandini, and D'Maris Coffman (Cham: Springer International Publishing, 2018), 186.

87 Jan de Vries and Ad van der Woude, *The First Modern Economy: Success, Failure, and Perseverance of the Dutch Economy, 1500–1815* (Cambridge University Press, 1997), 592. These data closely correspond to similar ratios found for wealthy citizens in Gouda and Hoorn.

up a further 14 percent of the Amsterdam population. The remainder of the accord population can clearly be classified among the urban elite or *grote burgerij* of merchants, rentiers, industrialists, doctors, as well as the highest government officials and the governing patriciate itself. They formed about 6 percent of the urban population.[88]

It is also interesting to compare the value of these estates with the classes of the burial tax that was introduced by the States of Holland in 1695. The first class, which consisted of those with assets worth more than fl. 12,000, made up 2.1 percent of the population in the years 1701–1705. The second class, consisting of those with assets worth between fl. 6,000 and fl. 12,000, formed a further 0.8 percent. Notaries, procurators, or other salaried professionals with an income between fl. 400 and fl. 800 were categorized in this second class, unless their personal assets warranted their inclusion in the highest tax category. For the marriage tax that was imposed at the same time, the percentages were slightly higher: in the same period 3.8 percent fell in the first class, 1.4 percent in the second class.[89] This means that at the end of the seventeenth century, less than 6 percent of the married couples and less than 3 percent of the deceased in Amsterdam had personal assets worth more than fl. 6,000. From an analysis of probate inventories between 1700 and 1710, it appears that citizens from the first class of the burial tax had average outstanding debts to their creditors of fl. 12,083. Citizens from the second class owed on average fl. 8,555 at the time of their death.[90] Of course, these estates were not necessarily insolvent, but allow us to determine the range of debts normally incurred by households from these social classes. When compared to the amounts of credit obtained by the majority of the insolvents in the accord population, this strongly suggests that most of them should be positioned among the higher strata of Amsterdam society.

[88] Ibid. 562–64.

[89] Simon Hart, "Een sociale structuur van de Amsterdamse bevolking in de 18e eeuw," in *Geschrift en getal. Een keuze uit de demografisch-, economisch- en sociaal-historische studiën op grond van Amsterdamse en Zaanse archivalia, 1600–1800* (Dordrecht: Historische Vereniging Holland, 1976), 183–91.

[90] Johannes A. Faber, "Inhabitants of Amsterdam and Their Possessions," in *Probate Inventories: A New Source for the Historical Study of Wealth, Material Culture and Agricultural Development*, ed. A. M. van der Woude and Anton J. Schuurman (Wageningen: Landbouwhogeschool, 1980), 149–55.

While partially based upon estimates, this data supports the general image of the Desolate Boedelskamer as an institution for broad groups of Amsterdam citizens. Among those able to conclude an accord, however, the small upper layer of society seems to have dominated. At first sight, one would consider this unsurprising, as the larger amounts of debts related to the estates of merchants, entrepreneurs, and industrialists both necessitated a more professional management in case of insolvency, and would yield enough to warrant the procedural costs. However, Oldewelt states that "really large insolvencies were usually resolved as if among friends, bypassing the court." He based this on the observation that in the 1690s, for instance, he was only able to identify two large insolvencies, with debts worth fl. 143,000 and fl. 193,000.[91] His analysis is clearly proven wrong by the data presented in this book.

As displayed in Figure 5.9, based upon my quantitative dataset, roughly a tenth of the insolvencies in which an accord was concluded concerned debts exceeding fl. 100,000. Furthermore, even in the dataset of insolvencies that were resolved through the benefice of *cessie van goede* in just three years of the 1690s in which Oldewelt only found two large insolvencies, I have located five insolvencies in which debts exceeded fl. 100,000 and a further nine in which the total debts crossed the fl. 50,000 mark. This evidence strongly suggests that the Desolate Boedelskamer was the principal forum for financial conflict resolution in case of insolvency in seventeenth-century Amsterdam. Even if important merchants were often able to arrive at an amicable resolution of their illiquidity, they did so through official, legal means such as an accord rather than informally, bypassing the city's legal and institutional structures. In the General Conclusion, I will compare the amount of debts found among the accord population with similar data found among the applicants for the benefice of *cessie*. This comparative analysis will allow us to draw interesting conclusions about the groups of people who could make use of either legal strategy.

[91] Oldewelt, "Twee eeuwen," 429. Van Eeghen also suggests that many insolvents (especially those with large estates) would have bypassed the Desolate Boedelskamer in the mid-eighteenth century: Chr. P. van Eeghen, "Het faillissement der firma Coenraad & Hendrick van Son in 1762," *Economisch-Historisch Jaarboek* 22 (1943): 82–187, 107–8.

Conclusion

Caspar Barlaeus may have been right about the risks of extending credit, but his description of the consequences of insolvency seems to have been atypical for at least the second half of the seventeenth century. The upper layer of the Amsterdam community of citizens became increasingly lenient towards unfortunate insolvents who could not repay their debts. Whereas in the first decades of the seventeenth century, accords drawn up by notaries almost always contained repayment schemes for the full amount of debts, the foundation of the Desolate Boedelskamer and especially the introduction of majority compositions around midcentury resulted in ever lower repayment percentages as part of such agreements. While this did not result in an official acquittal of the remaining debts, *de facto* creditors will have been forced to accept the loss of at times substantial claims. Sometimes, insolvents attempted to pressure their creditors into a profitable agreement by means of a retreat to asylum cities. Most often, however, the acceptance of a proposed accord reflected trust and good relations between all parties involved. In many cases, this trust in the insolvent's capacity to meet the accords' conditions was strengthened by the support and (social) capital of one or more guarantors.

While the development towards lower repayment percentages might seem disadvantageous for the creditors at first sight, the introduction of the Desolate Boedelskamer and its procedures strengthened the security of credit in two important ways. First, it increased the transparency of the insolvency procedure through its publicly regulated management of the insolvent estate. A notarial agreement could never provide the same degree of transparency, or guarantee that all creditors would be treated equally in all insolvencies. Second, the inclusiveness of the procedure was strengthened even further through far-reaching communication protocols. By publicly endorsing the privately developed practice of notarial accords between insolvents and their creditors, the Amsterdam authorities guaranteed the universality of the insolvency procedure and thereby strengthened the local institutional structure that served as a foundation for its economic prosperity. At the same time, however, this does not mean that notaries were completely excluded from the legal resolution of insolvencies in the second half of the seventeenth century. As the stories of Isacq Nunes Bernal and his relative Hester Vaez illustrate, at various moments notarial attestations or acts that had been drawn up as part of their private business dealings served as written evidence in legal procedures. Of even greater importance were the translation services supplied by various notaries, which enabled the Portuguese-speaking women involved in the aforementioned agreements to take part in the public procedures of the Desolate Boedelskamer.

Finally, even though the accords do not contain much information about the occupational background of the insolvents, it is possible to deduce some information about their position in society from the value of their debts. While all categories of citizens were represented, the urban elite clearly dominated the population of insolvents who were able to conclude an accord with their creditors. This means that the great majority of Amsterdam insolvents must have resolved their repayment conflicts in alternative ways, whether formal or informal. The main formal legal alternative to an accord was the benefice of *cessie van goede*. I will now turn to this procedure, which allowed the majority of Amsterdam insolvents in this period to arrive at an acceptable solution for their financial problems.

6

Cessie van Goede

There was not much "golden" about the last years of the seventeenth century for many people in the Dutch Republic. Mercantilist politics in England and France as well as the wars fought against these states since 1672 had harmed the formerly dominant international commercial position of the Republic, while burdening it with large debts. Even though most regents acknowledged the need to reduce state debt and heavy taxation, a lack of economic growth frustrated this ambition. The widespread unease about these developments is exemplified by a contemporary analysis of the economic situation, handed over to the States of Holland in 1684 by some Amsterdam regents. Since 1672, according to these merchants, both their general trading capital and real-estate value had diminished by 50 percent. This was primarily due to fact that the loss of a quarter of all maritime commerce or *commercie ende navigatie* had resulted in the halving of actual profits. Besides that, the internal market or *commercie van consumptie* was shrinking. The merchants strongly pleaded for sustaining the peace, as that would be the only way to relax the heavy taxation that made it so difficult to cut back on costs and increase profit margins. Soon, however, the changing international political climate forced them to continue to back stadtholder William III's expensive military schemes to the further detriment of the economy. This step into what would eventually become the Nine Years' War (1688–1697), which was quickly followed by the War of Spanish Succession (1701–1713), eventually proved to be a profitless investment. These conflicts would fiscally strangle the Republic for the remainder of the eighteenth century rather than recreating an international economic climate in which it could flourish once more.[1]

It is here that we must return to the story of Jan Arnout Wichelhuysen, whom we first encountered at the start of this book. Early in the year 1695, this Amsterdam merchant found himself in such dire financial conditions that few options remained but to draw up a *staet en inventaris* to request the "miserable benefice" or *miserabel beneficie van cessie van goede*, as it was commonly called at the time.[2] In this document, which was drawn up on March 7 but processed by the Desolate Boedelskamer ten days later, we find a short summary of Wichelhuysen's life and business up to the moment of his insolvency. About eleven years earlier, on December 21, 1683, he had married the Hulst-born Johanna Macaré, then living at the Steenschuur in Leiden. Wichelhuysen himself originally came from 's-Hertogenbosch, but by the time of his marriage he lived on the prestigious Amsterdam Herengracht. The Leiden Dutch Reformed congregation provided Johanna with the attestation that was required to successfully transfer the newly married couple to its Amsterdam counterpart.[3] This is confirmed by the Amsterdam registers, in which the marriage was officially inscribed two days after it had been concluded.[4]

Throughout the next decade, the merchant – who mainly dealt in wine and luxury goods such as saffron – continued to make good use of his connections in the peripheral regions of the Dutch Republic. This is illustrated by the outstanding claims noted in his *staet*, which include debtors in places as widespread as Veere, Tilburg, Maastricht, and Liège. Wichelhuysen apparently also continued to use a second house in 's-Hertogenbosch, as testified by two creditors there to whom he owed house rent. Whereas this strategy might have been a successful business model in more peaceful times, the endemic warfare and

[1] Jan de Vries and Ad van der Woude, *The First Modern Economy: Success, Failure, and Perseverance of the Dutch Economy, 1500–1815* (Cambridge University Press, 1997), 673–81; Arie Th. van Deursen, *De last van veel geluk. De geschiedenis van Nederland, 1555–1702* (Amsterdam: Bakker, 2004), 324–34 and 349–51.

[2] Gemeente Amsterdam Stadsarchief [GAS], 5072: Archief van de Commissarissen van de Desolate Boedelkamer [DB], inv. nr. 697, nr. 26. Derived from *cessio bonorum*, see Chapter 2 above.

[3] Erfgoed Leiden en Omstreken, 1004: Burgerlijke Stand: doop-, trouw- en begraafboeken [DTB] Leiden, inv. nr. 23, f. 149r.

[4] GAS, 5001: DTB, inv. nr. 512, f. 30r.

raids by various armies that plagued the Southern Netherlands and the Brabantine border regions in the 1690s must have been detrimental to Wichelhuysen's commerce. When too many of his own debtors were forced to default or postpone their payments, eventually turning to the Desolate Boedelskamer became inescapable. As is typical of *cessie* applications, the insolvent also mentioned two accidents as part of his tale of financial misfortune. In 1686, Wichelhuysen had to write off fl. 600 when a stock of barley was wasted when the 's-Hertogenbosch attic in which it had been stored collapsed. One year later, he lost a further fl. 750 due to the spoiling of thirty bales of hops. On March 15, 1695, Matijs Brouwer was appointed curator of Wichelhuysen's estate, the execution of which must have commenced soon after the commissioners provided a *favorabel advijs* or "positive, binding opinion" for *cessie* on March 24.[5]

While the Amsterdam *cessie* applications that have survived in great numbers from 1689 onwards provide intriguing snapshots of the lives and businesses of late seventeenth-century Amsterdam citizens, stories such as that provided by Jan Arnout Wichelhuysen are always colored by the insolvent's purpose, which was to convince the commissioners of their good intent in order to obtain the benefice. Solely based upon their accounts, we would be tempted to construct an even bleaker image of the economic conditions in this period than is warranted by other historical evidence. If we keep this in mind, however, these files provide detailed insight into the types of people who were forced to make use of this benefice, their occupations, the size of their debts at the moment of the insolvency, their own view of the cause of their financial demise, and, most importantly, they allow us to compare the attributes of these insolvents to those of the smaller population of insolvents who managed to obtain an accord with their creditors as discussed in Chapter 5. Unlike the latter procedure, which was heavily impacted by the introduction of the Desolate Boedelskamer, the basic principle and structure of *cessie* does not seem to have been greatly altered over the seventeenth century. What *was* revolutionary, however, was the radically more debtor-friendly stance

[5] GAS, 5072: DB, inv. nr. 480, f. 36r and inv. nr. 28, f. 79v. I will henceforth use the term *advijs* untranslated in similar contexts, since there is no English equivalent that entirely covers the legal meaning this concept had in seventeenth-century Holland.

of Amsterdam's legal institutions towards honest insolvents which developed over this same period. Through the benefice of *cessie van goede* as much as through an accord, Amsterdam insolvents received a second or even third chance to participate in social and economic life through a procedure that was stripped of its common defamatory connotations.

In the first section of this chapter, the *cessie* procedure as it was employed in this period will be described for both the local authorities and the High Court from the perspective of the Amsterdam insolvent Jan Verwey, in relation to contemporary legal scholarship. Second, the identity of the applicants for *cessie* will be analyzed in contrast with the characteristics of the accord-population that was discussed in Chapter 5. Third, the main factors that were provided by the applicants as an explanation for their insolvency will be categorized and critically examined. Finally, I will discuss the aftermath of *cessie* applications. Through this benefice, many Amsterdam insolvents clearly gathered sufficient trust and reputation to attempt to restart their businesses. Together, these elements will provide a fresh perspective on the economic and social conditions that confronted middle-class citizens in late seventeenth-century Amsterdam.

Procedure

Between 1462 and 1531, the benefice of *cessie van goede* seems to have been gradually received into the County of Holland.[6] As discussed in Chapter 2, in 1536 Charles V issued a *placaat* that officially introduced the possibility of *cessie van goede* for all honest insolvents in Brabant and "the lands of Overmaas" (the latter are presently part of both the Dutch and the Belgian provinces of Limburg). These regulations were extended to the entire Low Countries through the ordinances of 1541/1544. While the benefice was not immediately accepted and received in all local (urban) legal traditions, over time this resulted in a situation in which Amsterdam insolvents could

[6] Joannes van der Linden, *Verhandeling over de judicieele practijcq, of form van procedeeren, voor de Hoven van Justitie in Holland gebruikelijk*, 2 vols. (Leiden: A. en J. Honkoop, 1798), II:394–95.

generally seek protection against imprisonment for debt.[7] As Filips Wielant had already noted in his *Practijke Civile* in 1519:

Cessie van goede is een beneficie dat de Rechten geven den ghenen die niet machtich en zijn te betalen, want de Rechten en willen niet dat yemant van schult eewelijck gevangen zy.[8]

[*Cessie van goede* is a legal benefice granted to those unable to pay their debts, as the Law would not wish that an insolvent would remain incarcerated for all eternity.]

Originally, requests for *cessie* had to be addressed to the *Grote Raad* or Great Council in Malines. As we learn from the manuscript *Uit de praktijck van het Hof van Holland*, which was drawn up by an anonymous author in the third quarter of the sixteenth century, after the Dutch revolt this function was temporarily taken over by the Court of Holland after a resolution of May 8, 1573.[9] After its establishment in 1582, the *Hoge Raad* or High Court of Holland would handle such requests until the end of the *ancien régime*.[10] It is interesting to note how contemporary legal scholars defined the benefice as it was applied in seventeenth-century Holland. In his *Inleidinge*, Grotius states:

Boedel-afstand (L. Cessio bonorum) is een weldaed dat van de hooge overheid werd verworven, waer door een schuldenaer bevrijd werd van ghevanckenisse, ende oock de schulden niet vorder en is gehouden te voldoen, dan behoudens sijne nooddruft.[11]

7 On local resistance against the new top-down *cessie* as it was introduced by Charles V, see: De ruysscher, "Reconciling Old and New. Imprisonment for Debts and Cessio Bonorum, in Antwerp and Mechelen (c. 1500–c. 1530)."

8 Filips Wielant, *Practijcke ende maniere van procederen in materie civile na den ghemeynen stijl van dese Nederlanden* (Antwerp: Henrice van der Loe, 1573), 83, II.18.1.

9 L. J. van Apeldoorn (ed.), *Uit de practijk van het Hof van Holland in de tweede helft van de zestiende eeuw* (Utrecht: Uitgevers-Maatschappij Broekhoff NV, 1938), 14–15.

10 Maria-Charlotte le Bailly and Christel Verhas, *Procesgids Hoge Raad van Holland, Zeeland en West-Friesland (1582–1795). De hoofdlijnen van het procederen in civiele zaken voor de Hoge Raad zowel in eerste instantie als in hoger beroep* (Hilversum: Verloren, 2006); Christel Verhas, "De beginjaren van de Hoge Raad van Holland, Zeeland en West-Friesland" (PhD, Universiteit Leiden, 1997), 149–50.

11 Hugo de Groot, *Inleidinge tot de Hollandsche rechts-geleerdheid*, ed. F. Dovring, H. F. W. D. Fischer, and E. M. Meijers, 2nd ed. (Universitaire Pers Leiden, 1965), 327–29.

[*Cessie van goede* is a benefice granted by the central authorities, through which a debtor is freed from imprisonment, and cannot be held responsible to continue repaying his debts unless his possessions exceed his basic life necessities.]

A few decades later, Simon van Leeuwen included a very similar description of the benefice in his *Rooms-Hollands-regt.*[12] In the formulary or *Papegay* by Willem van Alphen, we find standard formats for the insolvent's applications that had to be addressed to the High Court as well as its usual responses.[13] Gerard van Wassenaer seems to have combined data from most of the aforementioned works in his 1669 *Practijk judicieel.*[14]

While neither the 1649 *Papegay* nor the Amsterdam ordinances on the Desolate Boedelskamer specify how the procedural costs incurred when attempting to obtain and impetrate a letter of *cessie* had to be paid, the extended 1682 version of the aforementioned formulary added that "the costs incurred for impetrating the *mandement van cessie* would have to be paid from the proceeds of the executed goods that had been ceded to the creditors."[15] Van Bijnkershoek confirms that "letters of *cessie* cannot be obtained free of charge."[16] Kersteman, too, agrees that these procedural costs theoretically held preference even over creditors who were in the possession of a legal hypothec. In practice, however, if the applicant had successfully obtained the benefice and could convincingly show that their insolvency had resulted from bad luck rather than fraud, they could appeal to be granted the benefice *pro deo* from the

[12] Simon van Leeuwen, *Het Rooms-Hollands-regt [etc.]* (Leiden/Rotterdam: Hackens, 1664), 444–45.

[13] Willem van Alphen, *Nieuw verbeterde en vermeerderde papegay, ofte formulierboeck van alderhande requestē, mandamenten, conclusien &c, ghelijck die ghebruyckt ende gepractiseert werden voor de respectieve hoven van iustitie in Hollandt* (The Hague: Johannes Verhoeve, 1649), 161–66; Willem van Alphen, *Papegay, ofte formulier-boek van allerhande requesten, mandamenten, conclusien, schrifturen, als anders, in de dagelijksche practijke dienende voor de respective hoven van justitie in Hollandt*, 2 vols. (The Hague: Johannes Steucker, 1682), I:222–27.

[14] Gerard van Wassenaer, *Practijk judicieel ofte instructie op de forme en maniere van procederen voor hoven en rechtbanken*, 2 vols. (Utrecht: Gijsbert van Zijll, 1669), I:244–56.

[15] Van Alphen, *Papegay*, I:226.

[16] Cornelis van Bijnkershoek, *Observationes Tumultuariae*, ed. E. M. Meijers, A. S. de Blécourt, and H. D. J. Bodenstein, 2 vols. (Haarlem: Tjeenk Willink, 1926), I:nr. 841.

local court to which its *interinement* (official registration) had been committed.[17]

The daily practice of *cessie* procedures in seventeenth-century Holland is best described through an example such as the case of Jan Verwey, a typical applicant for this benefice. On December 29, 1699, the commissioners of the Desolate Boedelskamer appointed Wijnand Toll as curator of Verwey's estate after they had been notified of his financial problems.[18] Toll swiftly proceeded to draw up an inventory of Verwey's possessions, which was completed on January 1, 1700. One day later, "sworn appraiser" Catharina Verlaen – who often fulfilled such tasks for the Desolate Boedelskamer – estimated that Verwey's estate was worth little more than fl. 134. From this intriguing document, we learn that Verwey had tried to make a living as *commenijsman* or grocer in a rented house "at the end of the Laurierstraet." The inventory includes a wooden *winckel* or "shop" and counter, some flour trays, and an oil container "lined with lead." "Five pair of small copper scales and balances" and "a copper weight of two pounds" were used to measure the goods. On January 20, 1700, the commissioners allowed Verwey's wife to redeem their furniture and possessions for the sum determined by Catharina Verlaen. As usual, she also had to pay for the costs of the inventory and taxation, as well as the "taxes [owed to] the city, concierge, and secretary."[19]

In the meantime, Verwey had sent an application for *cessie van goede* to the High Court of Holland. On January 12, 1700, its councilors delegated the request to the Amsterdam authorities through a *committimus*.[20] In previous decades, various cities had striven to keep close control of the letters of *cessie* granted to their citizens. In 1682, the States of Holland once more affirmed that the authorities of an insolvent's domicile or – if they lived in the countryside – those of the

[17] Franciscus Lievens Kersteman, *Hollandsch rechtsgeleerd woorden-boek* (Amsterdam: Wed. van Esveldt en Holtrop, 1777), 45.
[18] GAS, 5072: DB, inv. nr. 480, f. 144v.
[19] GAS, 5072: DB, inv. nr. 625, ff. 12–13r. According to Lesger, the wooden "winckel" or store should not be interpreted as a building in itself, but rather the (movable) set of shelves on which the goods were stored: Clé Lesger, *Het winkellandschap van Amsterdam. Stedelijke structuur en winkelbedrijf in de vroegmoderne en moderne tijd, 1550–2000* (Hilversum: Verloren, 2013), 121–22.
[20] National Archives in The Hague [NL-HaNA], Hoge Raad Holland en Zeeland, 3.03.02, inv. nr. 104, p. 401.

nearest city would always be the court to which the High Court had to delegate the investigation and *interinement* of such benefices. These local judges were in a much better position to inquire whether the applicant was honest or fraudulent.[21] On March 31, 1688, Rotterdam delegates to the States of Holland complained that, contrary to these rulings, their magistrates were not being notified about insolvents who had been incarcerated "abroad." In response, the States reconfirmed their earlier decision that such cases always had to be committed to the court of an insolvent's domicile rather than to that of the place in which they had been arrested.[22]

While creditors were included in the *cessie* procedure, they could only prevent the granting of this benefice by providing evidence of fraud on the part of their debtor. In order to enable the Amsterdam commissioners to locate his creditors, Verwey had to produce a *staet.* He signed the document on January 18, 1700, and it was then delivered at the Desolate Boedelskamer two days later. Presumably, it was no coincidence that on the same date his wife redeemed their furniture and other possessions.[23] These applications clearly constitute collections of original documents supplied by the debtors themselves, as they are all written in varying hands and sometimes even on varying sizes of paper. Their structure, however, always seems to follow a standard format. After a more-or-less standardized opening, the applicant's creditors are listed, as well as the amount of debts they owed them. An account of the outstanding debts and other possessions of the estate follows. Next, most applications include narratives of "damages and losses," in which the insolvent reinforces their request by describing the unfortunate circumstances that forced them to resort to what is often called a "miserable benefice." In Verwey's case, he simply had not earned enough in the seven years after his marriage in 1693 to pay off his creditors. In his own words, *slegte winste* and *banqueroeten* or "meagre earnings and bankrupt customers" had forced him to file the application. The document was concluded with a standard closing formula, in which the applicant swore that the information provided

21 NL-HaNA, Staten van Holland na 1572, 3.01.04.01, inv. nr. 115, p. 47–48 and p. 596.

22 NL-HaNA, Staten van Holland na 1572, 3.01.04.01, inv. nr. 121, p. 237–238 and p. 563–564.

23 GAS, 5072: DB, inv. nr. 702, nr. 5.

reflected the true condition of their estate and that they had withheld nothing from the commissioners. If any new information should come up, whether to the advantage or disadvantage of their creditors, the applicant promised to augment their *staet*. This oath was sealed by a signature.

The format of the applications was partially prescribed by the High Court of Holland and later added to by the Desolate Boedelskamer itself, to ensure an efficient processing of the relatively high number of cases. In an ordinance issued on June 14, 1649, the judges of the High Court complained about the "multitude of requests for letters of *cessie*." In order to successfully exclude fraudulent debtors from the benefice they prescribed that henceforth, besides the name and place of residence of the debtor, those of their principal creditors would also have to be included in the application.[24] It is important to note that the general applications or *mandementen* that were addressed to the High Court by applicants for *cessie* were much less elaborate than the official *staeten* that they would subsequently have to hand in at the Amsterdam Desolate Boedelskamer. In 1660, the Amsterdam authorities elaborated upon the basic requirements laid down by the High Court, demanding that every applicant for *cessie* would have to deliver a detailed *staet* "strengthened by an oath" to the curator, as well as a justification for their desperate economic condition, before the benefice could take effect.[25] These instructions clearly shaped the basic structure of late seventeenth-century Amsterdam *cessie* requests such as that of Verwey, and helped to turn them into very rich historical sources.

In 1664, a group of Amsterdam merchants, united in the short-lived *College van Commercie*, sought to elaborate the *cessie* applications even further. They demanded that an applicant would have to deliver their entire administrative documentation and correspondence

[24] Isaac Scheltus, *Groot placaat boek. Inhoudende de placaaten ende ordonnantien van de Hoog Mog. Heeren Staaten Generaal der Nederlanden ende van de Ed. Groot Mog. Heeren Staaten van Holland ende West-Friesland mitsgaders van de Ed. Mog. Heeren Staaten van Zeeland* (The Hague: Isaac Scheltus s'Lands Drukker, 1770), 936; see also: Van Alphen, *Papegay*, I:226–27.

[25] Hermanus Noordkerk (ed.), *Handvesten; ofte privilegien ende octroyen: mitsgaders willekeuren, costuimen, ordonnantien en handelingen der stad Amstelredam*, 4 vols. (Amsterdam: Hendrik van Waesberge, Salomon en Petrus Schouten, 1748), II:696–97.

from at least the three or four years leading up to their insolvency to the court, besides their *staet* and inventory, requiring them to swear that they had not alienated anything that would cause harm to their creditors. This was usual practice for the Desolate Boedelskamer, which always appointed a curator to manage insolvent estates. Besides this, however, they proposed that a public proclamation of the *cessie* would have to be made, inviting anyone who illegally possessed goods from the estate or knew of someone else holding such goods to make this known to the commissioners. According to the merchants, these proposals were meant to reduce the many occurrences of *vele bedriegerijen* or fraud, but they seem to have been neglected by the burgomasters.[26] Probably, the proclamations and even more detailed investigations were deemed too time-consuming for the great number of *cessie* applications that were received annually by the Desolate Boedelskamer.

Soon after Verwey's *staet* had been delivered to the commissioners, they investigated his case. On January 27, 1700, it was determined that none of his creditors had spoken against him, resulting in a favorable *advijs* on his *cessie* request.[27] Similar to their Rotterdam counterparts' demand for a proper *committimus* to the competent urban court, the Amsterdam authorities firmly guarded their power to approve or deny *cessie* requests. When in 1698 the High Court refused to provide Amsterdam citizen Johan Luden with his letter, even though the commissioners of the Desolate Boedelskamer had sent in a favorable *advijs*, the Amsterdam authorities asked the States of Holland to admonish the court. I will return to this interesting competence dispute in the final section of this chapter.[28] In Jan Verwey's case, the Amsterdam *rescriptio* was sent back to The Hague without further trouble. On February 27, 1700, the High Court granted Verwey his *cessie* in the form of a *brief* or "letter."[29]

[26] Hajo Brugmans, "De notulen en munimenten van het College van Commercie te Amsterdam, 1663–1665," *BMGN – Low Countries Historical Review* 18 (1897): 181–330, 249–52.

[27] GAS, 5072: DB, inv. nr. 30, f. 31v.

[28] NL-HaNA, Staten van Holland na 1572, 3.01.04.01, inv. nr. 131, pp. 156–59; a copy of this text from the Resolutions of the States of Holland was included in the Book of Resolutions of the Amsterdam Desolate Boedelskamer: GAS, 5072: DB, inv. nr. 58, ff. 57–58.

[29] NL-HaNA, Hoge Raad Holland en Zeeland, 3.03.02, inv. nr. 104, p. 401.

Once he had officially registered the benefice with the Amsterdam authorities through the *interinement* procedure, which entailed a final opportunity for protest from the side of his creditors, it would finally enter into effect. I will now proceed to analyze the characteristics of the other applicants in the *cessie* population, all of whom had to go through similar procedures.

Applicants' Identities

Unlike countries such as Belgium, Germany, or France, the Netherlands does not have a tradition of separating commercial from civil law, apart from a short period in the nineteenth century under Napoleonic influence.[30] Jan Wagenaar unjustifiably characterized the Amsterdam Desolate Boedelskamer as a predominantly mercantile institution.[31] The existing literature on insolvency in early modern Amsterdam has generally followed his assertion, focusing on the court's use for commerce while neglecting its impact on the thousands of middle-class artisans and shopkeepers whom we also encounter in its archives.

Actually, ordinary self-employed craftsmen and small shopkeepers formed the mass of the Amsterdam citizenry. This lowest level of burghers formed about a quarter of the urban total, always being close to social degradation due to the untimely death of the breadwinner, extended illness, or other vices and misfortunes. A further 10 to 14 percent consisted of a broad group of government servants (e.g. clerks, schoolmasters), artisans (e.g. bakers, butchers, modest innkeepers, or coopers), and specialized shopkeepers of all sorts, who

[30] Jan Hendrik Dalhuisen, *Compositions in Bankruptcy: A Comparative Study of the Laws of the E.E.C. Countries, England and the U.S.A.* (Leiden: A. W. Sijthoff, 1968), 36–38; Dave De ruysscher, "At the End, the Creditors Win: Pre-Insolvency Proceedings in France, Belgium and the Netherlands (1807–*c.*1910)," *Comparative Legal History* 6, no. 2 (2018): 184–206.

[31] Jan Wagenaar, *Amsterdam in zijne opkomst*, 4 vols. (Amsterdam: Yntema en Tieboel, 1767), III:461. Together with Marco in 't Veld, I have sought to nuance the image of seventeenth-century Amsterdam put forward by scholars such as Mary Lindemann, who characterize the city as a "merchant republic" in which all aspects of society were dominated by commerce. See Mary Lindemann, *The Merchant Republics: Amsterdam, Antwerp, and Hamburg, 1648–1790* (New York: Cambridge University Press, 2014); Marco in 't Veld and Maurits den Hollander, "Citizenship in Early Modern Amsterdam: An Artisanal Identity?," in *Citizenship, Identity, and Commerce in Legal History*, ed. Dave De ruysscher, Albrecht Cordes, and Heikki Pihlajamäki (Leiden: Brill, 2021).

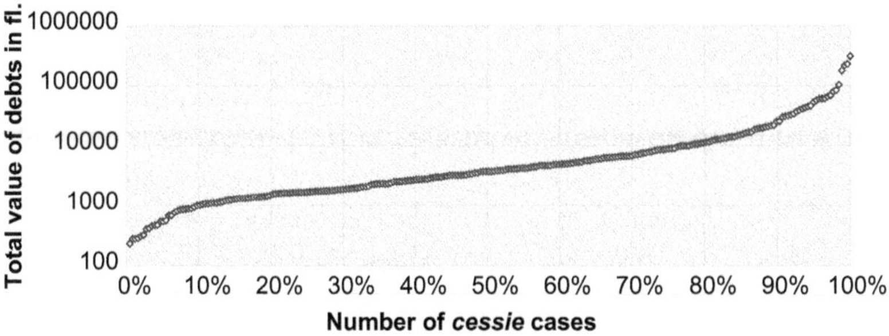

FIGURE 6.1 Value of debts per insolvent estate in the dataset of applicants for *cessie van goede* on a logarithmic scale

earned between fl. 600 and 1,000 on an annual basis. Only the top 6 to 8 percent of society could be described as proper "bourgeoisie" (e.g. merchants, notaries, and most of the Protestant clergy), few of whom were truly rich (those with an annual income exceeding fl. 5,000).[32] In the registers that contain the Amsterdam applications for *cessie van goede*, most of these groups are well represented, besides a few applications from the lower strata of urban society. In the case of grocer Jan Verwey, the total amount of his debts amounted to a relatively modest fl. 891. How typical was his case for the total *cessie* population?

When one compares the total value of debts for every application, a few trends can be observed (see Figure 6.1). The lowest debt in the sample was the fl. 233 owed by Adriaen van Hattem, whose possessions had all been "consumed in his poverty."[33] The highest debt was incurred by international merchant Alexander Hinderson, who owed his creditors more than fl. 300,000 at the time of his application for *cessie*.[34] He forms an exception, as it is clear that most cases concern relatively modest debts, 70 percent of the cases lying within the range of fl. 1,000–10,000. Out of the total sample, only five cases exceeded fl. 100,000. These outliers heavily influence the average debt value of fl. 12,441, as the average of the lowest 75 percent is only fl. 5,642. This means that the great majority of applicants for *cessie* came from the middle classes of Amsterdam society, even though important merchants occasionally also made use of the benefice when circumstances forced them to do so.

32 De Vries and Van der Woude, *First Modern Economy*, 563–64.
33 GAS, 5072: DB, inv. nr. 697, nr. 6. 34 GAS, 5072: DB, inv. nr. 702, nr. 56.

Even though Bart Willems found a strong correlation between the possession of real estate (as a potential security) and the amount of debt citizens were able to incur in eighteenth-century Antwerp, only thirty-nine applicants or 15 percent of the sample mention the possession of any form of real estate in their application.[35] This is unsurprising, as many Amsterdam entrepreneurs in this period rented the houses in which they lived and conducted business.[36] More than half of the applicants who did possess real estate belonged to the group that amassed the largest debts (more than fl. 10,000). More than half of the houses in Amsterdam were owned by the richest 14 percent of society, who were responsible for about 80 percent of the total real estate investments.[37] It is interesting to note that while – apart from a small peak around 1690 – rents for upper-class residences were relatively stable in the last quarter of the seventeenth century, those for middle-class houses display a steady rise from the 1680s onwards. This might have contributed to the financial stress of this social group.[38] What is more, the absence of real estate might also have negatively influenced the capacity of debtors to negotiate an accord. Land or houses were solid property against which loans could be secured, the lack of which would sooner have condemned an insolvent to resort to the benefice of *cessie van goede* due to a lack of trust on the part of their creditors. I will explore these different strategies at the end of this section.

An examination of various occupation groups in the dataset reinforces the image of a predominantly middle-class population of applicants (see Figure 6.2). The majority of applicants were either shopkeepers, merchants, traders, or artisans. Within the merchant category, three applicants were active in insuring, while six worked as

[35] Bart Willems, *Leven op de pof: Krediet bij de Antwerpse middenstand in de achttiende eeuw* (Amsterdam University Press, 2009), 166–69.

[36] Clé Lesger, "Merchants in Charge. The Self-Perception of Amsterdam Merchants, *ca.*1550–1700," in *The Self-Perception of Early Modern Capitalists*, ed. Margareth C. Jacob and Catherine Secretan (New York: Palgrave Macmillan, 2008), 84.

[37] Johannes A. Faber, "Inhabitants of Amsterdam and Their Possessions," in *Probate Inventories: A New Source for the Historical Study of Wealth, Material Culture and Agricultural Development*, ed. A. M. van der Woude and Anton J. Schuurman (Wageningen: Landbouwhogeschool, 1980).

[38] De Vries and Van der Woude, *First Modern Economy*, 334.

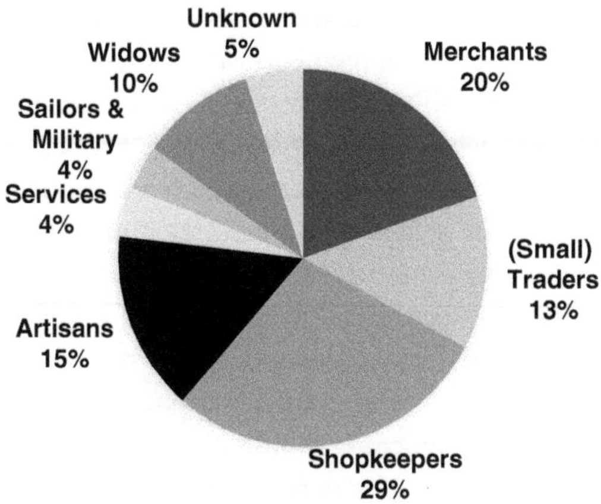

FIGURE 6.2 The occupations of Amsterdam applicants for *cessie van goede*

brokers. (Pastry) bakers were well represented among the shopkeepers, as well as grocers, beer or wine tappers, and innkeepers. Among the artisans, weavers and distillers were most common, followed by shoemakers. The service sector included a barber and two surgeons, as well as a schoolmaster. While the highest debts were incurred by merchants and artisans such as the distiller Dirk Muurman, whose capital-intensive business *De Groene Duiff* amassed a debt of fl. 45,783, there are significant differences within these categories.[39] Trader Moses Cohen del Medico, for instance, who got into financial trouble due to unsuccessful investments in various Venetian ships, only owed his creditors fl. 1,335 at the time of his application for *cessie*.[40] An interesting category is formed by widows and other independently operating women. Even though Roman Law stipulated that women could only be incarcerated for *misdaden*, or crimes, in 1664 the legal scholar Simon van Leeuwen observed that "presently, this is no longer taken into regard."[41] Therefore, women who found themselves in desperate economic conditions were also forced to apply for the benefice of *cessie*. While most had simply lost their spouses due to natural causes, two of them, Maria Swart and Susanna Aleman, were "legally separated" from their husbands. Their stories will be discussed in more detail in the next section.

39 GAS, 5072: DB, inv. nr. 702, nr. 6. 40 GAS, 5072: DB, inv. nr. 702, nr. 18.
41 Van Leeuwen, *Rooms-Hollands-regt*, 445–46, IV.41.1.

Six applications were signed with a series of Hebrew letters. This reaffirms the observation that members of the Jewish community made use of the services of the Desolate Boedelskamer.[42] In a few cases, the application is signed by a mark instead of a proper signature. An example is the case of Anthonij Maes, which was signed by his mark "X," according to the scribe who identifies himself as "Portmani," because he was unable to write himself: *vermits hij selfs niet schrijven kan*.[43] Generally, the degree of literacy in late seventeenth-century Holland was very high. This is exemplified by the fact that only 4 out of 259 applications were signed with a cross, and 2 with crude initials.[44] Even these six applicants should not necessarily be considered completely illiterate, as in this period the art of reading was taught before writing lessons started.[45]

It is intriguing that we find such small numbers of merchants with truly large businesses among the applicants for *cessie*. However, this is unsurprising when we take the general functioning and procedure of the Desolate Boedelskamer into account. In principle, the goal of this institution was to arbitrate between an insolvent and their creditors in order to reach an accord. Of course, as we saw in Chapter 5, this favorable solution required a degree of mutual trust between the parties. If it was impossible to reach an accord due to unwilling creditors, insolvents could attempt to force them to accept one by moving to legal places of asylum such as Culemborg or Vianen. For most of the middle-class insolvents in my dataset, this solution was simply too expensive. In the case of the larger merchants, seeking asylum was probably too cumbersome and uncertain if they wished to quickly revive their businesses after the insolvency had been wrapped up. Therefore, if the creditors were unwilling to cooperate, an insolvent's

42 GAS, 5072: DB, inv. nr. 689, f. 126v; inv. nr. 692, nrs. 14, 55, and 66; inv. nr. 702, nrs. 40 and 42.

43 GAS, 5072: DB, inv. nr. 697, nr. 56.

44 GAS, 5072: DB, inv. nr. 689, f. 2r; inv. nr. 697, nr. 56; inv. nr. 702, nrs. 50 and 70 were signed with a cross. Inv. nr. 697, nr. 73 was signed with mark "K" (for Christiaen van Keldenig), while inv. nr. 702, nr. 74 was signed with the mark "BB" (for Barent Barents).

45 Simon Hart, "Geschrift en getal. Onderzoek naar de samenstelling van de bevolking van Amsterdam in de 17e en 18e eeuw, op grond van gegevens over migratie, huwelijk, beroep en alfabetisme," in *Geschrift en getal. Een keuze uit de demografisch-, economisch- en sociaal-historische studiën op grond van Amsterdamse en Zaanse archivalia, 1600–1800* (Dordrecht: Historische Vereniging Holland, 1976), 130.

only option was to apply for the benefice of *cessie van goede*. While the creditors were consulted, they could only prevent its effectuation by providing proof of fraudulent acts on the part of the applicant. Even though a *cessie* did not safeguard insolvents from future litigation, it at least offered protection against a shameful debt imprisonment. Perhaps even more importantly, it resulted in a situation in which the applicants themselves, rather than their creditors, seized the initiative in the insolvency procedure.[46]

Roots of Insolvency

In 1670, Adriaen Hellendoorn borrowed a substantial sum of money in order to buy a wood sawmill named *The Wolf*. Soon after this transaction, however, the unfortunate miller was forced to break down the mill as well as the sheds and houses surrounding it due to the French military invasion in that "year of troubles." In 1674, just after he had rebuilt the mill, bad weather resulted in the collapse of the entire structure, which meant that Hellendoorn had to incur even more debts for its restoration. For years, the miller somehow managed to keep himself and his family alive, but by November 1695 the "war and great shortage of work" made it impossible to continue paying the interest on his loans. This sad combination of circumstances forced the miller to resort to the benefice of *cessie*.[47]

The great majority of applicants for *cessie* in my dataset provided stories about their financial and professional background similar to the account of Adriaen Hellendoorn. The main purpose of these personal stories was to stress their "good faith," by providing an explanation for their insolvency that put the blame on circumstances beyond their control. Even if we accept that these accounts are colored by the applicants' ulterior motives and necessarily subjective view, the rich variety of their contents is simply too valuable to neglect. At the very least, this section provides evidence of what late seventeenth-century insolvents themselves considered to be the prime causes of their financial demise. As a whole, the relative importance of the various factors that

[46] Marijke Gijswijt-Hofstra, *Wijkplaatsen voor vervolgden. Asielverlening in Culemborg, Vianen, Buren, Leerdam en Ijsselstein van de 16e tot eind 18e eeuw* (Amsterdam: De Bataafsche Leeuw, 1984).

[47] GAS, 5072: DB, inv. nr. 697, nr. 68.

TABLE 6.1 *Causes of financial problems among* cessie *applicants 1689–1700*

	Number of instances	Percentage of total (259)
Bad business	193	75
Illness	107	41
Fraud/lawsuits	45	17
Widows	35	14
Theft/piracy	35	14
Natural disaster	22	8

I have extracted from these qualitative accounts also sheds light on the common roots of insolvency in early modern Amsterdam. In this section, I will treat these factors or causes successively and illustrate them with some examples from the research population in order to provide further insight into the challenges that the Amsterdam middle class was facing in this period. When taking a closer look at the arguments provided in the applications for *cessie*, a number of important factors can be discerned. It should be noted that some applications (10 out of 259) did not provide any supporting argumentation at all. The instances of each factor have been listed in Table 6.1.

Unsurprisingly, disappointing business results were the factor that pushed almost all applicants over the brink. Almost half of them mention medical costs, often resulting from pregnancies and related issues, as supplementary reasons for their amassed debts. Smaller numbers of applicants mention problems related to deceased or abusive husbands (the "widows"); fraud committed by or against the applicant and the costs of lawsuits related to such disputes; or piracy and theft. Some were victims of natural disasters such as storms or lightning strikes, as in the case of Adriaen Hellendoorn. Many petitioners mention several causes. The less commonly reported smaller factors, in particular, are almost always supplementary to other main causes for financial troubles. Therefore, it is hard to determine and quantify the exact reason for every insolvency and subsequent *cessie* application. As was discussed in previous chapters, illiquidity and a subsequent insolvency almost always resulted from an intricate interplay of economic (business success or failure) and social (reputation) factors. Nevertheless, the relative occurrence of various arguments provided by the applicants themselves is a strong indication of the risks that merchants, shopkeepers, and other entrepreneurs were confronted with in late seventeenth-century Amsterdam. I will now elaborate on these factors and illustrate them with examples from the dataset.

Bad Business or Slegte neering

The great majority of applicants for *cessie* blamed unfortunate economic conditions for their insolvency. As mentioned in the introduction, the "upcoming war" resulted in higher food prices, while income from trade and its many related industries dwindled. This in turn resulted in trouble for shopkeepers and other small traders such as beer tappers or wine sellers, as many customers failed to repay their outstanding debts due to losing their own sources of income. Broker Roeloff Wonincman, for instance, had previously worked as a bread baker. As he had repeatedly lost great amounts of money on the grain market, however, in 1685 he had been forced to "quit baking and move into a smaller house," after which his unsuccessful attempts to make a living as a broker led to his insolvency in 1690.[48] Sailmaker Crijn Jansz. had borrowed fl. 1,600 in order to buy and reconstruct a house and yard called "De Drie Baersies" just outside the Rampoort when the economic prospects still seemed promising. Soon after this initial investment, he also bought a bleachery close to his business. The economic downturn led to dwindling profits, however, which probably made it hard for Jansz. to pay the interest on his investment loans. He, too, was forced to request *cessie* in order to escape from his creditors' clutches.[49]

Some applicants clearly became the victims of their own bad business decisions. Anna Meijers, for instance, widow of Jan Visbeek, had a small store selling products such as hats, stockings, ribbons, and fringes. She often had to write off batches of goods "due to the changing fashion," which she had apparently failed to anticipate. She also bought goods on credit against high interest, sometimes even selling them for less than their purchase price. This eventually led to her downfall in these "expensive times."[50] Master carpenter Barent van

[48] GAS, 5072: DB, inv. nr. 689, ff. 67v–69r.

[49] GAS, 5072: DB, inv. nr. 692, nr. 22.

[50] GAS, 5072: DB, inv. nr. 702, nr. 59.

Doorn got into financial trouble by taking on construction projects such as the *uytermeerse sluys* for too low a tariff.[51] In the case of wine trader Dirk Mol, the effects of the war and economic downturn were further exacerbated by his careless children. By their doing, a large barrel of brandy was broken so that it "ran out and emptied," which resulted in the loss of a further fl. 125.[52]

Illness

Early modern cities were not the healthiest places on earth. Even if it was sufficiently available, medical care was very basic and rudimentary. Many applicants mention the costs incurred in the numerous pregnancies that women endured in these times without successful birth control.[53] In three cases, an insolvent mentions that their wife suffered from *sweerende borsten* or "festering breasts," a malady connected with breast-feeding. For tapper Willem Pier, tinsmith Abraham van Hoeck, and shopkeeper Hendrick de Wolf, this resulted in high medical expenses for doctors and midwives.[54] Many infants died in or soon after childbirth, resulting in potentially substantial burial costs.

The disappearance of the plague after the 1670s resulted in a substantial decline of the mortality rates in Amsterdam. This most likely contributed to one of the rare premodern periods of birth surpluses between 1696 and 1700. The problems described by the applicants for *cessie* might in part be interpreted as an illustration and consequence of this increase in childbirth and survival rates in this period.[55] The subsequent costs of maintaining an enlarged family are often mentioned as a factor that contributed to the applicants' financial downfall. Cooper Gerrit Heerenzoon describes how his "children, who had become lame and blind" resulted in large expenses for "masters, doctors, and medicines."[56] The son of broker Elias Luijdens, who

[51] GAS, 5072: DB, inv. nr. 689, ff. 146r–148r.

[52] GAS, 5072: DB, inv. nr. 697, nr. 63.

[53] Hubert Nusteling, *Welvaart en werkgelegenheid in Amsterdam 1540–1860. Een relaas over demografie, economie en sociale politiek van een wereldstad* (Amsterdam: De Bataafsche Leeuw, 1985), 26.

[54] GAS, 5072: DB, inv. nr. 689, ff. 100v–101v; inv. nr. 697, nr. 3; inv. nr. 702, nr. 57.

[55] Nusteling, *Welvaart en werkgelegenheid*, 37–40.

[56] GAS, 5072: DB, inv. nr. 689, ff. 108v–109v.

lay down feeling "very wretched and miserable" for a long time, cost him more than fl. 1,000 in "doctors, apothecaries, and barbers."[57] Master mason Jan Jacobsz relates how in the twenty-two years since his marriage with Maritje Claesz, they had produced ten children, apart from five additional miscarriages. After one of these pregnancies, poor Maritje was struck by lameness for an entire year. To make things worse, one of their daughters, "now twenty years of age, was affected by the illness known as *Teeringe* soon after her birth … After all, she has been troubled by a wide variety of fevers and other maladies for twelve years, such that the applicants have been forced to buy great amounts of medicines."[58]

Another group of insolvents was personally incapacitated by a severe illness or accident. Karol Savonne, for instance, broke a leg in 1689, which made it impossible to work for an entire year.[59] Pieter Gerritsz. Veen, who had attempted to earn a living as shoemaker in a cellar near the Haarlemmersluis, *was van God de Heere besogt met een breuk aan sijn lichaam* or "was tried by the Lord our God with a fracture to his body" in 1694. Together with the bad times, this made it impossible for his business to stay afloat.[60] The unfortunate goldsmith Nicolaes Jakel was plagued by all aforementioned maladies. While the applicant himself was hit by "severe illnesses" in the years 1692, 1693, and 1694, his wife suffered from two miscarriages until she died in childbirth in 1692. She left him five young children, all of whom were "very miserably suffering from the pox" at the time.[61] Circumstances such as these must have made it very hard for citizens to keep their businesses afloat amidst the political and economic turmoil of the 1690s.

Fraud and Lawsuits

In this interesting category, we encounter a wide range of cases. First of all, some applicants personally committed fraud. The consequences of these actions sometimes resulted in a debt that they could not repay. Tobacco trader Joseph Polack, for instance, committed fraud when buying wares in Leiden and was incarcerated by that city for

[57] GAS, 5072: DB, inv. nr. 692, nr. 60. [58] GAS, 5072: DB, inv. nr. 689, f. 90.
[59] GAS, 5072: DB, inv. nr. 689, f. 58. [60] GAS, 5072: DB, inv. nr. 697, nr. 78.
[61] GAS, 5072: DB, inv. nr. 697, nr. 75.

twenty-eight days. This resulted in expenses of fl. 800, which he was forced to borrow on the spot, presumably against a very disadvantageous rate of interest.[62] Wine tapper Hermanus de Ruyter committed tax fraud. He relates how he was unfortunate enough to "fall into the hands of the tax tenant Van der Schalck," resulting in heavy fines. De Ruyter was also cheated himself, however, when a certain Willem van Nes failed to deliver wines that had been paid for in advance.[63]

De Ruyter was not the only applicant who was cheated by their suppliers. Isaac Brugman had to initiate a lengthy legal battle against Jan Langerak, who had promised to deliver furs worth fl. 3,000 from Danzig, but failed to honor the agreement.[64] In 1690, wine buyer Jan Lindemans bought twelve casks of brandy. Having received the goods, however, he discovered that the casks were "corrupt, and half-filled with cotton wool." This cost the unfortunate trader more than fl. 1,200.[65] Widow Grietje Evers, whose husband had left for the East Indies, had started a grocery store to sustain her family. However, some merchants sold her bad butter, which drove her customers away. Together with the bad economic conditions, this resulted in the failure of her business. A number of suppliers confiscated her house and effects, leaving her "on the street without any possessions."[66]

One applicant, barber Lambertus van Wesel, became the victim of an especially cunning scheme. When he came to Amsterdam, hoping to earn a living there, he stayed with a host named Tomas Tomase. At a certain point, the latter forced Van Wesel to sign a substantial debt obligation, after which he locked him up in his house as a hostage in order to enforce payment. This made it impossible for the unfortunate barber to practice his trade, after which Tomase even "robbed him of his garments" in lieu of payment. Even when Van Wesel's father offered to pay the fl. 50 which his son had consumed during his stay with the malicious host, Tomase refused to accept this offer, pointing at the obligation worth fl. 250. Completely desperate, Lambertus requested *cessie* to escape from this unfortunate situation.[67]

62 GAS, 5072: DB, inv. nr. 692, nr. 2.
63 GAS, 5072: DB, inv. nr. 702, nr. 27.
64 GAS, 5072: DB, inv. nr. 689, f. 59.
65 GAS, 5072: DB, inv. nr. 697, nr. 69.
66 GAS, 5072: DB, inv. nr. 689, ff. 65v–66r.
67 GAS, 5072: DB, inv. nr. 702, nr. 73.

A special group of applicants were not victimized by a malicious individual, but by a foreign state. After the revocation of the Edict of Nantes in 1685, the French government started a series of severe persecutions of Protestants. Some of these sought refuge in Amsterdam. The merchant Isaac Estienne, for instance, had to flee from Sedan, leaving behind most of his goods. After a short stay in Maastricht, he and his family came to Amsterdam. Here, further troubles awaited them. After eight months, his wife died, leaving him alone with four children and "his old mother of eighty years." Even though some friends extended credit to him in order to continue his trade in lacing, due to the "bad times" he used up his last reserves and was forced to apply for *cessie*.[68]

Another victim of the new French religious policy was the Jewish trader Fernando Cardoso. For many years, he and his family had lived in Bordeaux, also owning a storehouse in Toulouse. When it became public knowledge that he belonged to the Jewish nation, however, Cardoso and a number of other Jews were sentenced *om levendig verbrant te werden* or "to be burned alive." He immediately fled from France, forced to leave behind "his whole family and all of his goods," unable to take anything with him but "two shirts and a little travelling money." The royal death-sentence also resulted in the confiscation of all of Cardoso's goods. His creditors, "knowing the circumstances wherein he had fled France … and completely assured that it was not his fault that he now possessed insufficient means" to repay their claims, should have left him alone, the unfortunate trader sadly remarks. However, for some unknown reason they changed their mind, "to his great sorrow." Because he had been forced to leave behind all his books in France, Cardoso would be unable to effectuate his claims on his debtors there. Because all his goods in Toulouse had been confiscated on royal orders, he did not have any other option than to apply for *cessie* in his new place of residence.[69]

Theft and Piracy

The French did not only cause trouble through religious repression of Protestantism and Judaism, but also through more direct acts

[68] GAS, 5072: DB, inv. nr. 689, ff. 51v–52v.

[69] GAS, 5072: DB, inv. nr. 689, ff. 77v–78v. This case was previously discussed in a blog post on our project website: Maurits den Hollander, "Unfortunate Arguments for *Cessie van Goede*" (October 12, 2018), www.clls.eu.

of aggression. In 1687, the merchant Christiaan Philip Szals was captured by the feared Dunkirk privateers on order of the French king, together with his ship and merchandise. Soon after his liberation, in 1688 his "ship and goods" were confiscated by the king of Denmark. His wife Catharina Andries, who acted as his legal representative, was forced to apply for *cessie* after this chain of misfortunes.[70] Likewise, in 1698 the ship *The Hope*, owned by merchant Dionisius van Vlierden, was captured by French privateers. After he had redeemed it at great cost, a year later the same unlucky ship was "seized and confiscated by the *fiscael* of the navy office." Together with some losses on his trade, this pushed Van Vlierden over the edge into insolvency.[71]

In 1674, Lambert van Till had been granted *cessie* after a previous insolvency, after which he was free to restart his trading career from scratch. Possessing little more than his clothes, he decided to move to Denmark. Initially, this proved to be a good decision. Van Till managed to build up a "store in expensive wares" in Copenhagen, which was later specified as dealing in silk and other luxury textiles. The value of the business and its goods were estimated at about fl. 30,000. Unfortunately, it appears that the commercial success and wealth of this foreigner raised the envy of a number of important servants of the Danish Crown. In 1681, the assessor of the Danish king, Mauritz van der Tie, and his accomplice Evert Holst "violently struck [Van Till] to the ground, and denuded him of all his goods." They also destroyed Van Till's books and papers, after which he could "barely get into safety, nude and robbed of all his possessions." Still not giving up, the unlucky trader travelled throughout Sweden and Denmark with small amounts of textiles between 1681 and 1690. This did not allow him to rebuild his fortune, though, as "he made such small profits that he could barely keep himself alive." At the end of the day, the continuous misfortune drove Van Till to apply for *cessie* once more, unable to repay his creditors in Amsterdam and other places.[72]

Not all cases of theft were as spectacular as these examples of privateering or other state-condoned violence. Still, they could have a

[70] GAS, 5072: DB, inv. nr. 689, ff. 1v–2r. [71] GAS, 5072: DB, inv. nr. 702, nr. 12.
[72] GAS, 5072: DB, inv. nr. 689, ff. 150v–152r. This case was previously discussed in Den Hollander, "Unfortunate Arguments for *Cessie van Goede*."

substantial impact on the applicants' financial situation. Melchert Luursen, for instance, worked as a pastry baker's apprentice and started his own business after his marriage in 1689. Having rented a cellar to store his trade goods, the unfortunate Luursen became insolvent when his cheating landlord stole all of the goods from the cellar, leaving him nothing but debt.[73] Jan Cras and his wife Gratia Putten were robbed by "a certain woman in the Kalverstraat," losing merchandise worth more than fl. 500. Later, their own maid ran off with fl. 120 of possessions stolen from their house. Together with disappointing profits from their business, this made it impossible for the couple to repay their debts.[74] Widow Margriet Seeck, who had traded in horses together with her late husband Jacob Rijck, was robbed by her servant. He took gold and silver worth fl. 2,100 from her house. Soon thereafter, she rented a "riding horse with its accessories" to a man, who never showed up to return them. Together with declining trade, these losses forced her to apply for *cessie*.[75]

Natural Disaster

Pirates and privateers were not the only danger that could be encountered at sea. A number of applicants mention losses incurred due to investments in ships that had sunk in storms or other natural disasters. One of them, Pieter Prop, barely escaped alive from such a dreadful event. When his ship lay before Texel, a heavy storm drove away *De Nederigheyt* and twelve other ships. Leaking, with broken masts, the ship ran aground on the beach of Staveren in Friesland. All Prop's possessions and merchandise were spoiled by the water. To aggravate his financial situation, he lost hundreds of guilders that he had lent to the ship's boatswain, who was swept overboard and drowned during the storm. These events forced Prop to apply for *cessie*.[76]

As we saw before in the case of Adriaen Hellendoorn, natural disaster could also strike on land. An especially unlucky victim of such circumstances was pastry baker Daniel Keijser. In the *Allerheiligenvloed* of 1675, the Spaarne dike between Amsterdam and Haarlem broke

[73] GAS, 5072: DB, inv. nr. 692, nr. 20.
[74] GAS, 5072: DB, inv. nr. 689, ff. 66v–67r. [75] GAS, 5072: DB, inv. nr. 697, nr. 9.
[76] GAS, 5072: DB, inv. nr. 689, f. 69v.

at a place called Halfweg. The flood caused hundreds of guilders of damage to his business and house. Just when Keijser had recovered from these events, a new disaster hit the unfortunate baker in 1685 when a fire broke out in his bakery and once more reduced it to ruins. The loans resulting from these events could no longer be borne during the worsening economic climate of the 1690s, when Keijser had to apply for *cessie*.[77]

Widows and Other Independent Women

Even though we have already encountered various widows such as Anna van Loo (Chapter 1) who remained or became active in various trades after their husbands' deaths, there were some special challenges for members of this category. This was especially true for Antonia van Lommel, who did not lose one but two husbands in a row. First, she had been married to the grocer Andries van Odijk from Utrecht. After his death, she married the young Johannes Boote, who added nothing of value to her estate apart from his labor, and who sired an additional five children with her – besides the four from her first marriage. Of these nine children, "only one had passed away." Due to bad economic circumstances, they failed to earn enough to feed this extensive household. Hoping to do better in Amsterdam, they moved to this center of commerce in the summer of 1692, where Boote started to work as wine buyer on the Fluwelenburgwal near the Halsteeg. Bad luck seems to have clung to Antonia, as in that same year her second husband also passed away, while her children suffered from a *sware siekte* or "heavy illness." Even though "with the help of good people she was able to continue her trade," as time went on her profits dwindled and she did not earn enough to feed her children and to pay her debts. By 1700, her situation had deteriorated to the extent that she was forced to apply for *cessie*. Interestingly, the widow seems to have kept a *schuldboek* full of bad debts, the majority of which she never expected to be able to recover.[78]

[77] GAS, 5072: DB, inv. nr. 697, nr. 11.

[78] GAS, 5072: DB, inv. nr. 702, nr. 32. Books such as that of the widow Van Lommel must have been very common, but hardly any of them have survived to the present day in our archives. An intriguing example of a surviving *schuldboek* that has recently been published is that of the merchant Arend Kenkhuis, who operated in the region of Twente in the early seventeenth century: Tilly Hesselink-Van

Sometimes, women had to fight for their social and economic position due to spousal abuse. While it was generally frowned upon by the religious authorities, during the second half of the seventeenth century such problematic relationships increasingly ended in a "separation from bed and board" or even an official legal divorce.[79] Among the *cessie* applicants, I encountered two problematic marriages. In the case of Maria Swart, Jan de Koningh had failed to fulfil his duties towards his wife and two children. He spent all his time engaged in "countless debaucheries by day and night, being drunk as well as seeking the company of unfaithful women." Thereby, he consumed all their possessions, eventually even absenting himself from his wife and creditors for years. Having fallen into great poverty, Maria could see no other way out than requesting *cessie* to rid herself of the debts incurred by her unfaithful husband.[80] In a similar way, Susanna Aleman had "found herself to be cheated" by wine trader Hendrik Grol. While he promised to use her dowry to set up a business to maintain their family, he incurred large debts and even ended up being locked away in the *Gevangenpoort* of The Hague. In the Dutch Republic, marriages in principle resulted in a "community of property" or *gemeenschap van goederen*. When Aleman tried to legally divorce her husband, after a two-year process the shrewd Grol managed to convince her to conclude an amicable settlement, in which she even committed herself to his debts rather than finally being liberated from this liability. When the wine trader quickly reverted to his old ways, one of his creditors kept Susanna hostage "for about one whole year," completely disregarding her poverty. This eventually forced her to apply for *cessie*.[81]

The Aftermath of *Cessie van Goede*

After the letter of *cessie van goede* had been officially registered by the local court of the applicant's place of residence through an

der Riet, Wim Kuiper, and Cor Trompetter, *Het schuldboek van Arend Kenkhuis* (Amsterdam: Aksant, 2008).

79 Manon van der Heijden, *Huwelijk in Holland. Stedelijke rechtspraak en kerkelijke tucht, 1550–1700* (Amsterdam: Bert Bakker, 1998), 73–75 and 268–70.

80 GAS, 5072: DB, inv. nr. 697, nr. 23.

81 GAS, 5072: DB, inv. nr. 697, nr. 25. On marriage in early modern Amsterdam, see also René van Weeren and Tine De Moor, *Ja, ik wil! Verlief, verloofd, getrouwd in Amsterdam 1580–1810* (Amsterdam: Prometheus, 2019).

interinement, their estate would be executed according to the local procedures and the proceeds would be distributed among their creditors. Generally, of course, this execution sale would not suffice to repay all outstanding debts. In 1544, Charles V had provided that a successful – and thus innocent – applicant for *cessie* could retain a limited number of basic goods with which they could strive to arrive "at fatter fortune," as it was often expressed in those days. According to the ordinance, the applicant could retain a single bed and its appurtenances, besides a small number of *haeffelycke goederen* or movables. This expressly excluded any tin- or silverware, as well as additional furniture.[82] Grotius offers a rather stricter interpretation than that expressed in the imperial ordinance, stating that applicants "could retain nothing but their daily apparel"; however, in his view this also meant that someone who did not have any other goods left could still qualify for the benefice.[83] Van Wassenaer adds that artisans were allowed to keep "any tools, needed to carry out their craft and so make a living." This also meant that a university student would be allowed to keep the books that were essential for their studies, but this was contested by many others.[84] Generally, therefore, it seems that successful applicants were allowed to keep a set of clothing, the tools needed to practice their craft, as well as some very basic goods.[85]

As a *cessie* did not wipe out remaining debts, but simply protected the insolvent from incarceration, creditors might still hope to retrieve some of the remaining debts in the future if their debtor retained the opportunity to make a living after the legal procedure. As Van Leeuwen states, once the applicant had obtained any new means after their *cessie*, "[they are] obliged to repay as much [of their old debts] as [they] can afford to after having paid for [their] basic needs" or

[82] Lameere and Simont (eds.), *Recueil des ordonnances des Pays-Bas* [*ROPB*], *Deuxième série 1506–1700*, 8 vols. (Brussels: J. Goemaere, 1910), V:52–56 (May 10, 1544), preprint 36.

[83] De Groot, *Inleidinge*, 328, III.51.4.

[84] Van Wassenaer, *Practijk judicieel*, I:249, II.18.22.

[85] These Dutch authors largely seem to base themselves upon ideas that had already been expressed by legal scholars in late medieval Italy: Walter Pakter, "The Origins of Bankruptcy in Medieval Canon and Roman Law," in *Proceedings of the Seventh International Congress of Medieval Canon Law*, ed. Peter Linehan (Vatican City: Bibliotheca Apostolica, 1988), 494–96.

sijnen nood-druft.[86] This corresponds to what is stated by Grotius.[87] What precisely this *nood-druft* entailed, however, was not always clear. Van Wassenaer argues that creditors could not seek to execute goods obtained after a *cessie* if this would "fail to leave the *cedent* with enough to live a decent life," and furthermore "that such goods would have to be of sufficient value to give all creditors a substantial profit." A judge would have to consider whether a former insolvent had become wealthy enough to warrant a further execution of their goods.[88] This was intended to provide them with an incentive to try to rebuild their business, which would eventually allow the old creditors to regain all or part of their claims. The extended *Papegay* seems to confirm this procedure. It provides a case in which a creditor who had not joined in with the original *cessie* procedure attempted to execute their debt sometime after the insolvent had obtained the benefice. The insolvent did not deny the debt, but argued that they had handed over their estate to a curator, and could therefore not be forced to pay. The creditor argued that any goods obtained after the *cessie* were not deemed to be in the custody of the curator, but would be open for an execution, since the former insolvent had by now arrived *ad meliorem fortunam*. In response, the court ordered both parties to appear before the commissioners of the Desolate Boedelskamer, where the creditor would have to prove that the insolvent had indeed arrived at fatter fortune and could therefore be held responsible to repay (part of) their old debts. In this way, "even if the *cessie* had received its *interinement*, one could still seek to obtain a judgment on an unpaid debt."[89]

These scholarly opinions on the aftermath of applications for *cessie* raise two interesting questions: first, whether the benefice was ever refused in practice; second, whether successful applicants actually managed to revive their business with such success that they could start to repay their old creditors. Even though it is very hard to find reliable information about the lives of insolvents after they had been rehabilitated or otherwise removed from the direct supervision of the commissioners, this problem can at least partially be solved through an analysis of the fascinating category of repeat beneficiaries of *cessie*.

86 Van Leeuwen, *Rooms-Hollands-regt*, 446, IV.41.3.
87 De Groot, *Inleidinge*, 328, III.51.6.
88 Van Wassenaer, *Practijk judicieel*, I:254–55, II.18.34–35.
89 Van Alphen, *Papegay*, I:226.

The fact that it was legally possible to file an application for *cessie van goede* if one had already been granted the benefice at some point in the past is confirmed by Van Zutphen.[90] A closer analysis of such cases allows us to make some tentative observations on the practical impact of the *cessie* procedure on the lives of individual insolvents.

Before examining the cases found in my dataset, I would like to draw attention to an intriguing example from the 1650s of an applicant who was first refused, but subsequently admitted to the benefice. As part of his research into Rembrandt's insolvency, Machiel Bosman examined all Amsterdam *cessie* requests that were submitted in the years surrounding the painter's application in the archives of the High Court of Holland. During this source analysis, he also came across the case of Pieter van der Horst.[91] In this application, which was forwarded to the Amsterdam commissioners on December 14, 1655, the unfortunate Amsterdam citizen recalls how he had already tried to obtain *cessie* three months earlier. When the commissioners of the Desolate Boedelskamer asked his creditors if they had any objections to their issuing a favorable *advijs* in this case, a number of *gepassineerde*, or hot-tempered, creditors had unjustifiably argued that Van der Horst had not acted in good faith. Even though the insolvent had attempted to prove them wrong, the commissioners had still decided to refuse the *interinement* of his benefice. According to Van der Horst, this refusal to take note of his arguments destroyed the whole purpose of the *interinement*, in which he should have received a fair hearing *ter purge off om sich daer tegen deuchdelyck te defenderen* or "to purge or properly defend himself." As his wife and children "dearly needed his assistance to alleviate their great poverty," the applicant pleaded with the High Court to reconsider his case. Perhaps the councilors were sensitive to his final argument, that the granting of the benefice would allow him *om sich selff sijn wijff en kinderen de mont open te houden* or "to keep the mouths of himself, his wife and his children open [i.e. filled]," as they "once more" forwarded the benefice to the Amsterdam authorities. After a careful reconsideration of the case, the latter apparently altered their

[90] Bernhard van Zutphen, *Practycke der Nederlansche rechten vande daghelijcksche soo civile als criminele questien* (Leeuwarden: Dominicus Lens, 1664), 98.

[91] Machiel Bosman, *Rembrandts plan. De ware geschiedenis van zijn faillissement* (Amsterdam: Atheneum – Polak & Van Gennep, 2019), 171 (n. 21).

opinion and sent a positive *rescriptio* to the High Court, which officially arrived on January 12, 1656.[92]

While Bosman justifiably stresses the importance of the *interinement*, which has been somewhat neglected in the existing literature, his interpretation of the reason why Van der Horst's first application for *cessie* failed seems to be incorrect. According to Bosman, the *interinement* would not have taken place because the commissioners doubted the applicant's "good faith." From the insolvent's letter to the High Court, however, we learn that the *interinement* was the *reason* for the commissioners' refusal: they had based themselves upon the (false?) accusations of fraud by a number of Van der Horst's creditors. When the latter sought to redress this situation through a second application for *cessie*, the Amsterdam commissioners must have re-examined their evidence in this case, deciding that Van der Horst *was* innocent after all and therefore deserved to be granted the benefice.

How can this case be related to the examples of multiple applicants found in my dataset covering the 1690s? Of the seven insolvents in this category, only one states that his former application had been rejected. Daniel Alexander, a Jewish peddler, had applied for *cessie* in 1689, which failed due to *eenige wangunstighe menschen* or "some ill-affected people." It is somewhat surprising that Alexander's *staet* cannot be found among the other applications of that year. Fortunately, an entry from the commissioners' minutes sheds light on this case. After having convoked the creditors twice, on November 15, 1689 the Amsterdam commissioners decided to forward the case to the city of Gorinchem. Unfortunately, their reasons for doing so were not specified. It might be that this was seen as Alexander's main place of residence at the time of his insolvency, or that his family actually stayed there while he attempted to make a living abroad.[93] From the time of his first failed *cessie* application onwards, he had travelled through the countryside as a peddler, attempting to earn a little money by selling small pieces of cotton clothing to alleviate his family's great poverty. Due to the bad economic conditions, this had

92 NL-HaNA, Staten van Holland na 1572, 3.01.04.01, inv. nr. 60, pp. 21–22. Bosman seems to have misread the dates from the original manuscript, stating that Van der Horst's application was received on December 13, 1655 and that the final letters were granted on January 22, 1656.

93 GAS, 5072: DB, inv. nr. 26, f. 131r.

only resulted in larger debts and failing credit, leaving him nothing but another try at a *cessie* application in 1700.[94]

The most intriguing element of this case is that it seems to be exceptional. What is more, even this single refusal did apparently not really result from creditors of ill-will in Amsterdam, but took place after the case had been passed on to the Gorinchem authorities. All other former applicants for *cessie* seem to have been able to use it as a way to reintegrate into the civic community, even if their businesses got into trouble again at a later stage. Abraham van Casele, for instance, had received the benefice in 1680. After that time, he was able to continue his work as a broker in shares for ten years, until he lost large amounts of money on the Exchange and was again forced to apply for *cessie* in June 1691.[95] Artist Dirck Smidt had received *cessie* in 1683. Afterwards, a certain Sijbrandt Bas, who lived in the Agnietenstraet, was kind enough to lend him the money that he needed to pick up his "craft of drawing." Illness, theft, and bad business forced him, "as a sickly man," to resort to the benefice again in 1689.[96] The fact that someone was willing to extend credit to a former *cessie* applicant illustrates how the benefice allowed these insolvents to retain some honor and to reintegrate into the civic community. In that sense, it was not so much a final condemnation as a new start for honest but unfortunate insolvents.

Interestingly, it seems that the authorities in late seventeenth-century Amsterdam went even further than De la Court in their kindness towards citizens with financial difficulties. In the case of the stock fish trader Johan Luden, a fraudulent bankrupt was treated like one of De la Court's "honeybees" rather than being punished for his crimes. When Jan Bruin was appointed as curator of Luden's estate on January 14, 1694, the debtor himself was locked up in the "ordinary prison of this city."[97] He had been arrested in Bremen by Antoni van Oort, who received fl. 200 as a reward for his efforts to deliver the fugitive bankrupt "back into the shackles of this city."[98] Besides that, the curator

[94] GAS, 5072: DB, inv. nr. 702, nr. 40. [95] GAS, 5072: DB, inv. nr. 689, f. 142r.
[96] GAS, 5072: DB, inv. nr. 689, ff. 17v–18r. [97] GAS, 5072: DB, inv. nr. 28, f. 6r.
[98] GAS, 5072: DB, inv. nr. 28, ff. 14v–15r. On the *oversenden* of criminals from foreign jurisdictions, see Toon van Weel, "De interjurisdictionele betrekkingen in criminele zaken van het Amsterdamse Gerecht (1700–1810)," in *Nieuw licht op oude justitie. Misdaad en straf ten tijde van de Republiek*, ed. Sjoerd Faber (Muiderberg: Coutinho, 1989), esp. 33–43.

was to pay out fl. 119 – 16 "for some costs of the transport of Johan Luden from Bremen." The commissioners explicitly stated that Luden had been imprisoned because of his "trickeries," among which were "the hiding of money, goods, and effects," pointing to a clear intent to deceive his creditors.[99] It seems clear that Luden was a fraudulent bankrupt, who deserved imprisonment rather than a *cessie* that might save some of his honor.

Notwithstanding his fraudulent acts, Luden's *staet* (describing debts worth fl. 78,922) was received by the Desolate Boedelskamer on January 18, 1695.[100] On November 4, 1694, Luden's wife Joanna Joachina van Campen had already been allowed to redeem some gold and silver jewels from the estate, which had been valued at fl. 485 – 5 – 14 by Dirck Schelte.[101] Remarkably, none of Luden's Amsterdam creditors protested the *cessie* request, and the burgomasters sent their *rescriptio* with a favorable *advijs* to the High Court on February 8, 1695. The fact that this was rather unusual is shown by a conflict that arose between the High Court and the Amsterdam authorities. After hearing about Luden's fraudulent acts from a creditor from The Hague, who according to the Amsterdam representatives had "wrongfully informed [the Court], out of pure hate," the judges decided to neglect the favorable *advijs* from Amsterdam and gave a *nihil* on Luden's request. They argued that if the High Court could grant *cessie*, it could also independently refuse to do so on good grounds.[102]

This downplaying of their role in the *cessie* procedure infuriated the Amsterdam authorities. Together with and on behalf of Luden, they filed a complaint with the States of Holland against the High Court's ruling. In their reaction to this complaint, the States agreed that the High Court had overstepped its mark. As this court was the highest legal authority in Holland, if it one-sidedly decided to refuse a *cessie* request, an insolvent could potentially remain "incarcerated for eternity, or for so long as it would please even a single one of his creditors." For this very reason, the States argued, there were no prior examples of cases in which the High Court had refused to grant the benefice after a favorable *advijs* from the local authorities,

[99] GAS, 5072: DB, inv. nr. 28, f. 6r. [100] GAS, 5072: DB, inv. nr. 697, nr. 7.
[101] GAS, 5072: DB, inv. nr. 28, ff. 52v–53r.
[102] NL-HaNA, Staten van Holland na 1572, 3.01.04.01, inv. nr. 131, pp. 156–59.

against whose judgment the applicant could always file an appeal. The States ordered the High Court to retract its *nihil*, and to provide the letter of *cessie* according to the *advijs* of the Amsterdam authorities. In doing so, they clearly protected the jurisdiction of the city in such matters.[103]

Perhaps this dispute helped to further reduce the High Court's agency in the granting of *cessie* requests. A few decades later, when the councilors were confronted with a negative *advijs* from local authorities on a *cessie* application, they often simply decided to "put the request aside for a bit": *men besloot om het verzoekschrift nog wat te laten liggen*. If pressed to decide, as Van Bijnkershoek remarks, *sed cujus rationem fateor me non intelligere* or "even though I could not fathom the grounds for their reasoning," the councilors simply granted the letter even after a *kwaad* or "angry" *advijs* as, after all, "the creditors would still be able to counter it during its *interinement*" in the local court that was treating the insolvency. Clearly, his colleagues had had enough of the recurring competence disputes with the multitude of Holland urban authorities, who fiercely guarded their local jurisdictions in these matters.[104]

Even though the reaction of the Amsterdam authorities is understandable from the perspective of protecting the city's legal autonomy against interference by the central courts, it is intriguing that it accepted Luden's *cessie* request in the first place. I would like to argue that this points towards a pragmatic rather than moralistic approach towards such cases. De la Court acknowledged that even in the case of an already convicted fraudulent bankrupt, their creditors could still decide to conclude an accord or other type of composition with them if they felt that this was in their advantage. For them it was purely *res nummi* or "a matter of money."[105] An execution sale would usually result in much lower proceeds than the actual value of the auctioned goods and effects.[106] At the end of the day, a proper *cessie* rather than an endless imprisonment and execution of the estate could

[103] NL-HaNA, Staten van Holland na 1572, 3.01.04.01, inv. nr. 131, p. 159.

[104] Van Bijnkershoek, *Observationes Tumultuariae*, I:nrs. 795 and 942; and the second volume (Haarlem: Tjeenk Willink, 1934) II:nrs. 1470, 1527, and 1568.

[105] Pieter de la Court, *Interest van Holland, ofte gronden van Hollands-welvaren* (Amsterdam: Joan. Cyprianus vander Gracht, 1662), 85–86.

[106] Gijswijt-Hofstra, *Wijkplaatsen*, 136–37.

be beneficial to all parties involved. It was simply the most efficient procedural solution when faced with an impoverished debtor.

We should keep in mind that Luden had been in jail for a year before he applied for *cessie* in January 1695. Perhaps the authorities and his creditors considered this dishonor to be sufficient punishment for his fraudulent acts. When out of his shackles, Luden might revive his business and be able to pay back more of the remaining debt than could be expected of him if he remained stuck in his current situation. The fact that his sons continued a flourishing stock fish trade after 1700, their offspring in turn being involved in important eighteenth-century banking firms such as Hope & Co., shows that this was a sensible decision from his creditors' perspective.[107] Through *cessie van goede*, many Amsterdam insolvents were reintegrated into the civic community, which was ultimately to all parties' advantage.

Conclusion

The liberal application of the Roman-law inspired benefice of *cessie van goede* as it came to be used in seventeenth-century Holland, ensured that official, legal solutions for financial demise became available for a much broader range of social groups in early modern Amsterdam. While an accord drawn up before a notary or – after the middle of the seventeenth century – arbitrated by the commissioners, was usually not an option for the middle-class artisans and small traders who formed the bulk of the urban citizenry, *cessie* offered them a decent and even honorable way out of their financial quandaries. As it was observed in prior chapters of this book, while in many countries *cessie* was associated with criminal deeds and shameful acts, in the Dutch Republic even Calvinist preachers considered it to be the only acceptable act that was left to an insolvent. Perhaps this was in part caused by the procedural involvement of impartial and reliable legal institutions such as the Desolate Boedelskamer. Through the *interinement* or official registration of the benefice, all creditors were provided with the opportunity to report fraudulent acts to a court that was much closer and more accessible to them than the High Court in The Hague – let alone the Great Council of Malines that had

[107] GAS, 922: Archief van de Familie Luden en Aanverwante Families.

originally granted the benefice. Just as in the case of the fact-based *curatele* and accord procedures, the involvement of the commissioners added systemic trust that helped to glue together the shards of a broken commercial and social reputation. All of these factors must have contributed to the reappraisal of the benefice and its moral connotations, leading to its broad acceptance among seventeenth-century creditors, judges, and moralists alike.

Even though financial misfortune always resulted in a weakening of one's social position, in the Dutch Republic and especially in Amsterdam a decent legal solution for insolvency went a long way towards retaining one's social status. While an accord was always to be preferred, the majority of Amsterdam's insolvents in this period actually opted for an application for *cessie van goede* when facing illiquidity. The examples of applicants who were able to build up their businesses again after a former *cessie* procedure indicate that the benefice was a generally acceptable solution, both for insolvents of more modest means and those facing uncompromising creditors. Ultimately, this benefited not just individual insolvents and – if they managed to arrive "at fatter fortune" – their creditors, but also the Amsterdam civic community as a whole.

Having discussed the Desolate Boedelskamer's procedure, staff, and the main groups of insolvents that appear in its archives, we should now focus in on the important question of the impact of this institution on economy and society in both Amsterdam and the Dutch Republic as a whole. In the final chapter of this book, I will explore how this institution could actually attain its remarkable achievements.

General Conclusion

Old habits die hard. Even though the French-appointed mayor of Amsterdam, Rijksbaron W. J. van Brienen van de Groote Lindt, had ordered the last commissioners of the Desolate Boedelskamer to liquidate their remaining cases and wrap up its procedures "as soon as possible" on April 30, 1811, this committee clearly took its time. Only by August 1835 had every person who could still reasonably effect a claim on money in the possession of the court been satisfied, after which the committee presented its final account to the municipal council. Just as its foundation in the early seventeenth century was only realized after decades of deliberations, while many older legal traditions, both public and private, continued to influence the new court, by the nineteenth century Amsterdam clearly found it difficult to part with an institution that had served the interests of both citizens and foreigners so well for almost two centuries.[1] Even today, actually more so after the introduction of the 1893 *Faillissementswet* than in much of the nineteenth century, many elements of the old local Amsterdam insolvency legislation and practices continue to influence the way in which such matters are dealt with in the Kingdom of the Netherlands.[2]

[1] Goswin Moll, *De Desolate Boedelskamer te Amsterdam: bijdrage tot de kennis van het Oud-Hollandsch failliten-recht* (Amsterdam: De Roever-Kröber-Bakels, 1879), 201–3.

[2] For instance, according to art. 20 Fw, the *faillissementsbeslag* (insolvency attachment) intriguingly still excludes *het bed en beddengoed van de schuldenaar en diens*

As a recent volume on the history of social inequality states, this phenomenon is "to a large extent shaped by practices of governance, political decisions, and the overall organization of polities."[3] Historians have often related the creation of new legal and institutional solutions for insolvency to business cycle fluctuations. Do the Amsterdam data indicate any social levelling or polarizing effects of the functioning of its seventeenth-century insolvency legislation? How can these be related to the broader economic trends? And to what extent is the case studied in this book, Amsterdam, exemplary for related developments in the Dutch Republic as a whole? This final concluding chapter will engage with these broader questions, in order to suggest how the assembled empirical data can help historians to better understand the relations between institutional innovation and economic growth.

The Impact of Crisis

The year 1648 was the high point of both the outreach and the volume of the Dutch Republic's maritime commerce. Soon after this zenith of its Golden Age, however, a series of naval wars with England (1652–1654, 1665–1667, and 1672–1674), the last of which was accompanied by the French invasion of the *Rampjaar* in 1672, combined with new mercantilist policies in many European countries to disrupt Dutch trade. From the 1660s onwards, economic growth slowed down. Nominal wages stagnated at a high level while prices dropped, resulting in a "stationary state" of the economy that would last until the mid-eighteenth century. In 1672, investments in the construction sector had virtually ceased, at least partially caused by house rents that continued to drop by 10 percent for the cheapest dwellings to as much as 25 percent for the most expensive houses in Amsterdam. Atypically, the house rents started to rise again during the Nine Years' War (1688–1697), accompanied by an increase in the revenues of the

gezin or "the bed and its appurtenance of the insolvent and his family" from the insolvent estate. Insolvency legislation, as we have already seen in our examination of Roman, medieval, and early modern practices, seems to be remarkably stable in its development over time.

[3] Bruno Blondé et al., "The Low Countries' Paradox," in *Inequality and the City in the Low Countries (1200–2020)*, ed. Bruno Blondé et al. (Turnhout: Brepols, 2020), 32.

convooien en licenten, a tax on imports and exports that reliably reflects the volume of maritime commerce.[4]

The annual fluctuations in the number of Amsterdam registrations in the books of *curatele* (on which Oldewelt based his statistics) in the second half of the seventeenth century closely correspond to the general development of the *convooien en licenten*. This suggests that (1) the business cycle in this period was still closely connected to developments in maritime commerce and (2) that these fluctuations were accompanied by increasing or decreasing numbers of insolvencies.[5] Contrary to the general business cycle, the real interest rates for both short- and long-term capital do not seem to have borne any relation to the number of insolvencies in this same period. This reaffirms the observation that a singular focus on (credit) markets might blind us to the important subsidiary role of contextual factors such as trust and reputation, which in historical practice must have played a crucial role in the (il)liquidity and subsequent insolvency of individual entrepreneurs. The number of insolvencies does, however, seem to be closely linked to fluctuations in both contemporary real wages and inflation, suggesting that these were affected by the same underlying developments.[6]

In many European countries, the long sixteenth century had seen a dramatic increase in the amount of litigation, after which this declined again from the middle of the seventeenth century onwards. The people that were responsible for the most important increase in lawsuits are generally described as the "economically independent members of social groups from the lower middling ranks of society." Griet Vermeesch has argued that "a socially differentiated analysis of the uses of justice would help to improve our understanding of changing patterns of litigation" during the early modern period.[7]

[4] Jan de Vries and Ad van der Woude, *The First Modern Economy: Success, Failure, and Perseverance of the Dutch Economy, 1500–1815* (Cambridge University Press, 1997), 673–81; Clé Lesger, *Huur en conjunctuur. De woningmarkt in Amsterdam, 1550–1850* (Amsterdam: Historisch Seminarium van de Universiteit van Amsterdam, 1986), esp. pp. 48–50; Pit Dehing, *Geld in Amsterdam. Wisselbank en wisselkoersen, 1650–1725* (Hilversum: Verloren, 2012), 42–44.

[5] W. F. H. Oldewelt, "Twee eeuwen Amsterdamse faillissementen en het verloop van de conjunctuur (1636 tot 1838)," *Tijdschrift voor Geschiedenis* 75, no. 4 (1962): 421–35, 429–30 and 434.

[6] Dehing, *Geld*, 43–47.

[7] Griet Vermeesch, "Reflections on the Relative Accessibility of Law Courts in Early Modern Europe," *Crime, Histoire & Sociétés / Crime, History & Societies* 19, no.

Having discussed the collective characteristics of the insolvents in seventeenth-century Amsterdam who were able to conclude accords with their creditors, or had to make do with an application for *cessie van goede*, it is interesting to compare these groups and the ways in which they were able to use insolvency legislation to their advantage.

While the "working poor," such as sailors or day laborers, would be affected directly by any disturbance of maritime commerce, they generally did not hold citizenship and usually also lacked the possessions and debts that would have warranted their appearance in the archives of the Desolate Boedelskamer. One could argue that their absence from the archives of this court displays its inaccessibility for large parts of early modern society, but in reality this would most probably have been irrelevant, as these people would not have benefited from the court's procedure anyway.

Although the competitiveness of the Dutch economy gradually deteriorated over the last decades of the seventeenth century, because of the relatively high and stable real wages this should not have resulted in direct financial problems for the majority of the skilled workers who made up the greater part of the Amsterdam citizenry. However, this image does not seem to correspond at all with the lamentations found in the personal stories of applicants for *cessie van goede* that were discussed in Chapter 6. Around 1700, many Amsterdam innkeepers complained about *deze schrale, miserabel slechte of dure tijd* or "these meagre, miserably bad or expensive times."[8] Oldewelt's data indeed show a slight peak in the number of Amsterdam insolvencies in the years 1697–1702, but this is no worse than the situation during the First Anglo-Dutch War, while the crisis of the 1670s and especially the Second Anglo-Dutch War of the mid-1660s show much higher annual numbers.[9] How can we explain this phenomenon?

2 (2015): 53–76, 68–69. See e.g. Craig Muldrew, "Credit and the Courts: Debt Litigation in a Seventeenth-Century Urban Community," *Economic History Review* 46, no. 1 (1993); Craig Muldrew, *The Economy of Obligation: The Culture of Credit and Social Relations in Early Modern England* (Basingstoke: Macmillan Press, 1998).

[8] Maarten Hell, *De Amsterdamse herberg 1450–1800. Geestrijk centrum van het openbare leven* (Nijmegen: Vantilt, 2017), 275–78.

[9] Oldewelt, "Twee eeuwen," 434.

First, the years 1696–1700 saw one of the very rare occurrences of a birth surplus in Amsterdam, which in combination with macroeconomic tensions might have increased financial stress on individual households.[10] Second, 1698 appears to have been a year of harvest failures in Danzig, the most important source of grain imports for Amsterdam, which led to rising food prices and export bans that clearly put merchants at a disadvantage to the benefit of the common good.[11] Third, it is important to realize that the combination of stable nominal wages and a decreasing general price level, which protected wage laborers through rising real incomes, actually put the Amsterdam entrepreneurs who constitute the majority of the insolvents in my research population at a relative disadvantage. At the same time, however, just as the poor were protected from the worst shocks of economic crises through extensive social welfare policies (as described in Chapter 1), for Amsterdam merchants, shopkeepers, and other more well-to-do citizens insolvency legislation formed part of the solution for their financial troubles. This does not, however, mean that the legal system affected all members of the elite and middling groups in an entirely similar way.

When we compare the size or total debt value of the insolvent estates in the accord and *cessie* populations, it is immediately clear that the former were larger than the latter by roughly a factor of ten. Generally, the entrepreneurs who had been able to mobilize greater amounts of credit before their insolvency were also able to resolve their illiquidity through more favorable legal solutions than their less fortunate colleagues, who had to make do with an application for *cessie* (see Figure C.1).

Entrepreneurs who faced a sudden illiquidity that they could not resolve in an informal way could relatively quickly regain control over their estate after an accord had been ratified by the majority of their creditors, which was especially beneficial due to the protection

[10] Hubert Nusteling, *Welvaart en werkgelegenheid in Amsterdam 1540–1860. Een relaas over demografie, economie en sociale politiek van een wereldstad* (Amsterdam: De Bataafsche Leeuw, 1985), 40.

[11] J. G. van Dillen, "De duurte van het jaar 1698," *Onze Eeuw* 17, no. 1 (1917): 250–73. See also Daniel R. Curtis and Jessica Dijkman, "The Escape from Famine in the Northern Netherlands: A Reconsideration Using the 1690s Harvest Failures and a Broader Northwest European Perspective," *The Seventeenth Century* 34, no. 2 (2019): 229–58.

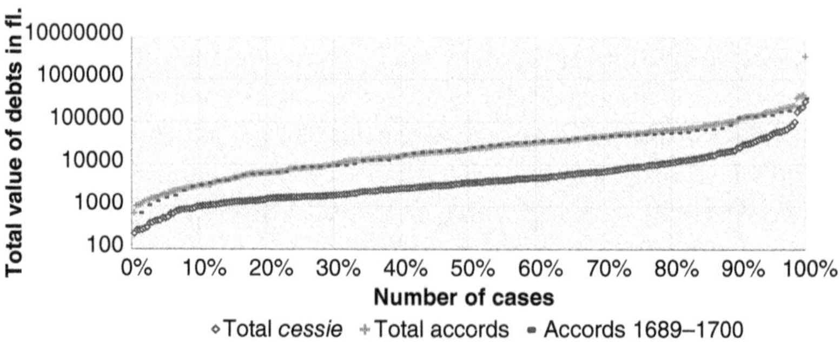

FIGURE C.1 Value of debts per applicant for *cessie van goede* compared to insolvent estates in which an accord was concluded in the qualitative dataset on a logarithmic scale (1631–1700)

from further litigation that was often part of such agreements. While an application for *cessie* was not the first choice for many Amsterdam insolvents, the liberal way in which this benefice was applied still offered broad categories of citizens protection against debt imprisonment and continuing harassment from particularly antagonistic creditors. As I have shown in this book, in many cases the legal benefice of *cessie*, even though it entailed the execution of an estate, did not necessarily result in the end of one's social and economic life. On the contrary, many former applicants were able to revive their businesses after the commissioners of the Desolate Boedelskamer had provided a decent legal solution for their repayment conflicts.

The miserable tales of applicants for *cessie van goede* might in part be overdone due to these insolvents' fear that they might otherwise fail to obtain the benefice. There is, however, another reason why the general economic situation might be portrayed too negatively in the lamentations of this group. Thomas Safley remarks that even though insolvencies "occur in the context of economic conjunctures, [they] result no less from managerial decisions." Business failure was never entirely caused by governmental acts, market conditions, or structural economic factors. A single rumor or a number of bad business decisions might push an enterprise over the brink of illiquidity that, had it been managed with greater skill, might have survived the crisis based upon its credit and good name.[12] It is this element of human

[12] Thomas Max Safley, "Business Failure and Civil Scandal in Early Modern Europe," *BHR* 83 (2009): 35–60, 59–60.

agency that is perhaps best reflected by the individual insolvencies that have been discussed in this book and that, notwithstanding their at times substantial annual numbers, never amounted to more than a fraction of the thousands of hard-working and enterprising Amsterdam citizens who actually stayed afloat even as its Golden Age drew to an end.

A well-functioning and broadly accessible legal treatment of insolvencies, such as that of the Desolate Boedelskamer in seventeenth-century Amsterdam, is generally seen as a good example of an "efficient" institution, which exists because it has a positive effect on economic growth by providing additional security to property rights. Such a classic interpretation in the tradition of the new institutional economics, however, should be amended on two grounds. First, even though insolvency legislation helps private contracting to recover after a breach of trust, it does so not by protecting or restoring past property rights, but rather by intervening in private contracts and reallocating wealth for the common good.[13] Second, to be truly successful in the long run, efficient systems of exchange need to be coupled with social balance.[14] The developments in Amsterdam insolvency legislation between 1647 and 1659, especially the introduction of majority compositions, constitute a clear example of institutional innovations that benefited the common good to the detriment of some individual creditors. The differentiated treatment of insolvencies through accord and *cessie* created sufficient flexibility to restore trust and commercial relations between broad groups of Amsterdam's inhabitants, smoothening the impact of crisis on both members of the city's elite and middling groups to the benefit of its economy and society as a whole.

Historians have often related the creation of such new and innovative legal and institutional solutions for insolvency to the demands raised by specific moments of crisis. According to Safley, for instance, the public scandal surrounding the 1529 insolvency of the Augsburg Höchstetter merchant banking firm would have led

[13] Jérôme Sgard, "Bankruptcy Laws: East versus West," in *Law and Long-Term Economic Change: A Eurasian Perspective*, ed. Debin Ma and Jan Luiten van Zanden (Stanford University Press, 2011), 207–9.

[14] Bas van Bavel, *Manors and Markets: Economy and Society in the Low Countries, 500–1600* (Oxford University Press, 2010), esp. 403–8.

to "the creation of formal, uniform regulations for business failure that would transform business practice and capital redistribution."[15] Oldewelt argues that his graph displaying the fluctuations in the annual number of insolvencies in Amsterdam between 1636 and 1838 "more than any other statistic, provides us with a good indication of the prosperity of its citizenry in a given period" thanks to its "high degree of sensitivity for changes in the business cycle."[16] Did the insolvency legislation and practices treated in this book indeed develop in response to crisis and widespread problems among certain groups of Amsterdam citizens?

While economic crises indisputably had an impact on individual citizens that found themselves confronted with illiquidity, their oft-assumed causal relation with legal innovations is much less evident. The Desolate Boedelskamer was established in the middle of the most opulent economic efflorescence that the city of Amsterdam had ever experienced, just before the 1648 high-point of its overseas trade. On the contrary, the "crisis decades" of the last quarter of the seventeenth century, which brought higher annual numbers of insolvencies, saw little change to either the institution itself or to its legal framework. The only exception to this rule might be the 1659 ordinance, the introduction of which could in part have been prompted by the preceding peak of insolvencies after the Second Anglo-Dutch War. The fact that it flowed from a number of official adaptations or *ampliaties* in the preceding decade, however, suggests that the ordinance evolved from the needs of practical experience rather than being prompted by a specific crisis. At least in the case of early modern Amsterdam, it seems safe to argue that instead of being driven by economic crises, innovations in insolvency legislation and the institutional framework dealing with its application were more likely to occur in times of economic efflorescence than amidst the shards of a depression. It is impossible to conclusively test this alternative hypothesis within the scope of this book, but the topic definitely merits further attention.

[15] Safley, "Business Failure," 60. See also Thomas Max Safley, *Family Firms and Merchant Capitalism in Early Modern Europe: The Business, Bankruptcy and Resilience of the Höchstetters of Augsburg* (Oxford: Routledge, 2020).

[16] Oldewelt, "Twee eeuwen," 430.

Insolvency in the Dutch Republic

From 1643 onwards, many cities in the Dutch Republic introduced local ordinances concerning *desolate boedels*, just like Amsterdam. Sometimes, such as in the preamble of the 1702 Haarlem ordinance, it is explicitly stated that such legislative initiatives had been inspired by "the example of other, neighboring cities." According to the Haarlem regents, it would be of the "greatest utility and necessity" to introduce better insolvency legislation, to maintain public order as well as to protect creditors' interests.[17] Besides Amsterdam and Haarlem, ten other cities issued ordinances concerning insolvent estates until the end of the *ancien régime*: Leiden (1652), Amersfoort (1654), Wijk bij Duurstede (1658), Gouda (1659), Middelburg (1661), Dordrecht (1668), Arnhem (1681), Rotterdam (1703), Utrecht (1708), and Zutphen (1742). Furthermore, ordinances were issued for the entire Province of Zeeland (1649) as well as the districts of Veluwe and Veluwezoom (1683/1738).[18] To what extent were Amsterdam's innovations in insolvency legislation and procedure also reflected in other contemporary Dutch cities?

Middelburg was the only Dutch city besides Amsterdam to create an independent *desolate boedelskamer*. From 1661, every two years five new commissioners would be appointed to supervise the local management and execution of insolvent estates, assisted by the urban secretary (*griffier*) and ushers. In other cities, such as Leiden, Gouda, or Dordrecht, two or three of the aldermen would be appointed as commissioners for insolvent estates besides their other duties. The Dordrecht commissioners would meet as often as necessary to fulfil this responsibility, but only when the timing would not interfere with their "administration of justice." Rotterdam and Utrecht followed a different model, in which a number of aldermen were delegated to

[17] Anon., *Keuren en ordonnantien der stad Haerlem*, 2 vols. (Haarlem: Izaäk en Johannes Enschedé en Jan Bosch, 1755), I:124.

[18] For an in-depth discussion of these ordinances up to 1713, on which most of this section is based, see Maurits den Hollander, "Failliet in de Republiek. Lokale ordonnanties over de omgang met desolate boedels, circa 1643–1713," *Pro Memorie* 24, no. 2 (2022): 190–217. For the Zutphen and Veluwe ordinances, see Anon, *Ordre en reglement over desolate en insolvente boedels binnen de stadt en schependom van Zutphen* (Zutphen: wed. J. van der Spyck, 1742); Anon., *Reglement soo omtrent verlatene, desolate of insolvente boedels … in Veluwen en Veluwen-zoom* (Arnhem: Hendrik van Goor, 1738).

supervise the management of an insolvent estate on a case-by-case basis. In Arnhem, exceptionally, the colonels of the urban militia were responsible for the supervision of local curators. Just like in Middelburg, in other cities the urban secretary and other staff such as ushers or clerks also assisted in the management of insolvent estates.

Whereas in Amsterdam, curators could be described as freelance specialists, some other cities followed different procedures for their appointment. In Wijk bij Duurstede, for instance, the curator was elected by the creditors and subsequently appointed by the aldermen after providing sufficient guarantees or "behoorlycke cautie." In Rotterdam, a number of "capable individuals" from among the creditors would be appointed as curators. Middelburg occupied a middle ground: here curators could either be selected from among the creditors or from a pool of external candidates. In Haarlem and Amsterdam, finally, it was possible to appoint *ghecommitteerden* or *opzienders* from among the creditors: official representatives who would both assist and keep an eye on the curators.

The preambles of the ordinances often contain interesting information about the regents' rationale. Often, they mention reports or complaints by citizens about irregularities in the wrapping-up of insolvent estates or the curators' conduct. We already saw how, for instance in the case of Haarlem, bylaws from other neighboring cities could serve as inspiration to introduce new or updated legislation on a certain topic. Many complaints concern severely delayed or erratic insolvency procedures, which would be to the detriment of creditors and insolvent alike. In the 1652 Leiden ordinance, it is even stated that some were advantaged over others as "friends and favorites." The ordinance orders the aldermen to prod and compel – "aen te porren ende te constringeren" – the local curators in order to ensure quick and fair insolvency procedures for all involved. These passages were subsequently copied into the 1659 Gouda ordinance. In general, a closer supervision and improved accountability of the curators seems to have been one of the main goals of this type of ordinance. This was simply the most effective way to ensure a good handling of insolvencies, while avoiding prohibitive expenses for the urban community as a whole.

The Dutch Republic witnessed a proliferation of urban legislation on how to deal with the problem of insolvency in the second half of the seventeenth century. The degree of professionalization varied by city according to the size of the population as well as the dynamism of the local economy. Whereas Amsterdam and Middelburg, as the most important contemporary maritime and commercial hubs, created separate courts to supervise the management of insolvent estates, other cities opted for a simpler solution that best fit local circumstances. Generally, the liberal application of a legal procedure such as *cessie van goede* was much to be preferred to the alternative as practiced in, for instance, contemporary England. There, the absence of well-functioning insolvency procedures for much of the population resulted in over-filled debtors' prisons.

Rather than limiting contractual freedom to combat fraud, as Emperor Charles V had done when restricting compositions between insolvents and their creditors, Dutch regents actively intervened in relations between creditors and debtors to stimulate the local economy. For them, this followed from a pragmatic consideration of costs and benefits. Religious authorities concurred: if an insolvent managed to resolve their illiquidity through an official legal solution, they were rehabilitated and reintegrated into the moral body of society in the form of the holy communion, even if they had not repaid all of their old debts as of yet. At the same time institutional innovations, like the professionalized supervision of the management of insolvent estates, enabled the controlled introduction of legal innovations such as the majority composition.

This was part of a broader contemporary development, in which both urban and village authorities actively intervened in numerous facets of the private life of their citizens to further the common good.[19] Rising population numbers and their related increase in tax income provided both the necessity and the administrative capacity for this increased governmental activity.[20] Even if Amsterdam's example was not copied one-on-one by other Dutch cities, its important innovations in insolvency legislation and objective, transparent procedure

[19] Gabrielle Dorren, *Het soet vergaren. Haarlems buurtleven in de zeventiende eeuw* (Haarlem: Arcadia, 1998); Arie Th. van Deursen, *Een dorp in de polder. Graft in de zeventiende eeuw* (Amsterdam: Bert Bakker, 1994).

[20] Manon van der Heijden, *Civic Duty: Public Services in the Early Modern Low Countries* (Newcastle upon Tyne: Cambridge Scholars Publishing, 2012), 106 and 131.

became sufficiently widespread to suggest a broader impact on the Dutch Republic as a whole. Further comparative empirical research would be most welcome, in order to help understand the full impact of these crucial legal and institutional innovations on both a Dutch and European scale.

Good Governance

When confronted with an insolvency, we would generally express our compassion and sympathy with its victims. For a long time, however, this primary response would have been alien to legal scholars and ordinary citizens alike. Insolvency was perceived to be a deeply problematic phenomenon for two main reasons. First, it put the economy at serious risk, as, in an era that was characterized by information deficits, a single insolvency could cause the collapse of a whole chain of other businesses. Second, it also imperiled the moral order of society. Because of imperfect information, trust and reputation were vital mechanisms for both the day-to-day functioning of business and the proliferation of credit. Insolvency, and even more so a fraudulent bankruptcy, violently ripped apart the moral fabric of society, which explains why in many parts of Europe both religious and worldly authorities actively and indiscriminately punished those who did not honor their financial obligations. Insolvency was not just a private economic phenomenon that concerned an individual debtor and their creditors. It represented a serious breach of trust that put the entire public order at risk. This meant that governments, especially the burgomasters of an important commercial hub such as Amsterdam, had to act in order to mitigate its potentially harmful effects. Insolvency legislation represents their solution to redress these issues in an orderly manner.

Past authorities' pragmatic concerns with regard to the handling of insolvents and their estates were often accompanied by symbolic measures such as humiliating public ceremonies. These sated the creditors' emotional desire to punish the insolvent, but at the same time displayed a degree of leniency after the event in order to serve the interests of society at large. Over time, there was a clear development towards less punitive and rather more pragmatic policies. As this book has sought to demonstrate, seventeenth-century Amsterdam is exemplary of this larger development. Just as the Amsterdam poor were provided with decent social aid that protected them from famine, the middle classes were granted a way out of social degradation through liberal, open-access insolvency procedures. These citizens were given an opportunity to reconstruct their businesses after an economic setback, much to the advantage of both their personal situation, public order, and the general economic climate. Even though not every insolvent in seventeenth-century Amsterdam had equal legal opportunities at his or her disposal, in practice the innovations in its insolvency legislation are a great example of how good governance could mitigate the effects of crisis for large parts of the population.

This pragmatic approach was not created out of thin air, but was firmly rooted in the transparent and professional procedures of the Desolate Boedelskamer. Contrary to what has often been assumed, the legal innovations in Amsterdam that helped both applicants for *cessie* and insolvents who managed to conclude a composition past moments of personal financial meltdown were not driven by the needs of a general economic emergency. Instead, the opulent economic and intellectual climate of the finest years of the Dutch Golden Age constituted the cradle of one of Europe's most innovative and effective insolvency regimes.

Widely available or "open access" insolvency legislation is often mentioned as a perfect example of the generalized institutions that are heralded as the foundation of economic success by legal and economic historians writing in the tradition of the new institutional economics. Because of its positive effects on the validity of contracts and the security of payments, good insolvency legislation is expected to have the potential to significantly reduce transaction costs. As growing social and economic complexity necessitated that early modern businessmen engage in contracts and exchanges with increasing numbers of foreign or otherwise unfamiliar parties, the personal trust and reputation that had traditionally served as the lubricant of economic life were increasingly found wanting. Through a range of institutional innovations that started in the late sixteenth century, the Amsterdam authorities successfully solved at least part of this problem by creating the possibility of replacing personal trust between individual merchants or businessmen by system trust. The introduction of the Desolate Boedelskamer in 1643 is a clear example of this development, in which new and impartial legal institutions reinforced the social and economic relations within the broader civic community. Because of its professional procedure and staff, its objective and transparent handling of individual cases, and its equal treatment of all creditors, the Desolate Boedelskamer was able to provide the systemic trust that was essential to ensure the continued securitization of credit in a world of growing complexity.

The Desolate Boedelskamer was so successful because it managed to not only solve the economic problem of insolvency with greater organizational efficiency than, for instance, notaries had been able to do in preceding decades, but it also found a way to reinforce and safeguard the traditional moral economy of trust and reputation networks. As Niklas Luhmann has argued, power turns into coercion if it monopolizes all decisions and dictates these to all parties involved in any kind of dispute. This might seem efficient, but fails to accomplish anything but shifting the burden of complexity to the power-holder.[21] The crucial accomplishment of the Desolate Boedelskamer was that it created an institutional environment in which parties could trust one another to arrive at an arbitrated composition or a controlled liquidation of an insolvent estate, because the information deficit was (partially) resolved by the trustworthy commissioners and their professional staff. The fact that one could always expect to have a fair chance to get back the credit extended to an Amsterdam citizen who later ran into financial problems must have helped immensely to make the city on the Amstel a favorable place to do business, the evident success of which remains visible even today.

This book has demonstrated how legal history will struggle to arrive at valid insights about the functioning of law in practice without taking the broader historical context in which it functioned into account. Likewise, one cannot hope to uncover the true functioning of institutions or the roots of economic growth if one does not realize that these were fundamentally embedded in this same sociocultural background. Much is still to be gained from future applications of the fruitful combination of an empirical research methodology and a fundamentally context-driven approach that has been pursued in

[21] Frens Kroeger, "Unlocking the Treasure Trove: How Can Luhmann's Theory of Trust Enrich Trust Research?," *Journal of Trust Research* 9, no. 1 (2019): 110–24, 120–21.

this book, both in legal history and other fields of the social, economic, and institutional analysis of past societies. It would be especially interesting if the findings for Amsterdam could be compared to equally detailed studies of other cities in Holland, the Dutch Republic, and other parts of Europe. Much remains to be said about the intricate relations between religion, morality, and normativity as well as their effect on past public mentalities. For seventeenth-century Amsterdam, it is safe to conclude that "honor" did not necessarily exclude "gold." Through its pragmatic, transparent, and professional application of innovative legal solutions for the problem of insolvency, the Amsterdam Desolate Boedelskamer restored credit for numerous industrious but unfortunate citizens. Legal innovations and the court thereby formed a foundation for the continued success and prosperity of this center of early capitalism.

Appendix: Accords Datasets

In this appendix, I will provide some further details about the two datasets I compiled based upon archival research into the accords. The first is a qualitative dataset. These accords were read and studied in detail, summarized, and supplemented by supportive evidence found in other series of registers such as the minutes of the commissioners of the Desolate Boedelskamer. The second is a quantitative dataset, containing all cases from the first qualitative dataset, but supplemented by a great number of accords categorized in an index file created by an anonymous Amsterdam archivist around 1892.[1] It categorizes the accords based on the insolvent's last name, providing the year in which the accord was concluded and – in about half of the cases – the repayment percentage and amount of debt. I corrected some small mistakes in this dataset where I could compare them to my own qualitative study, and added accords before 1644. While imperfect, the data in this index allow us to back up the findings from the qualitative dataset with similar results drawn from a much larger sample. For example, a comparison of the value of debts for accords in the qualitative dataset with those in the much larger quantitative sample shows that the former set constitutes a good sample of the total amount of accords which have been preserved in the archives (see Figure A.1).

[1] Gemeente Amsterdam Stadsarchief [GAS], 5072: Archief van de Commissarissen van de Desolate Boedelkamer [DB], inv. nr. 145: "Namenregister 1644–1777 met opgave der procenten van de accoorden en bedragen der faillissementen."

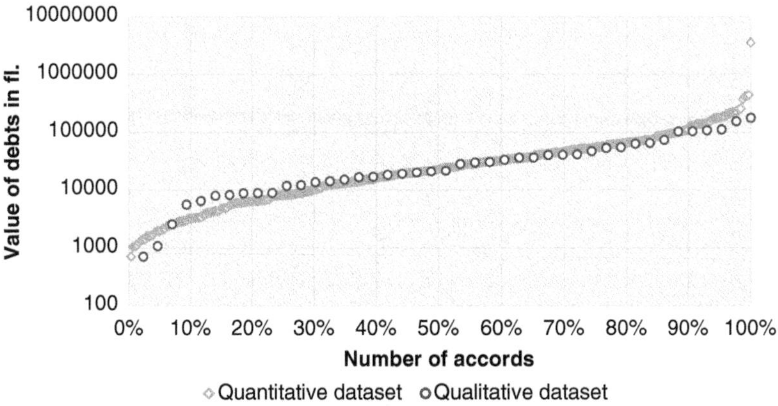

FIGURE A.1 Value of debts per insolvent estate in which an accord was concluded in the quantitative dataset compared to those in the qualitative dataset on a logarithmic scale (1592–1700)

Qualitative Dataset

The qualitative dataset contains two basic series of accords: (1) those created by notaries, found in various notarial protocols, and (2) those created after 1643, preserved by chance in the archive of the Desolate Boedelskamer in the collection *Restant* or "left-overs" (1.2.8.1 Accoorden). The first group of seventeen accords was found based upon references in secondary literature on Amsterdam insolvencies in this period, supplemented by references found in the card indexes on the notarial archives compiled by the Amsterdam archivist Simon Hart. These indexes contain a wealth of information on a great variety of topics that were treated by Amsterdam notaries in the early modern period.[2] The second group of accords forms a sample taken from the 1654 accords preserved from the period 1644–1778. Even this large group of records is not complete: the minutes contain references to many accords which have not been preserved in the archives of the Desolate Boedelskamer to this date. Nevertheless, a random selection provides a good understanding of the form and contents of these agreements and the ways in which they changed over the seventeenth century. In order to be able to study the effect of the new 1659 ordinance, I selected thirty accords from the first two decades of the

[2] GAS, 30452: Archief S. Hart.

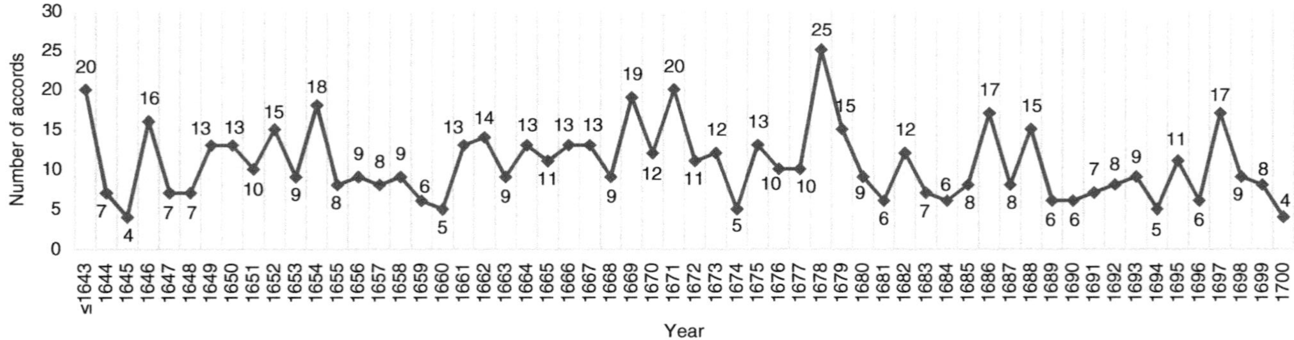

FIGURE A.2 Annual number of accords preserved in the Amsterdam archives (1592–1700)

TABLE A.1 *Completeness of the data in every preserved accord*

Information type	Number of accords
Name of insolvent and year of accord	615
+ Repayment percentage	449
+ Amount of debt	308
+ Repayment percentage + Amount of debt	296

court's functioning, and about ten from each of the last four decades of the seventeenth century.

Quantitative Dataset

The quantitative dataset contains all the information on seventeenth-century accords that could be found in the 1644–1777 index, which is based upon the compositions preserved in the *Restant* collection of the Desolate Boedelskamer's archive, supplemented by new accords found in other places, such as the notarial protocols. Figure A.2 displays the annual number of accords that have been preserved.

The amount of detail provided per accord varies, and can be quantified as set out in Table A.1.

It should be noted that for five accords, no percentage was mentioned, but certain possessions were assigned to the creditors for the fulfilment of the accord instead. These have been excluded from the "repayment percentage" numbers. In seven cases, a sum of guilders was specified, from which I calculated a percentage based upon the total debt value of the estate. The same was done for four cases in which the debt or payment ratio was expressed in Flemish pounds. In the three cases in which the value of the debt was listed in pounds, I have converted these sums into guilders based upon the prevailing ratio of 1 Flemish pound = 6 Holland guilders.[3] These eleven cases have been included in the "repayment percentage" numbers.

[3] Stichting Nederlandse Penningkabinetten, "Pond," http://wiki.muntenenpapiergeld.nl/index.php?title=Pond.

Archival Sources

Nationaal Archief, Den Haag (NL-HaNa)

3.01.04.01	Staten van Holland na 1572
3.03.01	Hof van Holland
3.03.02	Hoge Raad Holland en Zeeland

Gemeente Amsterdam Stadsarchief (GAS)

5001	Archief van de Burgerlijke Stand: doop-, trouw- en begraafboeken van Amsterdam (retroacta van de Burgerlijke Stand)
5023	Archief van de Burgemeesters: groot-memoriaal
5024	Archief van de Burgemeesters: dagelijkse notulen, resoluties en missivenboeken
5031	Archief van de Burgemeesters: stukken betreffende ambten en officiën
5061	Archieven van de Schout en Schepenen, van de Schepenen en van de Subalterne Rechtbanken
5072	Archief van de Commissarissen van de Desolate Boedelkamer
5073	Archief van de Weeskamer en Commissie van Liquidatie der Zaken van de Voormalige Weeskamer
5075	Archief van de Notarissen ter Standplaats Amsterdam
30452	Archief van S. Hart: (gedeeltelijke) toegang op de notariële archieven

Erfgoed Leiden en Omstreken

1004	Archief Doop-, trouw- en begraafboeken Leiden

Bibliography

Abels, Paul. *De nieuwe samenleving*, II: *Nieuw en ongezien. Kerk en samenleving in de classis Delft en Delfland 1572–1621*. Delft: Eburon, 1994.

Alphen, Willem van. *Nieuw verbeterde en vermeerderde papegay, ofte formulier-boeck van alderhande requestē, mandamenten, conclusien &c, ghelijck die ghebruyckt ende gepractiseert werden voor de respectieve hoven van iIustitie in Hollandt*. The Hague: Johannes Verhoeve, 1649.

Papegay, ofte formulier-boek van allerhande requesten, mandamenten, conclusien, schrifturen, als anders, in de dagelijksche practijke dienende voor de respective hoven van justitie in Hollandt. 2 vols., vol. I. The Hague: Johannes Steucker, 1682.

Ankum, J. A. *De geschiedenis der "actio Pauliana."* Zwolle: Tjeenk Willink, 1962.

Anon. *Amsterdamsche secretary [etc.]*. Amsterdam: Jacob van Royen, 1700.

Keuren en ordonnantien der stad Haerlem. 2 vols., vol. I. Haarlem: Izaäk en Johannes Enschedé en Jan Bosch, 1755.

Ordre en reglement over desolate en insolvente boedels binnen de stadt en schependom van Zutphen. Zutphen: wed. J. van der Spyck, 1742.

Reglement soo omtrent verlatene, desolate of insolvente boedels ... in Veluwen en Veluwen-zoom. Arnhem: Hendrik van Goor, 1738.

Apeldoorn, L. J. van, ed. *Uit de practijk van het Hof van Holland in de tweede helft van de zestiende eeuw*. Utrecht: Uitgevers-Maatschappij Broekhoff NV, 1938.

Arend, Oscar van den. *Zeven lokale baljuwschappen in Holland*. Hilversum: Verloren, 1993.

Asaert, Gustaaf. *1585. De val van Antwerpen en de uittocht van Vlamingen en Brabanders*. Tielt: Lannoo, 2004.

Bailly, Maria-Charlotte le. *Procesgids Hof van Holland, Zeeland en West-Friesland: de hoofdlijnen van het procederen in civiele zaken voor het Hof van Holland, Zeeland en West-Friesland zowel in eerste instantie als in hoger beroep*. Hilversum: Verloren, 2008.

Bailly, Maria-Charlotte le, and Christel Verhas. *Procesgids Hoge Raad van Holland, Zeeland en West-Friesland (1582–1795). De hoofdlijnen van het procederen in civiele zaken voor de Hoge Raad zowel in eerste instantie als in hoger beroep*. Hilversum: Verloren, 2006.

Banakar, Reza, and Max Travers. "Systems Theory." In *Law and Social Theory*. Ed. Reza Banakar and Max Travers. 2nd ed., 53–58. Oxford: Hart Publishing, 2013.

Barels, Jeronimo Mattheus. *Onderzoek over de pandingen binnen de stad Amsterdam in gebruik*. Amsterdam: Hendrik Gartman, 1780.

Barlaeus, Caspar. *Mercator Sapiens*. Trans. S. van der Woude. Amsterdam: Universiteitsbibliotheek, 1967.

Barreveld, Dirk J. *Tegen de Heeren van de VOC. Isaac le Maire en de ontdekking van Kaap Hoorn*. The Hague: SDU, 2002.

Bauer, Peter M. *Der Insolvenzplan. Untersuchungen zur Rechtsnatur anhand der geschichtlichen Entwicklung*. Berlin: Lit, 2009.

Bavel, Bas van. *Manors and Markets: Economy and Society in the Low Countries, 500–1600*. Oxford University Press, 2010.

Berman, Harold Joseph. *Law and Revolution*, II: *The Impact of the Protestant Reformations on the Western Legal Tradition*. Cambridge: Harvard University Press, 2006.

Bijnkershoek, Cornelis van. *Observationes Tumultuariae*. Ed. E. M. Meijers et al. 2 vols., vol. I. Haarlem: Tjeenk Willink, 1926.

Observationes Tumultuariae. Ed. E. M. Meijers et al. 2 vols., vol. II. Haarlem: Tjeenk Willink, 1934.

Blondé, Bruno et al. "The Low Countries' Paradox." In *Inequality and the City in the Low Countries (1200–2020)*. Ed. Bruno Blondé et al., 15–42. Turnhout: Brepols, 2020.

Blondé, Bruno, Oscar Gelderblom, and Peter Stabel. "Foreign Merchant Communities in Bruges, Antwerp and Amsterdam, c. 1350–1650." In *Cultural Exchange in Early Modern Europe*, II: *Cities and Cultural Exchange in Europe, 1400–1700*. Ed. Donatella Calabi and Stephen T. Christensen, 154–74. Cambridge University Press, 2013.

Bockel, Jeroen van. *Gevormde kaders. Bureaucratische en professionele regulering van het werk van ambtenaren in de Republiek der Zeven Verenigde Nederlanden*. Delft: Eburon, 2009.

Bontemantel, Hans. *De regeeringe van Amsterdam, soo in 't civiel als crimineel en militaire (1653–1672)*. Ed. Gerhard Wilhelm Kernkamp. The Hague: Martinus Nijhoff, 1897.

Bos, Sandra. *"Uyt liefde tot malcander." Onderlinge hulpverlening binnen de Noord-Nederlandse gilden in internationaal perspectief (1570–1820)*. Amsterdam: IISG, 1998.

Bosma, A. I. *Repertorium van notarissen residerende in Amsterdam Amstelland, ambachtsheerlijkheden en geannexeerde gemeenten 1524–1810*. Amsterdam: Gemeentearchief Amsterdam, 1998.

Bosman, Machiel. *Rembrandts plan. De ware geschiedenis van zijn faillissement*. Amsterdam: Atheneum – Polak & Van Gennep, 2019.

Braam, A. van. "Bureaucratiseringsgraad van de plaatselijke bestuursorganisatie van Westzaandam ten tijde van de Republiek." *Tijdschrift voor Geschiedenis* 90 (1977): 457–83.

Bredero, Gerbrand Adriaenszoon. *Klucht van de koe*. Amsterdam: Cornelis Lodewijckszoon van der Plasse, 1619.

Brissaud, Jacques. *Le Créancier "premier saisissant" dans l'ancien droit français*. Paris: Presses Universitaires de France, 1972.

Brugmans, Hajo. "De notulen en munimenten van het College van Commercie te Amsterdam, 1663–1665." *BMGN – Low Countries Historical Review* 18 (1897): 181–330.

Brundage, James A. *The Medieval Origins of the Legal Profession: Canonists, Civilians, and Courts*. University of Chicago Press, 2008.

Burke, Peter. *Venetië en Amsterdam. Een onderzoek naar elites in de zeventiende eeuw*. 2nd ed. Amsterdam: Agon, 1991.

Caesar, Martinus. *Ius hodiernum ofte hedens-daaghs recht beschreven ende gecolligeert naer ordre ende tot elucidatie van de vier boecken der institutien des keizers Justiniani*. Amsterdam: Dirck Meyer, 1656.

Carter, Alice Clare. *The English Reformed Church in Amsterdam in the Seventeenth Century*. Amsterdam: Scheltema & Holkema / Stadsdrukkerij Amsterdam, 1964.

Coeur, Jacob de. *Styl der notarissen; zynde een verzameling van actens, contracten en instrumenten, dagelyks dienende tot de notariale practyk*. The Hague: Cornelis van Zanten, 1740.

Coing, Helmut. "Die juristische Fakultät und ihr Lehrprogramm." In *Handbuch der Quellen und Literatur der Neueren Europaïschen Privatrechtsgeschichte*, I(2): *Neuere Zeit (1500–1800). Das Zeitalter des Gemeinen Rechts*. Ed. Helmut Coing, 3–102. Munich: C. H. Beck'sche Verlagsbehandlung, 1977.

Collins, Aidan. "Bankruptcy in the Court of Chancery, 1674–1750." PhD, University of York, 2020.

Commelin, Caspar. *Beschryvinge van Amsterdam*. Amsterdam: Wolfgang, Waasbergh, Boom, Van Someren, and Goethals, 1693.

Coornhert, Dirk Volkertsz. *Boeventucht of middelen tot mindering der schadelijke lediggangers*. Ed. A. J. Gelderbloem et al. Muiderberg: Coutinho, 1985.

Court, Pieter de la. *Interest van Holland, ofte gronden van Hollands-welvaren*. Amsterdam: Joan. Cyprianus vander Gracht, 1662.

Cox, Joost C. M. *Repertorium van de stadsrechten in Nederland*. 2nd ed. Oisterwijk, 2012.

Crenshaw, Paul. *Rembrandt's Bankruptcy: The Artist, His Patrons, and the Art Market in Seventeenth-Century Netherlands*. Cambridge University Press, 2006.

Curtis, Daniel R., and Jessica Dijkman. "The Escape from Famine in the Northern Netherlands: A Reconsideration Using the 1690s Harvest Failures and a Broader Northwest European Perspective." *The Seventeenth Century* 34, no. 2 (2019): 229–58.

Daalder, Remmelt, et al., eds. *Goud uit graan. Nederland en het Oostzeegebied 1600–1850*. Zwolle: Waanders Uitgevers, 1998.

Dalhuisen, Jan Hendrik. *Compositions in Bankruptcy: A Comparative Study of the Laws of the E.E.C. Countries, England and the U.S.A.* Leiden: A. W. Sijthoff, 1968.

De Munck, Bert. *Guilds, Labour and the Urban Body Politic: Fabricating Community in the Southern Netherlands, 1300–1800*. New York: Routledge, 2018.

De ruysscher, Dave. "Antwerp Commercial Legislation in Amsterdam in the 17th Century: Legal Transplant or Jumping Board?" *Tijdschrift voor Rechtsgeschiedenis* 77 (2009): 459–79.

"At the End, the Creditors Win: Pre-Insolvency Proceedings in France, Belgium and the Netherlands (1807–C1910)." *Comparative Legal History* 6, no. 2 (2018): 184–206.

"Business Rescue, Turnaround Management and the Legal Regime of Default and Insolvency in Western History (Late Middle Ages to Present Day)." In *Turnaround Management and Bankruptcy*. Ed. Jan Adriaanse and Jean-Pierre van der Rest, 22–42. New York: Routledge, 2017.

"Designing the Limits of Creditworthiness: Insolvency in Antwerp Bankruptcy Legislation and Practice (16th–17th Centuries)." *Tijdschrift voor Rechtsgeschiedenis* 76 (2008): 307–27.

Gedisciplineerde vrijheid. Een geschiedenis van het handels- en economisch recht. Antwerp: Maklu, 2014.

"Jurisprudence & The Formulation of Law in Antwerp: An Academic and Practice-Oriented Tradition in Commercial Law (Sixteenth to Nineteenth Centuries)." In *Nothing Will Come of Nothing: Science and Education in Antwerp since 1500*. Ed. Helma de Smedt, 227–45. University of Antwerp, 2019.

"Naer het Romeinsch recht alsmede den stiel mercantiel." Handel en recht in de Antwerpse rechtbank (16de-17de eeuw). Kortrijk-Heule: UGA, 2009.

"Reconciling Old and New. Imprisonment for Debts and Cessio Bonorum, in Antwerp and Mechelen (*c.*1500–*c.*1530)." In *European Traditions: Integration or Dis-Integration?* Ed. J. Oosterhuis and Emanuel van Dongen, 35–48. Oisterwijk: Wolf Productions, 2012.

De ruysscher, Dave, and Ilya Kotlyar. "Local Traditions v. Academic Law: Collateral Rights on Movables in Holland (*c.*1300–*c.*1700)." *Tijdschrift voor Rechtsgeschiedenis* 86, nos. 3–4 (2018): 365–403.

Decock, Wim, ed. *Handbuch zur Geschichte der Konfliktlösung in Europa*, III: *Konfliktlösung im Fruhen Neuzeit*. Berlin: Springer, 2021.

"Law, Religion, and Debt Relief: Balancing above the 'Abyss of Despair' in Early Modern Canon Law and Theology." *American Journal of Legal History* 57, no. 2 (2017): 125–41.

Dehing, Pit. *Geld in Amsterdam. Wisselbank en wisselkoersen, 1650–1725*. Hilversum: Verloren, 2012.

Demars-Sion, Véronique. "La Réglementation de la cession de biens dans les Pays-Bas méridionaux: copie ou modèle des solutions francaises?" In *Commerce et droit*. Ed. Jean-Marie Cauchies and Serge Dauchy, 131–54. Brussels: Facultes Universitaires Saint-Louis Bruxelles, 1996.

Deursen, Arie Th. van. *Bavianen en Slijkgeuzen. Kerk en kerkvolk ten tijde van Maurits en Oldenbarnevelt*. Assen: Van Gorcum & Comp, 1974.

De last van veel geluk. De geschiedenis van Nederland, 1555–1702. Amsterdam: Bakker, 2004.

Een dorp in de polder. Graft in de zeventiende eeuw. Amsterdam: Bert Bakker, 1994.

Mensen van klein vermogen. Het kopergeld van de Gouden Eeuw. Amsterdam: Bert Bakker, 1991.

Dievoet, G. van. "Notarisboeken en formulierboeken voor notarissen in de Zuidelijke Nederlanden van 1500 tot 1800." In *Forma Servata. Vijf opstellen over formulieren en formulierboeken in het notariaat van de middeleeuwen tot vandaag*. Ed. P. L. Nève and J. J. Verbeek, 51–84. Deventer: Kluwer, 1998.

Dijkhof, Eef. "Op weg naar autonomie." In *Geschiedenis van Amsterdam*, I: *Een stad uit het niets (tot 1575)*, 62–73. Amsterdam: SUN, 2004.

Dillen, J. G. van. "Amsterdam in Bredero's tijd." *De Gids* 99 (1935): 308–36.

"De duurte van het jaar 1698." *Onze Eeuw* 17, no. 1 (1917): 250–73.

Doesselaere, Elien. "Archiefvormer, bewaarplaats of constructie? Een onderzoek naar de context van de Antwerpse Insolvente Boedelskamer." MA Thesis Archivistiek, VUB, 2011.

Dondorp, Harry. "Partes Secanto. Aulus Gellius and the Glossators." *Revue Internationale Des Droits de l'antiquité* 57 (2010): 131–44.

Dorren, Gabrielle. *Het soet vergaren. Haarlems buurtleven in de zeventiende eeuw*. Haarlem: Arcadia, 1998.

Druwé, Wouter. "Dignity and Cessio Bonorum in Early-Modern Dutch Learned Legal Literature." Max Planck Institute for European Legal History Research Paper Series, 2016-08, 1–27, 2016.

Dudok van Heel, S. A. C. "Doopsgezinden en schilderkunst in de 17e eeuw – Leerlingen, opdrachtgevers en verzamelaars van Rembrandt." *Doopsgezinde Bijdragen* 6 (1980): 105–23.

"Rembrandt van Rijn (1601–1669). Een veranderend schildersportret." In *Rembrandt. De meester en zijn werkplaats*. Ed. Christopher Brown, 50–67. Amsterdam/Zwolle: Rijksmuseum/Waanders, 1991.

Dumolyn, Jan, and Bart Lambert. "Cities of Commerce, Cities of Constraints. International Trade, Government Institutions and the Law of Commerce in Later Medieval Bruges and the Burgundian State." *TSEG / Low Countries Journal of Social and Economic History* 11, no. 4 (2014): 89–102.

Dunbabin, Jean. *Captivity and Imprisonment in Medieval Europe 1000–1300*. Basingstoke: Palgrave Macmillan, 2002.

Dupouy, Claude. *Le Droit des faillites en France avant le Code de Commerce*. Paris: R. Pichon & R. Durand-Auzias, 1960.

Eeghen, Chr. P. van. "Het faillissement der firma Coenraad & Hendrick van Son in 1762." *Economisch-Historisch Jaarboek* 22 (1943): 82–187.

Eeghen, I. H. van. *De gilden. Theorie en praktijk*. Bussum: C. A. J. van Dishoeck, 1965.

"Het graf van Titus van Rijn." *Maandblad Amstelodamum* 76 (1989): 123–26.

Elias, Johan E. *De Vroedschap van Amsterdam 1578–1795*. Amsterdam: N. Israel, 1963.

Geschiedenis van het Amsterdamsche regentenpatriciaat. 's-Gravenhage: Martinus Nijhoff, 1923.

Ernst, Wolfgang. "Zur Epistemologie rechtsgeschichtlicher Forschung." *Rechtsgeschichte* 23 (2015): 256–59.

Evenhuis, R. B. *Ook dat was Amsterdam. De kerk der hervorming in de Gouden Eeuw*. 2 vols., vol. I. Amsterdam: Ten Have, 1965.

Ook dat was Amsterdam. De kerk der hervorming in de Gouden Eeuw. 2 vols., vol. II. Amsterdam: Ten Have, 1967.

Faber, Johannes A. "Inhabitants of Amsterdam and Their Possessions." In *Probate Inventories: A New Source for the Historical Study of Wealth, Material Culture and Agricultural Development*. Ed A. M. van der Woude and Anton J. Schuurman, 149–55. Wageningen: Landbouwhogeschool, 1980.

Finn, Margot. *The Character of Credit: Personal Debt in English Culture, 1740–1914*. Cambridge University Press, 2003.

Fockema Andreae, Sybrand J. *Het Oud-Nederlandsch burgerlijk recht*. Haarlem: Bohn, 1906.

Fontaine, Laurence. *The Moral Economy. Poverty, Credit, and Trust in Early Modern Europe*. New York: Cambridge University Press, 2014.

Forster, Wolfgang. *Konkurs als Verfahren. Francisco Salgado de Somoza in der Geschichte des Insolvenzrechts*. Cologne: Böhlau, 2009.

Frijhoff, Willem. "Graduation and Careers." In *Universities in Early Modern Europe (1500–1800)*. Ed. Hilde De Ridder-Symoens, 355–415. Cambridge University Press, 1996.

Ganshof, Louis F. *Le Droit de la faillite dans les états de la Communauté économique européenne*. Brussels: Centre Interuniversitaire de Droit Comparé, 1969.

Garrison-Estèbe, Janine. *Protestants du Midi, 1559–1598*. Toulouse: Privat, 1980.

Gehlen, A. F. L. "De notaris in de Republiek der Verenigde Nederlanden (17de-18de eeuw)." In *Gepasseerd. De rol en positie van notarissen in het verleden*. Ed. C. C. T. M. Van Haren, J. Ch. Janssens, and M. J. Swenker, 55–68. Nijmegen: Gerardt Noodt Instituut, 1987.

Gelder, H. A. Enno van. *De levensbeschouwing van Cornelis Pieterszoon Hooft, burgemeester van Amsterdam (1547–1626)*. Amsterdam: A. H. Kruyt, 1918.

Gelderblom, Oscar. *Cities of Commerce: The Institutional Foundations of International Trade in the Low Countries, 1250–1650*. Princeton University Press, 2013.

"Continuïteit en verandering in de handelsgeschiedenis van Amsterdam." *BMGN – Low Countries Historical Review* 118, no. 1 (2003): 49–57.

Zuid-Nederlandse kooplieden en de opkomst van de Amsterdamse stapelmarkt (1578–1630). Hilversum: Verloren, 2000.

Gelderblom, Oscar, Mark Hup, and Joost Jonker. "Public Functions, Private Markets: Credit Registration by Aldermen and Notaries in the Low Countries, 1500–1800." In *Financing in Europe: Evolution, Coexistence and Complementarity of Lending Practices from the Middle Ages to Modern Times*. Ed. Marcella Lorenzini, Cinzia Lorandini, and D'Maris Coffman, 163–94. Cham: Springer International Publishing, 2018.

Gelderblom, Oscar, and Joost Jonker. "Completing a Financial Revolution: The Finance of the Dutch East India Trade and the Rise of the Amsterdam Capital Market, 1595–1612." *The Journal of Economic History* 64, no. 3 (2004): 641–72.

"Enter the Ghost – Cashless Payments in the Early Modern Low Countries, 1500–1800." *SSRN*, 2015. http://dx.doi.org/10.2139/ssrn.2604089.

Geltner, Guy. *The Medieval Prison: A Social History*. Princeton University Press, 2008.

Gijswijt-Hofstra, Marijke. *Wijkplaatsen voor vervolgden. Asielverlening in Culemborg, Vianen, Buren, Leerdam en Ijsselstein van de 16e tot eind 18e eeuw*. Amsterdam: De Bataafsche Leeuw, 1984.

Godding, Philippe. *Le Droit privé dans les Pays-Bas méridionaux du 12e au 18e siècle*. Brussels: Académie Royale de Belgique, 1987.

Granovetter, Mark. "Economic Action and Social Structure: The Problem of Embeddedness." *American Journal of Sociology* 91, no. 3 (1985): 481–510.

Greif, Avner. *Institutions and the Path to the Modern Economy: Lessons from Medieval Trade*. Cambridge University Press, 2006.

Greif, Avner, Paul Milgrom, and Barry Weingast. "Coordination, Commitment, and Enforcement: The Case of the Merchant Guild." *Journal of Political Economy* 102, no. 4 (1994): 745–76.

Groot, Hugo de. *Inleidinge tot de Hollandsche rechts-geleerdheid.* Edited by F. Dovring, H. F. W. D. Fischer, and E. M. Meijers. 2nd ed. Universitaire Pers Leiden, 1965.

Häberlein, Mark. *Brüder, Freunde und Betrüger. Soziale Beziehungen, Normen und Konflikte in der Ausgburger Kaufmannschaft um die Mitte des 16. Jahrhunderts.* Berlin: Akademie Verlag, 1998.

Hall, M. C. van. "Verhandeling over het zinnebeeldige in de Oud-Nederlandse regten." In *Regtsgeleerde verhandelingen en losse geschriften*, 117–244. Amsterdam: Johannes van der Hey en Zoon / Ten Brink & De Vries, 1838.

Hart, Simon. "Een sociale structuur van de Amsterdamse bevolking in de 18e eeuw." In *Geschrift en getal. Een keuze uit de demografisch-, economisch- en sociaal-historische studiën op grond van Amsterdamse en Zaanse archivalia, 1600–1800*, 183–92. Dordrecht: Historische Vereniging Holland, 1976.

"Geschrift en getal. Onderzoek naar de samenstelling van de bevolking van Amsterdam in de 17e en 18e eeuw, op grond van gegevens over migratie, huwelijk, beroep en alfabetisme." In *Geschrift en getal. Een keuze uit de demografisch-, economisch- en sociaal-historische studiën op grond van Amsterdamse en Zaanse archivalia, 1600–1800*, 115–81. Dordrecht: Historische Vereniging Holland, 1976.

Hay, Douglas et al. *Albion's Fatal Tree. Crime and Society in Eighteenth-Century England.* 2nd ed. London: Verso, 2011.

Heersink, Wim. "'Van oude tijden bij alle volkeren geacht.' Amsterdamse notarissen van schrijftafel tot schepenbank, 1600–1800." In *Nieuw licht op oude justitie. Misdaad en straf ten tijde van de Republiek.* Ed. Sjoerd Faber, 48–63. Muiderberg: Coutinho, 1989.

Heersink, Wim et al. *Register Notarium. De notarissen van het Hof van Holland 1525–1811.* The Hague: Algemeen Rijksarchief, 1999.

Heijden, Manon van der. *Civic Duty: Public Services in the Early Modern Low Countries.* Newcastle upon Tyne: Cambridge Scholars Publishing, 2012.

Huwelijk in Holland. Stedelijke rechtspraak en kerkelijke tucht, 1550–1700. Amsterdam: Bert Bakker, 1998.

Heijden, Manon van der, and Ariadne Schmidt. "Public Services and Women's Work in Early Modern Dutch Towns." *Journal of Urban History* 36, no. 3 (2010): 368–85.

Hell, Maarten. *De Amsterdamse herberg 1450–1800. Geestrijk centrum van het openbare leven.* Nijmegen: Vantilt, 2017.

"De Oude Geuzen en de Opstand. Politiek en lokaal bestuur in tijd van oorlog en expansie 1578–1650." In *Geschiedenis van Amsterdam*, IIa:

Centrum van de wereld, 1578–1650. Ed. Willem Frijhoff and Maarten Prak, 240–97. Amsterdam: SUN, 2004.

Hengstmengel, Joost, and Henri Krop. "De gereformeerde religie en economie in de vroege republiek. Daniël Souterius (1571–1634) over de plichten van kooplieden." *Documentatieblad Nadere Reformatie* 42, no. 1 (2018): 2–22.

Hesselink-Van der Riet, Tilly, Wim Kuiper, and Cor Trompetter. *Het schuldboek van Arend Kenkhuis*. Amsterdam: Aksant, 2008.

Hollander, Maurits den. "Failliet in de Republiek. Lokale ordonnanties over de omgang met desolate boedels, circa 1643–1713." *Pro Memorie* 24, no. 2 (2022): 190–217.

"Grotius and Insolvency." *Grotiana* 44 (2023): 276–92.

"On the Relations between Law and History." *Forum Historiae Iuris* (online journal), 2019.

"Restoring Trust and Credit through Innovative Governance in 17th-Century Amsterdam." *Tijdschrift voor Rechtsgeschiedenis* 89, nos. 3–4 (2021): 481–99.

Hollander, Maurits den, and Remko Mooi. "Protecting the Foreign Creditor: International Insolvency in Early Modern Amsterdam and Frankfurt Am Main." *TSEG / Low Countries Journal of Social and Economic History* 16, nos. 3–4 (2020): 37–57.

Hooft, Cornelis Pietersz. *Memoriën en adviezen*. 2 vols., vol. I. Utrecht: Kemink & Zoon, 1871.

Huijbrecht, R. "Het notariaat in de gewesten Holland en Zeeland." In *Het notariaat in de Lage Landen (1250–1842)*. Ed. A. F. L. Gehlen and P. L. Nève, 145–90. Deventer: Kluwer, 2005.

Israel, Jonathan I. *Dutch Primacy in World Trade, 1585–1740*. Oxford: Clarendon Press, 1989.

Jacobs, Beatrix. "Ius Patrium en Ius Commune. Twee zijden van een medaille." *Pro Memorie* 19, no. 1 (2017): 22–46.

Jansen, L. *Geschiedenis van de Stads Bank van Lening te Amsterdam 1614–1964*. Amsterdam: Stads-kredietbank voor Roerende Zaken, 1964.

Jonker, Joost, and Keetie Sluyterman. *Thuis op de wereldmarkt. Nederlandse handelshuizen door de eeuwen heen*. The Hague: SDU, 2000.

Jousse, Daniel. *Nouveau Commentaire sur l'ordonnance du commerce des mois de mars 1673*. Paris: Jean Debure, 1777.

Kadens, Emily. "Cheating Pays." *Columbia Law Review* 119 (2019): 528–89.

"The Dark Side of Reputation." *Cardozo Law Review* 40 (2019): 1995–2027.

"The Last Bankrupt Hanged: Balancing Incentives in the Development of Bankruptcy Law." *Duke Law Journal* 59, no. 7 (2010): 1229–1319.

Kaplan, Yosef. *An Alternative Path to Modernity: The Sephardi Diaspora in Western Europe*. Leiden: Brill, 2000.

Kaptein, Herman. "Poort van Holland. De economische ontwikkeling 1200–1578." In *Geschiedenis van Amsterdam*, I: *Een stad uit het niets (tot 1575)*, 109–73. Amsterdam: SUN, 2004.

Kerkhoff, Toon et al. *A History of Dutch Corruption and Public Morality (1648–1940)*. Newcastle upon Tyne: Cambridge Scholars Publishing, 2020.

Kernkamp, Gerhard Wilhelm. *Regeering en historie van Amsterdam in de 17e eeuw*. Amsterdam: Emmering, 1900.

Kersteman, Franciscus Lievens. *Hollandsch rechtsgeleerd woorden-boek*. Amsterdam: Wed. van Esveldt en Holtrop, 1777.

Kessler, Amalia D. "Enforcing Virtue: Social Norms and Self-Interest in an Eighteenth-Century Merchant Court." *Law and History Review* 22, no. 1 (2004): 71–118.

Ketelaar, Eric. *Archiving People: A Social History of Dutch Archives*. The Hague: Stichting Archiefpublicaties, 2020.

"De procesgang bij het Hof van Holland, Zeeland en West-Friesland." In *Verslag en bijdragen Rijks Archiefschool 1969–1970*, 33–64. Utrecht: Rijksarchiefschool, 1971.

King, Michael. "The Radical Sociology of Niklas Luhmann." In *Law and Social Theory*. Ed. Reza Banakar and Max Travers, 2nd ed. Oxford: Hart Publishing, 2013.

Knevel, Paul. *Het Haagse bureau. Zeventiende-eeuwse ambtenaren tussen staatsbelang en eigenbelang*. Amsterdam: Prometheus / Bert Bakker, 2001.

Kooijmans, Luuc. "Risk and Reputation: On the Mentality of Merchants in the Early Modern Period." In *Entrepreneurs and Entrepreneurship in Early Modern Times: Merchants and Industrialists within the Orbit of the Dutch Staple Market*. Ed. Clé Lesger and Leo Noordegraaf, 25–34. The Hague: Stichting Hollandse Historische Reeks, 1995.

Kroeger, Frens. "The Development, Escalation and Collapse of System Trust: From the Financial Crisis to Society at Large." *European Management Journal* 33, no. 6 (2015): 431–37.

"Unlocking the Treasure Trove: How Can Luhmann's Theory of Trust Enrich Trust Research?" *Journal of Trust Research* 9, no. 1 (2019): 110–24.

Kuijpers, Erika, and Maarten Prak. "Burger, ingezetene, vreemdeling: burgerschap in Amsterdam in de 17e en 18e eeuw." In *Burger*. Ed. Joost Kloek and Karin Tilmans, 113–32. Amsterdam University Press, 2002.

"Gevestigden en buitenstaanders." In *Geschiedenis van Amsterdam*, IIa: *Centrum van de wereld, 1578–1650*. Ed. Willem Frijhoff and Maarten Prak, 188–239. Amsterdam: SUN, 2004.

Lagerwey, Antonie Cornelis. *Het accoord van den gefailleerde met zijne schuldeisers*. Utrecht: T. de Bruyn, 1862.

Lameere, J., ed. *Recueil des ordonnances des Pays-Bas. Deuxème série 1506–1700*. 8 vols., vol. III. Brussels: J. Goemaere, 1902.

Lameere, J., and H. Simont, eds. *Recueil des ordonnances des Pays-Bas. Deuxème série 1506–1700*. 8 vols., vol. IV. Brussels: J. Goemaere, 1907.
eds. *Recueil des ordonnances des Pays-Bas. Deuxème série 1506–1700*. 8 vols., vol. V. Brussels: J. Goemaere, 1910.
Langbein, John H. "Albion's Fatal Flaws." *Past & Present* 98 (1983): 96–120.
Lange, Tyler. *Excommunication for Debt in Late Medieval France: The Business of Salvation*. Cambridge University Press, 2016.
Leeuwen, Marco H. D. van. "Amsterdam en de armenzorg tijdens de Republiek." *NEHA-Jaarboek* 59 (1996): 132–61.
"Guilds and Middle-Class Welfare, 1550–1800: Provisions for Burial, Sickness, Old Age, and Widowhood." *Economic History Review* 65, no. 1 (2012): 61–90.
The Logic of Charity: Amsterdam, 1800–1850. London: Macmillan Press, 2000.
Leeuwen, Simon van. *Het Rooms-Hollands-regt [etc.]*. Leiden/Rotterdam: Hackens, 1664.
Lesaffer, Randall. "Law and History. Law between Past and Present." In *Law and Method. Interdisciplinary Research into Law*. Ed. Bart van Klink and Sanne Taekema, 133–52. Tübingen: Mohr Siebeck, 2011.
Lesger, Clé. *Handel in Amsterdam ten tijde van de Opstand. Kooplieden, commerciële expansie en verandering in de ruimtelijke economie van de Nederlanden ca. 1550–ca. 1630*. Hilversum: Verloren, 2001.
Het winkellandschap van Amsterdam. Stedelijke structuur en winkelbedrijf in de vroegmoderne en moderne tijd, 1550–2000. Hilversum: Verloren, 2013.
Huur en conjunctuur. De woningmarkt in Amsterdam, 1550–1850. Amsterdam: Historisch Seminarium van de Universiteit van Amsterdam, 1986.
"Merchants in Charge: The Self-Perception of Amsterdam Merchants, *ca.*1550–1700." In *The Self-Perception of Early Modern Capitalists*. Ed. Margareth C. Jacob and Catherine Secretan, 75–98. New York: Palgrave Macmillan, 2008.
Lindemann, Mary. *The Merchant Republics: Amsterdam, Antwerp, and Hamburg, 1648–1790*. New York: Cambridge University Press, 2014.
Linden, Joannes van der. *Verhandeling over de judicieele practijcq, of form van procedeeren, voor de Hoven van Justitie in Holland gebruikelijk*. 2 vols., vol. II. Leiden: A. en J. Honkoop, 1798.
Linebaugh, Peter. "(Marxist) Social History and (Conservative) Legal History: A Reply to Professor Langbein." *New York University Law Review* 60, no. 2 (1985): 212–44.
Loeff, I. J. *Inventaris Desolate Boedelkamer Amsterdam*. Amsterdam, 1892.
Lord Smail, Daniel. *Legal Plunder: Households and Debt Collection in Late Medieval Europe*. Cambridge: Harvard University Press, 2016.
Luhmann, Niklas. *Trust and Power*. Ed. Christian Morgner and Michael King. Cambridge: Polity Press, 2017.

Lupi, Marta. "Insolvent Merchants and Royal Jurisdictions in Early Modern Lyon (1600–1660). The Role of Royal Notaries and the Conservation Des Privilèges Royaux Des Foires." PhD, Tilburg University, 2023.

"Ius Mercatorum and Statutes of Florence during the 14th and 15th Centuries: The Case of Bankruptcy." *GLOSSAE. European Journal of Legal History* 16 (2019): 205–27.

Maassen, H. A. J. *Tussen commercieel en sociaal krediet. De ontwikkeling van de Bank van Lening in Nederland van Lombard tot Gemeentelijke Kredietbank 1260–1940*. Hilversum: Verloren, 1994.

Martino, Paolo Di, Mark Latham, and Michelangelo Vasta. "Bankruptcy Laws Around Europe (1850–2015): Institutional Change and Institutional Features." *Enterprise & Society* 21 (2020): 1–55.

Mathias, Peter. "Strategies for Reducing Risk by Entrepreneurs in the Early Modern Period." In *Entrepreneurs and Entrepreneurship in Early Modern Times: Merchants and Industrialists within the Orbit of the Dutch Staple Market*. Ed. Clé Lesger and Leo Noordegraaf, 5–24. The Hague: Stichting Hollandse Historische Reeks, 1995.

Meeteren, Aries van. *Op hoop van akkoord. Instrumenteel forumgebruik bij geschilbeslechting in Leiden in de zeventiende eeuw*. Hilversum: Verloren, 2006.

Mieris, Frans van, ed. *Bundel van handvesten [etc.] der stad Leyden*. Leiden: Abraham Kallewier, 1759.

Moine de l'Espine, Jacques le, and Isaac le Long. *De koophandel van Amsterdam*. Amsterdam: Andries van Damme en Johannes Ratelband, 1714.

Molengraaff, Willem L. P. A. *Leidraad bij de beoefening van het Nederlandsche handelsrecht*. Haarlem: Erven F. Bohn, 1925.

Moll, Goswin. *De Desolate Boedelskamer te Amsterdam: bijdrage tot de kennis van het Oud-Hollandsch failliten-recht*. Amsterdam: De Roever-Kröber-Bakels, 1879.

Monti, Annamaria. "Fallimento-impresa." In *Parole in Divenire. Un vademecum par l'uomo occidentale*. Ed. Alberto Sciumè and Aldo A. Cassi, 43–57. Turin: Giappichelli, 2016.

"Osservazioni sparse intorno alle vicende storiche del fallimento." In *Commentario alla legge fallimentare*. Ed. Cesare Cavallini, 4 vols., vol. IV. 165–95. Milan: Egea, 2010.

Mooi, Remko. "Without Regard to Foreignness. The Emergence of Equal Treatment in Early Modern German Insolvency, 1648–1806." PhD, Tilburg University, 2023.

Muldrew, Craig. "Credit and the Courts: Debt Litigation in a Seventeenth-Century Urban Community." *Economic History Review* 46, no. 1 (1993).

The Economy of Obligation. The Culture of Credit and Social Relations in Early Modern England. Basingstoke: Macmillan Press, 1998.

"Interpreting the Market: The Ethics of Credit and Community Relations in Early Modern England." *Social History* 18, no. 2 (1993): 163–83.

Nadelmann, Kurt. "Bankruptcy Treaties." *University of Pennsylvania Law Review* 58 (1944): 58–97.

Nederveen Meerkerk, Elise van. "Professionalization of Public Service: Civil Servants in Dordrecht, 1575–1795." *Journal of Urban History* 36, no. 3 (2010): 345–67.

Nierop, Henk van. "Popular Participation in Politics in the Dutch Republic." In *Resistance, Representation, and Community*. Ed. Peter Blickle, 272–90. Cambridge University Press, 1997.

"Van wonderjaar tot Alteratie 1566–1578." In *Geschiedenis van Amsterdam*, I: *Een stad uit het niets (tot 1575)*, 450–81. Amsterdam: SUN, 2004.

Noordam, Arnoud J. "Schuldsanering en goede trouw." PhD, Amsterdam, VU, 2007.

Noordkerk, Hermanus, ed. *Handvesten; ofte privilegien ende octroyen: mitsgaders willekeuren, costuimen, ordonnantien en handelingen der stad Amstelredam*. 4 vols., vol. II. Amsterdam: Hendrik van Waesberge, Salomon en Petrus Schouten, 1748.

North, Douglass C. *Institutions, Institutional Change, and Economic Performance*. Cambridge University Press, 1990.

Structure and Change in Economic History. New York: Norton, 1981.

North, Douglass C., and Robert Paul Thomas. *The Rise of the Western World: A New Economic History*. Cambridge University Press, 1973.

Nusteling, Hubert. *Welvaart en werkgelegenheid in Amsterdam 1540–1860. Een relaas over demografie, economie en sociale politiek van een wereldstad*. Amsterdam: De Bataafsche Leeuw, 1985.

Ochser, Schulim. "VAEZ." In *The Jewish Encyclopedia: A Descriptive Record of the History, Religion, Literature, and Customs of the Jewish People from the Earliest Times*. 12 vols. Ed. Isidore Singer, XII:394–95. New York: Ktav Publishing House, 1906.

Ogilvie, Sheilagh C. *Institutions and European Trade: Merchant Guilds, 1000–1800*. Cambridge University Press, 2011.

Ogilvie, Sheilagh C., and A. W. Carus. "Institutions and Economic Growth in Historical Perspective." In *Handbook of Economic Growth*. 2 vols. Ed. Philippe Aghion and Steven N. Durlauf, IIA:403–513. Amsterdam: Elsevier, 2014.

Oldewelt, W. F. H. "Twee eeuwen Amsterdamse faillissementen en het verloop van de conjunctuur (1636 tot 1838)." *Tijdschrift voor Geschiedenis* 75, no. 4 (1962): 421–35.

Oliel-Grausz, Evelyne. "Dispute Resolution and Kahal Kadosh Talmud Torah: Community Forum and Legal Acculturation in Eighteenth-Century Amsterdam." In *Religious Changes and Cultural Transformations in the Early Modern Western Sephardic Communities*. Ed. Yosef Kaplan, 228–57. Leiden: Brill, 2019.

"Patrocinio and Authority: Assessing the Metropolitan Role of the Portuguese Nation of Amsterdam in the Eighteenth Century." In *The Dutch Intersection. The Jews and the Netherlands in Modern History*. Ed. Yosef Kaplan, 149–72. Leiden: Brill, 2008.

Pakter, Walter. "The Mystery of 'Cessio Bonorum.'" *Index: Quaderni Camerti Di Studi Romanistici = International Survey of Roman Law* 22 (1994): 323–42.

"The Origins of Bankruptcy in Medieval Canon and Roman Law." In *Proceedings of the Seventh International Congress of Medieval Canon Law*. Ed. Peter Linehan, 485–506. Vatican City: Bibliotheca Apostolica, 1988.

Parker, Geoffrey. *Global Crisis: War, Climate Change and Catastrophe in the Seventeenth Century*. New Haven: Yale University Press, 2013.

Petram, Lodewijk. *The World's First Stock Exchange*. New York: Columbia University Press, 2014.

Planitz, Hans. "Der Schuldbann in Italien." *Zeitschrift der Savigny-Stiftung für Rechtsgeschichte. Germanistische Abteilung* 52, no. 1 (1932): 134–259.

Poelwijk, Arjan. "*'In dienste vant suyckerbacken'*." *De Amsterdamse suikernijverheid en haar ondernemers, 1580–1630*. Hilversum: Verloren, 2003.

Pol, Lotte C. van de. "Prostitutie en de Amsterdamse burgerij: Eerbegrippen in een vroegmoderne stedelijke samenleving." In *Cultuur en maatschappij in Nederland 1500–1800*. Ed. Peter Boekhorst, Peter Burke, and Willem Frijhoff, 179–218. Amsterdam / Heerlen: Boom / Open Universiteit, 1992.

Polanyi, Karl. *Great Transformation: The Political and Economic Origins of Our Time*. 2nd ed. Boston: Beacon Press, 2001.

Pool, Isaac. *De handelsgeest van Isaac Pool. Dagboek van een Amsterdammer in de Gouden Eeuw*. Ed. Laurence Duquesnoy and Jeroen Salman. Hilversum: Verloren, 2018.

Porta, Antonio. *Joan en Gerrit Corver. De politieke macht van Amsterdam (1702–1748)*. Assen: Van Gorcum, 1975.

Prak, Maarten. "Armenzorg 1500–1800." In *Studies over zekerheidsarrangementen. Risico's, risicobestrijding en verzekeringen in Nederland vanaf de middeleeuwen*. Ed. Jacques van Gerwen and Marco H. D. van Leeuwen, 49–90. Amsterdam: NEHA / Verbond van Verzekeraars, 1998.

Citizens without Nations: Urban Citizenship in Europe and the World, c.1000–1789. Cambridge University Press, 2018.

The Dutch Republic in the Seventeenth Century. Trans. Diane Webb. 2nd ed. Cambridge University Press, 2023.

"Guilds and Mutual Aid in the Northern Netherlands." In *Professional Guilds and the History of Insurance: A Comparative Analysis*. Ed. Phillip Hellwege, 47–62. Berlin: Duncker & Humblot, 2020.

"Individual, Corporation and Society: The Rhetoric of Dutch Guilds (18th. C.)." In *Individual, Corporate, and Judicial Status in European Cities*

(Late Middle Ages and Early Modern Period). Ed. Maarten Prak and Marc Boone, 255–79. Louvain/Apeldoorn: Garant, 1996.

Prak, Maarten, and Jan Luiten van Zanden. *Pioneers of Capitalism. The Netherlands 1000–1800*. Princeton University Press, 2023.

Price, J. L. *Holland and the Dutch Republic in the Seventeenth Century: The Politics of Particularism*. Oxford University Press, 1994.

Puyenbroek, Marleen. "Gezworen schatsters. Vakvrouwen in zeventiende-eeuws Amsterdam." *Amstelodamum* 108, no. 2 (2021): 103–17.

Raadschelders, Jos C. N. *Handbook of Administrative History*. Oxford: Routledge, 1998.

Radzinowicz, Leon. *A History of English Criminal Law and Its Administration from 1750*. 5 vols. London: Stevens, 1948.

Reitsma, J., and S. D. van Veen. *Acta der provinciale en particuliere synoden, gehouden in de Noordelijke Nederlanden gedurende de jaren 1572–1620*. 8 vols., vol. II. Groningen: J. B. Wolters, 1893.

Acta der provinciale en particuliere synoden, gehouden in de Noordelijke Nederlanden gedurende de jaren 1572–1620. 8 vols., vol. III. Groningen: J. B. Wolters, 1894.

Ressel, Magnus. "Norms and Practice of Handling Complex and International Insolvencies in Early Modern Venice." In *Dealing with Economic Failure: Between Norm and Practice (15th to 21st Century)*. Ed. Albrecht Cordes and Margrit Schulte Beerbühl, 115–38. Frankfurt am Main: Peter Lang, 2016.

Rhee, Remco van. "Geschiedenis van het deurwaardersambt. Van 'nederige dienaar' tot zelfbewuste professional." *Justitiële Verkenningen* 3 (1999): 19–30.

Richter, Rudolf. "The New Institutional Economics: Its Start, Its Meaning, Its Prospects." *European Business Organization Law Review* 6, no. 2 (2005): 161–200.

Roodenburg, Herman. *Onder censuur: de kerkelijke tucht in de gereformeerde gemeente van Amsterdam, 1578–1700*. Hilversum: Verloren, 1990.

Rooseboom, Gerard, ed. *Recueil van verscheyde keuren, en costumen; midtsgaders maniere van procederen binnen de stadt Amsterdam*. 2nd ed. Amsterdam: Jan Hendricks, 1656.

Safley, Thomas Max. "Business Failure and Civil Scandal in Early Modern Europe." *BHR* 83 (2009): 35–60.

Family Firms and Merchant Capitalism in Early Modern Europe: The Business, Bankruptcy and Resilience of the Höchstetters of Augsburg. Oxford: Routledge, 2020.

"Introduction: A History of Bankruptcy and Bankruptcy in History." In *The History of Bankruptcy. Economic, Social and Cultural Implications in Early Modern Europe*. Ed. Thomas Max Safley, 1–16. London: Routledge, 2013.

Sallila, Jussi. "Insolvency, Commercial Utility and the Principles of Justice: The Making of Bankruptcy Law in Sweden and Finland, *ca.* 1680–1868." PhD, University of Helsinki, 2015.

Santarelli, Umberto. *Per la storia del fallimento nelle legislazioni italiane dell'età intermedia*. Cedam, 1964.

Schama, Simon. *The Embarrassment of Riches: An Interpretation of Dutch Culture in the Golden Age*. New York: Alfred A. Knopf, 1987.

Scheltus, Isaac. *Groot placaat boek. Inhoudende de placaaten ende ordonnantien van de Hoog Mog. Heeren Staaten Generaal der Nederlanden ende van de Ed. Groot Mog. Heeren Staaten van Holland ende West-Friesland mitsgaders van de Ed. Mog. Heeren Staaten van Zeeland*. The Hague: Isaac Scheltus s'Lands Drukker, 1770.

Schick, Sandor E. "Globalization, Bankruptcy and the Myth of the Broken Bench." *American Bankruptcy Law Journal* 80, no. 2 (2006): 219–60.

Schnitzeler, Josje. "Financial Care for the Vulnerable: Rise and Decline of Holland Orphan Chambers." PhD, Utrecht University, 2022.

Schumpeter, Joseph A. *Capitalism, Socialism, and Democracy*. New York: Harper & Brothers, 1942.

Sgard, Jérôme. "Bankruptcy Laws: East versus West." In *Law and Long-Term Economic Change: A Eurasian Perspective*. Ed. Debin Ma and Jan Luiten van Zanden, 198–220. Stanford University Press, 2011.

Smail, John. "Credit, Risk, and Honor in Eighteenth-Century Commerce." *Journal of British Studies* 44, no. 3 (2005): 439–56.

Soman, Alfred. "Deviance and Criminal Justice in Western Europe, 1300–1800: An Essay in Structure." *Criminal Justice History* 1 (1980): 3–28.

Souterius, Daniel. *Praxis Banccaeruptorum*. Leiden: Godefridus Basson, 1615.

Spaans, Joke. "Stad van vele geloven 1578–1795." In *Geschiedenis van Amsterdam*, IIa: *Centrum van de wereld, 1578–1650*. Ed. Willem Frijhoff and Maarten Prak, 385–467. Amsterdam: SUN, 2004.

Spann, Michael. *Der Haftungszugriff auf den Schuldner zwischen Personal- und Vermögensvollstreckung. Eine exemplarische Untersuchung der geschichtlichen Rechtsquellen ausgehend vom Römischen Recht bis ins 21. Jh. unter besonderer Berücksichtigung bayerischer Quellen*. Berlin: Lit, 2004.

Speet, Ben. "Een kleine nederzetting in het veen." In *Geschiedenis van Amsterdam*, I: *Een stad uit het niets (tot 1575)*, 21–61. Amsterdam: SUN, 2004.

Sprunger, Mary. "Faillissementen. Een aspect van geestelijke tucht bij de Waterlands-doopsgezinde gemeente te Amsterdam in de zeventiende eeuw." *Doopsgezinde Bijdragen* 17 (1991): 101–30.

Staehelin, Adrian. "Zwangsvollstreckung in älteren Schweizer Stadtrechten." *Zeitschrift der Savigny-Stiftung für Rechtsgeschichte: Germanistische Abteilung* 93, no. 1 (1976): 184–256.

Stolker, Fleur. "The Forgotten History of Bankruptcy, 1543–1624." *The Journal of Legal History* 44, no. 3 (2023): 295–324.

Stolleis, Michael. "Methode der Rechtsgeschichte." In *Handwörterbuch zur deutschen Rechtsgeschichte (HRG) Konfliktbewältigung – Nowgorod.* Currently 4 vols., vol. III. Ed Albrecht Cordes, 1475–83. Berlin: Schmidt, 2016.

Straccha, Benvenuto. *De Mercatura.* Amsterdam: Jan Jacobsz. Schipper, 1669.

Sztompka, Piotr. *Trust: A Sociological Theory.* Cambridge University Press, 1999.

Temple, William. *Ambassadeur in de Lage Landen – Observations upon the United Provinces.* Ed. Daniel Jeen Roorda and Y. H. Foppema. Haarlem: Fibula – Van Dishoek, 1978.

Thompson, Edward P. "The Moral Economy of the English Crowd in the Eighteenth Century." *Past & Present* 50 (1971): 76–136.

Tielhof, Milja van. *The "Mother of All Trades": The Baltic Grain Trade in Amsterdam from the Late 16th to the Early 19th Century.* Leiden: Brill, 2002.

Trivellato, Francesca. *The Promise and Peril of Credit: What a Forgotten Legend about Jews and Finance Tells Us about the Making of European Commercial Society.* Princeton University Press, 2019.

Udemans, Godfried. *'t Geestlyck roer van 't coopmans schip.* Dordrecht: Françoys Boels, 1638.

Vaz Dias, A. M. "Geneeskundige archivalia. Sprokkels uit het oud notarieel archief te Amsterdam." *Nederlands Tijdschrift voor Geneeskunde* 76, no. 4 (1932): 5584–86.

Veld, Marco in 't, and Maurits den Hollander. "Citizenship in Early Modern Amsterdam: An Artisanal Identity?" In *Citizenship, Identity, and Commerce in Legal History.* Ed. Dave De ruysscher, Albrecht Cordes, and Heikki Pihlajamäki. Leiden: Brill, 2021.

Verhas, Christel. "De beginjaren van de Hoge Raad van Holland, Zeeland en West-Friesland." PhD, Universiteit Leiden, 1997.

Vermeesch, Griet. "Reflections on the Relative Accessibility of Law Courts in Early Modern Europe." *Crime, Histoire & Sociétés / Crime, History & Societies* 19, no. 2 (2015): 53–76.

Verus, Justinius. *Discurs von verdorbeten Kaufleuten, Bancorottirern und Falliten.* Frankfurt-Leipzig: Esaias Fellgibeln, 1669.

Vives, Juan Luis. *Over de hulp aan de armen.* Trans. Raf Debaene. Zoetermeer: Klement, 2015.

Voetius, Gisbertus. *Commentarius Ad Pandectas.* 2 vols., vol. I. Leiden: Johannes Verbessel, 1698.

Vries, Jan de. *The Price of Bread: Regulating the Market in the Dutch Republic.* Cambridge Studies in Economic History. New York: Cambridge University Press, 2019.

Vries, Jan de, and Ad van der Woude. *The First Modern Economy. Success, Failure, and Perseverance of the Dutch Economy, 1500–1815*. Cambridge University Press, 1997.

Vries, Oebele. "Geschapen tot ieders nut. Een verkennend onderzoek naar de Noordnederlandse ambtenaar in de tijd van het Ancien Régime." *Tijdschrift voor Geschiedenis* 90, nos. 3–4 (1977): 328–49.

Wachter, Jacob Pieterszoon. *Handtvesten ofte privilegien, handelingen, costumen ende willekeuren der stadt Amstelredam*. Amsterdam, 1639.

Wagenaar, Jan. *Amsterdam in zijne Opkomst*. 4 vols., vol. I. Amsterdam: Isaak Tirion, 1760.

Amsterdam in zijne Opkomst. 4 vols., vol. II. Amsterdam: Isaak Tirion, 1765.

Amsterdam in zijne opkomst. 4 vols., vol. III. Amsterdam: Yntema en Tieboel, 1767.

Wassenaer, Gerard van. *Practijk judicieel ofte instructie op de forme en maniere van procederen voor hoven en rechtbanken*. 2 vols., vol. I. Utrecht: Gijsbert van Zijll, 1669.

Water, Johan van de, ed. *Groot placaatboek*. Utrecht: Jacob van Poolsum, 1729.

Weber, Max. *Gezag en bureaucratie*. Ed. A. van Braam. Trans. J. J. M. de Blok. Universitaire Pers Rotterdam, 1972.

Weel, Toon van. "De interjurisdictionele betrekkingen in criminele zaken van het Amsterdamse Gerecht (1700–1810)." In *Nieuw licht op oude justitie. Misdaad en straf ten tijde van de Republiek*. Ed. Sjoerd Faber, 23–48. Muiderberg: Coutinho, 1989.

Weeren, René van, and Tine De Moor. *Ja, ik wil! Verlief, verloofd, getrouwd in Amsterdam 1580–1810*. Amsterdam: Prometheus, 2019.

Wessels, Bob, Bruce Markall, and Jason Kilborn. *International Cooperation in Bankruptcy and Insolvency Matters*. Oxford University Press, 2009.

Whitman, James Q. "The Moral Menace of Roman Law and the Making of Commerce: Some Dutch Evidence." *The Yale Law Journal* 105, no. 7 (1995): 1841–89.

Wielant, Filips. *Practijcke ende maniere van procederen in materie civile na den ghemeynen stijl van dese Nederlanden*. Antwerp: Henrice van der Loe, 1573.

Willems, Bart. *Leven op de pof: Krediet bij de Antwerpse middenstand in de achttiende eeuw*. Amsterdam University Press, 2009.

Witteveen, Menno. *Reinier Pauw (1564–1636) en Amsterdam. De macht van een man en een stad*. Amsterdam: Boom, 2022.

Wolf, Hendrik C. de. *Geschiedenis van het R.C. Oude-Armenkantoor te Amsterdam*. Hilversum: Uitgeverij Paul Brand, 1966.

Woud, Auke van der. *Koninkrijk vol sloppen. Achterbuurten en vuil in de negentiende eeuw*. Amsterdam: Bert Bakker, 2010.

Zanden, Jan Luiten van, and Arthur van Riel. *The Strictures of Inheritance: The Dutch Economy in the Nineteenth Century*. Trans. Ian Cressie. Princeton University Press, 2004.

Zandvliet, Kees. *De 500 rijksten van de Republiek. Rijkdom, geloof, macht & cultuur*. Zutphen: Walburg Pers, 2018.

Zijlstra, S. *Om de ware gemeente en de oude gronden. Geschiedenis van de dopersen in de Nederlanden 1531–1675*. Hilversum: Verloren, 2000.

Zutphen, Bernhard van. *Practycke der Nederlansche rechten vande dagheli-jcksche soo civile als criminele questien*. Leeuwarden: Dominicus Lens, 1664.

Index

Page numbers in *italics* refer to figure/table.

Studies in Legal History
(*continued from page ii*)

Christian G. Fritz, *Monitoring American Federalism: The History of State Legislative Resistance*
Ada Maria Kuskowski, *Vernacular Law: Writing and the Reinvention of Customary Law in Medieval France*
E. Claire Cage, *The Science of Proof: Forensic Medicine in Modern France*
Kristin A. Olbertson, *The Dreadful Word: Speech Crime and Polite Gentlemen in Massachusetts, 1690–1776*
Edgardo Pérez Morales, *Unraveling Abolition: Legal Culture and Slave Emancipation in Colombia*
Lyndsay Campbell, *Truth and Privilege: Libel Law in Massachusetts and Nova Scotia, 1820–1840*
Sara M. Butler, *Pain, Penance, and Protest: Peine Forte et Dure in Medieval England*
Michael Lobban, *Imperial Incarceration: Detention without Trial in the Making of British Colonial Africa*
Stefan Jurasinski and Lisi Oliver, *The Laws of Alfred: The Domboc and the Making of Anglo-Saxon Law*
Sascha Auerbach, *Armed with Sword and Scales: Law, Culture, and Local Courtrooms in London, 1860–1913*
Alejandro de La Fuente and Ariela J. Gross, *Becoming Free, Becoming Black: Race, Freedom, and the Law in Cuba, Virginia, and Louisiana*
Elizabeth Papp Kamali, *Felony and the Guilty Mind in Medieval England*
Jessica K. Lowe, *Murder in the Shenandoah: Making Law Sovereign in Revolutionary Virginia*
Michael A. Schoeppner, *Moral Contagion: Black Atlantic Sailors, Citizenship, and Diplomacy in Antebellum America*
Sam Erman, *Almost Citizens: Puerto Rico, the U.S. Constitution, and Empire*
Martha S. Jones, *Birthright Citizens: A History of Race and Rights in Antebellum America*
Julia Moses, *The First Modern Risk: Workplace Accidents and the Origins of European Social States*
Cynthia Nicoletti, *Secession on Trial: The Treason Prosecution of Jefferson Davis*
Edward James Kolla, *Sovereignty, International Law, and the French Revolution*
Assaf Likhovski, *Tax Law and Social Norms in Mandatory Palestine and Israel*
Robert W. Gordon, *Taming the Past: Essays on Law and History and History in Law*

Paul Garfinkel, *Criminal Law in Liberal and Fascist Italy*
Michelle A. McKinley, *Fractional Freedoms: Slavery, Intimacy, and Legal Mobilization in Colonial Lima, 1600–1700*
Karen M. Tani, *States of Dependency: Welfare, Rights, and American Governance, 1935–1972*
Stefan Jurasinski, *The Old English Penitentials and Anglo- Saxon Law*
Felice Batlan, *Women and Justice for the Poor: A History of Legal Aid, 1863–1945*
Sophia Z. Lee, *The Workplace Constitution from the New Deal to the New Right*
Mitra Sharafi, *Law and Identity in Colonial South Asia: Parsi Legal Culture, 1772–1947*
Michael A. Livingston, *The Fascists and the Jews of Italy: Mussolini's Race Laws, 1938–1943*

For EU product safety concerns, contact us at Calle de José Abascal, 56–1°, 28003 Madrid, Spain or eugpsr@cambridge.org.

www.ingramcontent.com/pod-product-compliance
Ingram Content Group UK Ltd.
Pitfield, Milton Keynes, MK11 3LW, UK
UKHW041042221025
464223UK00006B/19
9781009631051